Strategic and Tactical Advanced Combat Prayers

By: Evangelist Tony Laurent

STRATEGIC AND TACTICAL ADVANCED COMBAT PRAYERS
First edition. November 15, 2024.
Copyright © 2024 Tony A Laurent.
Written by Tony A Laurent.

ABOUT THIS BOOK

"Strategic & Tactical Advanced Combat Prayers" is a compact, highly formulated prayer Book, containing highly strategized prayer methods for disarming the powers of witchcraft and other satanic operations working against you.

The prayer format and structure of this book, together with scriptures and a depth of detailed knowledge of the secrets of the kingdom of darkness, makes this prayer book a dynamic tool in the hands of a Christian Warrior, and it is truly Heavy Artillery.

Utilizing the powerful name of Y'ahushua the Messiah, and the dominion given to us in scriptures and the Holy Spirit, make us weapons of wars and a battle Axe in the hand of the Most High God.

In this Book you will learn:
- Uncommon strategies in spiritual combat, which you can use to develop your own prayer life.
- You will understand the names of the categories of demons you are fighting within the cosmic and aquatic planes.
- You will understand the realms from which your attackers are operating from.

This makes the prayers very potent, detailed, strategic and tactical and dangerous to Witches, Warlocks, Satanists, Demons and fallen Angels.

This powerful prayer book is truly feared by the kingdom of darkness, as was shown to me in multiple visions, and is a great investment in your spiritual walk with God.

THE MISSION OF THIS PRAYER BOOK

Our main mission is God's people walk in victory and liberty. The outline and mission of the Jesus is mentioned in:
[Isaiah 61:1-4]

"The Spirit of the Lord GOD *is* upon me; because the LORD hath anointed me to preach good tidings unto the meek; he hath sent me to bind up the broken-hearted, to proclaim liberty to the captives, and the opening of the prison to *them that are* bound;"

"To proclaim the acceptable year of the LORD, and the day of vengeance of our God; to comfort all that mourn;"

"To appoint unto them that mourn in Zion, to give unto them beauty for ashes, the oil of joy for mourning, the garment of praise for the spirit of heaviness; that they might be called trees of righteousness, the planting of the LORD, that he might be glorified".

This prayer Book was specifically formulated to increase your prayer life as a Warrior, a Keeper or an Intercessor. To help you pray effectively, and in the process increase your knowledge, and to help you achieve in prayer the things that are duly yours.

As soldiers in the Lord's army, we are mandated to confront the high intelligence and sophisticated tactics of witchcraft and other crafts within the inner esoteric framework of darkness. Therefore, the prayer strategies in this Book equips one with the precise words for a smoother and more accurate deployment of your spiritual weapon. It helps one to navigate successfully through the lines of the enemy's defences.

Go higher, change your strategies in prayer, overcome greater levels of spiritual combat, and access higher dimensions in Christ, for God is with you Amen.

Endorsement

"I recently had the pleasure of listening to the Author prayed, and I must say, it has truly enriched my spiritual life. The book "Strategic and Tactical Advanced Combat Prayers" is beautifully organized, with prayers that resonate deeply and offer comfort and inspiration. Each section is thoughtfully crafted, making it easy to find the right prayer for any moment—whether you need guidance, gratitude, or solace."

"What I appreciate most is the author's ability to connect with readers on a personal level. The language is both uplifting and accessible, allowing me to engage with the prayers meaningfully. I've found myself returning to it daily, discovering new insights and reflections that have helped deepen my faith."

"I highly recommend this Prayer Book to anyone seeking solace, inspiration, or a deeper connection to their faith. It's truly a gem that will enrich your spiritual journey!"

- Apostle Dr. Jeanetta Woods

Table of Contents

Prayer Of Repentance 13

1. Prayer To Bring All Angelic And Demonic Forces Under Subjection To Your Authority 15

2. Dismantle Demonic National & International Boundaries & Border Security Against Your Life When You Travel To Another Country 23

3. Prayers Against The Destroyer Demon 29

4. Prayer Against Marine Kingdoms 35

   Destroying Ancient Water Covenants From Your Blood 36

   Destroying Witchcraft Against You From The Waters 38

   Recovering Your Life From Fresh & Salty Water Kingdoms 41

   Judgement Upon Human & Demon Water Occult Agents 43

   Arrows of Combat Decrees 45

5. Prayers Against Witchcraft Operating In Your Life By Night 50

6. Prayers Against Witchcraft Operating In Your Life By Daytime 55

7. Setting Yourself Free From Witchcraft Holds 59

8. Destroying Weapons Of Witchcraft 65

9. Prayer For The First-Born Child 68

10. Bringing Satan To The Courts Of Heaven For Your Star & Masterplan ... 75

11. Prayer Warfare To Recover Your Star, & Master Plan From Hell 81

12. Prayers Against Blind Initiation & Witchcraft 87

13. Taking Back Your Glory From Darkness 90

14. Prayer Against The Spirit Of Stagnancy 95

15. Prayers Against The Spirit Of Calamity 99

16. Recovering Your Garment That Was Stolen, Exchanged, Or Replaced 104

   Spiritual blessings 104

    Garment of beauty..104

    Marital Garment 105

    Garment of Praise 106

    Oil of Joy and Beauty 106

    Garment of Ministry 107

    Organ replacement 107

17. Prayer Against Magic Mirrors & Your Spirit Being Summoned 109

    Against Astral Surveillance Devices 110

    Against Magic Mirrors...112

    Against Footprint Being Taken..113

18. Prayer Against Witchcraft Candles Lit Against You......................116

    Destroying Black Magic Candles 116

    Destroying White Candles 118

    Destroying Red Candles 119

    Destroying Yellow Candles..121

    Destroying Green Candle 122

    Destroying Purple Candles 124

    Destroying Orange Candles 125

    Destroying Blue Candles 127

    Destroying Pink Candle 128

    Destroying Grey And Brown Candles...................................129

19. Prayers Against The Spirit Of Unbelief & Doubt 131

20. Prayers Against Miscarriage & Barrenness.................................136

21. Reclaiming Your Physical Items Taken By Witches.....................143

22. Prayer Against Witchcraft Prayers Done Against You..................147

23. Prayer Against Serpentine Spirit 151

24. Reclaiming Your Destiny And Life From Demons 157

25. Destroying Witchcraft Chains And Locks 161

26. Prayers Against Curses Of Death 168
    Against The Books Of Hell 170
    Against Astral Poisons Of Death 171
    Against The Spirit Of Mortality 172

27. Warfare Prayer Against Assassins Sent Against You 173

28. Prayers Against Satanic Councils, Plots, & Gatherings Against You .. 179

29. Prayer Against Spirit Imprisonment In The Shadow Of Captivity 183

30. Prayer Against Spirits Of Astral Projection 192

31. Prayers Against Evils Attacking Your Child 194

32. Petition To God For Your Marriage 208
    Prayer for Forgiveness and Healing 208
    Prayer for Communication 208
    Prayer for Love and Affection 209
    Prayer for Unity and Togetherness 209
    Prayer for Spiritual Growth 210
    Prayer for Protection 210
    Prayer for Gratitude and Appreciation 211
    Prayer for Commitment and Dedication 211

33. Combat Against Hell For Your Marriage 213

34. Prayer When In Trouble 218

35. Prayer To Break Ties With Cults, Curses, And Demonic Religion 221

36. Prayer Against Witchcraft Altars 227

37. Prayer Against The Tribunal Of The Night 234

38. Prayer To Invoke God's Supernatural Wealth 237

39. Prayer To Invoke God's Supernatural Blessings 240

40. Prayer Against Crooked Paths 246

41. Prayers Against Evil Mountains 249

42. Prayer For Mountain-Moving Faith 253

43. Fighting Against Hell To Keep Your Garment White	256
44. Restoration Of God's Goodness In Your Life	261
45. To Be Transformed By The Amber Fire Of His Secret Place	265
46. Prayer Against Demonic Communication And Monitoring Systems Against Your Life	268
47. PRAYER AGAINST THE CURSE OF ABORTION	270
For Men Who Participated	274
48. Prayer Against The Spirit Of Household Destruction	276
49. Haunted House/Paranormal Activities [Prayer Against Witchcraft Attack & Demonic Invasion In Your Home]	280
Home Submerged Under Spiritual Water	284
Home Trapped In An Enchanted Forest Kingdom	287
50. Prayer To Liberate Your Property From Being A Ground For Satanic Secret Operations	290
51. Prayers Against Demons That Haunt You	292
52. Prayers Against Curses Of Infirmities	297
Pray Against Blood Clot Conditions	299
Family history	300
Medications	300
Vitamin deficiencies	300
53. Prayers Against Curses Of Failures	304
54. Warfare Against The Spirit Of Abandonment & Rejection	307
55. Prayers Against Curses Of Fear	310
56. Prayer Against Past Hurts And Pains	315
57. Prayers Against The Spirit Of Abnormality	318
58. Prayers Against The Spirit Of Abuse	320
59. Prayers Against The Spirit Of Anger	323
60. Prayer For Your Unborn Baby	327

61. Prayer Against Venom Of Neutralization..331

62. Prayer To Deliver From Fragmented Soul...336

63. Destroying Witchcraft Fortresses From Your Mind And Thoughts....339

64. Prayer For Repairing The Breach Made In Your Life. 346

65. Prayers Against The Spirit Of Mind Wandering & Daydreaming.......349

66. Prayers Against The Spirit Of Bitterness, Hatred, & Unforgiveness. .352

    To Forgive a Friend 353

    Forgiving Family Who Have Caused Pain...354

67. Prayers Against The Spirit Of Oppression 357

68. Prayers Against The Spirit Of Contention And Discord......................360

69. Prayers Against The Demons Of Addiction & Bad Habits 363

70. Prayer Against The Spirit Of Suicide 367

71. Prayers Against The Spirit Of Backsliding. 371

72. Prayers Against The Spirit Of Camouflage & Disguise 375

73. Prayers Against The Spirit Of Nightmare 379

74. Prayers Against The Spirit Of The Occult 382

75. Prayer Against The Octopus Demons 385

76. Prayers Against Dreams Of Dead People 390

77. Prayer Against The Demon Of Sleep Disorder 396

    Sleep Apnea 398

    Against Narcolepsy 399

    Restless Leg Syndrome. 399

78. Prayer Against Demons Of Dream Invasion......................................401

79. Prayers Against Sexual Molestation 405

    Renounce Ties..406

    Rebuke Directly..407

    Banishment..407

80. Prayers Against The Spirit Of Paralysis 412

81. Prayers Against The Spirit Of Alcoholism..................................414
82. Prayers Against The Spirit Of Anorexia Nervosa.....................417
83. Prayers Against Spirit Of Backlash 419
84. Prayers Against The Spirit Of Spiritual Blindness.....................421
85. Prayers Against The Spirit Of Spiritual Deafness 424
86. Prayers Against The Spirit Of Regression And Backwardness 426
87. Prayers Against The Spirit Of Hard-Heartedness & Mercilessness....429
88. Prayers Against The Spirit Of Sabotage 432
89. Prayers Against Curses Of Cancer..436
90. Prayers Against The Spirit Of Monsters 442
91. Prayers Against The Spirit Of Anxiety 444
92. Prayers Against The Spirit Of Shame And Disgrace 448
93. Prayers Against Curses Of Spiritual Partitions 450
94. Prayers Against The Spirit Of Slothfulness................................453
95. Prayer Against The Spirit Of Guilt & Self-Condemnation 457
96. Prayers Against Hermaphrodite Demon (Bisexual Spirit)........461
97. Spirits Of Gaslighting..466
98. Protection From People Trying To Gaslight You 469
99. Spirits Of Guilt-Tripping 473
100. Protection From People Trying To Guilt-Trip You..................476
101. Spirits Of Blame Shifting 478
102. Prayers Against Curses Of Singleness 481
103. Prayer For Women Of God 486

    Decrees 486

    Declare your position among the coals of the altar. 487

    Be polished after the similitude of a palace: 489

    Warfare Against the Kingdom of Darkness...................................492

    Claiming A Judicial Order from the Courts of GOD......................494

104. Destroying Curses 498

105. Transformer Of Minds 501

106. Prayers Against Aquatic (Marine) Friends 505

107. Prayers Against Pestiferous Friends (Forest Demons) 509

108. Prayers Against The Spirit Of The Masturbation Demon 513

109. Prayers Against The Pornography Demon [Pornography Spirit] 521

110. Prayer Against The Demon Of Bully 529

111. Prayer Against Demons Of Stealing 531

112. Praying Against Estranged Marine Babies 535

113. Prayer To Deflect Evil Arrows 537

114. Prayers Against Curses Of Poverty And Lack 540

115. Pulling Your Life From The Rivers 549

116. Rounding Up Demons In Your Life For Perpetual Destruction 552

117. Prayer Arrows Of Declarations 554

118. 58 Scripture Prayers - God's Judgement Upon Your Enemies 557

119. Prayer Against The List Of Evil Spirits 561

120. Prayer Against Dying In Your Sleep 566

Prayer Of Repentance

My God and Father in Heaven, creator of the Heavens and the earth, you are exalted in all kingdoms, spheres, realms and dimensions of the heavens and the Earth. Through the Blood of Y'ahushua the Lamb of God, by Your Holy Spirit and in the Name of Jesus the Christ, I now come boldly to the Throne of Grace to obtain mercy and find grace to help in this time of need.

Father, today, I stand in spiritual combat to revolt against witchcraft, and the diabolical forces of the 12 gates of Hell, who are seeking to keep me from entering Heaven and into Your will for my life. But as I engage in this tactical warfare, declaring war against the Devil's war, I request a Royal pardon, forgiveness and cleansing for my sins, iniquities and transgressions, and for those of my family bloodline foundation.

Today, I repent for my sins and iniquities, both current and past, and for those of my ancestors and parents. I ask you to remove from me every stigma of sin, and cleanse me from the stench of the sins of my ancestors, from my mother's house and my father's house.

Most gracious Father, I detest all personal and family transgressions and trespasses that have subjected me to become a victim of constant witchcraft afflictions and demonic harassment.

I repent for any agreement, covenant, truce, and alliance I have entered into with the kingdom of darkness, directly or indirectly, consciously or unconsciously, through my personal sins or through that of my ancestors.
By the Judicial Council of Your mercy, judgement and compassion, revive the verdict of the judicial Blood of the Lamb and the Mercy Seat, and acquit me of all allegations, accusations and condemnations, and of all sins, evil and wickedness embedded in me from my youth till now.

I repent for every door that I have opened in my life which allowed the demons to execute demonic spells and curses upon me. I petition by the blood of the Lamb for Your forgiveness and cleansing through Jesus the Messiah.

Psalms 39:8, **"Deliver me from all my transgressions: make me not the reproach of the foolish"**.

By the death, burial, resurrection, and coronation of Jesus Christ as King of Kings, and through the outpouring of Your Holy Spirit, you have given me power to tread upon serpents and scorpions and over all the powers of the enemy, and nothing shall hurt me, according to Luke 10:19.

Therefore, I now put on Your power in the name of Jesus against the gates of Hell, Death, and the Grave, in the name of Jesus of Nazareth, Amen.

1. Prayer To Bring All Angelic And Demonic Forces Under Subjection To Your Authority

Revelation 5:11-12
"Then I looked and heard the voice of many angels, numbering thousands upon thousands, and ten thousand times ten thousand. They encircled the throne and the living creatures and the elders. In a loud voice, they were saying: 'Worthy is the Lamb who was slain."
Lord our God, King of the ages, All-powerful and All-mighty who sits between the Cherubim of burning coals, hallowed be Your name in all kingdoms of the heavens and the earth. Heavenly Father, indeed, you are the Most High God; Your name is holy, and you are exalted in all kingdoms, realms, dimensions, and spheres.
Father, Your word says in Psalms 115:16, **"The heaven, even the heavens, are the LORD'S: but the earth hath he given to the children of men."** Therefore, the earth belongs to us humans and not evil spirits.
Psalms 8:6, **"Thou madest him to have dominion over the works of thy hands; thou hast put all *things* under his feet:"**
You, O Lord, have placed all things under my feet.
So, on this basis of the word of God, I take upon myself the dominion that you have given me, and I weaponize it against the forces of darkness, and I ask You to amplify its dynamic force sevenfold.
I take up the mantle of fire and authority of God to activate my dominion.
In the name of Jesus of Nazareth, I now take charge over the realms of the heavens and the Earth, and I say, O heavens, O Earth, by the authority of Jesus the Messiah, his lightnings and thunderings and voices: and the seven burning lamps of fire which are the seven Spirits of God, [Rev 4:5], hear my command now, for I stand in the presence

of the Most High God. I say to you, O heavens and Earth, and all that dwell in you, be subjected to my dominion through Christ Jesus.

I speak into the Astral Realms and Terrestrial Realms by fire, and I say, hear my command now, for I stand in the presence of the Most High God; be subjected unto me, all you kingdoms, spheres, and dimensions of the Astral and Terrestrial Worlds.

By the power of the Seven Spirits of God, I now take dominion, hold, and possession of all gates within every zone, region, center, realm, kingdom, and astral plane of the Astral and Terrestrial realms, spheres, kingdoms, and dimensions; and I bring all demonic and angelic dark powers into subjection to me through the dominion and authority of Christ Jesus.

By the power of Jesus the Messiah, the King of kings, Lord of the Heavens and the Earth, through whom all things are created, I bind, disarm, neutralize, and banish from my life and home the aura, essence, and spirit of the "fallen Angel Azazel," and all evil spirits under his jurisdiction and regime, who taught men to make swords, knives, shields, and breastplates, and made known to them the metals of the earth and the art of working them, and bracelets, ornaments, and the use of antimony, and the beautifying of the eyelids, and all kinds of costly stones, and all colouring tinctures,

I bind, disarm, neutralize, and banish from my life and home the aura, essence, and spirit of the "fallen Angel Semjaza," and all evil spirits under his jurisdiction and regime who taught enchantments and root cuttings.

I bind, disarm, neutralize, and banish from my life and home the aura, essence, and spirit of the "fallen Angel Armaros." and all evil spirits

under his jurisdiction and regime who taught men the resolving of enchantments.

I bind, disarm, neutralize, and banish from my life and home the aura, essence, and spirit of the "fallen Angel Baraqijal," and all evil spirits under his jurisdiction and regime, who taught men astrology.

I bind, disarm, neutralize, and banish from my life and home the aura, essence, and spirit of the "fallen Angel Kokabel," and all evil spirits under his jurisdiction and regime who taught the mysteries of the constellations.

I bind, disarm, neutralize, and banish from my life and home the aura, essence, and spirit of the "fallen Angel Ezeqeel," and all evil spirits under his jurisdiction and regime who taught man the knowledge of the clouds.

I bind, disarm, neutralize, and banish from my life and home the aura, essence, and spirit of the "fallen Angel Araqiel," and all evil spirits under his jurisdiction and regime who taught man the signs of the earth.

I bind, disarm, neutralize, and banish from my life and home the aura, essence, and spirit of the "fallen Angel Shamsiel",, and all evil spirits under his jurisdiction and regime who taught man the signs of the sun.

I bind, disarm, neutralize, and banish from my life and home the aura, essence, and spirit of the "fallen Angel Sariel", and all evil spirits under his jurisdiction and regime who taught man the mysteries of the course of the moon.

I bring under subjection the Guardian Demons of the twelve Cardinal points, the powers of the four Elements, and all forces, tribes, classifications, and regiments of evil spirits of the Astral world.

I bring the Land, the Waters, and the Air, and all their inhabitants consisting of solids, liquids, gases, and plasma under subjection to my authority, power, and dominion in Christ, the King of kings and Lord of lords.

I neutralize all satanic and witchcraft travels, operations, movements, and techniques within the atmospheres and subject the evil battalions and forces of the air, water, and land to the judgement of the Fire of the Holy Spirit.

I speak into the heavens and the Earth, and I say to all occult kingdoms of the land, the sea, the subterranean region, and the air, before I pray the prayers in this book, all your efforts, power, manipulations, oppressions, oppositions, and attacks against me have already failed miserably, by the power of the Holy Spirit and the fire of the highest Altar in Heaven, in Jesus name.

Lord, confirm my word and perform my counsel. Bring all the witchcraft elements of psychic spirits and curses of death that others send upon me from the gates of the Sun, the Moon, and the Stars, or from the aquatic world and kingdoms of the sea, lakes, ponds, pools, streams, and rivers, or from the subterranean regions of the supreme elementals into subjection.

It is written in Jeremiah 51:20, **"Thou art my battle axe and weapons of war: for with thee will I break in pieces the nations, and with thee will I destroy kingdoms."**

Vs.21, "And with thee will I break in pieces the horse and his rider; and with thee will I break in pieces the chariot and his rider;"

Today, I come against all the powers of darkness, and I declare by divine declaration through the mouth of God Almighty, I am in the hand of the LORD, a battle axe and weapons of war [Jeremiah 51:20].

By the power of the prophetic and the jurisdiction of a divine decree, I declare that in the hands of Yah, I am like an intercontinental ballistic missile; I am a weapon of mass destruction; I am a grenade launcher; I am a weapon of total annihilation; I am like a nuclear bomb; I am like a drone in stealth operations unseen by the enemies, and I am a battle axe and a weapon of war. The Devil cannot annihilate me, nor can he destroy me.
I decree and declare, my light is too bright for the eyes of my enemies; my presence is terrifying to my adversaries; my anointing is too heavy for the Devil to hold, too hot for Satan to handle, and too potent for the ammunition of darkness to stand.

O Kingdom of Satan and the Devil; hear my voice this day and crumble before me in shame, defeat, and disgrace, in the name of Jesus of Nazareth, for I declare and decree, I am a terror to terror; I am destructive to destruction; I terrify Terror; I make fear fearful; I ambush ambushment; I terrify the darkness; I oppose oppositions; I am wiser than the wise of the night; I am stronger than the strong in the darkness; and I bring captivity into captivity, because it is written in Jeremiah 51:20, I am a weapon of war in the hand of the Lord.

I invoke the Shield of Faith and the Sword of the Spirit to quench the fiery darts of the Mephistophelian operations and decapitate, block, or stop all dragons in the continental, intercontinental, and cosmic realms, and dismantle and banish from all jurisdiction the principalities, powers - provincial representatives, rulers of darkness - [demon ruler of the bureau], highway & street demons, community witch, demon of the toilet, which are working against my life through esoteric and other occult powers.

Effective immediately, let every witchcraft and satanic signal, sound frequency, resonant frequency, telegram, transmission, reception, communication line, and infrastructure be blocked, stopped, broken, and neutralized between all occult boundaries, realms, kingdoms, zones, regions, and centers, within the land, sea, air, and the subterranean world of the occult and demons. Let all communication occult channels fail at every point, effective immediately, in the name of Y'ahushua HaMashiach.

I also separate, block, and stop all frequencies, signals, and receptions within the aquatic world of the lakes, ponds, rivers, seas, and oceans, and I dismantle all witchcraft and satanic signals, sound frequencies, televisual transmissions, receptions, and communication between the altars of the fresh and salty waters, and the altars of the land, air, and underworld, in Jesus Name.

Any evil power that would try to attack me with astral and psychic weapons and poisons, let the preparation of their attack against me invoke an immediate detonation by the power of Jesus Christ, and let the waters be separated from the waters, and let immediate confusion arise between the regions of the seven seas and the five oceans, the cosmic occult world, the devic world, the sub-aquatic world, and the subterranean world, in Jesus name.

Every demon using electromagnetic fluctuations to access the earthly realm to fight against my destiny or to destroy and kill me physically, mentally, socially, spiritually, psychologically, emotionally, I scatter you with arrows and discomfit you with lightning, [2 Samuel 22:15], and I render you speechless and motionless in shame, disgrace, and defeat in Jesus' name, for it is written in Psalms 18:38, **"I have wounded them that they were not able to rise: they are fallen under my feet."**

I say, let God arise, and the enemies of Yah, God of Abraham, Isaac, and Jacob, be scattered. My Lord Jesus, destroy the enemies and let every satanic regiment, satanic military base, satanic military barrack, satanic encampment, demonic artillery, and all their ammunition in the North, East, South, and West be demolished by fire, and turn to debris; they and all that are currently fighting against my life and family or will fight against us in the future, for it is written in Psalms

35:8, **"Let destruction come upon him at unawares; and let his net that he hath hid catch himself: into that very destruction let him fall."**

The Lord Jesus said to us in Luke 10:19, **"Behold, I give unto you power to tread on serpents and scorpions, and over all the power of the enemy; and nothing shall by any means hurt you."**
It is also written in Luke 10:17, **"And the seventy returned again with joy, saying, Lord, even the devils are subject unto us through thy name"**.
I stand upon this authority, in the mighty name of Y'ahushua Ha-Mashiach, and by the power of the Holy Spirit, I invoke heavy divine artillery, and I detain, restrain, bind, disarm, shatter, and scatter in ruins all spirits that I will be praying against in these prayers.

Before I war against you, O kingdom of darkness, I declare your defeat. Before you rise, you are already fallen before me; before you engage in war, you are already smitten in defeat and disgrace; before you come against me with destructive maneuvers and manipulations, you are already confronted and blocked by walls of consuming holy fire and lightnings of perpetual destruction; before you are gathered against me, you are scattered in confusion, and your conferences against my life are sabotaged by God's holy Angels.

It is written in Psalms 35:4-6, **"Let them be confounded and put to shame that seek after my soul: let them be turned back and brought to confusion that devise my hurt."**
"Let them be as chaff before the wind; and let the angel of the LORD chase *them.***"**
"Let their way be dark and slippery; and let the angel of the LORD persecute them."

Kingdom of Satan and the Devil, I say to you, before you plan against my life, your plans are already sabotaged, and any entity that you send against me will be dead on arrival, in Jesus' mighty name.

So, I bring into subjection under my dominion and authority in Christ Jesus the Messiah, all demi-gods, the Queen of Heaven, the Metallic Council, all Planetary Spirits, Avatars, Watchers, Guardians of the Flame, Solar Lords, Inter-Planetary Lords, Inter-Galactic Lords, Guardians of Fate and the Cycles of life, Principalities, Powers, Rulers of darkness, Legions of the air, Legions of the Waters, Subterranean forces, Earth masters, Mermaids and Sirens.

I bring into subjection under my dominion and authority in Christ Jesus the Messiah the Elemental spirits, and the Queen of the South, the Queen of Beta, the Queen of Shylon, the Queen of Yemunah, the Queen of Delta, the Queen of the Coast, the gods of the Titans, the Tritons, the Trigons, the Olympian gods, the Pantheon gods, guardians of the cardinal points, the Nymphs, the gods and goddesses, or anyone within the Inner Esoteric framework and the powers of Astral and Terrestrial Hierarchy, and I say fall and bow to the Lordship of Jesus of Nazareth, now, in the Name of the Lord God Almighty.

It is written in Isaiah 28:21, **"For the LORD shall rise up as in mount Perazim, he shall be wroth as in the valley of Gibeon, that he may do his work, his strange work; and bring to pass his act, his strange act."** I pray this in the name of Jesus, Amen and Amen.

2. Dismantle Demonic National & International Boundaries & Border Security Against Your Life When You Travel To Another Country

Heavenly Father, I give You thanks and praise for the presence of Your Holy Spirit, who is always with me.
Lord, I came to this county to [say what you came to do].
I trust in you because you are my guide, for it is written: **"The steps of a good man are ordered by the LORD, and he delighteth in his way"** [Psalms 37:23].

As I tread upon this new territory, cover me with fire, because the kingdom of darkness has already set its surveillance upon me. But, Lord, You ask me to destroy the works of the Devil.
My God and Father, today I bind, disarm, and dislodge every continental, regional, national, and territorial demon guardian of this continent and nation, and I possess the gates of this Nation.

I stand in spiritual combat to revolt against the forces of the Continental, International, National, and Regional Dragons, and the Dragons of Realms, Spheres, and Kingdoms, and their spiritual border securities, who are seeking to keep me from entering or prospering in another state or country that is not my birthplace.

By fire, I request that Your Angels engage the continental Dragonic forces, the international resistance, the regional resistance, and the national resistance, as I declare tactical combat and war against the Devil's war.
I also request that the Royal seals of Heaven intervene on my behalf and condition and configure the heavens to accommodate my coming forth and success by a judicial divine decree.

It is written, Psalm 24:1-3, **"The earth is the Lord's, and the fulness thereof; the world, and they that dwell therein."**

It is also written in Psalm 115:16, **"The heaven, even the heavens, are the Lord's; but the earth hath he given to the children of men."**

In Jesus' name, I pray against every power under the Dragon of this continent oppressing me through the people I meet and those with whom I am affiliated, directly or indirectly.
I pray that all protocols, systems, principles, and laws in this country, state, and continent that are contrary to the word of God, which are making it difficult for me to progress and succeed here; let these evil powers break from over my life, in Jesus' name.

Father, it is Your will that I succeed and prosper wherever I go, for you have given me the nations as an inheritance because the earth belongs to you. In Genesis 39, the Bible describes Joseph prospering and finding favour with the people of Egypt, even though he was in a foreign land.

Therefore, I break from over my life, all the territorial oppression, oppression from the environment, religious oppression, social oppression, and oppression by the systematic methods of the communities in this nation.
Every force that is programmed by demonic stimuli and astral poisons to work against me, let it be neutralized now, in Jesus' name.
I destroy the art of homogeneity and banish the power of the guardian of fate and cycles of life, who is interfering with and manipulating the paths of my destiny.
It is written in Genesis 26:3, **"Sojourn in this land, and I will be with thee, and will bless thee; for unto thee, and unto thy seed, I will give all these countries, and I will perform the oath which I sware unto Abraham thy father;"**
Lord God of hosts, I petition that every continental, demonic force standing against me, setting snares of opposition for me, pledging my

destruction because I am a foreigner, let Your power dismantle these attacks in Jesus' name.

I pray in the name of the Lord Jesus, every international agreement among the kingdoms of darkness, to pursue and destroy me beyond foreign borders and in foreign territories, let their agreements be nullified and liquidated now, effective immediately.

All Satanists, warlocks, witches, and other occult members who are seeking advisory opinions for the best way to annihilate me in this foreign land, let their evil councils fall upon themselves and let them be devoured by one another. It is written, Psalms 70:2, **"Let them be ashamed and confounded that seek after my soul: let them be turned backward, and put to confusion, that desire my hurt."**

Every evil meeting that is held for my cause because I entered into this new country, continent, and state, let these witchcraft meetings turn into a bloodbath. I pray by Jesus that these witches would fall upon one another in confusion and eat themselves and devour one another, for it is written in Psalms 71:13, **"Let them be confounded and consumed that are adversaries to my soul; let them be covered with reproach and dishonour that seek my hurt."**

Abba Father, I break every invisible barrier within every regional and international border that I tread beyond, and I burn down the wall of every guardian demon, and call lightning and thunder of fire upon all demons who would try to register me as unwanted and undesirable, and within this new country.
Let fire descend and scatter every border patrol, for it is written in the scriptures that all they that are incensed against me shall be ashamed and confounded: they shall be as nothing; and they that strive with me shall perish, [Isaiah 41:11].

By Faith, I call upon the amber fire of the Glory of Yah, to wash my garment with light. Make my garment radiant and charged with the power of the light of the face of Jesus. Let the waters before me separate into two so I can walk into my destiny, let the mountains on my sides be brought down to level ground, and let the valleys be exalted before me, and all crooked things made straight, and the rough places plain (Isaiah 40:4).

In the name of Jesus, I break the sphere of influence within every jurisdiction of this nation where I am currently located, and I command every frontier zone or boundary zone of demons to sink into the ground for my sake.
In the name of Jesus, I deliver myself from the threats of darkness and the use of force, seeking to subject me to zero point, or violate my international and spiritual rights.

I terminate and overthrow by the verdict of the Blood of Jesus all satanic legal consequences that are scheduled to be executed upon my life because I crossed over spiritual jurisdictions of Hell.

Lord God of the heavens and the Earth, I pray that you dismantle and confuse every continental, international, national, and territorial dispute that is going on about my life in the kingdom of darkness. Those who see me as an intruder and undesirable in this land in which I was not born, and are discussing my fate, let these agents of confusion be rendered in confusion and disgrace.

In the mighty name of Jesus of Nazareth, I separate territories by walls of fire, and I set the fire of the Holy Spirit between demonic boundaries and lines, and I separate the spheres of demonic influences among the borders of every nation that I enter by land, sea, or air.

I also place a distinction between boundaries by fire, and I say let the general assembly of witches be confounded, scattered, and banished who seek after my hurt in this foreign land. They that war against me shall be as nothing, and as a thing of naught (Isaiah 41:12).

By the word of the Almighty, I speak prosperity, peace, safety, and success around me in this new territory and country. I will not suffer, nor cry because of affliction, for the LORD is my Shepherd; I shall not want.
He makes me lie down in green pastures; he leads me beside the still waters (Psalms 23:1-2).

I decree by the word of the Lord of hosts, every valley shall be exalted, and every mountain and hill shall be made low; and the crooked shall be made straight for me, in Jesus' name.
I therefore stand firm that I have the right to move anywhere on the Earth, and I declare that as a human, I have dominion, and I will walk in this dominion through Christ.
I say, "Yea, though I walk through the valley of the shadow of death, I will fear no evil, for the Lord Jesus is with me; his rod and his staff, they comfort me." [Psalms 23:4].
I will not be victimized, bullied, or be an object of oppression in a strange land.

Wherever I go, I rule, possess, and dominate in that territory, because greater is he who is in me than he who is in the world.
It is written in Psalms 2:8, **"Ask of me, and I shall give thee the heathen for thine inheritance, and the uttermost parts of the earth for thy possession."**

I rebuke every rebuke that is following me around, and every tongue that rises against me across territorial borders; I condemn these tongues in Jesus' name.

Every spirit that is seeking to hide my boldness and potential, I shake off this beast in the fire and will feel no harm (Acts 28:5).

I decree that I will eat of the good of the land wherever I go, and I will not walk in shame or disgrace in any city or state.

Let no continental agent of Satan or the Devil stand before me, for I bear in my body the marks of our Lord Jesus Christ.

Lord Jesus, thank you for Your presence, and for helping me in my time of distress, and for answering me by this prayer, in Jesus' name, Amen and Amen.

3. Prayers Against The Destroyer Demon

Almighty and ever-living God, I come before Your Throne of Grace seeking Your divine help from Heaven, through Jesus Christ Your Son, my Saviour.
You who sit between the two Cherubim of fire coals are exalted, and I therefore acknowledge Your sovereignty and authority over all spiritual forces, including Abaddon (Apollyon), the destroyer from the Abyss, Zeus, Kali, and every destroyer demon from the 999 Occult Seal, and the 7 kingdoms of darkness within land, sea, air, and underworld, and their works of darkness.

Father, according to Your word in Ephesians 6, I stand strong in You and in the power of Your might by faith in Jesus, Your Son.
Remove all generational curses, maledictions, or negative patterns from my life that have opened doors for this demon of destruction.
I acknowledge that You are the Almighty, and there is nothing too difficult for You; therefore, I ask that Your power descend upon me for spiritual warfare right now.
It is written in Psalm 27:2, **"When the wicked, *even* mine enemies and my foes, came upon me to eat up my flesh, they stumbled and fell."**

According to Matthew 16:19, Matthew 12:29, and Mark 3:27, I bind with hot chains and shackles of holy fire the hands and feet of every demon of destruction and their subjects and projects that are operating in my life to subject my life to captivity. I command you destructive forces holding me in captivity to go into captivity now, for it is written, captivity shall go into captivity.

I stand and revolt against the spirit of Abaddon or Apollyon, the destroyer angel from the abyss, and against his destroyer armies, the armies of hybrid grasshopper demons, or any other destroyer spirit who roams the shadows of death in search of my blood, life, and destiny.

Today I pray against and nullify, eradicate, and liquidate every psychic command given in the astral layers to construct monuments, strategies, traps, and snares of destruction in, around, and against my life.

I pray against, nullify, and eradicate the sound frequency, vibration, incantation, curses, spells, and hexes which carry the mandate to enforce Demons of destruction between June and September, which will be finalized, agreed upon, signed, and sealed in the month of September. I say to you arch demons, I will not be your candidate and victim, and therefore render these evil decisions and council fruitless, barren, useless, powerless, and dissolved by severe confusion, in Jesus' name.

I scatter every organized, sudden, and premature deployment of the demons of destruction, sent to annihilate me between the autumn equinox and the winter solstice (from September to December), which are the months of Blood. Also, I speak to the Four Elements—wind, water, fire, and earth, and I say my blood will not be taken, nor spilled; neither will any evil plan against me be successful.

I declare that all satanic missions that failed during the year in the kingdom of darkness will fail miserably as they attempt to accomplish their goals during these specific months of June to September, in Jesus' name.

Through the power of the council of God in Heaven, I declare war, as I revolt and destroy all satanic powers of the third Esoteric Seal of the Seal 999, which is the Seal of Destruction, within the five Mephistophelian Occult seals. It is written in Psalms 71:13, **"Let them be confounded *and* consumed that are adversaries to my soul; let them be covered *with* reproach and dishonour that seek my hurt."**

Let destruction above me and destruction below me implode and be destroyed, and let the emperor of death eat up every spirit of destruction that is pursuing me.

It is written, in Psalms 16:8, **"I have set the LORD always before me: because he is at my right hand, I shall not be moved;"** therefore, every destructive path set before my feet, be condemned now, by the word and blood of Jesus of Nazareth.

By the authority of the faith of Jesus Christ the Nazarene, I destroy any destruction pursuing me via the diabolical techniques of various astral poisons, psychic manipulation, and astral stones during the hourly gates of the day and in the hourly gates of the nocturnal time system. I pray against and destroy these weapons of mass destruction, and by the power of the Living God of Abraham, Isaac, and Israel, I neutralize and destroy the metaphysical intercourse and all manipulations of corrupt occult and esoteric powers operating with the highest rate of occult velocity against my life for my death and destruction physically, mentally, emotionally, and spiritually.

By the eternal power of Jesus, the Son of the Almighty God, and by the power invested in me by the seal of my redemption through the blood of Jesus and His holy name, I revolt and destroy the powers of the five Mephistophelian seals of the seven kingdoms of darkness, and their degrees of evil strongholds ambushing and working against my life in every aspect, and I uproot all their evil planted and operating in and against my life.

I break every authoritative chain of command within the esoteric spheres of the pandemonium world, and I neutralize the forces of the provincial representatives, the rulers of darkness, and all demon rulers of the bureau.

I pray against the elemental spirits of destruction and chaos, the emperor of death and the demons of high destruction, the wolverine spirits, the Tritons, the trigons, the armoured demons, the werewolves, and the night hunters that have been set against me in psychic motions, and every weapon, technique, and monitoring device they are utilizing against my life for my annihilation. I call on the power of the Lord Jesus of Nazareth to destroy them now, with immediate effect.

I condemn and nullify any declaration and verdict of the sentence of slow, progressive, and sudden destruction by the elemental forces of the land, sea, air, and underworld, and I, by the power of the Spirit of the Living God, destroy every dangerous power of diverse esoteric crafts, manipulations, weapons, systems, and techniques that are formed against my life by any human occult agent, demon, or spirit.

By the power of Jesus, I say, Blood of Jesus, arise against the highest council of darkness and condemn their verdict to destroy me in sleep, on the street, at home, by sudden sickness, or by any other way.

Fire of El-Eliyahu, descend for my sake, and let every psychic command given to the elemental forces through the Gnomes, the Sirens, members of the brotherhoods, representatives of the upper and lower darkness be tormented with fire and brimstone in the presence of the holy angels, and in the presence of the Lamb, according to Rev 14:10.

Every high altar of witchcraft, sorcery, satanism, and every other form of esoteric crafts and manipulations, assigned and programmed against me through the gate of the midday sun, midnight moon, full moon, new moon, waxing moon, and waning moon, or using the gates of any of the seven seas, the five oceans, continental rivers, forests, mountains, or the Zodiac signs, planetary alignments, or volcano openings, let the LORD, the God of heaven, and the God of the earth, rain down fire, brimstone, tempest, and terror upon these evils and destroy their rays, altars, fortitude, and power. It is written in Psalms 11:6, **"Upon the wicked he shall rain snares, fire and brimstone, and a horrible tempest: this shall be the portion of their cup."**

In the name and by the power of Jesus the Christ, Son of the Living God, may I be uprooted from the grounds of destruction, from the depths of hell, and from the grave of Hades.

May all these evil altars and powers explode, and their stronghold be demolished in the North, South, East, and West, and in any dimension where they are operating against and in my life.
It is written in Psalms 18:13, **"The LORD also thundered in the heavens, and the Highest gave his voice; hailstones and coals of fire."**
Let hailstones and coals of fire and fires of lightning and thunder release dynamic and spectacular detonations in every place where their altars are standing against my life for the destruction of my mind, soul, body, and destiny.

By the power of the Sapphire Throne of the Lamb of God, by the authority of his sceptre, by the power of the 7 horns and 7 eyes of the Lamb of God, and by the power of the fire, the lightnings, the voices and the seven thunders within the presence of the enthroned and exalted Jesus, and by the authority of his name King of Kings and Lord of lords, I command destruction upon you evil spirits of Destruction fashioned and working in my life to destroy me by the astral and metaphysical forces that operate at the highest velocity of Astro-metaphysical acceleration, through psychic manipulations, through the cosmological verdict, through metaphysical intercourse, by the powers of the Astro-Omnidictator and under the power and velocity of the five Mephistophelian seals of the occult.

Therefore, by the lightnings of fire in the name of Jesus Christ, I command my freedom from the powers of the works of these evil spirits of death, hell, and destruction, and I declare that every destroyer demon and astral poison assigned against me by witchcraft, sorcery, and any psychic commands be bound and rendered powerless, useless, ineffective, and I command them to leave my presence and my life immediately.

I thank you, Lord, for Your faithfulness and Your unfailing love. Your Word declares in Psalm 34:7, **"The angel of the Lord encamps all around those who fear Him and delivers them."** I trust in Your deliverance and protection.

Thank you for delivering me from this destroyer demon. Allow my seal unto the day of redemption to remain, according to Ephesians 4:30, and keep me in the will of Your Holy Spirit, now and forever, world without end. Amen.

I pray for all these things in the powerful and matchless name of Jesus Christ. Amen and Amen.

4. Prayer Against Marine Kingdoms

Lord our God, King of the ages, All-powerful and All-mighty who sits between the Cherubim of burning coals, hallowed be Your name in all kingdoms of the heavens and the earth. Heavenly Father, indeed, you are the Most High God; Your name is holy, and you are exalted in all kingdoms, realms, dimensions, and spheres.

In the name of Y'ahushua, the Son of Yah, I command and charge all you occult kingdoms of the waters, all water dragons, mermaids, sirens, hybrids, serpents, etc., on earth and under the earth to bow at the Lordship of Jesus of Nazareth, as I take authority over you through Christ Jesus.

It is written, Revelation 5:13, **"And every creature which is in heaven, and on the earth, and under the earth, and such as are in the sea, and all that are in them, heard I saying, Blessing, and honour, and glory, and power, *be* unto him that sitteth upon the throne, and unto the Lamb for ever and ever."**

By the power of Jesus the Messiah, the King of kings, Lord of the Heavens and the Earth, through whom all things are created, I bind, disarm, neutralize, and banish from my life and home the aura, essence, and spirit of the fallen Angels: Leviathan, Enki, Rahab, Azazel, and all ruling spirits who are connected to the water manipulations, enchantment, and spirits.

By Jesus Christ, Son of the Living God, I invoke the jurisdiction of the throne of Jesus, the Lamb of God, and the scepter of His right hand, and call forth Angelic reinforcement now from the presence of Jesus, and bring to judgement Leviathan, Enki, Rahab, Azazel, and all subordinate water spirits who function under Blue Magic and other dark magical formulas.

It is written in Isaiah 51:9, **"Awake! Awake! Put on strength, O arm of the LORD. Awake, as in the ancient days, in the generations of old. Was it not You who cut Rahab into pieces, piercing the serpent?"**

Isa 51:10, **"Was it not You who dried up the sea, the waters of the great deep; who made the depths of the sea a way for the redeemed to pass over?"**

I come against every water witchcraft speaking to my destiny and commanding my paths in ways contrary to the blueprint of God for my life.

I now deploy fiery arrows of mass destruction into the nucleus of every water witchcraft, sorcery, spell, hex, and incantation done upon the waters and in the sub-aquatic regions, in the continental intersections beneath the waters and in the Northern, Southern, Eastern, and Western borders of the marine waterscapes.

Destroying Ancient Water Covenants From Your Blood

By the name of the God of Noah who unlocked the waters from the heavens above and loosed the gates of the waters in the Earth, I break, destroy, and nullify every water altar built against my family foundation, my marital foundation, my destiny, and my life, which the Hydriads (the hydro-spirits) have built within the kingdoms of the salt and fresh waters upon and beneath the earth.

I speak to the realms of the waters, and I say, water of the Earth, be in subjection to me now, and become acidic to every evil essence that uses you to fight against my life.

I say let God arise for me this day, and let the voice of His majesty scatter, destroy, and banish from my life all powers, influence, essence, belongings, marks, new name, special powers, altars, and covenant that my ancestors received from the Sea and River spirits on my behalf, negotiated on my behalf, erected on my behalf, and invoked on my behalf.

Every friendship, embargo, contract, alliance, affiliation, connection, link, communication, covenant, partnership, and placement that my blood, my family bloodline, and my DNA have with the Bermuda Triangle, the Mediterranean Sea, the Adriatic Sea, the Black Sea, the Red Sea, the Sargasso Sea, the Arabian Sea, the Caspian Sea, the Baltic Sea, the Persian Gulf, or with the North Atlantic Ocean, the South Atlantic Ocean, the North Pacific Ocean, the South Pacific Ocean, the Arctic Ocean, the Southern Ocean, or the Indian Ocean, and with the Queen of Beta and her husband, the Queen of the Coast and her husband, the Queen of Shylon and her husband, the Queen of Yemunah and her husband, or the Queen of Delta and her husband, let all known and unknown, personal and ancestral contracts, alliances, connections, links, covenants, partnerships with these water spirits be broken, liquidated, dissolved, and nullified, effective immediately, by the power of Jesus the Christ, in Jesus' name.

I pray that all monuments representing my image, and the image of my family bloodline, be destroyed beyond usage, and I scatter and destroy every astral psychic aquatic weapon that is programmed and sent into my life. Let all witchcraft, mermaid and siren operational ground, naval artillery, aquatic barracks, naval military bases, forts and weapons in the salty waters within all five major zones of the marine kingdom sustain severe destruction for my sake and for the sake of my children and children's children.

I destroy all powers and strongholds in my life that are tied, connected, and empowered by ancient altars or kingdoms of "Okeanos," the "Mediterranean Sea," the "Atlantic Ocean," the "Indian

Ocean," or to the Pillars of Hercules, and to Lumani, Banni, Lemuria, Gamma, and Atlantis by the voice of God, by fire, and by thunder.

I pray and call down consuming holy fire and lightning from the Lord God of the Heavens and the Earth upon all you water forces attacking my life and who have been attacking my life since childhood.

I declare by the seven flames of fire that I am no more under the bondage of you water demons and psychic spirits, and all water covenants that are over my life from the ancient foundations of my ancestors; they are hereby nullified, liquidated, and dissolved, effective immediately.

Destroying Witchcraft Against You From The Waters

Every witchcraft incantation and invocation taking place on the seaside or river mouth, bearing my name, item, or image, or the image, photo, or item of my child/children, I call lightning to scatter these river mouth rituals and strike down any witch, warlock, satanist, or sorcerer performing this incantation; for it is written in Psalms 18:14, **"Yea, he sent out his arrows, and scattered them; and he shot out lightnings, and discomfited them."**
Psalms 58:7, **"Let them melt away as waters which run continually: when he bendeth his bow to shoot his arrows, let them be as cut in pieces."**

In the name of Jesus, and by the power of the Holy Spirit, I invoke the power and authority given to me in Luke 10:19, and I call forth a destructive earthquake within the ocean floor of the astral realm, and I command an immediate shifting and collapse of the tectonic plate beneath the grounds of every witchcraft, mermaid, and siren operational center located in the ocean floor, in the deep-ocean basins, in the mid-ocean ridges, in the continental margin, in the continental crust, in the continental rise, in the continental slope, in the continental shelf, and in the oceanic crust under the coastal waters.

Let every form of voodoo, blue witchcraft, white witchcraft, black witchcraft, red witchcraft, or even green witchcraft that is done or working against my life and generation from within any of the five submarine basins of the Caribbean Sea—the Yucatán Basin, the Cayman Basin, the Colombian Basin, the Venezuelan Basin, and the Grenada Basin—let the star from Heaven fall into the Caribbean Sea and destroy all witchcraft within this body of water for my sake, in Jesus' name I pray.

By the power and name of Jesus Christ of Nazareth, I bind, destroy, and banish from my life, from my home, my ministry, and from my bloodline, the presence, influence, manipulations, and powers of Oceanus, the Atlanteans, the Pleiadeans, the Oceanids, Nixies, water Nymphs, the Naiads, Mermaids, Merfolk, Undines, Hippocampi, Nereus, the Nereids, the Alseids (nymphs of the groves), the Potamoi, the Naiads - nymphs of the springs, streams, and rivers, and the offspring of the vast aquatic family of Oceanus or Poseidon (Neptune) and their subjects, confidants, allies, counterparts, and all the forces of the fountains, ponds, streams, rainwater, and the salt and fresh waters of the world.

By the authority of the Throne of Yah, my God and King, I say to the sub-aquatic occult world, let your operations, ceremonies, rituals, formulas, and curses fall, be broken asunder, be dismantled, and be rendered impotent, powerless, defenseless, weaponless, unrectified, ineffective, disqualified, useless, and clueless against my life from this very moment, effective immediately, in Y'ahushua's name, for it is written in Psalms 35:8, **"Let destruction come upon him at unawares; and let his net that he has hid catch himself: into that very destruction let him fall."**

I decree by the decree of the Blood of Jesus and the Council of the Most High, a second time, and I say, I will not be food or meat for water nymphs, mermaids, or sirens; neither will I be a sacrifice of any kind for the deities and dynasties of the waters.

By the power of Jesus Christ, who is exalted above all, let the waters above the earth, on the earth, and under the earth glorify the God who is the Living God.

Any astral poison, aquatic magic, and blue magic under the command of any water deity or dynasty, projecting into my home for vicious psychic attacks and manipulations, swift and progressive destruction, persistent predicaments, recurring calamities, repetitive failures, blockages, hindrances, disappointments, contamination, sensual defilement, marriage dismantlement, disgrace, and mutation of afflictions, shame, disgrace, and backwardness, and a mandate for my death, annihilation, madness, and destruction of my joy, peace, finances, health, and success, I call upon the Voice of the Lord in Psalms 29:3 to neutralize, disarm, and dismantle the force of these water occult powers and psychic manipulations.

I also call upon the Lord God of Psalms 18:8 and I say, O Lord God of David, breathe smoke out of Your nostrils, and devouring fire out of Your mouth, upon these evil powers of oceanic witchcraft, and release the rebuke of the LORD, and the blast of the breath of Your nostrils, upon these marine spirits, in Jesus' name. [2 Samuel 22:16].

All you water nymphs, sirens, gods and goddesses, kings and queens, princes and princesses, all marine creatures, tritons, mermaids, sirens, and all other forms of aquatic elemental spirits, water dragons and serpents, and all you aquatic troops, and members of the water dynasties within the different zones, wielding tridents or other aquatic weapons and devices of captivity, torture and calamities, and all squads of the naval forces of darkness, working and conspiring and devising evil and destruction against my life, my destiny and my home in the water occult world, in the rivers, lakes and seas, be burned and consumed by the electric fire and dynamic thunderclaps from Heaven, and let all your astral poisons from the supreme elementals and the astral forces become useless, ineffective and powerless, and their force and velocity dissolved and come to naught, effective immediately, by the God of Abraham, Isaac, and Jacob.

Recovering Your Life From Fresh & Salty Water Kingdoms

Lord, my life has been ambushed by water spirits. Intervene, O God, by lightning and thunder, for it is written in Psalms 81:7, **"You called in trouble, and I delivered you; I answered you in the secret place of thunder."**

Therefore, I declare a holy war of fire and light against the laws, principles, powers, and jurisdictions of the Aquatic Occult World, their princes, gods, goddesses, queens, princesses, and subordinates.

By fire, lightning, and thunder, in the name of Y'ahushua, I pull out my life, my destiny, my health, my mind, my children, my household, my career, my glory, my anointings, my ministry, my soul, my star, my success, my business, my future, and my wealth from the Bermuda Triangle, from the Mediterranean Sea, the Adriatic Sea, the Black Sea, the Red Sea, the Sargasso Sea, the Arabian Sea, the Caspian Sea, the Baltic Sea, the Persian Gulf, and from the North Atlantic Ocean, the South Atlantic Ocean, the North Pacific Ocean, the South Pacific Ocean, the Arctic Ocean, the Southern Ocean, the Indian Ocean, and from the Congo River, the River Nile, the Mississippi River, the Amazon River, the Orinoco River, the St. Lawrence River, the Niger River, and all lesser rivers, where my life was thrown through witchcrafts.

It is written in 2 Samuel 22:17-18, **"He sent from above, he took me; he drew me out of many waters; He delivered me from my strong enemy, *and* from them that hated me: for they were too strong for me."**

Wherever my life, destiny, health, mind, children, household, career, glory, anointings, ministry, soul, star, success, business, future, and wealth are bound beneath a River, a "Tributary," an "Estuary," a "Strait," "Channels," "Canals," a "Fjard," a "Bay," a "Gulf," a "Fjord," a "Bight," a "Sound," a "Cove," an "Inlet," or a "Polynya," I loose my life, destiny, and belongings from beneath these waters. I command that all that was stolen from me be set free, rise to the surface, and be recovered from the hands of every water entity connected to these dark water kingdoms, effective immediately.

I call upon the God of Jeshurun, who rides upon the heaven in my help, in his excellency on the sky [Deut 33:26], and by faith I say let the Angel Micha'el, Gabri'el, Rapha'el, and Uri'el place a hook of brass and iron in the jaw and nostril of every water Dragon, Serpent, Python, Eel, and Anaconda from these fresh and salty waters, who are programmed, mandated, and scheduled to fight against my life. Let the Angels of the Lord of hosts drag out these water Dragons, Serpents, Pythons, Eels, and Anacondas from the 7 oceans, the 76 Seas, and from the rivers mentioned above, in chains of fire and despair in Jesus' name.

By Jesus, I cast these water creatures into desert places, and I bind them in chains of fire to the dry, hot sand of the desert. Let them be persecuted by the flames of the Sun seven times, and let the creatures of the desert devour these water creatures in the mighty name of Jesus.

I come against the fallen Angel Azazel, and all water spirits under his jurisdiction, who are in charge of bracelets, ornaments, cosmetics, and the beautification industries of the marine kingdom.

Any beauty item manufactured beneath the waters that the water queens have used to entrap me and my destiny, and items under the waters, and any beauty product they would try to seduce me with; perfumes, assorted types of cosmetics: lipsticks, face powders, eye shadows, eyes and lip liners, eyelash extensions, face primers, foundation, contour powder/cream, creams, concealers, blusher, highlighters, bronzers, setting spray/powders, eye primers, mascara, lip gloss/balms, applicators, O Lord, remove these far from me, and destroy these enchanted things from my life.

Also, everything that carries the signature of the occult in my home, office, job, business, and school exposes them to the light of fire, in Jesus' name.

Judgement Upon Human & Demon Water Occult Agents

In Jesus' name, I address the occult kingdoms of the seas, oceans, lakes, rivers, streams, ponds, waterfalls, and fountains, and all psychic spirit creatures within them, who are competing for my mental, financial, physical, sexual, social, and psychological destruction and death. I say by the word of the Most High, I will NOT be food or meat for water nymphs, mermaids, or sirens, nor for the water dragons and pythons; neither will I be a sacrifice of any kind for the deities and dynasties of the waters because, according to Psalms 91:9-11, I have made the LORD, who is my refuge, even the Most High, my habitation.

No evil shall befall me, nor shall any plague come near my dwelling. For it is written in Psalms 91:11 that the Lord shall give His angels charge over me to keep me in all my ways.

Heavenly Father, my Lord and my God, I call upon the thunderous voice of "Ha'Ari Yahudah" [the Lion of Judah] to roar against my enemies beneath the waters.

Let Your eternal roar destroy the foundations of the waters beneath, in the occult astral realms. It is written in Psalms 29:3, **"The voice of the LORD is upon the waters; the God of glory thunders; the LORD is above many waters."**

Therefore, thunder with a great thundering upon the waters, O Lord God of the Heavens and the Earth, and stir up a 24.0 earthquake and tectonic shift beneath the foundations of the aquatic psychic occult civilizations, and let their monuments, mirrors, surveillance infrastructure, communication infrastructure, metropolitan infrastructure, idols, images, and laboratories be demolished to rubble and debris. For it is written in 2 Samuel 22:16, **"And the channels of the sea appeared, the foundations of the world were discovered, at the rebuking of the LORD, at the blast of the breath of his nostrils."**

Through this judgement upon the occult, Lord Jesus, let it be known to all occult kingdoms of darkness that I cannot be destroyed by the evil powers of the gates of Hell, because it is written, "I will build my church; and the gates of hell shall not prevail against it [Mat 16:18]; No weapon that is formed against me shall prosper [Isaiah 54:17]; I am in Christ and Christ is in me [John 6:56]; my life is hid in Christ [Col 3:3]; I am of God, and have overcome them: because greater is he that is in me than he that is in the world [1 John 4:4.

In the exalted name of Y'ahushua, I release confusion in the technologies of the water occult psychic kingdoms, and spoil their most sophisticated equipment by fire, and I bind and disarm all psychiatrists, scientists, technical engineers, psychologists, and designers, etc., who are working and devising evil plots and destruction against my life, home, and family.

By the God of hosts, let all agents who are responsible for the demise, destruction, setbacks, failures, sicknesses, and premature deaths in

my family, and have used weapons against me in the past, and are currently working with occult devices to annihilate me and my family, let the judgement of 12 legions of Angels fall upon them, and let these marine workers be brought to severe judgement, in the name of Jesus, for it is written in 2 Samuel 22:7-8, **"In my distress I called upon the LORD, and cried to my God: and he did hear my voice out of his temple, and my cry *did enter* into his ears."**
"Then the earth shook and trembled; the foundations of heaven moved and shook, because he was wroth."

Arrows of Combat Decrees

Any water sorcery under the rivers, seas, and oceans, remotely controlling my life, children, and household, let there be a breaking forth of lightning and fire storms upon you in the night, and be destroyed before dawn, in Jesus name.

In the name of Jesus of Nazareth, by the power of the Holy Spirit, I jam every radio wave, signal, transmission, and all frequencies within the waters that are carrying information about me, my children, household, and family members, and I break all telecommunications within the fresh and salty waters, and between the waters and the air, or land, or subterranean occult worlds.

In the name of Y'ahushua, I strike the eyes of the waters, and I destroy the powers of the Animus third eye, and blind all aquatic reflections projecting my life beneath the waters.

In the name of Jesus, I release the blast of the breath of God's nostrils written in 2 Samuel 22:16, and I shatter to pieces all evil monitoring mirrors, black obsidian mirrors, crystal balls, scrying devices, water reflections, gemstones, and all witchcraft art of scrying located under the waters, which are being used to monitor me, my children, and household.

Every marine witchcraft that has introduced a spirit husband or wife, or marine children in my dreams, be vanquished in oblivion by fire and lightning, in the name of Jesus.

Every agent of marine witchcraft physically or spiritually attached to my marriage to frustrate it, I strike you down and destroy your witchcraft powers in Jesus' name.

Every agent of marine witchcraft attacking my finances, my business, or employment through dreams, I command you to fall and perish by a lightning strike in the name of Jesus.

By the jurisdiction of Jesus as my Lord and Savior, and the indwelling Holy Spirit within my spirit, I file a counter report in the Courts of Heaven against all prayers, petitions, decrees, proclamations, and occult court orders made against my life, my family, my children, and my household by fresh and saltwater spirits.

I pull down every stronghold of bewitchment, enchantment, jinx, or divination fashioned against me by marine witches and spirits in the Devil's Triangle. Let all marine witches and spirits within the Bermuda Triangle who are fighting against my life be banished into the Sargasso Sea and be entangled in the Sargassum for three seasons, effective immediately, in all the names of the Son of the Most High God in Heaven.

Let the thunderbolts of God locate and destroy every marine witchcraft coven, sub-aquatic judicial council, high court, and congress where discussions and decisions are made against my life, my children, and my household.

Any body of water in my village in which my umbilical cord was thrown, I call forth the fire of El Eliyahu to descend and dry up this water in the spirit and let the Angels of God retrieve my umbilical cord, in Jesus name.

Any body of water in my village in which my eyes, ears, organs, health, marriage, education, and job opportunities were thrown into, I call forth the fire of El Eliyahu to descend and dry up this water in the spirit and let the Angels of God retrieve my sight, hearing, and life, in the name of Jesus.

Let every spiritual weapon of wickedness fashioned against me from under any river or sea be destroyed by the fire of the God of hosts, whose voice is upon many waters (Psalm 29:3), in the name of Jesus.

In the name of Jesus, I say every arrow shot into my life from under any water by witchcraft powers, come out of me and return upon the demons who sent you, or are behind you, evil arrows, effective immediately.

Any spiritual bondage in my life that may be associated with dreams where you are always around water or in water, let my soul be pulled out from blind water witchcraft, and let my soul be delivered from the psychic realm of occult manipulation in my dreams, in Jesus name.

Every curse of "Aquaphilia": where I am aroused by water and/or in watery environments, including bathtubs or swimming pools, rivers, etc., I curse this curse and pray that this curse of Aquaphilia be cast out from my life, and all water demons be gone from me, effective immediately, in Jesus name.

I pray against every form of higher psychic manipulation placed upon my life through my family bloodline in my mother's house or my father's house, because of the use of sex toys, porn videos, porn magazines, or adult magazines, pictophilia, sexual arousal creams, studs, and condoms, or manipulation placed upon me because of my use of these sensual paraphernalia. Let every water spirit that is attached to these items be banished from my life, as I renounce the queen of the Coast and the queen of India, and break their holds on my life, in Jesus' mighty name.

I command any evil material and water elemental demon that entered my body through contact with any marine witchcraft agent or items to be cast out of me now. I banish these materials and elemental spirits by fire and order them to leave my body, effective immediately, in Jesus' name.

Every sexual pollution from marine spirits that has entered my body through unclean sex, dreams, substances ingested (spiritually or physically), through rituals done on my behalf, or through marine spirit-cursed items, let these pollutants be flushed out of my body, soul, and mind by the blood of Jesus, effective immediately, in Jesus name.

Any evil name given to me under any water occult kingdom, I reject it and cancel it from over my life with the blood of Jesus. Wherever this evil name has been registered and is named over my life, let the records and registers be burned to ashes, effective immediately, in the name of Jesus of Nazareth.

Every image constructed under any water to represent my bondage, destruction, shame, and setback, and every marine witchcraft oppression and manipulation brought about by these images, I dismantle all these images, water powers, enigmas, and blue magic, and I dismantle every siege of the enemy made against my life and household, effective immediately.

Let the blood of the Lamb of God erase every evil record about my life, past and present, and remove my name from the book of death and the book of evil deeds, in the name of Jesus of Nazareth.

I pollute every occult river, sea, stream, pool, and pond with the blood of Jesus, and I command the water to stink [Exodus 7:21, **"And the fish** that *was* in the river died; and the river stank"]. I kill all evil creatures in proximity, and I command all water occult kingdoms fighting against my life from the womb, from childhood, teenagerhood, or adulthood to begin to stink with the rotting corpse of these evil creatures, now, effective immediately, in Jesus' name; for it is written in Exodus 8:13-14, **"And the LORD did according to the word of Moses; and the frogs died out of the houses, out of the villages, and out of the fields. And they gathered them together upon heaps: and the land stank."**

Father, thank you that you have been good to me on Earth and have delivered me and my family from the hold of the occult water kingdoms.
Worthy is the Lamb that was slain to receive power, and riches, and wisdom, and strength, and honour, and glory, and blessing. [Rev 5:12].

5. Prayers Against Witchcraft Operating In Your Life By Night

Heavenly Father, I give you thanks and praise because you are the God of my life. You are exalted above every mountain, height, and kingdom. Be magnified in the heavens and the earth, for you are holy.

Isaiah 44:26 says, **"You confirm the word of your servant, and performs the counsel of your messengers;"**
I stand upon the authority of the word of God where the Lord Jesus said to us in Luke 10:19, **"Behold, I give unto you power to tread on serpents and scorpions, and over all the power of the enemy; and nothing shall by any means hurt you."**
The Word of God commands me in Proverbs 6:5 where it says, **"Deliver thyself as a roe from the hand of the hunter, and as a bird from the hand of the fowler."**
It is also written in Proverbs 12:6, **"but the mouth of the upright shall deliver them."**

Therefore, according to Proverbs 6:5 and Proverbs 12:6, I speak with my mouth by faith, and I deliver myself from you, demon of all variants of witchcraft, as a roe from the hand of the hunter, and as a bird from the hand of the fowler.
As I venture into this arena of warfare against the nocturnal powers of evil, I bind the kingdom of the Prince of Darkness and all its subjects.

Your word says that the Moon is to rule by night, but the kingdom of the occult is using the Moon to fight against us. However, Your word says that the Moon will not smite us by night.
In this regard, by Jesus of Nazareth, I bind, disarm, neutralize, and banish from my life and home the aura, essence of the fallen Angel

Sariel, and all evil spirits under his jurisdiction, who have revealed to man the mysteries of the course of the moon in witchcraft.

All witchcraft operations against my life using the gate of the midnight moon, the full moon, new moon, first quarter, last quarter, the waxing moon, or the waning moon,

I banish you witchcraft operations, forces, and realms, using the planetary alignment, the enigma of the four elements, water, fire, earth, and air, or with the enigma of the night forest, intergalactic forces, interstellar forces, planetary forces, and cosmic elements to work witchcraft against me, I render you powerless, void, ineffective, dead, and broken from my life now, in the name of Jesus, Son of the Living God.

In Jesus' name, I block, stop, shut down, and destroy from over my life every signal, frequency, transmission, velocity, and telegram communicating between the occult realms and altars and antennas, orchestrating my destruction and annihilation across the astral layers of the land, sea, and air during the night.

Also, in Numbers 23:23 it is written, **"Surely *there is* no enchantment against Jacob, neither *is there* any divination against Israel: according to this time it shall be said of Jacob and of Israel, what hath God wrought!"**
It is also written in Micah 5:12, **"And I will cut off witchcrafts out of thine hand; and thou shalt have no *more* soothsayers:"**

In the name of Jesus, I break the power and activities of all witches, warlocks, Satanists, Wiccans, Freemasons, and sorcerers that are set over my life, body, soul, and mind during the nights in times past, which are currently working against me; and I strike these occult agents with blindness, deafness, and dumbness for a season, and I

send them into captivity, effective immediately, in the name of Jesus of Nazareth.
It is written in Isaiah 30:27, **"Behold, the name of the LORD comes from far, burning with His anger, and in thick uplifting of smoke; His lips are full of fury, and His tongue like a devouring fire."**

By the power of the burning with the anger of the Lord, and by the thick uplifting of smoke; by the fullness of fury of His lips, and by His tongue which is like a devouring fire, [Isaiah 30:27], I break and destroy the cycles of witchcraft, curses, and satanic holds over my life. I banish the power of the Order of Demi-gods, the Metallic Council, the Planetary Spirits, Avatars, Fallen Angels, Guardians of the Flame, Solar Lords, Inter-Planetary Lords, Inter-Galactic Lords, Guardians of Fate, and the Cycles of Life.

I also banish the Astral Poisons, Powers, Rulers of Darkness, Legion of the Air, and Subterranean forces. I reject the powers of the Astral and Terrestrial Hierarchy, the Order of the Queen of Heaven, the Queen of the South, Aquatic forces, the Queen of Beta, the Queen of Shylon, the Queen of Yemunah, the Queen of Delta, and the Queen of the Coast. I reject the Mother Anaconda, the Queen of Hades, the ancient spirits of fallen civilizations, the Mermaids, the Sirens, and the Nymphs. I reject the gods and goddesses of rivers, lakes, ponds, and waterfalls.

I reject the dragon entity of the city of Gupha in the Bermuda Triangle, the spirits of the dead, and the spirits of the psychic elementals, including the Sylphs, Salamanders, Gnomes, and Undines. I banish all powers within the Inner Esoteric framework that seek to destroy my life through witchcraft and fight against my blessings and destiny.

I rise in power, the name and the velocity in the Spirit of the Messiah Jesus, and I destroy all witchcraft attacks, manipulations, and curses

that are currently operating upon my life from the Book of Shadows, the Book of Technique Tactic, the Book of the Dead, the Book of Grimoire, The Satanic Bible, or from the ambiance and enigma of water, the ambiance and enigma of the soil, the ambiance and enigma of the air, the ambiance and enigma of sound frequency, the ambiance and the enigma of nature.

I also pray that all witchcraft powers that are operating in and over my life from the Bermuda Triangle, from the Mediterranean Sea, the Adriatic Sea, the Black Sea, the Red Sea, the Sargasso Sea, the Arabian Sea, the Caspian Sea, the Baltic Sea, the Persian Gulf, or from the North Atlantic Ocean, the South Atlantic Ocean, the North Pacific Ocean, the South Pacific Ocean, the Arctic Ocean, the Southern Ocean, or from the Indian Ocean, that they be neutralized, destroyed, and banished into oblivion, and every link, pack, covenant, soul tie that I have with these waters, that they be liquidated and nullified now, by the power of Jesus Christ the Nazarene, effective immediately.

By the authority of the Word of Almighty God, I destroy by lightning, thunder, and fire every witchcraft power that has infiltrated my life in the gates of the nighttime with blockages, setbacks, hindrances, poverty, lack, barrenness, calamities, misfortunes, darkness, shame, disgrace, failures, infirmities, and premature death. With the power of the Lord Jesus, I break these witchcraft powers and the pestilence that walks in darkness.

Reveal Your Pillar of Fire by night, O Lord God, and let darkness become a snare for all witches and demons working in the night against me.

By the fire of the Holy Spirit in Jesus' Name, I destroy all witchcraft that is operating in my life for setbacks, for hindrances, blockages, unfruitfulness, and unproductivity; attacks set to cause sicknesses, attacks to cause mental problems and psychological and emotional shutdowns, witchcraft to cause continual disappointments, shame, and disgrace, attacks to cause incompleteness and incompetence, witchcraft to cause poverty, lack, insufficiency, and always wanting and never getting, attacks to cause unachievements and incompleteness in everything that I have started.

I pray, if there be any cauldron pot, kettle, basin, hearth, furnace, or altar, boiling and roasting my life by means of witchcraft, I destroy these witchcraft vessels and altars by lightning and thunderclaps. I invoke the descending fire from the throne of Jesus Christ of Nazareth to consume these witch items to ashes now, by the authority of the name of Jesus Christ.

I stand against the kingdom of darkness using the moonlight against me, and I pray by the name of Y'ahushua Son of the Most High God Yah, and say, let the moonlight become 7 times more radioactive than radium and 7 times more lethal than polonium to any witch, warlock, Satanist, or occult practitioner who uses moonlight to work magic, spells, incantations, and rituals against me.
I pray that it be done as I have asked in Jesus' name, Amen and Amen.

6. Prayers Against Witchcraft Operating In Your Life By Daytime

I pray against destruction pursuing me via the diabolical techniques of various astral poisons and psychic manipulations operating in the light of the Day.

I dismantle, bind, disarm, neutralize, and banish from my life and home the aura, essence, and spirit of the fallen Angel Shamsiel, and all evil spirits under his jurisdiction and regime, who taught man the signs of the sun, and who are over the sun and are using the sun to attack me and my family.

I now dismantle the spirit of the ancient sun gods, "Enlil," "Ra," "Sol Invictus," "Utu," "Helios," "Apollo," "Eos," "Hemera," and "the spirit of Surya".

I pray against and destroy their solar weapons of mass destruction.

By the power of the Living God of Abraham, Isaac, and Israel, I neutralized and destroyed the metaphysical intercourse and all manipulations of corrupt occult and esoteric powers, operating with the highest rate of occult velocity against my life through the gates of the Sun, in order to bring about my mental, spiritual, and physical death and destruction.

I invoke the Pillar of Cloud by day to disarm all diurnal operations of the evil forces of Hell.

I destroy all diabolical strategies, satanic traps, and snares from the book of "Technique Tactic," the Book of Shadows, the Book of Grimoire, and the Book of the Dead that someone programmed against me in the psychic layers during the night and that are set to start working and operating with the energy of sunlight and radiation energy, in Y'ahushua's name.

In the name of Y'ahushua, I demolish by fire the lowest to the highest level of diabolical assaults projecting from the Book of Grimoire against me and my household, and I destroy every Satanic formula of death, destruction, and elimination that is sent upon me at 12 Midday.

Send Your judgement oh Lord, and give all these categories of demons and agents of Hell the portion of their cup, for it is written in Psalms 11:6, **"Upon the wicked he shall rain snares, fire and brimstone, and a horrible tempest: this shall be the portion of their cup."**

Heavenly Father, let the voices and the Seven Thunders within the presence of Your enthroned and exalted Son Jesus roar against every demonic and satanic throne that is exalted above the stars seeking to be like God, be pulled down and be scattered and banished in chains and disgrace into deserted places of oblivion within the universes.

Let each of these evil powers seeking to manipulate me be met with resistance and defences of lightning.

Judge them by fire and destroy them by fire, and let every stronghold be broken down to ash and become as useless ash and debris, in Jesus name.

I stand in the light of Yah's Glory, in the name of Jesus, Messiah of Nazareth, and I quench all fiery darts, deflect flying arrows, neutralize satanic forces, demolish satanic regiments, dismantle evil plots, scatter diabolical plans, unset spiritual snares, banish witchcraft incantations, disqualify satanic formulas, strike witches with madness, and unleash terror upon demons assigned against me.

Let the cosmic evil forces of the air, the naval forces of the marine kingdom, the Cro-Magnon forces of the subterranean world, the Pestiferous forces of the forest, and all psychic arsenals that are formed against my life within the seven kingdoms of darkness explode to pieces by the terror of God's divine judgement.

Let every witch, warlock, sorcerer, wizard, or occult practitioner working witchcraft of any form against me, during this daylight, receive fire, and sustain extreme and severe friction burns, cold burns, thermal burns, radiation burns, chemical burns, and electrical burns from the fiery presence of the Lord Jesus and His Angels, as I have spoken it, for it is written in Isaiah 44:26, **"That confirms the word of his servant, and performs the counsel of his messengers;"**
I stand against the kingdom of darkness using the sunlight against me, and I pray by the name of Y'ahushua Son of the Most High God Yah, and say, let the sunlight become 7 times hotter, more radioactive than radium, and 7 times more lethal than polonium to any witch, warlock, satanist, or occult practitioner who uses moonlight to work magic, spells, incantations, and rituals against me.
Lord Jesus, you are the Word, and you are saying to us in Isaiah 54:17, **"No weapon that is formed against thee shall prosper;"**

Oh Lord my God and Saviour, destroy the "Guardians of Fate and the Cycles of life" who are taking shifts, each programmed to fight and manipulate me for 52 days, and destroy the elemental forces using sound vibrations and frequencies to attack me, and also destroy all astral poison set to fight me for cycles of 1,095 days," all seeking to subject me to zero point.

I call upon the fire of the Most High God to burn in all cosmic crevices, cosmic space, regions, zones, and centers, and let the lightnings of fires burn, scatter, and destroy all cosmic forces, cosmic nets, and cosmic barriers working and fighting against my life under the jurisdiction of the dragons, gods, and goddesses.

I say to you evil powers, you have failed terribly by the laws of the Kingdom of Heaven, in Jesus name.

Father, thank you for giving me the victory in Christ Jesus according to 2 Corinthians 2:14 that says, **"Now thanks be unto God, which always causes us to triumph in Christ, and makes manifest the savour of his knowledge by us in every place"**. Amen and Amen!

7. Setting Yourself Free From Witchcraft Holds

Any spirit of witchcraft that is causing me to always be hiding, always scared, always terrified, always running away, always suspicious, and every spirit that causes me to walk in paranoia, lack of confidence, easily frightened, powerless in confrontations, ineffective in applying boldness, useless in offensive warfare, and barren in my victory against evil spirits, by the Blood of Jesus and the fire of the judicial altar of God Almighty, I break this curse of witchcraft from my life.

All witchcraft operations against my life using the gate of the midnight moon, the full moon, new moon, first quarter, last quarter, the waxing moon or waning moon, or using the gates of any of the seven seas, the five oceans, continental rivers, forests, mountains or the 12 Zodiac signs, the Requiem Mass, Satanic holiday, Black Mass, Black Sabbath, and all Samhain rituals, Yule rituals, Imbolc rituals, Ostara rituals, Beltane rituals, Litha rituals, planetary alignment, weather patterns, the enigma of the four elements, water, fire, earth and air, or with the enigma of the forest, intergalactic forces, interstellar forces, planetary forces and cosmic elements; I banish you witchcraft operations, forces and realms and I render you powerless, void, ineffective, dead, and broken from my life now, in the name of Jesus, Son of the Living God.

All witchcraft and sorcery that are eating, drinking, and destroying my life, or are feeding on my life, my glory, my destinies, I destroy these evil workings of witchcraft once and for all, now in Jesus' name.
All witchcraft that is operating in my life to strike me with financial, physical, and spiritual barrenness, I destroy and banish from my life these evil powers now, in Jesus' name.
All witchcraft that is operating in my life to cause me to have a broken and sad life, sorrowful encounters in life, advanced distress

syndromes, foreclosure of my home, bankruptcy, loss of my job, shut-up heavens, loss of memory, childlessness, etc.,

I break, banish, and destroy from my life these witchcraft powers, effective immediately, in Jesus' name.
All witchcraft that is operating in my life, causing me to sow good seeds and not receive a harvest, and is causing me to work hard and not see or enjoy the fruits of my labour, I break the curse and banish these witchcraft powers from my life, with immediate effect, in Jesus' name.

I pray, counter, and destroy every witchcraft power and manipulation that is currently operating upon my life to make me a victim of advanced calamities, a victim of advanced terror and living nightmares, a victim of advanced bullying and victimization, criticism, and rejection. I revoke, destroy, and banish these witchcraft operations from my life, effective immediately, in Jesus name.

All witchcraft attacks causing good jobs to pass me by and go to less qualified people, I renounce, revoke, destroy, and banish these demonic operations from my life, in Jesus' name.
I say, every psychic element by witchcraft assigned to waste away my life, I revoke, bind, and condemn these attacks, and I say, waste away, like salt placed upon a slug, all you witches and elemental spirits, now, in Jesus' name.

All witchcraft upon my life, causing my less qualified friends, family, and enemies to get good opportunities and jobs in life, while I sit here waiting, I destroy this curse of witchcraft from my life. By the power of the Lord Jesus Christ, break now, for this evil will not be my portion, in Jesus' name.

I command every witchcraft prayer, household, water, or coven witchcraft power that has been programmed and assigned to waste my life to waste itself instead, in the name of Jesus.
Let all astral stones and weapons of death, magical formulas, and occult principles set against my destiny on earth be hereby destroyed by the fervent heat of Jesus Christ.
All witchcraft curses causing me to give birth to sorrows, calamity, and emptiness, I break the power of these witchcrafts from my life, in Jesus name.

I revoke, break, and banish all witchcraft curses that are placed upon my life by a voodoo priest, witch doctor, shaman, native doctor, and I destroy any voodoo altar or shrine activated against my life, effective immediately.

I revoke, destroy, and banish all witchcraft powers that are sitting upon my life because of my parents, grandparents, or great-grandparents, both biological and non-biological, or by any other family members, or because of my friends, acquaintances, neighbours, schoolmates, teachers, or a school principal. I am set free from this witchcraft curse now, in Jesus name.

I pray against all satanic and diabolical attacks that are currently ruling and manipulating my life because of Catholic prayers, the Catholic rosary, the Catholic cross, any Catholic prayer book, the statues of Catholic saints, the Catholic holy water, the Catholic paschal candle, the Monstrance, or any prayer done against my life within any Catholic fraternity or secret society.
I say to you evil powers of Catholic magics and holy magics, break now and be destroyed from my life and generation perpetually, effective immediately, in Jesus name.

In addition, I nullify, liquidate, and banish all evil attacks sent upon my life by the legionaries of the Legion of Mary, the Confraternities, and every secret society under the Vatican. I say, be gone now from me, in Jesus' mighty name.

Every and any coven or witch who is using the enigmas of nature as a point for accessing the astral powers of the five esoteric seals of darkness against my life, to curse me and destroy me, let lightning strike this witch or coven now, in Jesus name.

For it is written in Psalms 71:13, **"Let them be confounded *and* consumed that are adversaries to my soul; let them be covered *with* reproach and dishonour that seek my hurt."**

I also renounce and revoke in Jesus' name all witchcraft attacks that are sitting upon my life because of the incantations, rituals, and witchcraft made in a Black Mass, on a Black Sabbath, on Easter, on Good Friday, on Christmas Day, through Halloween, through Saturnalia, All Souls' Day, All Saints' Day, or on any satanic and Paganic holiday.

Destroy them by Your judgement, oh Lord, and give all these categories of demons and agents of Hell the portion of their cup, for it is written in Psalms 11:6, **"Upon the wicked he shall rain snares, fire and brimstone, and a horrible tempest: this shall be the portion of their cup."**

It is written in Ezekiel 13:20, **"Wherefore thus saith the Lord GOD; Behold, I *am* against your pillows, wherewith ye there hunt the souls to make *them* fly, and I will tear them from your arms, and will let the souls go, *even* the souls that ye hunt to make *them* fly."**

Eze 13:21, **"Your kerchiefs also will I tear, and deliver my people out of your hand, and they shall be no more in your hand to be hunted; and ye shall know that I *am* the LORD".**

I speak through the fire of the Blood of Jesus and say, let every witchcraft curse set upon my life by day and by night, to destroy my life, my reputation, my dignity, my mind, my purpose, future, and destiny, and to suck the potency, exuberance, and resplendency of my star, be electrocuted by the lightning of God's presence; catch fire and be burned to ashes now, in the name of Jesus of Nazareth.

I speak through the fire of the Blood of Jesus, and decree that every witchcraft placed upon my life by day and by night, working through psychic vibrations, seeking to transmute, change, alter, and demote my destiny of success, wealth, happiness, and completeness, and seeking to make my life a life of shame, poverty, failure, incompetence, disgrace, and incompleteness, be subjected by force and be decapitated, disassembled, and banished by lightning, thunder, and the fire of Jesus Christ of Nazareth. You evil powers, I say to you, be electrocuted by the lightning of God's presence; catch fire and be burnt to ashes now, in the name of Jesus of Nazareth.

I speak through the fire of the Blood of Jesus and say, every transmission and communicable command carrying the code and formula for my death and destruction, utilizing the psychic elementals in the subtle layers of psychic operations, be electrocuted by the lightning of God's presence; catch fire and be burned to ashes now, in the name of Jesus of Nazareth.

I speak through the fire of the Blood of Jesus, and I renounce, revoke, shatter, and destroy all familiar curses and combined elements of Astral spirits who are programmed to sustain daily psychic attacks against my household for 1,095 days through witchcraft manipulations. You evil powers, be electrocuted by the lightning of God's presence; catch fire and be burnt to ashes now, in the name of Jesus of Nazareth.

I say let every astral poison and venom of secret witchcraft be neutralized and lose all power and effectiveness in my life, for I release destruction, desolation, degradation, annihilation, liquidation, and eradication upon all you elemental spirits plotting and concocting an attack and assassination on my life.

I burn to ashes all roots of familiar, family, and mysterious witchcraft and sorcery, and all you evil spirits, I burn to the ground your regiment, your fortress, your kingdom, and barrack that you have built in my life, by coals of fire, which hath a most vehement flame; [Jonah 4:8].

Oh Lord Jesus, protect me from all evil by Your light and destroy all diabolical strategies and satanic traps sent against me.

Be exalted, O my loving Father, and thank you for giving me the victory today against and over witchcraft. For this, I give you praise and glory. Amen and Amen.

8. Destroying Weapons Of Witchcraft

I stand upon the authority of the Word of God where the Lord Jesus said to us in Luke 10:19, **"Behold, I give unto you power to tread on serpents and scorpions, and over all the power of the enemy: and nothing shall by any means hurt you."**
It is also written in Luke 10:17, **"And the seventy returned again with joy, saying, Lord, even the devils are subject unto us through thy name"**.

I send the fire of amber from the presence of Jesus Christ into every occult sphere, region, and realm, and I dismantle and scatter in perpetual confusions and terrors every Requiem Mass, Satanic holiday, Black Mass, Black Sabbath, and all Samhain rituals, Yule rituals, Imbolc rituals, Ostara rituals, Beltane rituals, Litha rituals, and the rituals of the midday sun, rituals of the midnight moon, rituals of the full moon, rituals of the new moon, rituals of the waxing moon, and rituals of the waning moon that are held for my sake and are programmed to fight against my life for my destruction.

I rebuke Satan and the Devil, and I stand in revolt against every witchcraft and satanic paraphernalia that is used or is being used to destroy my life by witchcraft powers. It is written in Psalms 68:2, **"as wax melts before the fire, let the wicked perish in the presence of God."**

In the name of Jesus, by the devouring fire of the tongue of the LORD in Isaiah 30:27, I come against the powers of Darkness as the LORD'S battle axe *and* weapons of war [Jer 51:20].
I destroy from my life, spirit, soul, and body, all witchcraft manipulations and curses that are currently operating by satanic formulas, codes, vibrations, frequencies, and incantations from the

Book of Shadows, The Book of Technique Tactics, Book of the Dead, Book of Grimoire, the Satanic Bible, a Paten, a Magical Wand, a Chalice, or Goblet, Magic Candles, a Requiem Monstrance, a Besom or Broom, Boline, a Cauldron, Censer, Cingulum, Johnny Walker, a Scourge, a Spear, a Stang, a Smudge Stick, Voodoo Doll, Tarot Card, Rune Stone, Rune Card, Crystals, Incense, Magical Powders, Dust of my feet, My photo, Clothes, or other items containing my sweat, witch's bag, witches' black box, Palm Tree Leaves, Pumpkin heads, Rooster's head and feet, Urine of Animals, Faeces of Animals, Witch's Herbs, Spell Jars, Salts, Obsidian Mirror, Obsidian Stone or Pendulum, Altar Cloth, Bowl, Bell, and Spoon, etc., things being used in witchcraft spells, rituals, and ceremonies against my life.

I invoke a Divine Judicial Order from the Courts of the Divine Council of the Almighty God, who is the Grand Judge of the Heavens and the Earth, and I command by this Divine Judicial Order and jurisdiction through the Blood of the Lamb that any one of these witchcraft items that would be used to conjure, sustain, or reactivate a curse upon my life turn to powder, in Jesus' holy and mighty name.

Therefore, I call upon the fiery breath of the Holy Spirit and say, Lord Jesus, breathe fire upon and consume to ashes all these witchcraft items and tools mentioned here by the devouring fire of the tongue of the LORD in Isaiah 30:27.
Also, by the power of the Holy Spirit of Jesus Christ, I destroy, confuse, and eradicate all curses of the Sigils, Talisman, Seals, Calls, Binding Ceremonies, Keys, Prayers, Chant, Rituals, smiting, Scrying, Spell work, Divinations, and Incantations sent into and against my life, which are fighting my life on a daily basis. I render these occult ceremonies, rituals, formulas, and witchcraft paraphernalia that worked against me in the night to be rendered impotent, powerless, defenceless, weaponless, unrectified, ineffective, disqualified, useless, and clueless, effective immediately, in Y'ahushua's name, for

it is written in Psalms 35:8, **"Let destruction come upon him at unawares; and let his net that he hath hid catch himself: into that very destruction let him fall."**

Any Obsidian mirror or any other type of mirror that has been placed upon an altar or in a sacred space to amplify evil energy against me, or create a focused atmosphere and amplify evil energy against me, or is used to aid in meditation, energy work sessions, provide spiritual insight about my life, or to deepen spiritual insight and reveal hidden things about my life, or is used as a mirror to my inner self, let these mirrors be shattered to debris by lightning and fire explosions, in Jesus' name.
It is written in Psalms 18:3, **"I will call upon the LORD, who is worthy to be praised: so, shall I be saved from mine enemies."**

For it is written in Isaiah 30:26, **"And the light of the moon shall be as the light of the sun, and the light of the sun shall be sevenfold, as the light of seven days, in the day that the LORD binds up the bruise of His people and heals the stroke of their wound."**

Hear me, all powers of the darkness of occultism. By coals of fire, which have a most vehement flame, and a vehement east wind; [Jonah 4:8], I burn your roots to ashes, and I burn to the ground your regiment, your fortress, your kingdom, and barrack that you have built in my life, and I say let every astral poison and venom of serpents and scorpions be neutralized and lose all power and effectiveness in my life, for I release destruction, desolation, degradation, annihilation, liquidation, and eradication upon all elemental spirits of Pornography.

9. Prayer For The First-Born Child

Father, I praise you in spirit and declare that the Lamb who was slain is worthy to receive power, riches, wisdom, strength, honour, glory, and blessing [Rev 5:12].
Thank you for giving me the grace to stand before you in faith. Lord, I invoke the opening of the gate of warfare by the code name of Elohei Tzevaot, the Lord of hosts, creator of the heavens and the earth.

Jesus, I implore and ask for the intervention of Your divine council, and the ruling of Your 7 Eternal Flames of wisdom and light, requesting that Your 7 golden altars will render Your judgement against the 12 gates of Hell, especially against the destroyer demon of the 999 Mephistophelian seal of darkness, who came to steal, kill, and destroy me as the firstborn child of my mother.
At midnight, smite the kingdom of darkness, O Lord, for my sake and for Your glory.
It is written in Psalms 71:13, **"Let them be confounded and consumed that are adversaries to my soul; let them be covered with reproach and dishonor that seek my hurt."**
O Lord God, you said in Numbers 3:13, **"For every first-born is mine; in the day in which I smote every first-born in the land of Egypt, I sanctified to myself every first-born in Israel: both of man and beast, they shall be mine: I am the Lord."**
You also say in Exodus 13:2, **"Sanctify unto me all the firstborn, whatsoever openeth the womb among the children of Israel, *both* of man and of beast: it *is* mine."** I am sanctified unto you personally, because I am the firstborn that opened the womb.

Likewise, you say in Exodus 13:13, **"and all the firstborn of man among thy children shalt thou redeem."** I am redeemed by the blood of Christ according to Ephesians 1:7 that says, "In **whom we**

have redemption through his blood, the forgiveness of sins, according to the riches of his grace;"

Therefore, I henceforth claim deliverance from all demons through the jurisdiction of my sanctification and redemption in You according to Exodus 13:2, Ephesians 1:7, and Numbers 3:13.
Abba Father, let the fire of Jesus of Nazareth expose and scatter all destructive forces of the seven kingdoms of darkness and the Mephistophelian seals of Hell that I oppose today in prayer. It is written in Psalms 144:6, **"Cast forth lightning, and scatter them: shoot out thine arrows, and destroy them."**
It is written in 2 Samuel 22:15, **"And he sent out arrows, and scattered them; lightning, and discomfited them."**
Therefore, Lord Jesus, I stand in Your word that says to us in Luke 10:19, **"Behold, I give unto you power to tread on serpents and scorpions, and over all the power of the enemy: and nothing shall by any means hurt you."**

On this authority, in the Name of Y'ahushua HaMashiach of Nazareth, by the power of the judgement and the authority of the Word of God in Luke 10:19 and 2 Corinthians 10:4, I bind with hot chains of holy fire, and neutralize, arrest, and bring into captivity under subjection all evil spirits sent to annihilate me because I am the first born.

With the weapons of warfare and total destruction written in Isaiah 41:15-16, Psalms 11:6, and Exodus 9:24, I now call forth an immediate rain of fiery hailstones, snares, terrors, fires, brimstone, horrible tempests, and the fiery terror of God's divine judgement upon all categories and sects of evil spirits assigned and programmed for my destruction in every realm.

By authority in Christ written in Luke 10:19 and Mark 16:17, I cast out and banish by force and fire, lightning and thunder all psychic entities from the third Esoteric Seal 999, the Seal of Destruction, and from the Fourth Esoteric Seal 1330, the Terrestrial Occult Seal, and all psychic entities of calamity, catastrophe, strange phenomena, every demon dominator, elemental psychic entity, the destroyer demons, carnage demons, the demons of high destruction, venom, the armored demons, and the terror of death from the Occult Seals 333, Seal 666, and Seal 003, that are projected against me and are following me, pursuing me, strategizing against me, fighting me, and destroying me in various ways.

Heavenly Father, in Jesus I come to you, seeking deliverance from the strongholds of demonic tribes and clans, and from the powers and visual scope of all surveillance astral devices: the Astral Television, Celestial Mirror, Etheric Gemstone, the tele-dynamite, Akashic Black Stone, Astral Gemstone, Animus Third Eye, Psychic Camera, the Astro-Omnidictator, watcher and peeping spirits, and also from all vicious astral assaults, weapons, traps and snares of the evil powers of the Cro-Magnon world, the Aquatic world, the Pestifera world, the cosmic world and the subterranean world, and all other forces working under the 5 Mephistophelian Occult Seals, which are seeking to ambush and destroy my life and destiny, especially at midnight because I am the first-born child.

I rain tongues of fire upon all these evil spirits, astral poisons and weapons mentioned above, in Jesus' name.
I set myself free from all onslaughts and the harness of the kingdom of darkness that is specifically designed for the firstborn of families.
Exodus 12:29 says, "**And it came to pass, that at midnight the LORD smote all the firstborn in the land of Egypt, from the firstborn of Pharaoh that sat on his throne unto the firstborn of the captive that was in the dungeon.**"

I say in the name of Jesus of Nazareth, by the power of the glory of Fire, all evil entities seek to smite me with death because I am the firstborn; let their firstborn be smitten in my place.

All evil entities who have dug a grave to bury me, because I am the firstborn, let their firstborn be buried in this grave in my place.
Destroy their tridents, sickles, darts, spears, javelins, and arrows of destruction that are fashioned against me, and let me not be led into the secret snares of the ambushment of the esoteric crafts of darkness; for you said in Isaiah 41:11, "**Behold, all they that were incensed against thee shall be ashamed and confounded: they shall be as nothing; and they that strive with thee shall perish.**"

Let Heaven release upon all these astral forces and midnight powers of Hell severe destruction, desolation, degradation, annihilation, liquidation, and eradication within all spheres, kingdoms, regions, and zones for my sake.
All psychic entities of the four elements, powers, personalities, and principalities assigned to destroy my greatness, my upliftment, my spiritual promotion, my next level because I am the firstborn of my parents, I command you to be wasted, you evil beings, by the tongues of holy fire.

You demonic entities, by the three witnesses in the earth, the Spirit, and the water, and the blood: which agree in one, I rebuke and banish you now by fire, effective immediately! In the name of Jesus.

Psychic entities of the four Elements, Powers, personalities, and principalities assigned to plant destructions to my breakthroughs, my testimonies, my miracles, because I am the firstborn of my parents, I pray, by the three witnesses in the earth, the Spirit, and the water, and the blood: which agree in one, I rebuke and banish you now by tongues of fire, effective immediately! In the name of Jesus.

Psychic entities of the four elements, powers, personalities, and principalities assigned to oppose and stop my movement forward, progress, and success, I declare that I am unstoppable; I am moving forward, and I am making good progress by fire.

You psychic entities of the four Elements, Powers, personalities, and principalities assigned to oppress me at midnight, to make me suffer lack and suffer reproach because I am the firstborn of my mother, by the three witnesses in the earth, the Spirit, and the water, and the blood: which agree in one, I rebuke and banish you now by tongues of fire, effective immediately! In the name of Jesus.

You psychic entities of the four Elements, Powers, personalities, principalities, witches, and warlocks assigned and programmed to plant disgrace, shame, and humiliation in my life at midnight, so that in the day I could reap calamity because I am a firstborn of my parents, I pray, by the three witnesses in the earth, the Spirit, and the water, and the blood: which agree in one, I rebuke and banish you now by tongues of fire, effective immediately! In the name of Jesus.

I speak to the kingdom of Hell today and I say, You psychic entities of the four Elements, Powers, personalities, and principalities who are assigned to kill me in my sleep with an astral black stone - "Nkpitime", I say your expectation for me is now intercepted, confronted, and opposed by the Fire of the Holy Spirit. Your deployed astral poisons and manipulations that are programmed, weaponized, and commissioned to find and destroy me will be dead on arrival. By the three witnesses in the earth, the Spirit, and the water, and the blood: which agree in one, I rebuke and banish you now by fire, effective immediately, in the name of Jesus.

Battles of contestation, confrontations, and all astral powers programmed to lock me in a cycle of back to square one, reversal, dismissal, backwardness, and extreme hardship, because I am the firstborn of my parents, I say, by the three witnesses in the earth, the Spirit, and the water, and the blood: which agree in one, I rebuke and banish you now by fire, effective immediately, in the name of Jesus.

Problems assigned in my life at midnight, or any other hours that are programmed to make me beg my enemies for help, and beg strangers for handouts and alms, because I am the firstborn of my parents, by the three witnesses in the earth, the Spirit, and the water, and the blood: which agree in one, I rebuke and banish you now by fire, effective immediately, in the name of Jesus.

I pray against the astral poison of "sleep-wave," which is launched into the invisible layers of the astral system by every 12:00 midnight, specifically designed and programmed to fight against me between 3:00 a.m. to 6:00 a.m.

Alongside the angelic forces of the hosts of the Lord, I charge against these midnight astral poisons, and by the name of the King of kings and Lord of lords and with fire, lightning, and thunder, I destroy the law of metaphysical homogeneity, and all astral forces programmed to fight against me, the firstborn.
Father, I say, in the name of Jesus, let every witch and demon operating these monitoring devices be scattered and banished in chains of torments, and let the token of evil against me be frustrated; let the wise men of the occult be turned backward, and their knowledge turn to foolishness, and all diviners be struck with madness, for it is written in Isaiah 44:25, "**That frustrateth the tokens of the liars, and maketh diviners mad; that turneth wise *men* backward, and maketh their knowledge foolish;**"

I release the Weapon of the Divine Flame – the power of the Pillar of Fire by night [Exodus 13:21] against all forces of darkness using the Astro-Omni-dictator, the art of homogeneity, and operating under the five Mephistophelian occult seals and psychic manipulations against me as the firstborn child of my parents.

I also release the Weapon of the Thunderous Cloud, the power of the Pillar of cloud by day composed of thunders and lightnings (Exodus 13:21), against all forces of darkness operating under the five Mephistophelian occult seals and using the art of homogeneity, and the Astro-Omni-dictator and every form of psychic manipulation against me as a first-born child.

It is written, He shall deliver me in six troubles: yea, in seven there shall no evil touch me [Job 5:19].

Yea, though I walk through the valley of the shadow of death, I will fear no evil; for thou *art* with me; thy rod and thy staff, they comfort me [Psalms 23:4].

There shall no evil befall me, nor shall any plague come near my dwelling [Psalms 91:10].

Heavenly Father, thank you for Your protection as the firstborn and for helping me overcome Satan, in Jesus' name.

10. Bringing Satan To The Courts Of Heaven For Your Star & Masterplan

Lord God and Saviour, You are the restorer of all things, and I hereby come to Your Throne of Grace to obtain mercy and find help against the demons who have stolen, replaced, and displaced my destiny before I was conceived.

Father, Your word says that You have given to me all things that pertain to life and godliness. It is you who have blessed me with all spiritual blessings in heavenly places in Christ (Eph 1:3). Your word says that I am blessed of the LORD who made heaven and earth (Psalms 115:15). Your word says we who are of faith are blessed with faithful Abraham (Gal 3:9). Your word says that You have made us meet to be partakers of the inheritance of the saints in light [Col 1:12].

But Lord, I am inheriting another destiny that does not testify to that which You have ordained for me according to Your word.
Your word says that Your blessings make rich, and You add no sorrow with it. But behold my life.
Father, my people and I have sinned against you, and my ancestors have transgressed Your law and violated laws and covenants and broken truces and covenants.

The multitude of our sins is before You, and by transgression, the kingdom of darkness has ambushed my star and destiny.
Now, O Lord, I repent for my sins and iniquities, and those of my ancestors and parents from my mother's house and my father's house. I detest all personal and family transgressions and trespasses, and ask You to remove from me every sin, evil covenant, and iniquity that has given demons astral rights to capture my Star, Masterplan, and destiny.

Have mercy upon me, O God, according to thy lovingkindness: according unto the multitude of thy tender mercies, blot out my transgressions, according to Psalms 51:1.
Turn thee unto me, and have mercy upon me; for I *am* desolate and afflicted, Psalms 25:16.

Father, I come before You, who is the Great Judge of the Universe, through the Blood of Jesus and Your precious Holy Spirit of Love. You are the just and righteous Judge, Head of the Divine Council, and You are the God of justice. I petition that Your Divine Council be seated for my sake, and that my case against the Devil and Satan's kingdom be brought before Your Divine Council today, so that you can render judgement between me and the enemy who stole, replaced, or displaced my Star and master plan and destiny.

Right now, Father, let Your Judicial Court hearing and tribunal summon the kingdom of darkness that is responsible for the ruin of my life. Cause them to appear before Your Courtroom this day and be prosecuted.
There are allegations, accusations, and condemnations that the Devil is bringing against me, from my past and from the past of my family and ancestors. He is using my past faults and sins, and the sins of my mother's house and my father's house to keep me in bondage and is using them to ruin and hinder my life and ministry in Christ.

All the evil things I did in the past, place them under the Blood of the Lamb of God, and now that they are under the blood, let the Blood of Jesus speak for me in this Court, to defend me, to justify me, and remove all accusations and condemnation of darkness against my life.
Great Judge of the Heavens and the Earth, my life has been a shame and disgrace, and I cannot please You because of the kingdom of

darkness. Your word says, **"Let them shout for joy, and be glad, that favour my righteous cause: yea, let them say continually, Let the LORD be magnified, which hath pleasure in the prosperity of his servant."** [Psalms 35:27].

You Lord, takes pleasure in the prosperity of Your servants, yet you cannot take pleasure in my prosperity because the kingdom of darkness has robbed me of my prosperity by replacing, displacing, and ambushing my master plan and destiny.
By doing this, the kingdom of darkness is preventing you from taking pleasure in my prosperity as Your servant, which is not in alignment with Your character.
Therefore, consider and let Your judgement be rendered because of the sacrifice of Your Son Jesus.

Great Judge, I have been suffering for years because of the legal grounds and dark links the Devil has found in my blood. He has been using them against my life to torment and strike me. The Devil has plundered my goods, ruined most of my destiny, sabotaged my plans, disrupted my going forth, stolen my finances, blocked my ministry, sent terrors against me by night, arrows against me by day, pestilences by darkness, and destruction at noonday. He has placed a death sentence upon my head so that I will not fulfill Your work on earth.
Great Council, the things that I knew I had to do in life or become in life, I have not accomplished, nor do I see any possibility.

Everything I try fails; none of my desires are coming to pass; all my expectations in life come to naught, and the things I receive in life are always inadequate and insufficient. Also, the things I am receiving are below what I know should be my portion in this life. I apply the principles, and yet get little to no good results. What others do and succeed at, I have done and failed. From my childhood, I have been experiencing inadequacy, failures, setbacks, and my own is always different.

My Star and Masterplan contains Your will, guidelines, and purposes for my life. If my Destiny remains under the control of Satan's kingdom or the Devil's power, I will be living a life that is not what you have ordained, and I will walk into a destiny that you have not ordained.
My life has been laid on a scale, and I am found wanting. So, I am now seeking this Court's intervention in these matters.
Lord Jesus, I take hold of the four horns of the altar; I call upon You, Father, and great Judge.
I am asking Your seated Council in Heaven to rule on my behalf and for the Court of the Most High to rule against all handwritings and ordinances that are against me, which are contrary to me, that which the Devil has ordained for my destruction.
Hear, O LORD, *when* I cry with my voice; have mercy also upon me, and answer me according to [Psalms 27:7].
Hear, O LORD, and have mercy upon me: LORD, be thou my helper, according to [Psalms 30:10].
Have mercy upon me, O LORD, for I am in trouble: mine eye is consumed with grief, *yea,* my soul and my belly, according to [Psalms 31:9].

Render a verdict that will disarm Satan for my sake. Plead my cause and rule in my favour, and render judgement on my behalf because of the Blood of the Lamb of El-Shaddai, which was shed for me.
Righteous Judge, because Christ has suffered for my sins and transgressions (according to Isaiah chapter 53), let me not suffer by the hands of Satan, nor be hindered, stopped, blocked, or killed prematurely by the hands of the agents of darkness because of my past sins and transgressions, or that of my parents and Ancestors.

I am hereby requesting and petitioning the Great High Courts of the Most High God to rule in my favour, and by the judicial verdict of the judicial blood of Jesus, may these demons restore my Star, Masterplan, and Destiny, by a holy Court Order from Heaven.

Now, Lord, acquit me from my personal sins and the sins and iniquities of my ancestors and parents from my mother's house and father's house. Blot out my sins and unrighteousness, for You said in Your word in Isaiah 1:18, **"Come now, and let us reason together, saith the LORD: though your sins be as scarlet, they shall be as white as snow; though they be red like crimson, they shall be as wool."**

Now I am reasoning in Your courts. Your word says, **"Let your will be done in earth, as *it is* in heaven"**. If my destiny is not restored to me, Your will cannot be done on earth in my life as in Heaven. [Matt 6:10]. I am hereby asking Your Divine Council to release me from the condemnation and allegation and let the blood of Y'ahushua, restore my life with Your bounty and favours and blessings in double.

Let my Star, Masterplan, and Destiny be restored unto me, so that I can walk in alignment with my destiny in the areas that are still awaiting me.
Remove from me all ancestral or personal faults that are giving the kingdom of darkness legal right to hold my Star, Masterplan, and Destiny.
Your word says in Titus 2:14, "Who **gave himself for us, that he might redeem us from all iniquity, and purify unto himself a peculiar people, zealous of good works.**
Your word says in 1 Corinthians 6:11, "**And such were some of you: but ye are washed, but ye are sanctified, but ye are justified in the name of the Lord Jesus, and by the Spirit of our God."**

Your word says in Ephesians 1:**7, "In whom we have redemption through his blood, the forgiveness of sins, according to the riches of his grace."**
Your word says in Hebrews 9:12, "**Neither by the blood of goats and calves, but by his own blood he entered in once into the holy place, having obtained eternal redemption** *for us*".
Your word in 1 John 3:8 says, **"For this purpose the Son of God was manifested, that he might destroy the works of the devil."**
Now, Great Judge, Righteous and Holy One, let Your Council issue a verdict based on Your lovingkindness, tender mercies, and compassion.

I thank You for Your divine intervention; all praise be to God Most High. Amen!
Psalms 68:4, **"Sing unto God, sing praises to his name: extol him that rides upon the heavens by his name YAH, and rejoice before him."**
For this, I give You praise, glory, and honour, in the name of Jesus of Nazareth.

11. Prayer Warfare To Recover Your Star, & Master Plan From Hell

In the mighty name of Y'ahushua Ha-Mashiach, by the power of the emerald rainbow around the Throne of God [Rev 4:3], by the authority of the sceptre of God's kingdom [Psalms 45:6], by lightnings and thunderings and voices, and the seven burning lamps of fire which are the seven Spirits of God [Rev 4:5], I stand in the capacity of a warrior clothed with the power and authority of the name King of Kings and Lord of lords, and I now declare warfare against the 12 gates of hell and their jurisdictions, armies, and myriads of mortal and immortal agents.

Lord God Almighty, You have given me power and authority to destroy the works of the Devil. Today, I stand in my position in Christ, for it is written in Ephesians 2:6, **"God has raised *us* up together, and made *us* sit together in heavenly *places* in Christ Jesus"**
Also, Your word says in 2 Corinthians 2:14, **"Now thanks *be* to God, who always causes us to triumph in Christ, and He revealing through us the fragrance of the knowledge of Him in every place."**

I also claim upon myself right now the power of the Holy Spirit to overshadow me with fire for spiritual combats of retrieval and reclamation of my Star, Masterplan, and Destiny.
Thus says the Lord Jesus to us in Luke 10:19, **"Behold, I give unto you power to tread on serpents and scorpions, and over all the power of the enemy: and nothing shall by any means hurt you."**

Within the jurisdiction of Luke 10:19, and the authority given to me by the Son of God, my Saviour, I now **tread on serpents and scorpions, and over all the power of the enemy, in the land, sea, air, and underworld.**

By the power of Jesus of Nazareth, I bind, disarm, neutralize, and banish from my life and home the aura, essence, and spirit of the fallen Angel Baraqijal and Kokabel and all evil spirits under their jurisdiction and regime, who are in charge of astrology and the mysteries of the constellation, and the reading of the stars in order to reveal mysteries. Yet, astrology is forbidden by God Almighty.

Therefore, in Jesus' name, I, by the verdict of the highest Order of the Council of Yah, bind, disarm, renounce, denounce, revolt against, and destroy by fire the powers and jurisdiction of the cosmological verdict, the powers of the Astro Omni-dictator, and the psychic and astral forces of darkness, which have accelerated and are accelerating against my life under the velocity of the 5 Mephistophelian seals of the occult, which are also responsible for the confiscation of my Star and Destiny, and are responsible for the countless failures, dilemmas, and calamities in my life. These have cast shadows over my Star, ambushed my destiny, confiscated my Masterplan, things that do not belong to the kingdom of darkness.

In the name of the Lord Elohei Tzeva'ot, through the jurisdiction and verdict of the Mercy Seat by which I am redeemed, sanctified and have my being in Christ, I invoke the power of the Son of God, who has his eyes like unto a flame of fire, and his feet like fine brass [Rev 2:18]; and I invoke Angelic warfare for the immediate destruction, annihilation, eradication and liquidation of all ruling evil spirits of the rank of Arch-spirit, Captain, General, Headhunter, Commander in chief, Dragon, god, Supreme Elemental, Guardian of the Flames, Guardian of Fate and the Cycles of life, Masters, and all ruling evil spirits of the five Continents, of the 7 Seas, of the realm of the Dead, of the realms of the Air and outer cosmos, of the realm of the Forest, of the Deserts, of the Rivers, of the North Pole, of the South Pole, and upon all other ruling evil spirits, hybrid demons and all subordinate spirits who are holding my Star, my destiny and my Masterplan bound, captive, hidden, and locked up since I was a foetus or a child.

Let all you demons and psychic entities who have done evil to my destiny and star be banished in chains of unbearable torment and incomprehensible heat from the coals of the holy altar in Heaven, as your grip and darkness over my star, Masterplan, and destiny are broken now, effective immediately.
It is written in 1 Samuel 30:8, "**...And the Lord answered him, Pursue: for thou shalt surely overtake them, and without fail recover all."**

Therefore, by the authority of 1 Samuel 30:8, the verdict of the blood of Jesus, the authority of the Throne of Yah, and the lightnings and thunderings and voices: and *the* seven lamps of fire burning before the throne, which are the seven Spirits of God, [Rev 4:5, Exodus 19:16, I now pursue, overtake, and without fail recover and reclaim my Star, my Masterplan, and my Destiny, and all other components of my Star from the captivity, the powers, and the holding chambers of the Astral kingdom, the Eso-Terrestrial Kingdom, the Azura kingdom, the Kalami kingdom of the Air axis, or from the Water kingdom of Gupha, [headquarter of the water occult kingdom within the 'Bermuda-Triangle', from the Delvic kingdom, or from the subterranean occult realm - the realm of fire, and from the captivity, the powers, and the hold of the Queen of Beta and her husband, the queen of the Coast and her husband, the Queen of Shylon and her husband, the Queen of Yemunah and her husband, or the Queen of Delta and her husband, or from within any of the five occult zones of the marine kingdom: the zone Lumani, Banni, Lemuria, Gamma, and the zone Atlantis.

I say to you spirit queens, your husbands, the dragons of the waters, air, subterranean, and land mentioned here, be oppressed, tormented, afflicted, frustrated, and disassembled by the power of

Jesus Christ, as I command you to release my Star, Masterplan, and Destiny now, immediately effective.

Now, by the three that bear witness in earth, the Spirit, and the Water, and the Blood: [1Jn 5:8] and by holy fire, I take back my Star, my Masterplan, and my Destiny from the hands and powers of the Gates of Hell and from all these evil spirits.

Master plan, Star and Destiny given to me by God Almighty, hear my command now, for I stand in the presence of the Most High God, and I say to you, come forth unto me, and be restored in my life now with all your glory, effective immediately, in Jesus' exalted name.

Heavenly Father, I pray right now, let the Angels of the Lord Jesus bind and draw out all these Demonic entities of the vicious Occult world with hooks of fire in their mouths, and ropes of flames tying down their tongues as in Job 41:1, with hooks into their noses and thorns of fire boring into their jaws, as in Job 41:2. **"Let God arise, let His enemies be scattered;"** [Psalms 68:1].

It is written, **"let those who hate Him flee before Him. As smoke is driven away, so drive them away; as wax melts before the fire, so let the wicked perish in the presence of God"** [Psalms 68:2]. So now, let all demons, Sirens, and Arch evil spirits vomit up, release, and restore my Star, Masterplan, and Destiny back to me with all its glory, effective immediately, in the name of Jesus of Nazareth.

Lord God, You said in Isaiah 41:11-12, **"Behold, all they that were incensed against thee shall be ashamed and confounded: they shall be as nothing; and they that strive with thee shall perish."**
"Thou shalt seek them, and shalt not find them, even them that contended with thee: they that war against thee shall be as nothing, and as a thing of nought."

By the name of God, the LORD of hosts. [Elohei Tsevaoth] I declare war and combat of reclamation and retrieval, and I retrieve all and reclaim my Star, my Masterplan, and my Destiny from any cemetery, from the wastelands, from the barren lands, from the desolate places, from the woodlands, the wetlands, from any catacomb or grave, from any enchanted forest, the monsoon forest, the tropical forest, from the Swamp, from the sacred grove, from the mangroves, from the everglades, from the crossroad, the fork road or the roundabout, or from any metropolitan, megapolitan, jurisdiction, principality, municipality, Neighbourhood, township, borough, city, town, urban, exurb, suburb, county, district, state, nation, and from the power of the serpentine spirits, the crocodilian spirits, the reptilian spirits, and from the depths of the rivers, seas and oceans, and from the heights of the heavens above, and from the valleys and plains and mountains on the earth beneath, effective immediately.

By fire, by force, and by the finger of God, I take back my life, my organs, health, life, success, business idea, godly desires, expectations, endeavours, destinies, my future, my children, my generations, my wealth, health, mind, virtues, talents, gifts, character, potential, my precise intellectual capacities, intelligence, pristine articulation of my expression of morals, self-worth, integrity, knowledge, and love for Jesus, my Star and Destiny from the powers, hands, and hold of the Earth Masters, Guardians, Demi-gods, Astral forces, Planetary Spirits, Prithas, [White *giant demon Anacondas]; Watchers,* Yandavas, Devas, Devatas, *[psychic entities of the air]; Yamadutas, [spirits of death];* Guardians of the Flame, Ascended Masters, Principalities, Solar Lords, Inter-Planetary lords, Inter-Galactic Lords, Guardian of Fate and the Cycles of life, etc., who were specifically assigned to spiritually confiscate my Star, Destiny, assets, and everything contained in the master plan of my destiny on Earth.

Any dust of dark matter and black energy that was placed in the palm of my hand before birth, to replace the dust of light of my destiny and my star, I call upon the God of Israel to destroy this evil in my hands.

It is written that men should pray everywhere, lifting up holy hands, without wrath and doubting. [1Timothy 2:8].

Any black energy that was placed in the palm of my hand by the kingdom of darkness so that the works of my hands will be cursed and fail; in order to counter the Word of God, I rebuke it now and pull down every high thing that exalts itself against the knowledge of God.

[Now Lift Up Your Hands To Heaven Facing East And Repeat These Words]

"Right now, I lift up my hands towards the Eastern Gates, and to the Highest Heaven, to the Name of Yah and towards the Holy Oracle [Psalms 28:2 & Chp. 63:4], and I say lift up your heads, O Ye Gates, and be lifted up, ye Everlasting Doors. By the holy and divine invocation, I now invoke into my hands the Celestial Amber Fire of the Throne of God Almighty and of the Lamb, and I say, descend upon me O Holy Fire and burn out all evil marks, black light, dark matter, and evil stars placed in the palms of my hands by the kingdom of darkness, which are programmed to represent my false destiny, failures, infirmities, calamities, shames, disgraces, death, or any other form of destruction."

Holy Spirit of Yah, burn these evils from my hands and feet, destroy them in the name of Jesus of Nazareth, and restore my destiny into my hands, in Jesus' name.

It is said and written to us in Deuteronomy 2:7, **"For the LORD thy God hath blessed thee in all the works of thy hand"**

Father, I thank You for restoring my Masterplan. This is the Lord's doing, and it is marvelous in our eyes. Therefore, I thank You for Your awesome wonders in helping and saving me, in Jesus' mighty name, Amen.

12. Prayers Against Blind Initiation & Witchcraft

Lord God of the Heavens and the earth, in every place where I am being used as a blind witch because of Blind Initiation, I ask You to deliver me from the hold of Hell.
Let any witchcraft prison bar and gates begin to melt from the fervent heat of Your divine presence, as I call upon Your vehement flame of holiness.

Every mark of destruction placed upon me, and any initiation that I was initiated into unconscious witchcraft through edibles in my dream, which has subjected me to become mere food or meat for the powers of darkness, let these be neutralized, nullified, and removed from my body and soul, effective immediately.

But today, Lord, this blind initiation is broken by Your mercy and power, for it is Your will that I be set free from all evil, for it is written in Isaiah 61:1, **"The Spirit of the Lord GOD *is* upon me; because the LORD hath anointed me to preach good tidings unto the meek; he hath sent me to bind up the brokenhearted, to proclaim liberty to the captives, and the opening of the prison to *them that are* bound;"**

I hereby invoke a Judiciary Court Order from the Judicial Council, the Mercy Seat, and the Blood of the Lamb of God, to condemn in the courts of the Almighty any mark of blind witchcraft placed on my body and soul, and any initiation with which I was initiated into secret and unconscious witchcraft.
By the Blood of the Lamb of God, I revolt against and reject any witchcraft spirit, manipulation, and evil soul tie, where the witches are able to use my spirit in astral missions as a witch's agent.

I loose myself from the hold of blind witchcraft, and break by fire all evil powers sitting upon my life, in the North, South, East and West.
Let these doorways be removed and break the power of homogeneity and release me from the hands and powers of the Guardians of Fate and the Cycles of life, who have set boundaries, limitations, and manipulations in my life unto destruction.

Heavenly Father, any mark of destruction placed upon me by witchcraft spirits, and any secret initiation that took place with my soul in the astral realm, through sexual intercourse with an evil spirit in the dream, or sexual immorality, through eating in my dreams, [things served by demons], by smoking a cigar or drinking alcohol in the physical or in a dream; by visiting a fortune teller, by receiving so-called healing through occult powers, or reading occult books, or any other way, remove the allegations of these sins, and acquit me of these evil accusations and condemnation. Wash me from all evil deeds and sins of my mind, words, and actions. Let the legal luminaries of darkness who are projecting my case into the tribunal of condemnation of the night be destroyed, in Jesus name.
Deliver me from the symptoms of blind witchcraft where I always find it difficult to live the way I should on Earth; where I always indulge in evil acts beyond my control; where I always find myself fluctuating between joy and sorrow on a daily basis; where I am not hungry, but would indulge in excessive eating; where I am attached to hard drugs, alcohol, or smoking; where I am always submitting to the gratification of sexual propensity; where I am possessed by the psychic entities of somnambulism (sleepwalking); where I am most times filled with thoughts of suicide and violence; and where I am always susceptible to onsets of sudden depression.

It is written in Psalm 70:1-5, **"Make haste, O God, to deliver me; make haste to help me, O Lord.** Vs. 2 **Let them be ashamed and confounded that seek after my soul: let them be turned backward,** and put to confusion, that desire my hurt. Vs. 3 **Let them be turned back for a reward of their shame that say, Aha, aha.** Vs. 4 **Let all those that seek thee rejoice and be glad in thee: and let such as love thy salvation say continually, Let God be magnified.** Vs. 5 **But I am poor and needy: make haste unto me, O God: thou art my help and my deliverer; O Lord, make no tarrying."**

In the name of Jesus, let the token of evil in me be frustrated and broken. Let the wise men of the occult be turned backward, and their knowledge turn to foolishness, and all diviners be struck with madness, for it is written in Isaiah 44:25, **"That frustrateth the tokens of the liars, and maketh diviners mad; that turneth wise *men* backward, and maketh their knowledge foolish;"**

It is written - Isaiah 49:24, **"Shall the prey be taken from the mighty, or the captives of a tyrant be rescued?"**
Isaiah 49:25, **"But thus says the LORD, 'Even the captives of the mighty shall be taken away, and the prey of the fierce ones shall be rescued, for I will contend with him who contends with you, and I will save your children."**
"And I will feed those who oppress you with their own flesh; and they shall be drunk with their own blood, as with sweet wine; and all flesh shall know that I, the LORD, *am* your Savior and your Redeemer, the mighty One of Jacob."

At this moment, I banish all witches assigned to initiate me, all witches who have in times past initiated me, and all witches who will be responsible for initiating me in the future. Let fire fall upon them and burn them, and let all their powers, holds, cages, hexes, and curses be broken off me, and all chains fall off my body and soul, effective immediately, now, in Jesus' name, Amen and Amen.

13. Taking Back Your Glory From Darkness

Father, creator of Heaven and Earth, it is Your will for me to grow in spirit and stature from glory to glory.
But I recognized that my life has been tampered with by the psychic elements of Hell.
I therefore request Angelic assistance to reclaim my glory, by the name and fire of Elohei Tzeva'ot., and therefore request that You release Angels of battalions to fight for my glory within the second Heaven, within the fifth Heaven, within the Forest, the Underground, the Desert, Sun, Moon, Planets, Stars, Constellations, Galaxies and within the gates of the four Cardinal hemispheres, [North, South, East and West], within the sub-cardinal hemispheres and within the four intercardinal hemispheres, In Jesus name.

Right now, I declare a war of reclamation and retrieval of my glory, and I bind and disarm every category, clan, tribe, and species of demons, sirens, demi-god, avatar etc.
I address the kingdom of Pandemonium and the Mephistophelian world, and I say, Powers of Satan and the Devil that have taken my glory and its components in exchange for disgrace and shame, or have replaced my glory with the evil components of demons, let this exchange and replacement be undone now.

Let the shame, disgrace, reproach, contempt, criticism, condemnation, denunciation, disapproval, humiliation, discredit, disrepute, scorn, and degradation that the kingdom of darkness has given to me in place of my glory be destroyed and sent back to hell by the power of Jesus Christ of Nazareth, and let my glory revive and be restored to me.

Any witch, or coven, warlock, satanist, ritualist, grand master, ascending master, shaman, witch doctor, native doctor, wise man, avatar, ascended master, mermaid, siren, voodoo priest, deva, devata, [male and female "guardian spirits"], guru, secret society, lodge, freemason, illuminati, guardian of the flame, brotherhood, the order, and the sisterhood, who are currently holding my glory, or who are directly or indirectly involved in the stealing of my glory from me, before birth or after birth, I break, liquidate, and banish their spells, hexes, incantations, cages, curses, and evil powers from over my glory, star, and destiny, and I loose and liberate my glory from the bowels, grip, and chambers of Hell, in the mighty name of Jesus of Nazareth.

Every agent of the Occult world, within the land, waters, air, and subterranean regions who has taken my glory from me, or is holding my glory, star, and destiny, I release upon you the judgements and destructions by the fire from the Eyes of Jesus [Rev 1:14].
Let the fiery flames of the throne of the Ancient of Days, and the heat of his wheels of burning fire, [Daniel 7:9] be invoked upon you evil spirits and agents of darkness for your immediate neutralization, liquidation, destruction, desolation, degradation, annihilation, and eradication, and I hereby render you demons, sirens, and witches powerless, defenceless, weaponless, unrectified, ineffective, disqualified, useless, and clueless.
Be destroyed by the fiery coals of Almighty God, according to Psalms 140:10, which says, **"Let burning coals fall upon them: let them be cast into the fire; into deep pits, that they rise not up again."**

I command you to release and restore my glory to me now!
By fire of the Holy Spirit, I speak into the layers of the Heavens, the Earth, and within the subterranean worlds, and I call upon and invoke the fiery flames of the throne of the Ancient of Days, and the burning fire of his wheels [Daniel 7:9], to descend upon and burn upon the

Astral kingdom, the Eso-Terrestrial Kingdom, the Azura kingdom, the Kalami kingdom, the Delvic kingdom, and the subterranean occult kingdom, and upon the Queen of Beta and her husband, upon the queen of the Coast and her husband, upon the Queen of Shylon and her husband, upon the Queen of Yemunah and her husband, and upon the Queen of Delta and her husband, and upon all spirits of the five occult zones of the marine kingdom: the zone Lumani, Banni, Lemuria, Gamma, and the zone Atlantis, and I command the immediate release of my glory now, with full compensation.

I command that my glory be restored unto me in all its splendour sevenfold according to [Proverbs 6:31], effective immediately.

I command the second Heaven and the fifth Heaven, the Forest, the Underground, the Desert, Sun, Moon, Planets, Stars, Constellations, Galaxies to let loose their hold and release my glory from the North, South, East, and West, and restore to me my glory with its full splendour sevenfold, In Jesus name.

Every demon of the winter solstice, spring equinox, summer solstice, and autumn equinox that is feeding on my glory, I scatter and banish you demons into deserts of no return by turbulent firestorms, in Jesus' name.

In Jesus' name, I withdraw my glory from any evil altar, shrine, or from any place where it is held captive and heavily guarded.

My glory, which was taken through fornication, through my blood, my sperm [if you are a man], my vaginal fluids [if you are a woman], and placed upon altars of spirits, let these altars be broken down to debris, in Jesus name.

Any principality or evil power sitting on my glory, I overthrow you by a divine, heavenly, incomprehensible force, and I banish you and all your subject demons into chains of despair and destruction by the power of Jesus Christ.

Every negative word, proclamation, and decree that is helping to cast shadows over my glory, be dispelled now, effective immediately, in Jesus' name.

Let every family sin and iniquity that has become chains of bondage upon my glory, I subject these sins and iniquities to the fire of the blood of Jesus and break the power of ancestral abominations and influence over my glory.
Let my glory become too hot, vibrant, and dynamic for the kingdom of darkness to hold in the occult world any longer, in Jesus name.

I speak into the universe, and I say by the power of the Holy Spirit that all astral poisons and psychic manipulations that are programmed, weaponized, and commissioned to find and destroy me will be neutralized, bound, and rendered ineffective, powerless, and nullified upon arrival.

It is written in Psalms 57:8, **"Awake up, my glory; awake, psaltery and harp: I myself will awake early."** Therefore, by the power of Jesus of Nazareth, I say, O my glory, awake, O my glory, awake, hear the word of the Lord and hear my command now. I stand in the presence of the Most High God, and I now call you back into my life. I say to you, my glory given to me by the Father in Heaven and all your components, substance, and essence, come forth unto me, and be restored to my life now with all your resplendence.

I call forth and command the restoration of my elegance, my grandeur, my magnificence, my nobility, my wonderfulness, my gloriousness, my resplendency, my brilliance, and my nobleness, and I say, be restored back into my life in all fullness now, effective immediately.

Lord God, I beat all these evil spirits with a hammer of fire now that they rise not again, for it is written in Psalms 18:37, **"I have pursued mine enemies, and overtaken them: neither did I turn again till they were consumed."**
Psalms 18:38, **"I have wounded them that they were not able to rise: they are fallen under my feet."**
Psalms 18:39, **"For thou hast girded me with strength unto the battle: thou hast subdued under me those that rose up against me."**

Father in Heaven, now, as I have prayed, so let it be done, for You are worthy to be praised in all kingdoms and realms. Lord

Jesus, I thank You for restoring my glory, in the name of the Father, and of the Son, and of the Holy Spirit, Amen and Amen.

14. Prayer Against The Spirit Of Stagnancy

Father in Heaven, You are in Heaven; hallowed be Your name. Let Your kingdom come and let Your will be done on Earth, as it is in Heaven. I praise Your great name today, for You are worthy to be praised in all kingdoms and realms. Thank You for the Blood of the Lamb of God, through which I can stand in Your presence to declare my victory, blessings, and deliverance in Christ.

In the name of Jesus Christ, I destroy every curse and malediction of stagnation affecting my life as a result of my negative actions, thoughts, or words that I have spoken in the past, which have given the kingdom of darkness legal ground to inflict my life with various forms of stagnation, or as a result of the place where I live, or have lived, or as a result of the people I lived with or had sexual relations with.

Your word says, in Romans 8:37, **"Nay, in all these things we are more than conquerors through him that loved us."**
The Word of God commands me in Proverbs 6:5, where it says, **"Deliver thyself as a roe from the hand of the hunter, and as a bird from the hand of the fowler."**
It is also written in Proverbs 12:6, **"but the mouth of the upright shall deliver them."**

Therefore, according to Proverbs 6:5 and Proverbs 12:6, in the powerful name of Jesus, I speak with my mouth by faith, and today I deliver myself from you, demon of stagnation, that has ambushed my life through occult manipulations, techniques, and multi-dimensional combined psychic elements of darkness.
In the name of HaMashiach Y'ahushua the King of kings and Lord of lords, who is clothed with a vesture dipped in blood [Rev 19:13], I

unleash incomprehensible and unquenchable fires of warfare of mass destruction against the demon of heavy, the slug and snail demons, the demons of tar and sticky astral substances, and all psychic entities and elemental spirits of stagnancy in my business, family, job, health, marriage, projects, plans, vision, and endeavour. Every astral poison and all venom of tranquilization and neutralization that demons would try to vaccinate me with for stagnancy, let them be neutralized now, in the powerful name of Jesus.

Heavenly Father, I also call upon Your eternal light of fire, and Your violent flames of amber, the lightning and the thunder from Your sapphire throne to descend and neutralize, shatter, destroy, and banish from my life all manipulative techniques, all oppressive and restrictive forces programmed and keeping me apprehended, stagnant, dormant, unproductive, and neutralized on the same level, the same spot, and the same position and situation for years, and all self-imposed limitations, curses, demons of hindrance, lockdowns, shutdowns, boundaries, constraints, restrains, borders, blockages, failures, disgraces, shame, setbacks, and all connected dark psychic forces of the same category, and all occult astral and human agents of darkness who are conspiring and devising destruction against my destiny through implementations of stagnancy.

Also neutralize, shatter, destroy, and banish from my life by fire all forms and variants of stagnation sitting upon me as a result of my place of residence, the place where I have lived, the place where I work or worked, my sinful actions, evil thoughts, negative words, the law of metaphysical homogeneity, astral poisons, mind bending, mind blinding, mind manipulation, mental blocks, hypnotic poison, mental puzzle, mental perplexity, illusion, delusion, deception, stubbornness, lack of vision, misunderstanding, confusion, mind control, or as a result of the people I lived with, had sexual relations with, or as a result of inheritance from my family or ancestral bloodline. Let all these doorways, root causes, and foundations to the demon of stagnancy be confronted with fire, resistance, and be destroyed by destruction, desolation, degradation, annihilation, liquidation, and eradication, effective immediately, in Jesus' mighty name.

By faith, I bring under the judgement of the Blood of Christ each of these doorways and legal rights mentioned above, which I also renounce, revoke, and destroy their evil jurisdiction and legal ground, doorways, and roots of stagnation in my life.

Lord God and Abba Father, it is written in Isaiah 61:1, "**The Spirit of the Lord GOD** *is* **upon me; because the LORD hath anointed me to preach good tidings unto the meek; he hath sent me to bind up the broken-hearted, to proclaim liberty to the captives, and the opening of the prison to them that are bound;**"

Now, Lord, proclaim my liberty from captivity, and open the prison to me who is bound.

Today, in the authority of Jesus the Christ, let all you spirits of stagnancy and setback that have lured me into your lair, or have subjected me under your manipulations, laws, jurisdiction, and powers, and have established over my life a strongman, or have planted a seed of failure, a root of stagnation, retardation, and blockage, be confronted with fire, resistance, and be destroyed by destruction, desolation, degradation, annihilation, liquidation, and eradication.
It is also written in Luke 10:17, "**And the seventy returned again with joy, saying, Lord, even the devils are subject unto us through thy name**".

Holy Father in Heaven, if there is any sticky substance on the ground in the spirit realm that is making it difficult for me to move or walk from where I am towards my destiny and advancement, I revolt against this evil power today and hereby call for the light of fire to descend from Heaven and vaporize this astral sticky substance.

Holy Spirit of Jesus, I pray let each of these evil powers collide with God's holy fire, judged by this fire, and be destroyed by this very same fire.

Father, I claim full functionality of my strength, will and power to rise and go forward, according to Deuteronomy 1:6, **"The LORD our God spake unto us in Horeb, saying, Ye have dwelt long enough in this mount: Turn you, and take your journey..."**

Let every stagnant water in my life be stirred by the Angels of God and begin to flow.

Let my gifts be activated and begin to make room for me and bring me before great men.

I decree by fire, I am not a slacker and sluggish person, but I have the potential to rise to great success using the limited resources that I have at my disposal.

It is written in Philippians 4:13, **"I can do all things through Christ who strengthens me."**

I thank You for Your mercy and grace to sustain my protection in Christ my saviour, and Your will to protect me from the evil one.

2 Corinthians 2:14, **"Now thanks *be* unto God, which always causeth us to triumph in Christ, and maketh manifest the savour of his knowledge by us in every place."**

15. Prayers Against The Spirit Of Calamity

Lord God of the Heavens and the Earth, I come before Your throne of grace through the Holy Spirit and the judicial and redeeming blood of Jesus. My life is surrounded by continual calamities and continual disastrous occurrences, which have greatly caused sorrow, pain, misfortune, and mishaps in my life, and have compromised my destiny and the purposes of God in my life. Your word says in 1Co 6:20 that we are bought with a price; therefore, we must glorify God in our body and in our spirit, which are God's.

Therefore, look upon me with mercy. Let me not be led into temptation but deliver me from all evil.
It is written in Psalms 57:1, **"Be merciful unto me, O God, be merciful unto me: for my soul trusteth in thee: yea, in the shadow of thy wings will I make my refuge, until these calamities be overpast."**

Father, the kingdom of darkness has broken protocol, violated my rights, overstepped its bounds, and weaponized classified information against my life.
Therefore, bow the heavens, O Lord, and let the realm of Angels, the universe, and the Earth be conditioned to accommodate my deliverance and help, and come to my rescue, Lord Jesus.
Your word also says in Ephesians 2:10 that we are Your workmanship, created in Christ Jesus unto good works, which God hath before ordained that we should walk in them.

It is written in Psalms 116:3-4, **"The sorrows of death compassed me, and the pains of hell got hold upon me: I found trouble and sorrow. Then called I upon the name of the LORD; O LORD, I beseech thee, deliver my soul"**.

Also in Psalms 18:5, it says, **"The sorrows of hell compassed me about: the snares of death prevented me."**
Psalms 18:6, **"In my distress I called upon the LORD, and cried unto my God: he heard my voice out of his temple, and my cry came before him, even into his ears."**
Psalms 18:7, **"Then the earth shook and trembled; the foundations also of the hills moved and were shaken, because he was wroth."**
Psalms 18:8, **"There went up a smoke out of his nostrils, and fire out of his mouth devoured: coals were kindled by it"**.
Psalms 18:9, "He **bowed the heavens also and came down; and darkness was under his feet."**

Therefore, let the darkness of calamity and demonically programmed natural and unnatural situations be placed under the feet of the Lord, in Jesus' name.
In like manner, by the power of El-Shaddai, in the Name of Jesus of Nazareth, with hot chains of seraphic fire and fetters of hot iron heated by the Cherubic coals of fire [Eze 10:2], I strategically bind the neck, the hands, and the feet, all evil spirits of calamity, casualty, tragedy, injury, catastrophe, mishap, misfortune, and accident that are surrounding my life with spontaneous troubles, recurring disasters, and continual destructions and evils, and by the power of Jesus, Messiah of Nazareth, Son of the Living God, disarm, banish, and destroy the powers of all you demons operating in and against my life.

In the name of Jesus, let every witch and demon operating heavy demonic artilleries against me be scattered and banished in chains of torments, and let the token of evil against me be frustrated; let the wise men of the occult be turned backward, and their knowledge turn to foolishness, and all diviners be struck with madness, for it is written in Isaiah 44:25, **"That frustrateth the tokens of the liars, and** maketh diviners mad; that turneth wise *men* backward, and maketh their knowledge foolish;"

By the authority and power of the 7 horns and 7 eyes of the Lamb of God, and by the power of the fire, the lightnings, the voices, and the seven thunders within the presence of the enthroned and exalted Jesus, and by the authority of his name King of Kings and Lord of lords, I take hold of the powers in Psalms 11:6, where it is written, **"Upon the wicked he shall rain snares, fire and brimstone, and a horrible tempest: this shall be the portion of their cup."**

I command tongues of fire to destroy from my life the laws and strongholds of Calamity, and I command rains of fire, brimstone, a horrible tempest, and terror to descend and destroy the power and influence of all demi-gods, astral forces, planetary spirits, avatars, grand masters, witches, warlocks, satanists, wiccans, sorcerers, watchers, guardians of the flame, ascended masters, solar lords, inter-planetary lords, inter-galactic lords, guardians of fate and the cycles of life, dark principalities, powers, rulers of darkness, legions of the air, aquatic forces, subterranean forces, earth masters, highlanders, mermaids, sirens, the elemental spirits, and every other demon who has formed artillery of destruction, calamities, and systems of evil operations against my life through the subtle psychic manipulations.

I revolt with lightning and thunders of the amber fire of Jesus Christ, and I banish every combined element of psychic and esoteric powers, astral poisons and demons of calamities, disaster and chaos, and I command destruction by fire upon, and I deconstruct by fire, revoke, destroy and banish from my life the satanic ambushment, the psychic manipulations and the spirit of the queen of heaven, the queen of the south, the Queen of Beta, the Queen of Shylon, the Queen of Yemunah, the Queen of Delta, the Queen of the Coast, the gods of the

Titans, the Olympian gods, the supreme elemental spirits, the evil guardians of the cardinal points, the grand cardinals, the Mermaids, the Sirens and the Nymphs, and all other evil powers that have subjected me to be a victim of continual calamities and frequent mysterious recurring disasters.

Lord God, let these evil spirits be tormented with fire and brimstone in the presence of the holy angels, and in the presence of the Lamb. [Rev 14:10] Destroy them by Your judgement, O Lord, and give all these categories of demons and agents of Hell the portion of their cup, for it is written in Psalms 11:6, **"Upon the wicked he shall rain snares, fire and brimstone, and a horrible tempest: this shall be the portion of their cup."**

By the Lord God of Israel, I destroy the rays, altars, fortitude, and power of all astral and metaphysical forces that are operating at the highest velocity of Astro-metaphysical acceleration, which are combating my life through cycles of psychic manipulations, through the cosmological verdict, through metaphysical intercourse, or by the powers of the Astro-Omnidictator and the power and velocity of the five Mephistophelian seals of the occult. It is written in Psalms 71:13, **"Let them be confounded *and* consumed that are adversaries to my soul; let them be covered *with* reproach and dishonour that seek my hurt."**

I render you powers of darkness, death, calamity, disaster, and humiliation powerless, defenceless, weaponless, unrectified, ineffective, and useless against me, as I now tear down and destroy your rays, altars, fortitude, and powers in the mighty name of Jesus of Nazareth.

Angels who are given charge over me according to Psalms 91:11 excel in strength and fight for me according to Psalm 34:7. Psalms 35:5 says,

"Let them be as chaff before the wind: and let the angel of the LORD chase them".
These prayers I pray in the name of the Father, the Son, and the Holy Spirit of Yah.

Father, thank You for delivering me from all these evil forces of calamity and making me a liberated worshiper in Jesus' name. Amen and Amen.

16. Recovering Your Garment That Was Stolen, Exchanged, Or Replaced

Every power from the realm of the kingdom of darkness that has replaced anything in my life with something that is a counterfeit for a similar, different, or opposite function, I command this counterfeit replacement to be banished from my life now, and my original belonging to be restored to me from the realm of oblivion, or wherever it is, effective immediately.

I pray against any exchange that has taken place in my life, where something from me was taken and made to take the place of something in the kingdom of darkness, and something from the kingdom of darkness was made to take the place of an item in my life, specifically for the simultaneous functioning of a strange kind.

Spiritual blessings

Wherever my life, my organs, health, life, success, business idea, godly desires, expectations, endeavours, destinies, my future, my children, my generations, my wealth, health, mind, virtues, talents, gifts, character, potential, my marriage, my money, my intellectual capacities, intelligence, moral values, self-worth, integrity, knowledge, or love is displaced, misplaced, exchanged, or replaced by Sirens, mermaids, demigods, high witches, or transporter demons, or any other spirit of darkness, by fire, by force, and by the finger of God, I take it back and command the release of my virtues now, in Jesus' holy name.

Garment of beauty

In any way, my garment of glory and beauty has been replaced with an astral garment of unattractive and unappealing, or with a garment of unattractiveness, a garment of unlikeable, a garment of disgust, repulsion, revulsion, distaste, contempt, abhorrence, dullness, unbeauteous, uninviting, or a garment of lust and sensual desires; I tear off these garments from me, and I call upon the flame of fire in the eyes of the Son of God [Rev 2:18] to burn these evil garments to ashes.
I command that my God-given garments of beauty, glory, joy, praise, etc., be restored to me with all their glory, effective immediately.

Marital Garment

Every agent of darkness that has replaced my marital garment with a garment of divorce, marital dysfunction, marital shame and disgrace, marital abuse, and humiliation, etc. I call upon the throne of the Almighty from which proceed lightnings and thunderings and voices; and I pray that the fire of the seven lamps of fire burning before the throne, which are the seven Spirits of God [Rev 4:5], will now descend and destroy to ashes these evil garments and the demons responsible for this evil replacement, in the name of Jesus, the Christ of Nazareth. Every fake beauty given to me by the Sirens, Demons, and witches of the kingdom of darkness through the psychic elemental spirits, which is causing my spouse to lose taste in me because I look unattractive to the eyes, I break this demonic symptom, curse, and manipulation right now in Jesus' name.

I tear off from me every marital garment of unattractive, unappealing, unattractiveness, unlikeable, disgust, repulsion, revulsion, distaste, contempt, abhorrence, dullness, unbeauteous, uninviting, which is causing me to not be appealing to my spouse.
I release myself from this evil bondage of psychic manipulation. I cast out these evil garments back to hell, and I claim, recover, and take

back my true beauty as a spouse, for it is written in Psalms 1639:14, "**I will praise thee; for I am fearfully** *and* **wonderfully made: marvellous** *are* **thy works; and** *that* **my soul knoweth right well.**"

Garment of Praise

Every power from the realm of the kingdom of darkness that has replaced my garment of praise with a demon of heaviness, I call this replacement or exchange into order, and I say, you demon who has done this, destruction and chains of unbearable torment be upon you now, effective immediately.
I tear off any garment of heaviness placed upon me, and I receive and put on the garment of praise, for it is written in Psalms 107:8, "Oh that men would praise the LORD for His goodness, and for His wonderful works to the children of men!"

Oil of Joy and Beauty

Every power from the realm of the kingdom of darkness that has replaced my garment of beauty with ashes, and has replaced my oil of joy with a spirit of mourning, I call this replacement or exchange into order and undo this evil operation.

I say, you demon who has done this, destruction and chains of unbearable torment by the incomprehensible heat of the coals of the holy altar in Heaven be upon you now, effective immediately.

It is written in Isaiah 61:3, "**To appoint unto them that mourn in Zion, to give unto them beauty for ashes, the oil of joy for mourning, the garment of praise for the spirit of heaviness; that they might be called trees of righteousness, the planting of the LORD, that he might be glorified.**"

By Heaven's decree, I am called a tree of righteousness and the planting of the Lord (Isaiah 61:3).

I declare that Joy is my portion. I have joy unspeakable and full of glory according to [1Peter 1:8].

I am dwelling in the secret place of the Most High and I am abiding under the shadow of the Almighty, in the presence of the Lord my Savior [Psalms 91:1]; therefore, I am receiving the fullness of joy, for it is written in Psalms 16:11: **"in thy presence *is* fullness of joy; at thy right hand *there are* pleasures for evermore."**

Garment of Ministry

Father, every power from the realm of the kingdom of darkness that has replaced my garment of ministry, causing me to be an unfaithful, incompetent steward, and worthless servant as in Your parables, I rebuke these evil powers in Jesus' name.

I reclaim by fire my ministerial garment, and I command the kingdom of darkness in all realms and spheres to release my ministerial garment that was replaced or exchanged, effective immediately.

I say to my garment, release yourself from any realm of evil, and be restored upon me as ordered by the Lord, now, in Jesus' name.

Organ replacement

Every demon of the subterranean or any other realm of darkness that has replaced my healthy body organs with a sick organ, failing organ, I rebuke you now in the name of the Lord God, and I command you by fire to restore my healthy organ now, effective immediately, because the blood of Jesus of Nazareth compels you; the throne of the God Most High commands you.

Wherever my healthy organs are held within any crevice, storehouse, grave, water, witchcraft black box, jar, vase, witch bag, etc., let my healthy functioning organs be restored to me now, by the jurisdiction of the stripes of Jesus's broken body.

I call upon the fire of Rapha to burn out every demonic thing in my body and set in order my health and stature, in the name of Jesus of Nazareth.

Father, I thank you, that you have this day given me deliverance and the breakthrough requested.
Be exalted O God, as I thank you for what you have just done, in Jesus name, Amen and Amen.

17. Prayer Against Magic Mirrors & Your Spirit Being Summoned

Heavenly Father, by the authority of the Blood, fire, and Spirit of the Living God, I come to Your Throne of Grace to obtain Your mercy, grace, and protection.

Behold, Lord, I am under the monitoring system of the Kingdom of Satan and other powers of darkness.
Father, I have been afflicted by various astral forces because I was subjected to the forces of psychic manipulations.

But Your word says in Galatians 5:1, **"Stand fast therefore in the liberty wherewith Christ hath made us free, and be not entangled again with the yoke of bondage."**
I ask for Your forgiveness for everything that I have done and for things that I have or have had in my possession that have subjected me to become a focus of attention and a heavily monitored person of interest in the kingdom of Satan.
By this authority, in the name of Jesus of Nazareth, I will no longer be a prisoner of unconscious witchcraft, afflicted and tossed by demonic manipulations, wherein I am demonically accessed and manipulated via psychic mirrors and other surveillance devices of Hell.

Therefore, with the power of Jesus the Christ, I call upon the vehement fire of Yah, the God, Adonai Tzeva'ot, to descend from the Altar of El-Shaddai, in the Name of Y'ahushua HaMashiach, and intervene for me by the fire of amber.
Lord God, I now take up the authority of Christ mentioned in Luke 10:19, and through the fire and the blood of Y'ahushua, I address the kingdom of Satan and the Devil.

Hear me, all hosts of the kingdom of darkness, the Lord Y'ahushua of Nazareth has given me authority in Luke 10:19, where He says, **"behold, I give unto you power to tread on serpents and scorpions, and over all the power of the enemy: and nothing shall by any means hurt you"**.

Against Astral Surveillance Devices

By the authority of the Word of God in Luke 10:19, by the power of the emerald rainbow around the Throne of God [Rev 4:3], by the authority of the sceptre of God's kingdom [Psalms 45:6], by the authority of God's throne of Sapphire, by lightnings and thunderings and voices; and the seven burning lamps of fire which are the seven Spirits of God [Rev 4:5].

I stand in the capacity of a warrior clothed with the power of the eternal and Pentecostal fire of Elohei Tsidkenu, and I now wage warfare, and renounce, denounce, revolt against, and destroy by fire and by the blood of Jesus, all visual scopes, surveillance intelligence, astral monitoring devices, spiritual drones, the Astral Televisions, Celestial Mirrors, Etheric Gemstones, Akashic Black Stones, Astral Gemstones, Animus Third Eye, Psychic Cameras, tele-dynamites, the Astro-Omnidictator, watchers, peeping spirits, whistling spirits, etc., that are programmed over my life by the high demons of darkness.

Let all these monitoring devices of the occult working against me be shattered, destroyed beyond repair, and banished by fire, lightnings and thunders, effective immediately.

In the name of Jesus, let every witch and demon operating these monitoring devices be scattered and banished in chains of torment, and let the token of evil against me be frustrated; let the wise men of the occult be turned backward, and their knowledge turn to foolishness, and all diviners be struck with madness, for it is written

in Isaiah 44:25, **"That frustrates the tokens of the liars, and makes diviners mad; that turns wise men backward, and makes their knowledge foolish;"**
Isaiah 44:26, **"That confirms the word of his servant, and performs the counsel of his messengers;"**

Let all demonic triggers, activators, programs, laws of metaphysical homogeneity, spells, hexes, psychic commands, occult sound frequencies, vibrations, and all subtle psychic manipulation by witchcraft, necromancy, injuring, conjuring, projecting, voodoo, herb mixtures, incantations, rituals, altars, and every plot, plan, weapon, curse, snare, lair, or any other esoteric craft deployed to destroy me through the Astro-Omnidictator or other monitoring devices and magic mirrors, which are set up for me in every corner of the universe, in the crevices of the earth, within covens, in underground witchcraft chambers, beneath the waters in the occult world, in all occult zones, regions, astral planes, be shattered by the power of Jesus the Christ of Nazareth.

Let them be bound, condemned, annihilated, liquidated, dissolved, eradicated, and rendered impotent, useless, and clueless against my life, effective immediately.
I call every servant of occultism into alignment to the Judgement of the Word of Yah Almighty; now, let every witch, warlock, satanist, ritualist, grand master, ascending master, shaman, witch doctor, native doctor, wise man, avatar, ascended master, mermaid, siren, voodoo priest, Devas and Devatas (male and female "Guardian Spirits"), Guardian of the Flame, brotherhood, the Order, the sisterhood, and Guru who are secretly sniffing, switching, snitching, projecting, and plotting my destruction and death through astral surveillance devices of the occult be confronted, apprehended, and neutralized by advanced defences of lightning, whirlwinds, and uncompromizing, unquenchable, and incomprehensible terrifying fire

of disastrous proportions and mass destruction. Destroy them, O Lord God, for You reign over the heavens and the Earth.

Also, I break, block, and stop every transmission, signal, frequency, and wireless communication between the realms and the Pandemonium kingdom that is channeling information to one another about my life, and is carrying information about my life, for my life is hidden with Christ.
I pray against the monitoring systems of the witches' central tower of communication, and all "obelisks," "towers," "pyramids," and every power of the air that is monitoring my phone calls, texts, photos, and social information in order to cast incantations upon me at 12 midnight.

Against Magic Mirrors

Every witch, warlock, sorcerer, Wiccan, or any agent of darkness who has called my name upon a magic mirror, or is calling my name upon a magic mirror, or who would try to call my name upon a magic mirror within any witchcraft coven on earth, or in the marine kingdom, or in the astral kingdom of the Air, or in the subterranean kingdom, let my name become destructive lightning and thunder in the mouths of these occult agents, releasing a detonation and explosion of destruction upon these evil workers. Let the mirrors be shattered to pieces and the ground split open and swallow up every living and non-living thing.

Also, I pray, O Father, every agent of darkness and witchcraft that would seek to summon my spirit to appear in their magic mirror, let this mirror explode into pieces when my name is called.
I also pray that whoever is doing the incantation and using a magic mirror against me would be trapped in their own mirror.

Every evil power that has or is trying to sexually violate me or initiate me through sex using a magic mirror, let these agents of darkness be bound, restrained, and constrained by chains of fire from the altar of Heaven, and their mirror be shattered, in Jesus' name.

Every evil power that has or is trying to bind me to the marine or water kingdoms using a magic mirror, let these agents of darkness be bound, restrained, and constrained by chains of fire from the altar of Heaven, and their mirror be shattered, in Jesus' name.

Every evil power that has or is trying to trap me in a magic mirror, or steal my money, wealth, health, success, family, etc., using a magic mirror, let these agents of darkness be bound, restrained, and constrained by chains of fire from the altar of Heaven, and their mirror be shattered, in Jesus name.
Wherever my name is written upon parchment, a stone, or anything with demonic pens or tools of death, let my name be erased by the fire of the Spirit of God, now, in Jesus' name.

Against Footprint Being Taken

In the name and Spirit of Jesus of Nazareth, and by the power of the Most High God in the highest heaven, I pray that my footprints be engulfed in holy fire and become detrimental to every witch or Satanist.

I pray that every and any power from Hell that would try to take the dust of my footprint in order to summon my soul and my spirit upon an evil mirror, let this agent be arrested by fire and thick smoke from the Altar of God and go into epilepsy, and be vanquished into another dimension, among merciless, vicious, demonic wild beasts with no way of return.

I pray and decree and declare by the judgement of God, that every evil power that has, or is trying to take my footprint using subtle esoteric powers of divination and witchcraft, in order to summon my spirit upon magic mirrors in water reflections, or to strike me with curses of various sorts, enchantments and manipulations, let these agents of darkness be bound, restrained and constrained by chains of fire from the altar of Heaven, and let their hands dry up and become stiff and withered as a dried tree branch, and their feet be stuck to the ground that they cannot be moved for a season, times, time and a half a time, in the majestic name of Jesus, Son of God Almighty.

Right now, by the jurisdiction of Proverbs 6:5 that says to us, "**Deliver yourself as a roe from the hand *of the hunter*, and as a bird from the hand of the fowler,**" I now deliver myself from all satanic holds, traps, snares, and imprisonments, and I pray, let dynamic fires, lightning, and thunders shatter every astral prison facility where my soul is held in captivity by demonic spirits.
The scriptures say to us in Psalms 91:3, **"Surely he shall deliver thee from the snare of the fowler, and from the noisome pestilence."**

Let me be delivered from the snare of the fowler, and from the noisome pestilence, now, and from all vicious astral assaults, weapons, traps, and snares of the evil powers of the Cro-Magnon world, the Aquatic world, the Pestifera world, the cosmic world, and the subterranean world, and all other forces working under the five Mephistophelian Occult Seals, effective immediately.
It is written in Psalms 124:7, **"Our soul is escaped as a bird out of the snare of the fowlers: the snare is broken, and we are escaped."**
Lord Jesus, let the stronghold and pattern of this wickedness in my life be broken, and the manipulations of demonic spirits of the surveillance infrastructure of the Occult who are seeking to transmute, change, alter, and demote my character, personality,

behaviors, thinking systems, and practical methods be banished by force, in Jesus' name.

Let every witchcraft curse set upon my life to destroy my life, my reputation, my dignity, my mind, my purpose, future, and destiny, through any psychic surveillance device, be banished and destroyed now, in Jesus' name.
Sanctify and separate me from sin and worldly adornments, vanities, greed, love of money, etc., that I may become invisible to these magic mirrors, and thank You for fighting for me against the monitoring systems of Hell and setting me free in the name of Jesus. Amen.

18. Prayer Against Witchcraft Candles Lit Against You

By the power of the Spirit of the Most-High God, I pray against evil powers conjured against my life through rituals and incantations using candles, chants, and evil prayers.

Your word said, O Lord, in Psalms 71:13, **"Let them be confounded *and* consumed that are adversaries to my soul; let them be covered *with* reproach and dishonour that seek my hurt."**

With hot chains of fire and by force, I bind and bring into captivity and under subjection all forces of darkness working against my life and destiny, through rituals and incantations using candles, chants, and evil prayers, and by the name of Jesus of Nazareth I pray for the destruction of all Beeswax Candles, Paraffin Wax Candles, Soy Wax Candles, Palm Wax Candles, Liquid Wax Candles, Bayberry Wax Candles, Pillar Candles, Tea Light Candles, Votive Candles, Taper Candles, Cartridge Candles etc.

Destroying Black Magic Candles

In the Name of Jesus of Nazareth, if there are, or have been, or will be any candles of death, or black magick rituals utilizing black candles within any of the terrestrial kingdoms or astral planes against my life, I pray against them now.

Any candle that is programmed with a curse tied to a date of my death, let it be blown to pieces, and all curses of death destroyed, in Jesus' name.

In the Name of Jesus of Nazareth and by the power of the Holy Spirit, I pray against and destroy any and every black occult Candle of Death burning against my life in the astral or physical realm, with the mandate to absorb, devour, consume, and banish my destiny, or to bind my life within inanimate objects, and to shorten my lifespan upon the earth by the workings of destruction.

I banish the black energy of any black candle connected to the waning Moon, the root chakra, or the planet Saturn with the mandate to secure hexes against me, or compromise my spiritual identity, induce grief, terror, nightmares, fearfulness, phobias, sorrows, negativities, mysterious karmas, afflictions, calamities, catastrophes, sudden and premature death, or to ignite upon me slow destruction.

I render every black candle of black magick and any candle of death inadequate, incapable, and ineffective in channeling any incantation and psychic commands to the elemental forces throughout the psychic layer and astral planes against me. By the power of the judicial blood of Jesus of Nazareth, these incantations and psychic spirits are now disqualified and rendered useless against my life.

I pray and command these orange candles of death and destruction to melt by the fervent heat of the Holy Spirit and disappear beyond recovery by the power and name of Jesus of Nazareth.
By Jesus Christ of Nazareth, I render these candles of black magick inadequate, incapable, and ineffective in channeling any psychic commands to the elemental forces throughout the psychic layers and astral planes against me.

By the power of the Name of Jesus of Nazareth, every human agent of darkness working with candles and black witchcraft against my life in the land, sea, and air, let them go into spasm and convulsion now, and by the power of the judicial blood of Jesus of Nazareth, let all incantations and psychic spirits now be disqualified, become redundant, and be rendered useless against my life.

Therefore, effective immediately, let every black magic ritual of death and swift destruction against my life be liquidated, annihilated, eradicated, and become inadequate, incapable, ineffective, ineligible, and useless in any incantation being done against me through the psychic elemental spirits.

May the priest and acolytes of these altars be destroyed and banished now, Amen and Amen!

Destroying White Candles

In the Name of Jesus of Nazareth, if there are, or have been, or will be any black witchcraft rituals utilizing white candles within any of the terrestrial kingdoms or astral planes against my life, I pray against them now.

In the Name of Jesus of Nazareth and by the power of the Holy Spirit, any white candle used in the workings of black magick, connected to the psychic channels of the Moon, to Monday, and the energy of the third eye, which is burning against my life with the mandate of black and white magick to incite corruption, bring impotence, create weaknesses, induce neurosis, paranoia, fear, coercive control, or psychological, emotional, sexual, and spiritual destruction, by the Name of Jesus of Nazareth and by the power of the Holy Spirit, I pray against and destroy by fire these white occult candles.

I render every white candle of black magick inadequate, incapable, and ineffective in channeling any incantation and psychic commands to the elemental forces throughout the psychic layer and astral planes against me. By the power of the judicial blood of Jesus of Nazareth, these incantations and psychic spirits are now disqualified and useless against my life.

I pray and command these orange candles of death and destruction to melt by the fervent heat of the Holy Spirit and disappear beyond recovery by the power and name of Jesus of Nazareth.

By Jesus Christ of Nazareth, I render these candles of black magick inadequate, incapable, and ineffective in channeling any psychic commands to the elemental forces throughout the psychic layers and astral planes against me.

By the power of the Name of Jesus of Nazareth, every human agent of darkness working with candles and black witchcraft against my life in the land, sea, and air, let them go into spasm and convulsion now, and by the power of the Blood of Jesus of Nazareth, let all incantations and psychic spirits now be disqualified, become redundant, and be rendered useless against my life.

Therefore, effective immediately, let every black magic ritual of death and swift destruction against my life be liquidated, annihilated, eradicated, and become inadequate, incapable, ineffective, ineligible, and useless in any incantation done against me through the psychic elemental spirits.

May the priest and acolytes of these altars be destroyed and banished now, Amen and Amen!

Destroying Red Candles

In the Name of Jesus of Nazareth, if there are, or have been, or will be any black magick rituals utilizing red candles within any of the terrestrial kingdoms or astral planes against my life, I pray against them now.

In the Name of Jesus of Nazareth and by the power of the Holy Spirit, I pray against and destroy any and every burning red occult candle being used in the workings of black magick against my life in the astral or physical realm, with the mandate of black magick to kill me, or invoke upon me **various categories of accidents, sudden psychic attacks, sexual captivities, depravities,** or that are programmed to harvest my blood, drink my energy, and take my life through the commands of astral sound vibrations.

I render every red candle of black magick inadequate, incapable, and ineffective in channeling any incantation and psychic commands to the elemental forces throughout the psychic layer and astral planes against me. By the power of the judicial blood of Jesus of Nazareth, these incantations and psychic spirits are now disqualified and rendered useless against my life.

I pray and command these orange candles of death and destruction to melt by the fervent heat of the Holy Spirit and disappear beyond recovery by the power and name of Jesus of Nazareth.

By Jesus Christ of Nazareth, I render these candles of black magick inadequate, incapable, and ineffective in channeling any psychic commands to the elemental forces throughout the psychic layers and astral planes against me.
By the power of the Name of Jesus of Nazareth, every human agent of darkness working with candles and black witchcraft against my life in the land, sea, and air, let them go into spasm and convulsion now, and by the power of the judicial blood of Jesus of Nazareth, let all incantations and psychic spirits now be disqualified, become redundant, and be rendered useless against my life.

Therefore, effective immediately, let every bl magic ritual of death and swift destruction against my life be liquidated, annihilated, eradicated, and become inadequate, incapable, ineffective, ineligible, and useless in any incantation being done against me through the psychic elemental spirits.
May the priest and acolytes of these altars be destroyed and banished now, Amen and Amen!

Destroying Yellow Candles

In the Name of Jesus of Nazareth, if there are, or have been, or will be any black magick rituals utilizing yellow candles within any of the terrestrial kingdoms or astral planes against my life, I pray against them now.

By the power of the Holy Spirit, I renounce, revoke, and destroy the power of any and every yellow candle burning by the enchantment of black magic, psychic forces of the solar chakra, the throat chakra, the planet Jupiter, or any constellation, zodiac, or interstellar energy field, or the psychic powers of Wednesday and Sunday, and charged with a satanic mandate to ambush my communication skills, my intellectual capacity, my happiness, my inspiration, my intuition, my knowledge, my wisdom, and my pleasures.

May the power of the holy fire of Jesus bind and disarm the power of any enchanted yellow candle programmed to subject my soul to astral travel and burning with enchanted forces to ambush and take over my logic, consciousness, communication abilities, and audible expression, or to incite in me infidelity, cowardice, decay, disease, dying, insanity, and inconsistency.

I render every yellow candle of black magick inadequate, incapable, and ineffective in channeling any incantation and psychic commands to the elemental forces throughout the psychic layer and astral planes against me. By the power of the judicial blood of Jesus of Nazareth, these incantations and psychic spirits are now disqualified and rendered useless against my life.

I pray and command these orange candles of death and destruction to melt by the fervent heat of the Holy Spirit and disappear beyond recovery, by the power and name of Jesus of Nazareth.

By Jesus Christ of Nazareth, I render these candles of black magick inadequate, incapable, and ineffective in channeling any psychic commands to the elemental forces throughout the psychic layers and astral planes against me.

By the power of the Name of Jesus of Nazareth, every human agent of darkness working with candles and black witchcraft against my life in the land, sea, and air, let them go into spasm and convulsion now, and by the power of the Blood of Jesus of Nazareth, let all incantations and psychic spirits now be disqualified, become redundant, and be rendered useless against my life.

Therefore, effective immediately, let every black magic ritual of death and swift destruction against my life be liquidated, annihilated, eradicated, and become inadequate, incapable, ineffective, ineligible, and useless in any incantation being done against me through the psychic elemental spirits.

May the priest and acolytes of these altars be destroyed and banished now, Amen and Amen!

Destroying Green Candle

If there are, or have been, or will be any black magick rituals against my life, utilizing green candles within any of the terrestrial kingdoms or astral planes, I pray against them now.

In the Name of Jesus of Nazareth and by the power of the Holy Spirit, I destroy any green candle used in the workings of black magick against my life to harmonize me with the sacred creatures and astral entities of the forest occult kingdom.

Any green candle burning against my life, with destructive flames for the consumption of my spirit, soul, body, and destiny, through various satanic formulas of black magick, being connected to the waxing Moon, the heart chakra, the planet Venus, or any constellation,

Zodiac, or interstellar energy field, and programmed to incite jealousy, greed, suspicion, resentment, sickness, disease, and disharmony, or to entangle and cover my life with forest vines, forest moss, and chaos, I destroy by fire this green candle incantation and ritual of black and green magic now, in the name of Jesus.

Also, I banish green witchcraft, green energy, and the power of any green candle with the mandate to secure hexes against me, or compromise my spiritual identity, induce grief, sorrows, negativities, mysterious karmas, afflictions, calamities, catastrophes, sudden and premature death, or to ignite upon me slow destruction.

I render every green candle of black magick inadequate, incapable, and ineffective in channeling any incantation and psychic commands to the elemental forces throughout the psychic layer and astral planes against me. By the power of the judicial Blood of Jesus of Nazareth, these incantations and psychic spirits are now disqualified and rendered useless against my life.
I pray and command these orange candles of death and destruction to melt by the fervent heat of the Holy Spirit and disappear beyond recovery by the power and name of Jesus of Nazareth.

By Jesus Christ of Nazareth, I render these candles of black magick inadequate, incapable, and ineffective in channeling any psychic commands to the elemental forces throughout the psychic layers and astral planes against me.
By the power of the Name of Jesus of Nazareth, every human agent of darkness working with candles and black witchcraft against my life in the land, sea, and air, let them go into spasm and convulsion now, and by the power of the judicial Blood of Jesus of Nazareth, let all incantations and psychic spirits now be disqualified, become redundant, and be rendered useless against my life.

Therefore, effective immediately, let every black magic ritual of death and swift destruction against my life be liquidated, annihilated, eradicated, and become inadequate, incapable, ineffective, ineligible, and useless in any incantation being done against me through the psychic elemental spirits.

May the priest and acolytes of these altars be destroyed and banished now, Amen and Amen!

Destroying Purple Candles

In the Name of Jesus of Nazareth and by the power of the Holy Spirit, I pray against, renounce, and revoke any purple candle used in the workings of black magick against my life through the full Moon, through the channels and forces of psychic powers, through the energy of the sixth chakra and the third eye, through the planet Jupiter, and through the gates of Thursdays and Mondays.

Let every channel created by these candles for astral projection be clogged with chaos and confusion, as I now command the destruction of any purple candle ritual invoking the calamities of divination against me through astrological symbols, through magical cubes, and the zodiac elements.
Any purple candle used in black magic to incite tyranny, abuse of power, sadness, and treachery to me, my family, and others, business failure, and negative influence towards people in power, let these powers wither away like powder in the south wind and die now.

I render every purple candle of black magick inadequate, incapable, and ineffective in channeling any incantation and psychic commands to the elemental forces throughout the psychic layer and astral planes against me. By the power of the judicial Blood of Jesus of Nazareth, these incantations and psychic spirits are now disqualified and rendered useless against my life.

I pray and command these purple candles of death and destruction to melt by the fervent heat of the Holy Spirit and disappear beyond recovery by the power and name of Jesus of Nazareth.

By Jesus Christ of Nazareth, I render these candles of black magick inadequate, incapable, and ineffective in channeling any psychic commands to the elemental forces throughout the psychic layers and astral planes against me.
By the power of the Name of Jesus of Nazareth, every human agent of darkness working with candles and black witchcraft against my life in the land, sea, and air, let them go into spasm and convulsion now, and by the power of the Blood of Jesus of Nazareth, let all incantations and psychic spirits now be disqualified, become redundant, and be rendered useless against my life.

Therefore, effective immediately, let every black magic ritual of death and swift destruction against my life be liquidated, annihilated, eradicated, and become inadequate, incapable, ineffective, ineligible, and useless in any incantation being done against me through the psychic elemental spirits.
May the priest and acolytes of these altars be destroyed and banished now, Amen and Amen!

Destroying Orange Candles

In the Name of Jesus of Nazareth and by the power of the Holy Spirit, I pray against, renounce, and revoke any orange candle used in the workings of black magick against my life to consume and destroy my Abundance, my Adaptability, Ambition, Celebration of good things, Confidence, Creativity, Courage, Discipline, Vitality, Independence,

Freedom, Goals, Justice, Money, Positivity, Pleasure, Reconciliation, Inspiration, Strength, and even my mobility. May the fire of Jesus Christ descend upon these candles to destroy their ability to channel curses through the astral layers against me.

I render every orange candle of black magick inadequate, incapable, and ineffective in channeling any incantation and psychic commands to the elemental forces throughout the psychic layer and astral planes against me. By the power of the judicial Blood of Jesus of Nazareth, these incantations and psychic spirits are now disqualified and rendered useless against my life.

I pray and command these orange candles of death and destruction to melt by the fervent heat of the Holy Spirit and disappear beyond recovery, by the power and name of Jesus of Nazareth.
By Jesus Christ of Nazareth, I render these candles of black magick inadequate, incapable, and ineffective in channeling any psychic commands to the elemental forces throughout the psychic layers and astral planes against me.

By the power of the Name of Jesus of Nazareth, every human agent of darkness working with orange candles in black witchcraft against my life in the land, sea, and air, let them go into spasm and convulsion now, and by the power of the judicial Blood of Jesus of Nazareth, let all incantations and psychic spirits now be disqualified, become redundant, and be rendered useless against my life.
Therefore, effective immediately, let every black magic ritual of death and swift destruction against my life be liquidated, annihilated, eradicated, and become inadequate, incapable, ineffective, ineligible, and useless in any incantation being done against me through the psychic elemental spirits.
May the priest and acolytes of these altars be destroyed and banished now, Amen and Amen!

Destroying Blue Candles

In the Name of Jesus of Nazareth and by the power of the Holy Spirit, I pray against, renounce, and revoke any blue candle used in the workings of black magick against my life. Any black magick ritual utilizing blue candles within any of the terrestrial kingdoms or astral planes against me, to consume and destroy my honesty, my trust, communication skills, my dreamwork, my wisdom, leadership abilities, my career, my visions of success, my productivity, my mental stability, and competency, may fire from Jesus Christ descend upon these candles to destroy their ability to channel curses through the astral layers against me.

I banish the blue energy of all blue candles connected to the psychic powers of continental oceans and seas, the psychic powers of the blue moon, or to the psychic powers of the crown chakra, the throat chakra, the planet Jupiter, or any other planetary body, phase, and alignment.

I also pray against and destroy any and every blue occult Candle of Death burning against my life in the astral or physical realm, with the mandate of black magick to fight against my spirituality, my meditation, reverse my healing, work against my sincerity, block me from obtaining the truth, corrupt my influential fidelity and loyalty, bring chaos to my inner peace, my knowledge, my wisdom, and banish harmony from my home.

I pray against and destroy any program of black magic set in cosmic motion for the incitement of depression, sadness, hopelessness, lack of sympathy, coldness, and gloominess in my life.

Any blue magic incantation done to summon water demons against me, to increase occult marine power operations in my life, or to establish evil spiritual protections and spirit guides in my life, I pray for the destruction of this witchcraft operation and astral poisons.

By Jesus Christ of Nazareth, I render these blue candles of black magick ritual and incantations inadequate, incapable, and ineffective in channeling any psychic commands to the elemental forces throughout the psychic layers and astral planes against me.

By the power of the Name of Jesus of Nazareth, every human agent of darkness working with candles and black witchcraft against my life in the land, sea, and air, let them go into spasm and convulsion now, and by the power of the judicial Blood of Jesus of Nazareth, let all incantations and psychic spirits now be disqualified, become redundant, and be rendered useless against my life. May these blue candles of death and destruction melt by the fervent heat of the Holy Spirit and disappear beyond repair and recovery by the power of Jesus of Nazareth.

Therefore, effective immediately, let every black magic ritual of death and swift destruction against my life be liquidated, annihilated, eradicated, and become inadequate, incapable, ineffective, ineligible, and useless in any incantation being done against me through the psychic elemental spirits.
May the priest and acolytes of these altars be destroyed and banished now, Amen and Amen!

Destroying Pink Candle

In the Name of Jesus of Nazareth and by the power of the Holy Spirit, I pray against and destroy any and every pink occult Candle of Death burning against my life in the astral or physical realm, with the satanic mandate through black magick to lock my life in a vortex of false Acceptance, false Affection, false Beauty, false Compassion, false Reconciliation, marine Children, cycles of Abuse, infidelity, Family feud, false and destructive Friendship, fake Kindness, false Love, bad Marriage, false Passion, and false Sensuality.

May these pink candles of divination and destruction melt by the fervent heat of the Holy Spirit and disappear beyond repair and recovery by the power of Jesus of Nazareth.

Therefore, let every black magic ritual of death and swift destruction against my life be liquidated, annihilated, eradicated, and become inadequate, incapable, ineffective, ineligible, and useless in any incantation being done against me through the psychic elemental spirits, effective immediately.
May the priest and acolytes of these altars be destroyed and banished now, Amen and Amen!

Destroying Grey And Brown Candles

In the Name of Jesus of Nazareth and by the power of the Holy Spirit, I pray against and destroy any and every grey occult Candle of Death burning against my life in the astral or physical realm, with the mandate of black magick to incite mourning and sadness, death, illness, etc., by the workings of destructive magicks.

I render every grey candle of black magick inadequate, incapable, and ineffective in channeling any incantation and psychic commands to the elemental forces throughout the psychic layers and astral planes against me. By the power of the judicial Blood of Jesus of Nazareth, these incantations and psychic spirits are now disqualified and useless against my life.
Any grey or brown candle that is used to represent my demise and unity with the soil and humus, melt and be destroyed now.

In the Name of Jesus of Nazareth and by the power of the Holy Spirit, I destroy any candle of ambushment that is lit or burning against my life.

In the Name of Jesus of Nazareth and by the power of the Holy Spirit, I destroy any candle of terror that is lit or burning against my life to terrify my mind and privacy.

In the name of Jesus of Nazareth and by the power of the Holy Spirit, I destroy any black and white candles lit against me for calamity.

In the name of Jesus of Nazareth and by the power of the Holy Spirit, I destroy any candle lit upon waters.

In the Name of Jesus of Nazareth and by the power of the Holy Spirit, I destroy all candles burning upon the graves against me.

In the Name of Jesus of Nazareth and by the power of the Holy Spirit, I destroy any candle lit with strange fires to burn my life and destiny to ashes.

In the Name of Jesus of Nazareth and by the power of the Holy Spirit, I destroy any candle lit upon any dark altar against my life.

19. Prayers Against The Spirit Of Unbelief & Doubt

Lord our God, King of the ages, All-powerful and All-mighty who sits between the Cherubim of burning coals, hallowed be Your name in all kingdoms of the heavens and the earth. Heavenly Father, indeed, You are the Most High God; Your name is holy, and You are exalted in all kingdoms, realms, dimensions, and spheres.

I come to you today acknowledging that You are the author and finisher of my faith. However, I have been struggling with doubts and unbelief and am having difficulty trusting in Your word, and for this, I petition by the blood of the Lamb for Your mercy.

Father, Your word says in Hebrews 11:6, **"But without faith it is impossible to please him; for he that cometh to God must believe that he is and that he is a rewarder of them that diligently seek him."**
I repent for my sins, transgressions, and the iniquities of doubt and unbelief associated with my bloodline that may have passed on to me. I also repent for my sins, transgressions, and the iniquities of doubt and unbelief that I may have opened a door to in my life.

Every sin of doubt and unbelief from my mother's house, or from my father's house that the enemy is using as a legal right to build legal cases against me, to sabotage and ruin my destiny, and to keep me in an impoverished state, let the fire of Your holy word burn out this evil of doubt and unbelief in me. Let all astral poisons of doubt and unbelief that are programmed to cause me to miss the blessings of God be destroyed now, by the velocity of the fire of the altar mentioned in Revelation chapter 8.

Father, Your word says, **"Delight yourself also in the Lord, and He shall give you the desires of your heart" (Psalm 37:3-4)**; therefore, I claim Your mercy and grace to have the desires of my heart granted. But Your word says in James 1:6, **"But let him ask in faith, nothing wavering. For he that wavereth is like a wave of the sea driven with the wind and tossed. For let not that man think that he shall receive anything of the Lord."**

With this verse, I identify and acknowledge that I am a victim of doubt and unbelief, which is the reason for the absence of the miraculous hand of God in my life. It is confirmed **in Mark 6:5, "And he could there do no mighty work, save that he laid his hands upon a few sick folks, and healed** *them."*

Mark 6:6, "And he marvelled because of their unbelief."

O Lord, I pray that You send me Your Spirit of faith and open the channels of trust for Your word in my soul and spirit, and give me great faith, even the gift of faith.

It is written in Romans 10:17, **"So then faith cometh by hearing, and hearing by the Word of God."** Therefore, on this verse I request the enlightenment of my understanding for Your revelatory word, the opening of my ears to hear, and the conditioning of my heart to receive this word.

Heavenly Father, configure my heart to be an ark of great faith, and my life to testify of my great faith, [James 2:14-24] for Your word says in Mark 9:23, **"Jesus said to him, If you can believe, all things** *are* **possible to him who believes."**

It is also written that Your will be done on earth as it is in Heaven.

It is Your will for me to have faith; therefore, I am requesting the faith of Matthew 21:21 which says, **"Jesus answered and said unto them, Verily I say unto you, If ye have faith, and doubt not, ye shall not only do this** *which is done* **to the fig tree,"** and Mark 11:23 that says, "For **verily I say unto you, that whosoever shall say unto this mountain, Be thou removed, and be thou cast into the sea; and shall not doubt in his heart, but shall believe that those things** which he saith shall come to pass; he shall have whatsoever he saith."

I am asking that You light the fire of Your greatness in my heart and melt the stoniness that is preventing my heart from being a ground for great productivity and harvest.
Erase the mark of doubt and unbelief (ancestral or personal) from my forehead, heart, and DNA that has caused me to attract calamity and many sins, for it is written, **"... for whatever is not of faith is sin"** (Romans 14:23).

Let the eternal fire of Your altar burn out from my heart and soul the spirit of doubt, hardness of heart, rebellion, disobedience, fear, skepticism, distrust, agnosticism, faithlessness, perversion, suspicion, unbelief, and an augmentative spirit of argument, as I renounce the forces of darkness that are manipulating my perception, thought processes, and paradigm.

Lord Jesus, Your word says to us in Luke 10:19, **"Behold, I give unto you power to tread on serpents and scorpions, and over all the power of the enemy; and nothing shall by any means hurt you."**

Therefore, by my authority through Jesus of Nazareth, I now take authoritative command over all spirits of the four kingdoms of the Air, the kingdom of the waters below, the kingdom of the Land, and the kingdom of the subterranean region, and over the four elements of the four cardinal dimensions, and I demand the release of my great faith in Christ, now, with immediate effect.

In the name of Jesus of Nazareth, I take authority over every generational curse of unbelief and doubt inherited from my father's house and from my mother's house, and every arrow of doubt that has been fired into my mind and heart, into my body and destiny, that it be vaporized by fire.

Every demon of doubt, unbelief, and delay, who through my doubt and unbelief has created a breach in my career/business, or has blocked my children from receiving from God, delayed my healing, robbed my relationship of spiritual benefits from Heaven, has blocked divine resources from flowing into my life and atmosphere, delayed my breakthrough, my deliverance, and every spirit of doubt and unbelief that has been assigned to sabotage my opportunity to witness and testify to miraculous demonstrations of the power of God in my life, be bound and disarmed with hot chains of holy fire from the altar of God now!

I banish you foul spirits out of my life and body and now command you to get out and leave me now, effective immediately, and go into places of desolation and oblivion with no opportunity to return, in the name of the Lord God of hosts, Creator of the heavens and the earth. It is written in Luke 10:17, **"And the seventy returned again with joy, saying, Lord, even the devils are subject unto us through thy name"**.

In Jesus' Name, I decree and declare by my jurisdiction in the Blood of the altar of the highest Heaven that I have the code and intelligence of divine wisdom to harness the substance and power of Great Faith.
In Jesus' Name, I decree and declare by my jurisdiction in the Blood of the altar of the highest Heaven that I am a vessel of Great Faith, and Faith is like a garment upon me.
In Jesus' Name, I decree and declare by my jurisdiction in the Blood of the altar of the highest Heaven that I have mountain-moving and sycamore uprooting faith.

In Jesus' Name, I decree and declare by my jurisdiction in the Blood of the altar of the highest Heaven that I have the faith that quenches fiery darts, neutralizes satanic forces, scatters battalions of armies, and overthrows occultic regiments.

In Jesus' Name, I decree and declare by my jurisdiction in the Blood of the altar of the highest Heaven that my faith is as a wall of terrifying, uncompromising fire, as a barrier of electricity with the highest capacity of voltage, and an invisible force of incomprehensible power against my enemies.

In Jesus' Name, I decree and declare by my jurisdiction in the Blood of the altar of the highest Heaven that I have chain-breaking, shackle-destroying, burden-lifting, demon-chasing, miracle-invoking, disease-healing, and God pleasing Faith.

In Jesus' Name, I decree and declare by my jurisdiction in the Blood of the altar of the highest Heaven that any evil creature that seeks to swallow my faith, let them swallow themselves instead.

Father, thank You for changing my disposition and giving me the faith of Your kingdom, in Jesus' Name, Amen.

20. Prayers Against Miscarriage & Barrenness

Lord God of Israel, King of the ages, All-powerful and Holy One of Jacob. You sit between the two Cherubim who are made from burning coals and are clothed with the splendour of Your magnificence and hold the power of times and seasons.

I come boldly unto the throne of grace, that I may obtain mercy, and find grace to help in time of need (Heb 4:16), as I revolt in faith against the curse of miscarriage, or infertility, or barrenness.
Today, by force, I pull Your sword of the Spirit out from its sheath, and I charge against the kingdom of darkness with the full force of the Word of God and power, for you said in Isaiah 43:26, **"Put me in remembrance: let us plead together: declare thou, that thou mayest be justified."**

Holy Spirit, I implore the judicial authority of the wounds of the Lamb who was slain, and I seek help from the verdict of Your judicial council, and I petition by the blood of the Lamb that the Council of the Most High God be seated on my behalf and discuss my case. I pray that the council of the Lord God, with the 24 Elders, the 4 Seraphim, and the 6 Cherubim would agree upon my healing and deliverance from the dilemma and repetitive cycle of miscarriages. It is written, Psalms 50:15, **"call on Me in the day of trouble; and I will deliver you, and you shall glorify Me."**
According to Your word in Exo 23:25-26, it is written, **"And you shall serve the LORD your God, and He shall bless your bread and your water. And I will take sickness away from the midst of you. None shall cast their young, nor be barren in your land. The number of your days I will fulfill."**
You also said in Deut 7:13, **"And he will love thee, and bless thee, and multiply thee: he will also bless the fruit of thy womb,"**

In thee, O LORD, do I put my trust; let me never be ashamed: deliver me in thy righteousness. [Psalms 31:1]

"Bow down your ear to me; deliver me speedily: be my strong Rock, for a house of defence to save me", according to Psalms 31:2. Right now, I sever, nullify, and destroy beyond repair or replication any personal connection, ancestral connection, or direct and indirect, current and past, conscious and unconscious agreement, covenant, truce, alliance, or any secret link that my womb and reproductive system have with any familiar spirit, spirits of the grave, with the emperor of death, the death hunter, death reaper, with the art of white witchcraft, black witchcraft, blue witchcraft, green witchcraft, red witchcraft, with Moloch, the Queen of Beta, the queen of the Coast, the Queen of Shylon, the Queen of Yemunah or the Queen of Delta, or with the spirit of the mother anaconda, the spirit of the Pritha, the spirit of serpentine, the spirit of the merfolk, nymphs, sirens, dragons, demons, gods, goddesses, or spirits of the four elements of nature, or any other creature of darkness within the land, waters, subterranean, and air.

I revoke and withdraw any secret sworn oaths, all confessions, professions, acclamations, proclamations, decrees, allegiances, written contracts, blood signatures, and agreements that were made between my womb and the kingdom of the Devil, directly or indirectly, consciously or unconsciously. Hence, let all family altars with these demons be demolished, effective immediately, in Jesus' name.

Lord Jesus, thou Son of David, have mercy upon me according to the multitude of Your lovingkindness and Your tender mercies as I seek deliverance from the curse and spirit of miscarriage or infertility, or barrenness. It is written in Isaiah 53:4-5 **"Surely he has borne my infirmities and carried my diseases..."**

Let my cry for help and my state of despair trigger an emergency alarm in Heaven to accelerate the velocity of mercy for intervention on my behalf. Psalms 70:1 says, **"Make haste, O God, to deliver me; make haste to help me, O LORD."**
Psalms 127:3 **Lo, children *are* an heritage of the LORD: *and* the fruit of the womb *is his* reward.**

Upon the authority of Your word in Exodus 23:25 and Deuteronomy 7:13, I stand erect in the spirit and invoke the authoritative capacity of the Kavod glory and the fire of the Shekhinah in my mouth, in my prayers, and around me right now.
I curse the demons of miscarriage, infertility, barrenness, and I revolt against the spirits, the curses, and any altar for miscarriage that is in my life.
In Jesus' Name, I destroy all cycles of miscarriage that have been robbing me of the fruit of the womb, by which I have been emotionally dismantled and torn. Your word says, O Lord, a broken spirit, who can bear?

I cover my womb and all its contents and components with the bronze fire of the feet of Jesus and the light of his countenance. Every evil power of witchcraft, every repetitive curse that is programmed to operate at a specific time, and any cycle in my womb which is tied to and activated by a specific season or physical condition or is activated by the presence of a pregnancy, let it be broken with immediate effect, in Jesus' name.
Therefore, I summon a "Holy Rebuke" from the Courtroom and Divine Council in Heaven against all spirits of miscarriage that have imprisoned me and have set themselves upon me to afflict me through ancient astral rites, legal grounds, and ethereal bridges coming from my ancestral genealogy.

Arise, O Lord, let my womb and reproductive system now be released from captivity, and from the sin and curses from paternal and maternal sides up to ten generations of both my mother's house and my father's house, and open the prison of my bondage to liberate me, spiritually, emotionally, socially, psychologically, and mentally, in the Almighty Name of Jesus.

Acquit me from the iniquity and sin of abortion, neonatal murder, or any sin and iniquity, whether personal or ancestral, that has subjected me to be a victim of miscarriage, infertility, or barrenness.

It is written in Isaiah 61:1, "The **Spirit of the Lord GOD is upon Me because the LORD has anointed Me to preach the Gospel to the poor; He has sent Me to bind up the brokenhearted, to proclaim liberty to the captives, and the opening of the prison to those who are bound."**

By the power of the fire, the lightnings, the voices, and the seven thunders, by the power of the 7 horns and 7 eyes of the Lamb of God, and by the authority of the name King of Kings and Lord of lords, I declare a battle of retrieval and reclamation.

Psalms 68:1-2, **"Let God arise, let His enemies be scattered; also let those who hate Him flee before Him."**

"As smoke is driven away, so drive them away; as wax melts before the fire, so let the wicked perish in the presence of God."

In the name of Jesus, let every witch and demon operating monitoring devices and curses against my womb be scattered and banished in chains of torments, and let the token of evil against me be frustrated; let the wise men of the occult be turned backward, and their knowledge turn to foolishness, and all diviners be struck with madness, for it is written in Isaiah 44:25, **"That frustrateth the tokens of the liars, and maketh diviners mad; that turneth wise *men* backward, and maketh their knowledge foolish;"**

Wherever my womb is locked up, shut up, ambushed within the terrestrial realm, sub-aquatic region, astral layer, occult plain, zone, region, or kingdom, or is held in a glass jar, black box, tree, in a calabash, a vase, or upon an altar, or is buried in a cemetery, thrown in a river, sea, pond, or lake, I retrieve, reclaim, and recover by fire my ovaries, my entire womb, and all other components of my reproductive system now, for it is written in 1Sa 30:8, "...**Shall I go after this troop? Shall I overtake them?**" And He answered him, "**Go! For you shall surely overtake and will without fail recover all.**"

I address every demon of miscarriage, infertility, or barrenness planted in my body by any baby snake, brooding serpent, worm, larva, or pupa through a dream, spiritual procedure, sexual intercourse, erotic condoms, the use of a dildo, sex toys, or any other avenue that has captured my womb or is feeding on my womb.

By thunders of fire and lightnings, I disarm, bind, and banish by the power of Jesus Christ all baby snakes, brooding serpents, worms, larvae, pupae, or any other creature inside my womb, eating, drinking, or swallowing my pregnancies, causing or contributing to my having miscarriages. It is written in Psalm 27:2, "**When the wicked,** *even* **mine enemies and my foes, came upon me to eat up my flesh, they stumbled and fell.**"

I crush and burn to ashes by fire the eggs of any serpent, the eggs of any cockatrice, or the eggs of any other evil creature that have been laid in my womb, and I crush any worm, larva, or pupa that were also placed in my womb.

Let the Blood of Jesus flush out every demonic substance and deposit that was left in my womb or reproductive system from past doorways of sexual perversion, or sexual, medical, or hygienic procedures and invasions.

Let every rope, chain, or item used to tie my womb be burned to ashes.

Any anaconda, python, Pritha, dragon, or evil beast that has swallowed my womb, let it vomit up my womb and restore it to my body, and let the two-edged sword of the Holy Spirit cut off the heads of these demons afflicting my womb and reproductive system.

I block, stop, shut down, and destroy by lightning, by thunder, and by fire every witchcraft operation, message, signal, frequency, transmission, velocity, and telegram that is in communication with higher powers, orchestrating the destruction and annihilation of my pregnancies and life.

All spirit of Hell responsible for my miscarriages, infertility, or barrenness be burned and consumed by the electric fire and dynamic thunderbolts from Heaven, and let the transporter demons and all astral forces of evil, voodoo, hex, spell, cage, tie, weight, witchcraft, programs, agenda, technique, formula, code, esoteric occult sciences, orders, channels, vibration and frequencies, etc., and all demons and sirens attached to these evils working against me and my womb become useless, ineffective, powerless, and let their force and velocity dissolve and come to naught, effective immediately, by the God of Abraham, Isaac, and Jacob, for it is written in Psalms 34:19, **"Many are the afflictions of the righteous: but the LORD delivereth him out of them all"**.

Arise, my God, and set me free, and overthrow any demon sitting upon my womb, for it is written in Psalms 68:1-2, **"Let God arise, let his enemies be scattered: let them also that hate him flee before him. As smoke is driven away, so drive them away: as wax melteth before the fire, so let the wicked perish in the presence of God"**.

I thank you, Father, for Your help and angelic assistance in setting my womb free from the powers of darkness. For this, I give you all the glory and honour, as I wait to see Your glory in the land of the living, in Jesus' Name, Amen.

21. Reclaiming Your Physical Items Taken By Witches

Heavenly Father, I seek the intervention of Your Eternal Flame, requesting that Your fire will render Your judgement against every agent of darkness for my sake, and the thief who came to steal, kill, and destroy me.

Abba Father, let the fire of Jesus of Nazareth expose and destroy the gimmicks, traps, and snares of the evil powers that have ambushed my life and destiny. It is written in Psalms 71:13, "**Let them be confounded** *and* **consumed that are adversaries to my soul; let them be covered** *with* **reproach and dishonour that seek my hurt.**" In the Name of Jesus of Nazareth, I declare war by fire against every altar upon which my bodily or household items were placed in order to sacrifice my life.

In whatever occult realm, occult zone, occult centre, occult region, terrestrial kingdom, or astral plain where my life is held imprisoned, or held upon witchcraft altars as a sacrifice because of my fingernail, toenail, my clothes, my hair or hair items, my blood, my semen/sanitary napkin, my photo, my footwear, my sock, my saliva, my sweat, or skin tissues, which were taken and buried in a cemetery, or wrapped in magical twines, placed under an object, tied to the four elements, tied to a gravestone, tied to the rotting corpse of a human or animal, or placed between a crevice, under a bridge, or thrown at the bottom of a lake, a pond, a pool, a river, sea or ocean, or wherever my item is being burnt upon an altar, submerged in a witchcraft solution, or flushed down the toilet as a ritual, I render these incantations and rituals inadequate, incapable, and ineffective in channeling any incantation and psychic command to the elemental forces, throughout the psychic layers and astral planes against me.

Whatever part of my life that has been placed upon an altar as food for the gods, by the judicial verdict of the judicial blood of Jesus, may these demon gods restore my life force and destiny by heaven's demand. May fire from Jesus Christ descend and destroy this altar with a detonation by lightning of fire, fires of amber, and by lightnings of thunderclaps.

In the name of Jesus of Nazareth and by the power of the Holy Spirit, I pray against and destroy any and every operation of black, white, red, blue, or green magic that is burning against my life in the secret places of the covens of Wicca, witchcraft, Satanism, and every other esoteric and astral psychic force.

By Jesus Christ of Nazareth, I pray against every ethereal bridge programmed to access my subconsciousness, my intuition, my perception, and my home, or that was programmed to set at naught my potential to get wealth, my successful future, and my ability to live a victorious life over sin, evil, and poverty.

Every piece of paraphernalia that is used in rituals against my life using my items, and magick which has access to me through my items that are placed upon cemetery altars, home shrines, church altars, teraphim, or forest altars, etc., by the power of the fire of the sanctified Blood of Jesus of Nazareth, let all incantations and psychic spirits now be disqualified, become redundant, and be rendered useless against my life. I renounce and revoke all witchcraft spells, hexes, and cages that are in my life because of my items placed in witchcraft rituals or ceremonies using prayers, hymns, chants, or religious signs, symbols, and sigils.

I now retrieve my items from the hands of every occult practitioner by fire.

Let lightning and thunderclaps rattle, explode, and detonate in every place where my clothes, hair items, hairs, nails, blood, semen/sanitary napkin, photo, skin tissues, shoes, sandals, socks, saliva, or sweat are held by occult powers. Henceforth, let my success become like a burning fire coal, too hot for the kingdom of darkness to hold concealed, use, or manipulate, I pray.

Every dragon or python in the sea, land, air, or subterranean region in whose belly are my bodily items, or items taken from my home, I pray that it will vomit up my items by force in Jesus' name.

Every pot and cauldron boiling my item, explode now in Jesus' name.

Every altar, holding my items in a witchcraft ritual, explodes to pieces now in Jesus' name.

The fire of the Holy Spirit of Yah now dries up the waters and solutions in which my items are submerged.
Let every human agent of darkness using my bodily items in witchcraft against my life in the land, sea, and air go into spasm and convulsion now! Psalms 35:6, **"Let their way be dark and slippery: and let the angel of the LORD persecute them,"** by the power of the Name of Jesus of Nazareth, let them run to and fro in terror and madness.

Let all black, white, green, blue, or red witchcraft working against my life within all seven kingdoms of darkness explode to pieces by the invisible force of a terrible windstorm, a terrible firestorm, a terrible earthquake, a terrible tempest, and fire mixed with brimstone and hail.

Therefore, effective immediately, let every black magic ritual of death and swift destruction against my life be liquidated, annihilated, eradicated, and become inadequate, incapable, ineffective, ineligible, and useless in any incantation being done against my life across the occult zones, planes, regions, and occult centers, in the name of Jesus of Nazareth.

Father, I thank you that Your Angels are already recovering my items, and my life is already making a full recovery.
Thank you for all the answers to my prayer, in Jesus name, Amen and Amen.

22. Prayer Against Witchcraft Prayers Done Against You

Heavenly Father, I seek the intervention of Your Eternal Flame, requesting that Your fire will render Your judgement on my behalf, against every agent of darkness who came to steal my substance, kill, and destroy me. Behold, they have set snares and aroused the vibrations of the astral forces within all dimensions against my life through their prayers, chants, and fasting.

By the light and fire of the Holy Spirit, I pray and counter every prayer that was made against my life by any Avatar, Grand Master, Witch, warlock, satanist, Wiccan, ascending master, Freemason, Sorcerer, or anyone within the Inner Esoteric framework, who operates by the 'powers of Astral and Terrestrial Hierarchy.

In the name of Jesus of Nazareth and by the power of the Holy Spirit, I renounce and revoke all witchcraft prayers that were made against my life to the Queen of Heaven, to the Queen of the South, to the Queen of Beta, to the Queen of Shylon, to the Queen of Yemunah, to the Queen of Delta, and to the Queen of the Coast, in the mighty name of Jesus of Nazareth.

I also renounce, condemn, and revoke all evil prayers made against my life to the gods of the Titans, to the Olympian gods, to the king demons of the four elements, to the evil guardians of the cardinal points, to the Mermaids and the Sirens, to the Nymphs, or to the gods and goddesses of the waters, rivers, lakes, ponds, waterfalls, or to the spirits of the dead, the spirit of the psychic elementals such as the Sylphs, the Salamanders, the Gnomes, and the Undines, or to the entities of the city of Gupha within the Bermuda Triangle, or to any of the supernatural beings of the land, sea, air, or the underworld, or to the continental dragon of Europe.

I call the fire of the verdict of the judicial Blood of Jesus to dispel the verdict of the satanic council, which has given jurisdiction to the astral spirits to work against my life because of evil prayers offered up to the gods against me. It is written in Psalms 71:13, **"Let them be confounded** *and* **consumed that are adversaries to my soul; let them be covered** *with* **reproach and dishonour that seek my hurt."**

By the fire of the Holy Spirit in Jesus' Name, I condemn and revoke all prayers that were made against my life for setbacks, hindrances, and blockages; prayers for unfruitfulness and unproductiveness; prayers for illnesses, mental problems, and psychological shutdown; prayers for continual disappointments, shames, and disgraces; prayers for incompleteness and incompetence; prayers for poverty, lack, insufficiency, and always wanting and never getting; prayers for always starting something good and not finishing it. Let all these prayers that were made on my behalf be canceled, nullified, and liquidated, effective immediately, in Jesus name.

In the powerful name of Jesus, the Lamb of God, I banish from my life any magical dust, dry bone powder, black powder, enchanted mist, magical herb, cursed water or liquid, enchanted water, magical twine, talisman, enchanted stick, magical wand, astral stone, every mystical arrow, astral poison, and pestilence of darkness that is programmed to sustain cycles of manipulation against my life via psychic vibrations etc.

I condemn and revoke all prayers that were made against my life for childlessness, for a broken and sad life, for sorrowful discoveries in life, for advanced distress syndromes, for the foreclosure of my home, for bankruptcy in my business, for loss of my job, for prayer for me to become a victim of advanced calamities, a victim of advanced terror and living nightmares, a victim of advanced bullying and victimization, criticism, and rejection. I renounce, revoke, and condemn these prayers in Jesus' name.

It is written in Psalms 57:6, **"They have prepared a net for my steps; my soul is bowed down: they have dug a pit before me, into the midst whereof they are fallen themselves. Selah"**.

All evil prayers that are causing good jobs to pass me by and go to less qualified people, I renounce, revoke, and condemn these prayers in Jesus' name.

Every evil prayer by household or Coven witchcraft power is assigned to waste my life; I renounce, revoke, and condemn these prayers in Jesus' name.

All prayers to cause my less qualified friends and enemies to get good opportunities in life while I stand here waiting. Every evil prayer, household, or Coven witchcraft power assigned to waste my life, be wasted in the name of Jesus. Psalms 27:2, **"When the wicked, even mine enemies and my foes, came upon me to eat up my flesh, they stumbled and fell."**

All prayers to cause me to give birth to sorrows, calamity, and emptiness, I renounce, revoke, and condemn these prayers in Jesus' name.

I renounce and revoke all witchcraft prayers that were made against me by a voodoo priest or practitioner at a voodoo altar.

I renounce and revoke all witchcraft prayers that were made against me by my parents, grandparents, or great-grandparents, both biological and non-biological, or by any other family members.

I renounce and revoke all witchcraft prayers that were made against me by any of my friends, acquaintances, neighbors, schoolmates, teachers, or a school principal.

I renounce and revoke all witchcraft prayers that were made against me in a Black Mass, on a Black Sabbath, on Easter, on Good Friday, on Christmas Day, through Halloween, through Saturnalia, All Souls Day, All Saints' Day, or on any satanic and Paganic holiday.
I pray against every Catholic prayer that was made against my life using the Catholic rosary, the Catholic cross, any Catholic prayer book, the statues of Catholic saints, the Catholic holy water, the Catholic paschal candle, the monstrance, or any prayer done against my life within any Catholic fraternity or secret society.
I nullify, defy, and revoke all prayers done against my life and destiny by the legionaries of the Legion of Mary, the Confraternity of the Holy Cross, the Confraternity of the Rosary, the Legion of Christ, the Sons of Divine Providence, St. Vincent de Paul, Man of Order, or the Confraternity of Our Lady, Mother of Perpetual Help, or any other secret society under the Vatican.

Every prayer made against my life over a pot of blood, a chalice of blood, a goblet, or prayers made within a shrine, upon a grave, etc., I renounce and revoke all witchcraft prayers in the name and power of Jesus Christ of Nazareth.

All evil prayers made against my life using the ambiance and enigma of water, the ambiance and enigma of the soil, the ambiance and enigma of the air, the ambiance and enigma of sound frequency, the ambiance and the enigma of nature, I break the powers of the Sirens of these different spheres which use the enigma as a point for accessing the astral powers of the five esoteric seals of darkness against my life.

23. Prayer Against Serpentine Spirit

Heavenly Father, I come boldly before Your Throne of Grace, seeking Your divine intervention against every serpentine spirit in my life who is programmed and carrying the mandate from the Order of the Old Serpent, who is called Satan.

It is written in Mark 3:27, **"No man can enter into a strong man's house, and spoil his goods, except he will first bind the strong man; and then he will spoil his house."**
Therefore, upon this authority, by the power of the Spirit of Jesus, according to Matthew 12:29 and Mark 3:27, I bind with hot chains and shackles of holy fire the hands and feet of every serpentine spirit, and their subjects and projects that are operating in my life.

It is also written in Luke 11:21, **"When a strong man armed keepeth his palace, his goods are in peace:"**
I now remove the peace of every strong man's asset in my life by the judicial velocity of the forces of the Angelic order and council of Almighty God. Every serpentine strong man armed and keeping his evil palace and goods in my life, I subject this spirit to destruction by the fire of the Spirit of God.

It is also written in Luke 11:22, **"But when a stronger than he shall come upon him, and overcome him, he taketh from him all his armour wherein he trusted and divides his spoils."**
I call upon you, Jesus, to send Your angels to overcome and strip away the trusted armour of every serpentine spirit, and I strip all demonic serpents, their subjects and their projects from their defences, weapons, artillery, and weapons of combat and manipulation.
I sever, block, and stop every reception, communication, channel, signal, frequency, and intel that is communicated between altars of the land and altars of the waters and the air against my life, through

the evil powers of the serpentine spirits. Every serpentine communication and transmission of evil info between altars and realms, zones, regions, and centres against my life, I command the telecommunication to backfire, jam, and be broken, in Jesus' holy name. It is written in Psalm 27:2, "**When the wicked, *even* mine enemies and my foes, came upon me to eat up my flesh, they stumbled and fell.**"

I call for the fire of the living Blood of Jesus to arise against the highest council of the serpentine spirit and condemn and overthrow the serpentine council and overrule and dismantle their verdict to destroy my life.

I pray and call for judgement of fire to destroy any Astro-Omnidictator through which evil spirits receive jurisdiction and capacity to project evil into my life for astral modification.

I speak to the Sun, the Moon, the heavens, and the Earth, and I say fight against the serpentine beings and forces that seek to occupy your territories with witchcraft against me, right now, through the authority of Jesus of Nazareth; I command.

I now rise in faith with the highest velocity of the power of Jesus Christ of Nazareth, and invoke the living Blood of Jesus, to flush out every venom and astral poison the serpent has released into my life, my body, my home, my destiny. I invoke the power of the living blood of the Lamb of God and the name of Jesus to neutralize and flush out the venom and poison of serpents of the dust. [Deut 32:24], the poison of dragons [Deut 32:33], the cruel venom of asps [Deut 32:33], the poison of asps [Job 20:16], the poison of the lady anaconda, the poison of the emperor of death, the Prithas, the viper, the cobra demon and the serpentine king that was placed in my body, soul, destiny, and mind, and every poison placed under my tongue and in my lips.

I pray against and banish the spirit of the mother anaconda, every Pritha and every serpentine and satanic throne that is exalted in the air, in the waters, at the gates between the realms, on the land and in the forest and is feeding on my blood, feeding on my lifeforce, eating my destiny, my success and has swallowed my life and my future. It is written in Psalm 27:2, **"When the wicked, *even* mine enemies and my foes, came upon me to eat up my flesh, they stumbled and fell."**

Any serpentine demon that has coiled or twisted itself around my brain, my mind, my body, my spine, sacral region, my cardiovascular system, skeletal system, muscular system, nervous system, endocrine system, lymphatic system, respiratory system, digestive system, urinary system, and my reproductive system, by the power of God, I address you coiled serpentine spirits with the language and artillery of the holy fire of amber from the Throne of the Lord, God of Israel, and I command you foul spirits to self-destruct, and the grip of your twisted stronghold to be destroyed by the Fire.

Wherever my joy, peace, destiny, happiness, success, praises, and health were replaced with shackles, shame, disgrace, and embarrassment through psychic manipulations, through the cosmological verdict, through metaphysical intercourse, by the powers of the Astro-Omni-dictator and under the velocity of the 5 Mephistophelian seals of the occult, I reverse this evil transaction and demand release and 7-fold restoration of everything you serpentine demons have taken from my mother's house and from my father's house.

Let judgement and destruction come upon every serpentine spirit who has scattered and dispersed or swallowed up my wealth, health, destiny, mind, virtues, talents, gifts, potential, future, my money, and my life, etc. It is written in Psalms 71:13, **"Let them be confounded**

and consumed that are adversaries to my soul; let them be covered with reproach and dishonour that seek my hurt."

By the authority of the Word of God in Luke 10:19, by the power of the emerald rainbow around the Throne of God [Rev 4:3], by the authority of the sceptre of God's kingdom [Psalms 45:6], by the authority of God's throne of Sapphire, by lightnings and thunderings and voices: and the seven burning lamps of fire which are the seven Spirits of God [Rev 4:5], I stand in the capacity of a warrior clothed with the power and authority of the name King of Kings and Lord of lords, and I command by fire and by the blood of Jesus, you Serpentine demon, and all you unclean demons, effective immediately, that you release and restore to me 7-fold all my life, the health of all my organs, success, business ideas, godly desires, favorable fulfillments, expectations, endeavors, God-given destinies, my future, my generations, my wealth, my health, and my mind from the mouth, or from the belly of the serpentine demon and subordinates, and from the power of the serpentine spirits located in the four cardinal points, and from the depths of the rivers, seas, and oceans, and from the heights of the heavens above, and from the valleys between kingdoms, and from every and any place where they are held.

By the power and authority of God's throne of Sapphire, and by the power of the fire, the lightnings, the voices and the seven thunders within the presence of the enthroned and exalted Jesus, by the power of the 7 horns of the Lamb of God, by the 7 eyes of the Lamb of God, and by the authority of the name King of Kings and Lord of lords, I command you, Serpentine demon, and all you unclean demons, effective immediately! that you release and restore to me 7-fold all my virtues, talents, gifts, character, potential, future, finances, favours with God and with man, and my good opportunities, open doors of promotion and success, my dignity, character, my faith, my glory, my anointing, my ministry, and my wisdom to gain wealth from your mouth, or from your belly, or from the four cardinal points, and from the depths of the rivers, seas and oceans, and from the heights of the heavens above, and from the valleys between kingdoms, and from every and any place where they are held.

Lord Jesus, let these serpents and dragons vomit out my assets and family wealth inheritance by the fire of Jesus of Nazareth, and let them restore to me sevenfold what they took from me.
In every terrestrial realm, sub-aquatic region, and in every astral layer, plain, zone, region, and kingdom where I am the monopoly and playground for the serpentine spirits, and in every spiritual crevice where I am ambushed and trapped, or am held in prison by the serpentine forces who operate at the highest velocity of Astro-metaphysical acceleration, I invoke the power of Elohei Tzevaot to release me from within every realm, plane, and region of the psychic kingdoms of space, land, and water, effective immediately, by the verdict of the judicial blood of Jesus in whom I have redemption through his blood, the forgiveness of sins, according to the riches of his grace; [Eph 1:7, Col 1:14].

I call upon the two-edged sword of the Holy Spirit to decapitate every serpent and let the Sword of the Spirit cut off the head of any anaconda, python, or Pritha who has vomited upon my life, is vomiting, or will seek to vomit upon me.
I call to destruction any serpent and cockatrice egg laid in any part of my life. In the name of Jesus, I release the rod of God to swallow up every serpent that would come against me to strangulate my life physically and spiritually.

By the power of Jesus the Christ, I tread upon you serpentine and your subordinate brood of serpents, and I call forth fire to roast to ashes every egg laid.

I am untouchable to you vipers and brood of serpents, and you cannot harm me according to Mark 16:18 in the name of Jesus.

Every alliance that was formed between me and the serpentine spirit through ancestral worship and idolatry in my family foundation, I cut off every soul tie with any demonic serpent spirit in the name of Jesus.

I repent of all serpent worship, and the worship of animal deities and forces of the air, fire, water, the underworld, and nature, in the name of Jesus.

You demonic serpents and viper demons, and all astral and psychic powers of various ranks operating against my life, are rendered venomless, teethless, powerless, ineffective, defenceless, weaponless and useless against me right now.

From this day onwards, I am no longer a victim, candidate, or prisoner of the manipulations of the serpentine spirit, or witchcraft altar, rural incantation, and satanic and diabolic prayers of destruction, effective immediately, henceforth, by warfare of fire, lightning, and faith in Jesus Christ, I am released from the strongholds of python, mother anaconda, and serpentine, and from every covenant, bondage, and cage, in the Mighty Name of Jesus of Nazareth.

24. Reclaiming Your Destiny And Life From Demons

In the mighty name of Y'ahushua Ha-Mashiach, by the power and authority of God's throne of Sapphire, and by the power of the fire, the lightnings, the voices and the seven thunders within the presence of the enthroned and exalted Jesus, by the power of the 7 horns of the Lamb of God, and by his 7 eyes, I declare war and combat of reclamation and retrieval, and by the power of God's word in 1 Samuel 30:8, by fire and by force I call forth, pursue, overtake and without fail recover *all, retrieve all* and reclaim my destiny and life, and all other components of my destiny and life from any cemetery, from the wastelands, from the barren lands, from the desolate places, from the woodlands, the wetlands, from any catacomb or grave, from any enchanted forest, the monsoon forest, the tropical forest, from the swamp, from the sacred grove, from the mangroves, from the everglades, from the crossroad, the fork road or the roundabout, or from any metropolitan, megapolitan, jurisdiction, principality, municipality, neighborhood, township, borough, city, town, urban, exurb, suburb, county, district, state, nation, archive, and from any of the seven kingdoms of darkness according to 1Samuel 30:8.

It is written in 1 Samuel 30:8, **"And David enquired at the LORD, saying, Shall I pursue after this troop? shall I overtake them? And he answered him, Pursue: for thou shalt surely overtake them, and without fail recover all."**
I call and open the celestial gates by the name of:
Jesus
Lamb that was slain
Almighty God
God of hosts
Rising us

Sun of Justice
Morning star
Y'ahushua
Word of God
Saviour of the World
King of kings and Lord of lords
El Shaddai,
and I command the release of all my items, assets, faculties, destiny, and blessings which were replaced with shackles, shame, disgrace, and embarrassment through psychic manipulations, through the cosmological verdict, through metaphysical intercourse, by the powers of the Astro Omni-dictator and under the velocity of the five Mephistophelian seals of the occult.

I stand by the jurisdiction of the Blood upon the Mercy Seat, and I reverse these evil transactions and exchanges and replacements, and I demand release and restoration, and retrieve by the Bronze and Amber fire of Mount Zion my organs, health, life, success, business idea, godly desires, expectations, endeavours, destinies, my future, my generations, my wealth, health, mind, virtues, talents, gifts, character, potential, my precise intellectual capacities, pristine intelligence, pristine articulation of my expression of morals, self-worth, integrity, and my knowledge from the belly and power of the serpentine spirits, dragons, and beasts located in the four cardinal points, in the depths of the rivers, seas, and oceans.

Let all my mental assets, spiritual assets, emotional assets, psychological assets, financial assets, marital assets, economic assets, and material assets, love for Jesus, and everything contained in my destiny that you evil spirits and demons have taken from me, be released back into my hands and life from the four corners and heights of the heavens above, from the valleys between kingdoms, and from the earth beneath, effective immediately, in Jesus name.

Hence, I reclaim the full functionality of my faculties: intellectually, spiritually, emotionally, psychologically, and mentally.

In every terrestrial realm, sub-aquatic region, and in every astral layer, plain, zone, region, and kingdom where I am secretly initiated as a blind witch, and is used as a monopoly and playground for the serpents and scorpions and other psychic entities, and in every spiritual crevice where I am ambushed and trapped, or am held in prison by the serpentine, reptilian, amphibian, spectral, and hybrid demonic forces who operate at the highest velocity of Astro-metaphysical acceleration, I invoke the power of Elohei Tzevaot to release me from within every realm, centre, plane, region, realm, and world of the psychic kingdoms of space, land, water, and underground, effective immediately, by the verdict of the judicial blood of Jesus in whom I have redemption through his blood, the forgiveness of sins, according to the riches of his grace; Eph 1:7 Col 1:14.

Through the Holy Spirit, I also call for judgement of fire and destruction to rain upon every Demon, Demi-god, and Siren god and goddess who are operating as Earth Masters, Guardians, Demi-gods, Astral forces, Planetary Spirits, Prithas, Watchers, Yamadutas, Yandavas, Guardians of the Flame, Ascended Masters, Archangels, Solar Lords, Inter-Planetary Lords, Inter-Galactic Lords, or as a seraphim or as a Guardian of Fate and the Cycles of life, who are specifically assigned to put my life under lockdown, and spiritually confiscate my destiny, assets, and everything contained in the master plan of my destiny on earth.
All spirits who are also sitting on my future, upon my life, the destiny of my ministry, my wealth, my health, my destiny, virtues, talents, gifts, and money, with darkness and heaviness, be destroyed now, by the power of Jesus Christ, effective immediately.

In Jesus' name, I shake off the beast in the fire, and I call upon the Fire of amber from the Throne of God to consume and ambush by fire all demonic ambushment, witchcraft cages, hexes, and occult curses placed upon me by the serpentine spirit, every twisted, crooked, coiled, nesting, and brooding serpent of the darkness assigned to destroy my life and harvest my soul.

By the power of the emerald rainbow that hovers over the Throne of the Lamb of God, by the authority of the sceptre of the Lamb of God and the presence of the enthroned and exalted Jesus, and by the authority of the name King of Kings and Lord of lords, I command every realm, sphere, dimension, cosmic zone, and region to release my life and destiny now, effective immediately, in the name of Jesus of Nazareth.

25. Destroying Witchcraft Chains And Locks

Lord our God, King of the ages, All-powerful and All-mighty who sits between the Cherubim, hallowed be Your name in all kingdoms of the heavens and the earth. Heavenly Father, indeed, You are the Most High God; Your name is holy, and You are exalted in all kingdoms, realms, dimensions, and spheres.
My God, I bring my life before you because of the afflictions that I am suffering due to spiritual chains and locks on my life.
I seek Your intervention and mercy to deliver me from the hold of the kingdom of darkness for Your name's sake.
You have given me authority in Your name, and therefore, I come here today to revolt and banish every evil power of these demonic chains and locks.

Father, by Your command that says curse be the man who keeps his sword from blood, I pull my sword out of its sheath and declare war on the Kingdom of darkness.
I call fire, terror, and degradation upon every evil force of the combined elements of astral spirits, capable of sustaining daily psychic attacks against my life for one thousand and ninety-five days.

I break the power of any witchcraft curse, lock and chain placed upon my life by incantations using a Calabash, the blood of a rooster, the blood of a frog, the blood of a goat, the blood of a raven, the blood of a bat, the blood of a ferret, the blood of a toad, the blood of a rabbit, the blood of a pig, the blood of a snake, the blood of a rat, the blood of a crow, or any herb or mandrake. By lightning, thunder, and the fire of Jesus Christ of Nazareth, I renounce, revoke, shatter, and destroy these witchcraft chains and locks in the name of Jesus the Christ.

It is written in Psalm 27:2, "**When the wicked, *even* mine enemies and my foes, came upon me to eat up my flesh, they stumbled and fell.**"

It is also written in Psalms 71:13, "**Let them be confounded *and* consumed that are adversaries to my soul; let them be covered *with* reproach and dishonor that seek my hurt.**"

I pray against any and every curse, lock, and chain placed upon me by witchcraft manipulations, using the cosmic network of the five Satanic seals of darkness.

Every curse placed upon my life through the occult Mephistophelian Level 333, 666, 999, 1330, 555, 777, 888, or 003, by lightning, thunder, and the fire of Jesus Christ of Nazareth, I renounce, revoke, shatter, and destroy these witchcraft codes, formulas, degrees, strongholds, chains, and locks in the name of Jesus the Christ.

I break the power of any witchcraft curse, lock, and chain placed upon my life through the velocity of the 'Five Esoteric Seals' and the acceleration of the forces of darkness and psychic elementals. By lightning, thunder, and the fire of Jesus Christ of Nazareth, I renounce, revoke, shatter, and destroy these witchcraft chains and locks, in the Name of Jesus the Christ.

I pray against and break the power of any witchcraft curse, lock, and chain that is placed upon my life through the 400,000 categories of demonic strongholds, which are compressed into the five Mephistophelian seals, occult levels, and psychic strongholds. By lightning, thunder, and the fire of Jesus Christ of Nazareth, I renounce, revoke, shatter, and destroy these psychic strongholds. chains and locks from my life now, in the Name of Jesus the Christ.

I pray and revolt against every witchcraft curse, lock, and chain placed upon my life by incantation done using diverse esoteric, occult, and psychic crafts.

Every witchcraft placed upon my life that was done in the seven psychic realms of darkness, in the Axis of the Earth, or through metaphysical projection, by lightning, thunder, and fire of Jesus Christ of Nazareth, I renounce, revoke, shatter, and destroy these witchcraft chains and locks, in the Name of Jesus the Christ.

I break the power of any witchcraft curse, lock, and chain placed upon me through the consummate agents of the cosmic forces, cosmic rites, psychic basis, and legions of the air.
I break every curse where my life is held by the invisible powers of the Forest, Desert, Air, and Water.
By lightning, thunder, and fire of Jesus Christ of Nazareth, I renounce, revoke, shatter, and destroy these witchcraft chains and locks in the name of Jesus the Christ.

I break the power of any witchcraft curse, lock, and chain placed upon my life through astrology, the Zodiac signs, the influences of the stars, and combined elements of astral spirits. By lightning, thunder, and fire of Jesus Christ of Nazareth, I renounce, revoke, shatter, and destroy these witchcraft chains and locks in the name of Jesus the Christ.
In the Name of Jesus of Nazareth and by the power of the Holy Spirit, I break the power of witchcraft manipulation, chains, and locks placed upon my life through esoteric mysteries, esoteric sciences, esoteric techniques, and occult knowledge.
By lightning, thunder, and fire of Jesus Christ of Nazareth, I renounce, revoke, shatter, and destroy these witchcraft chains and locks in the name of Jesus the Christ.

In the Name of Jesus of Nazareth and by the power of the Holy Spirit, I break the power of the witchcraft lock and chain that are placed upon my life, through divination and incantation using the influences of

Pleiades, the bands of Orion, the season of Mazzaroth, or the forces of Arcturus and his sons thereof.
By lightning, thunder, and fire of Jesus Christ of Nazareth, I renounce, revoke, shatter, and destroy these witchcraft chains and lock in the name of Jesus Christ.

I break the power of witchcraft manipulation, law, lock, and chain placed upon my life through astro-metaphysics, esoteric metaphysics, and demonic subtle atmospheres.
By lightning, thunder, and fire of Jesus Christ of Nazareth, I renounce, revoke, shatter, and destroy these witchcraft curses in the name of Jesus the Christ.

I break the power of any witchcraft operation, curse, lock, and chain placed upon my life, using the laws of homogeneity, psychic vibrations, and demonic frequencies.
By lightning, thunder, and fire of Jesus Christ of Nazareth, I renounce, revoke, shatter, and destroy these witchcraft curses in the name of Jesus the Christ.

I break the power of witchcraft manipulation placed upon my life using psychic manipulation by the supreme elementals.
By lightning, thunder, and fire of Jesus Christ of Nazareth, I renounce, revoke, shatter, and destroy these witchcraft curses in the name of Jesus Christ.

In the Name of Jesus of Nazareth and by the power of the Holy Spirit, I break the power of any witchcraft curse, lock, and chain placed upon my life by satanic mantras, um, om, chants, songs, occult prayers, and supplications.
By lightning, thunder, and fire of Jesus Christ of Nazareth, I renounce, revoke, shatter, and destroy these witchcraft curses in the name of Jesus the Christ.

I break any witchcraft curse, psychic manipulation, lock, and chain placed upon my life by any Guardian of the Flame, Avatar, Living Grand Master, Ascended Master, brotherhood, sisterhood, Witch, warlock, Satanist, ritualist, Guru, witch doctor, native doctor, wise man, fraternity, or any Cult organization.

By lightning, thunder, and fire of Jesus Christ of Nazareth, I renounce, revoke, shatter, and destroy these witchcraft curses in the name of Jesus the Christ.

In the mighty Name of Jesus of Nazareth and by the power of the Holy Spirit, I break the power of witchcraft chains and locks placed upon my life by the Gomes and Gnomes, and other subterranean spirits, and I break the power of witchcraft curses placed upon my life by the spirits of the four elements—fire, water, earth, and wind.

By lightning, thunder, and fire of Jesus Christ of Nazareth, I renounce, revoke, shatter, and destroy these witchcraft manipulations, curses, locks, and chains in the name of Jesus the Christ.

In the name of Jesus of Nazareth and by the power of the Holy Spirit, I break the power of the witchcraft curse of zero-point, and the vaccine of the law of repetition and resistance placed upon my life by witchcraft. I revolt and pray against every organized setup laid upon my life from within the Mephistophelean sphere. By lightning, thunder, and fire of Jesus Christ of Nazareth, I renounce, revoke, shatter, and destroy these witchcraft curses, chains, and locks in the name of Jesus the Christ.

By the power of the Holy Spirit, I break the power of any witchcraft curse, chains, and lock of the "Aramau astral poison" placed upon my life by sorcery, which is set to fight me for 1,095 days. By lightning, thunder, and fire of Jesus Christ of Nazareth, I renounce, revoke, shatter, and destroy these witchcraft chains and locks in the name of Jesus the Christ.

In the Name of Jesus of Nazareth and by the power of the Holy Spirit, I break every curse, lock, and chain placed upon my life by witchcraft done using metaphysical intercourse, metaphysical projection, and esoteric mysteries. By the lightning, thunder, and fire of Jesus Christ of Nazareth, I renounce, revoke, shatter, and destroy these witchcraft curses in the Name of Jesus the Christ.

All witchcraft chains, locks, and curses that are set upon my life and are monitored and kept in place by any Astral Television, Celestial Mirror, Etheric Gemstone, Akashic Black Stone, Astral Gemstone, Animus Third Eye, Psychic Camera, etc., by the lightning, thunder, and fire of Jesus Christ of Nazareth, I renounce, revoke, shatter, and destroy these witchcraft curses in the name of Jesus the Christ.

I break every curse, lock, and chain placed upon my life by witchcraft done in the river mouth, over running water, over a basin of water, or by using an ethereal bridge, or by any of my items containing my sweat secretion. By lightning, thunder, and fire of Jesus Christ of Nazareth, I renounce, revoke, shatter, and destroy these witchcraft curses in the name of Jesus the Christ.

Abba Father, I pray in the name of Your Son Jesus of Nazareth, that every magical substance, mixture, and ritualistic material will turn to useless and unusable dust in the hands of every occult practitioner who intends to do me harm by witchcraft.

Destroy every witchcraft in my life that is attached to ley lines, burial grounds, demonic sacred grounds, river mouths, chambers, water, covens, weather, full moons, or animals. Let this chain and lock by these witchcrafts break now, with immediate effect.

In the Name of Jesus of Nazareth and by the power of the Holy Spirit, I break any witchcraft curse of hypnotism and sensory manipulation, disorientation, hallucination, and memory loss placed upon my life by witchcraft or any form of sorcery. I renounce, revoke, and shatter it in the Name of Jesus the Christ.

I break the power of any witchcraft chain and prison lock placed upon me through the sins of illicit sex, fornication, sex toys, fetishes, philias, pornography, masturbation, voyeurism, adultery, karma-sutra etc.
By lightning, thunder, and fire of Jesus Christ of Nazareth, I renounce, revoke, shatter, and destroy these witchcraft curses in the name of Jesus the Christ.

I destroy any spiritual chain and witchcraft lock placed upon my life by witchcraft through Dream Catchers, Talismans, magic charms, etc.; I renounce, revoke, and shatter it in the name of Jesus the Christ.

26. Prayers Against Curses Of Death

O Lord my God, King of the ages, Omnipotent Yah who sits between the Cherubim, hallowed be Your name in all kingdoms of the heavens and the earth. Heavenly Father, indeed, You are the Most High God; Your name is holy and exalted in all kingdoms, realms, dimensions, and spheres.
You have given me authority to fight against the powers of darkness and prevail, and have anointed me with the fire to disarm the powers of darkness.

O death, you are an enemy according to [1Co 15:26], but it is written in Psalms 60:12, **"Through God we shall do valiantly: for he it is that shall tread down our enemies."** Therefore, O spirit of death, my God shall tread you down and shall deliver me from Your power and hand, for thus says the Lord in Isaiah 49:24-26, **"Shall the prey be taken from the mighty, or the captives of a tyrant be rescued?"**
Vs.25, **"But thus says the LORD, 'Even the captives of the mighty shall be taken away, and the prey of the fierce ones shall be rescued, for I will contend with him who contends with you, and I will save your children."**
Today, in Your holy name, I declare war against death in the name of the Lord.

In Jesus' name, I revolt against the death hunters of Hell and against all other death curses set upon me by witchcraft.
I declare by the Blood of the New Covenant of Christ to live and not die; therefore, by the power of the Holy Spirit, I now take up the authority of Jesus of Nazareth, and I pray against, bind, disarm, neutralize, and render powerless and useless every curse and spirit of death that is projected from any shrine, altar, or witchcraft coven, from within the land, sea, air, cemetery, and underworld to kill me

physically. It is written in Psalms 31:15, **"My times are in thy hand: deliver me from the hand of mine enemies, and from them that persecute me."**
By the authority of the throne of Elohei Tseva'ot, I bind, disarm, banish, and eradicate every evil verdict of death and any sentence of death that is decreed upon my life, which carries the mandate for my sudden or slow destruction. It is written in Psalms 71:13, **"Let them be confounded *and* consumed that are adversaries to my soul; let them be covered *with* reproach and dishonour that seek my hurt."**

Effective immediately, let electric fire and dynamic thunderclaps from Heaven annihilate, liquidate, dissolve, and eradicate the verdict of premature death, sudden death, death by my own lands, death by the hand of another, death by nature and natural disaster, sickness, or injury.

I hereby, with the verdict of the shed blood of Jesus, and the power of his resurrection, bind, disarm, and banish every spirit of swift destruction, demon of high destruction, spirit of slow and progressive destruction, spirit of death, death hunter, death reaper, and bounty hunter that is programmed and assigned against my life, health, and destiny. It is written in Psalms 27:2, **"When the wicked, *even* mine enemies and my foes, came upon me to eat up my flesh, they stumbled and fell."**
By the seraphic judgement and the amber fire of Yah, I cancel and destroy any death curse, death incantation, bounty, death plot, death plan, death warrant, and death sentence that is placed upon my life, effective immediately. By the power of Jesus Christ, I declare through His blood that untimely death is not my portion and inheritance and shall not locate me.

According to Psalms 118:17, **"I shall not die, but live, and declare the works of the LORD,"** in Jesus name.

The Word of God commands me in Proverbs 6:5, where it says, **"Deliver thyself as a roe from the hand of the hunter, and as a bird from the hand of the fowler."**
It is also written in Pro 12:6, **"but the mouth of the upright shall deliver them."**

Therefore, according to Proverbs 6:5 and Proverbs 12:6, I speak with my mouth by faith and deliver myself from you, demon of pornography, sexual lust, and lewdness, as a roe from the hand of the hunter, and as a bird from the hand of the fowler.
I stand upon the authority of the Word of God where the Lord Jesus said to us in Luke 10:19, **"Behold, I give unto you power to tread on serpents and scorpions, and over all the power of the enemy: and nothing shall by any means hurt you."**
It is also written in Luke 10:17, **"And the seventy returned again with joy, saying, Lord, even the devils are subject unto us through thy name"**.

Against The Books Of Hell

In the Name of Jesus of Nazareth and by the power of the Holy Spirit, I pray against the Book of Technique Tactic, the Book of Grimoire, and the Book of the Dead, so that their satanic formulas, codes, and witchcraft instructions will become useless, unusable, unstable, and ineffective in any incantation against my life.

Let there be a macro detonation and explosion whenever the Book of Technique Tactic, the Book of Grimoire, or the Book of the Dead is opened, read, or used against my life and destiny.
By the decree of Psalms 11:6, I call down rain of snares, fire, brimstone, a horrible tempest, and a terror to come upon every witch, warlock, Satanist, ritualist, grandmaster, ascending master, shaman, witch doctor, native doctor, wise man, avatar, ascended master, mermaid,

siren, voodoo priest, and vicious psychic entity who tries to recite satanic formulas and spells over my life for my physical death.

Wherever my name is written in the death register of the butchery of Diablo, in the book of death, on the bulletin for assassination, on the death wish list, or amongst the names of victims documented and scheduled to be slaughtered with premature and sudden death, by the power of the Holy Spirit, I call upon the lightning, the fire, and the light of Almighty God to erase my name from every book and realm of darkness – in the name of Jesus of Nazareth.

I pray that the pages of the book of the slaughterhouse of the Devil, or any book of destruction containing my name for the destruction of my spirit, soul, body, mind, and emotions, let these pages catch fire and burn to ashes now.

Abba Father, Your Word says, in Psalms 91:16, **"With long life will I satisfy him, and shew him my salvation."** Therefore, I am not and shall never be a candidate and victim of untimely death, unfortunate death, sudden death, death by accident, or any other form of death. Any mark of death placed upon my forehead, including the date for my annihilation, I call upon the fire of the Blood of Jesus the Lamb of God to burn out this mark and sigil. I claim immunity by Isaiah 54:17 that says, **no, weapon that is formed against thee shall prosper**.

Against Astral Poisons Of Death

By the blood of Christ Jesus, therefore, I pray against the weapon of the Voltra Bolt and the velocity of its psychic force that is programmed from 1:00 a.m. to 2:30 a.m. to annihilate me.
In Jesus' name, let the gate of 1:00 a.m. to 2:30 a.m. not accommodate any voltra bolt, Stampa, or witchcraft velocity organized against me by any witch, warlock, wizard, occult grandmaster, or avatar. Save me,

O Lord God, according to Psalms 31:2 that says, **"Bow down thine ear to me; deliver me speedily: be thou my strong rock, for a house of defence to save me."**

I also pray against every astral stone called "Nkpitime" that is organized to kill me in my sleep. I claim immunity by Isaiah 54:17 that says, **No weapon that is formed against thee shall prosper;** and every tongue that shall rise against thee in judgement thou shalt condemn.
I call upon the name of Jesus of Nazareth to shatter and destroy this astral poison by lightnings, thunders, and fire. Amen, and Amen!

By the power of the Holy Spirit, I bind in chains of holy light and fire, neutralize, and banish any spirit of death from the graveyard hovering over me or following me around, in the name of Jesus Christ.

Any grave clothes that have been tailored for me in the realm of the spirit, in expectancy of my physical death, I rip this garment of death apart and tear it to threads, and sabotage the expectancy of the wicked and say, your expectation, O death, shall not come to fruition; by the power of the Holy Spirit of Jesus of Nazareth, I pray.

Any coffin constructed for me in the spirit realm, let it explode and be shattered to pieces by lightning, thunder, and the fire of Almighty God now! In the name of Jesus of Nazareth!

Against The Spirit Of Mortality

By the power of the Holy Spirit, I pray that any catacomb, or burial grave that has already been dug for me in the astral realm, representing and awaiting my physical burial, let this grave bury the gravedigger who dug it now, in the name of Jesus of Nazareth.

Any tombstone or headstone in the spirit realm, upon which my name, date of birth, and the date of my death are inscribed, by the power of the name of Jesus, I demolish and shatter this gravestone to powder; let it be blown to pieces now!

Any stone image or monument in the astral world of the 2nd heavens that represents me, or my death and destruction, by the power of the Holy Spirit, I now call forth the great stone of Daniel 2:34 to shatter and destroy this stone image of me and monument of death, in the name of Jesus of Nazareth.

Wherever ceremonies are being held in celebration of my premature and sudden death, I call for the terrifying fire of God upon every occult graveyard worker, custodian of the cemetery, upon every memorial mason of the valley of death, upon every occult gravedigger, upon every mortician for those killed within the astral world, upon every guardian of the tombs, and upon all other occult participants who are involved in the ceremony and preparation for my premature and sudden death.

I bind them in chains of terror and dread, and I say let them be tormented and annihilated by fire, and may their expectations fail, according to Proverbs 10:28 which says, **"the expectation of the wicked shall perish."**

It is written in Psalms 21:11, "For they intended evil against thee: they imagined a mischievous device, which they were not able to perform."

27. Warfare Prayer Against Assassins Sent Against You

O Lord my God, King of the ages, Omnipotent Yah who sits between the Cherubim, hallowed be Your name in all kingdoms of the heavens and the earth. Heavenly Father, indeed, You are the Most High God;

Your name is holy and exalted in all kingdoms, realms, dimensions, and spheres.
Lord God, it is Your will that I dwell in safety according to Your word (Psalms 4:8) and have hidden my life in you through Christ.

You have also given me the authority to fight against the powers of darkness and prevail. You have anointed me with fire to disarm the psychic forces and powers of the gates of Hell, and Your word says that I shall possess the gates of my enemies.

Right now, I stand in the power of the Lord who says to me, in Isaiah 41:11, **"Behold, all they that were incensed against thee shall be ashamed and confounded: they shall be as nothing; and they that strive with thee shall perish."**
Also, it is written in Psalms 60:12, **"Through God I shall do valiantly: for he it is that shall tread down our enemies."**
Lord Jesus, I humbly place myself under Your loving care, as you surround me with Your shielding presence. Let Your light and fire be my armour, and guide my steps, leading me along the paths of righteousness by Your divine wisdom, for Your word says, those who find wisdom find life.
Keep me safe from the unforeseen dangers of the day and the night, and guard my mind against negative thoughts of fear and terror.

As I interact with others, let me be a beacon of Your love and peace, reflecting Your goodness in all that I do.
As the shepherd watches over his flock, watch over me, protecting me from harm and leading me away from the snares of the enemy, and deliver me from all evil according to Your word.

Oh Lord God, fight for me against my enemies and adversaries, as I pray in Your name with faith against the powers of darkness.

Today, in the holy name of the Lord God of hosts, Adonai Elohei Tzeva'ot, I declare war in the name of the Lord against demon and human assassins, destroyer demons, werewolves, and demons of high destruction from the occult kingdoms, sent to assassinate me.

I speak into the realms of the heavens, earthly dimensions, and water psychic channels, and I say the power of Jesus the Christ of Nazareth, every Aquatic assassin sent from the Bermuda Triangle, from the Mediterranean Sea, the Adriatic Sea, the Black Sea, the Red Sea, the Sargasso Sea, the Arabian Sea, the Caspian Sea, the Baltic Sea, the Persian Gulf, or from the North Atlantic Ocean, the South Atlantic Ocean, the North Pacific Ocean, the South Pacific Ocean, the Arctic Ocean, the Southern Ocean, or the Indian Ocean, to assassinate and annihilate me with astral arrows, stings of death, enchanted rings, poisonous darts, astral missiles, astral poisons, magical powders, webs, nets, tridents, sickles, or by a dagger or an athame, let the fire of God's terror fall upon you spirits and agents of darkness now, and be roasted to ashes by the fervent heat of the coals of the Altar of the Most High God.

According to Psalms 68:1-2, you assassins from Hell, be scattered, and be driven as smoke is driven away, and melt like wax in the fire and perish in the presence of the Lord of hosts, in the name of Jesus the Christ.

According to Psalms 11:6, I call forth the heavens to rain snares, fire and brimstone, and a horrible tempest upon all assassins, demon hunters, annihilators, and demons of high destruction assigned from Hell to kill and annihilate me physically.

By the power of the Holy Spirit, according to 2 Samuel 22:15 and Psalms 144:6, I scatter, destroy, and banish these witchcraft and satanic assassins by lightning from the east, by thunder from the thick cloud, and by the fire of amber in the name of Jesus Christ of Nazareth.

All assassins sent to kill me, let them be bound in hot heavy chains of fire and brimstone, and I pray they be assassinated in shame and disgrace, for captivity shall go into captivity. It is written in Psalm 27:2, **"When the wicked, *even* mine enemies and my foes, came upon me to eat up my flesh, they stumbled and fell."**

Let every assassin from the astral or terrestrial Occult kingdom of darkness sent to assassinate me through my dream, by mysterious death, sudden death, or some other form of physical assassination, be confronted with resistance and defences of lightning, and with uncommon and incomprehensible disasters and destruction by fire. Let them be roasted to dry ash, vaporized by fire, and vanished in thin air without a trace, in the mighty name of Jesus I pray.

Arise, oh Yah, God of Abraham, Isaac, and Jacob, and destroy my enemies from the gates of Hell. Let every military operation of darkness be liquidated, dissolved, and banished for my sake, by the terror of God's divine judgement, by thunderclaps and lightnings of indisputable fire.

It is written in Psalms 60:12, **"Through God we shall do valiantly: for he it is that shall tread down our enemies."** Therefore, O Assassins from the gates of Hell, my God shall tread you down and shall deliver me from your power and hand, for thus says the Lord in Isaiah 49:24-26, **"Shall the prey be taken from the mighty, or the captives of a tyrant be rescued?"**

Vs.25, **"But thus says the LORD, 'Even the captives of the mighty shall be taken away, and the prey of the fierce ones shall be rescued, for I will contend with him who contends with you, and I will save your children."**

All you Assassins from the kingdom of darkness, eat your own flesh and drink your own blood, for thus says the Lord God to us in Isaiah 49:26, "**And I will feed those who oppress you with their own flesh; and they shall be drunk with their own blood, as with sweet wine; and all flesh shall know that I, the LORD, *am* your Savior and your Redeemer, the mighty One of Jacob.**"

Break their teeth, O Lord, and let the lion and adder be trampled under our feet. Psalms 27:12, "**Deliver me not over unto the will of mine enemies: for false witnesses are risen up against me, and such as breathe out cruelty.**"

You promised in Isaiah 54:17, and it says, "**No weapon that is formed against thee shall prosper; and every tongue that shall rise against thee in judgement thou shalt condemn.**" Therefore, by this authority in the Word of God, in the Name of Jesus of Nazareth, I call forth a barrier of fire to block every psychic channel, every portal, and gate that any assassin would use to get to my location or dwelling place.

It is written in Psalms 71:13, "**Let them be confounded *and* consumed that are adversaries to my soul; let them be covered *with* reproach and dishonour that seek my hurt.**"

I barricade myself, my home, my workplace, and wherever I am; let there be barriers of fire, and permanent walls of reinforced resistance and defences of lightning, to protect me from assassins sent by the prince of darkness.
It is written in Isaiah 59:19, "**So shall they fear the name of the LORD from the west, and his glory from the rising of the sun. When the enemy shall come in like a flood, the Spirit of the LORD shall lift up a standard against him.**"

Heavenly Father, thank you for Your divine protection over me and my loved ones, and thank you for surrounding me and my household with Your angels, creating a hedge of safety around us, dismantling any assassinations.

To you, O Lord, be all the glory and honour and praise, for You are worthy, Lord God, in Jesus' name, Amen and Amen.

28. Prayers Against Satanic Councils, Plots, & Gatherings Against You

Heavenly Father, indeed, You are the Most High God, and Your name is holy and exalted in all kingdoms, realms, dimensions, and spheres. Great *is* the LORD, and greatly to be praised; and His greatness *is* unsearchable. One generation shall praise thy works to another, and shall declare thy mighty acts.
I will speak of the glorious honour of thy majesty, and of thy wondrous works.

And *men* shall speak of the might of thy terrible acts; and I will declare thy greatness (Psalms 145:3-6).
Oh Lord, the counsels of evil have gathered themselves against my life. I call upon you, for it is written in Psalm 64:2, **"Hide me from the secret counsel of the wicked; from the insurrection of the workers of iniquity."**
It is written in Esther 8:5, **"And said, If it please the king, and if I have found favour in his sight, and the thing seems right before the king, and I am pleasing in his eyes, let it be written to reverse the letters devised by Haman the son of Hammedatha the Agagite, which he wrote to destroy the Jews who are in all the king's provinces:"**

Now, Lord, reverse every decree and death sentence that has been decreed for me through secret plots. If it pleases you, the King of kings, and if I have found favour in Your sight, and the thing seems right before you, the King of Glory, and I am pleasing in Your eyes, let it be written to reverse the letters devised by my enemies and adversaries, both in the terrestrial and astral planes, in the name of Jesus.

By the power of the Holy Spirit, and in the name of Jesus Christ of Nazareth, I now pray against, sabotage, and scatter by lightning, thunder, and fire every witchcraft gathering, meeting, counsel, conference, court hearing, tribunal, summoning, conjuring, and any other diabolic meeting that is being held against my life by the counsel of witches, or any diabolical, satanic, and metallic counsel. It is written in Psalm 27:2, **"When the wicked, *even* mine enemies and my foes, came upon me to eat up my flesh, they stumbled and fell."**

It is written in Psalms 71:13, **"Let them be confounded *and* consumed that are adversaries to my soul; let them be covered *with* reproach and dishonour that seek my hurt."**

With hot chains of fire and by force, I bind and bring into captivity and under subjection all forces of darkness working, conspiring, and devising evil and destruction against my life and destiny in the occult world.

By fire, lightning, and thunder let every evil counsel against me turn to foolishness like how you turned the counsel of Ahithophel into foolishness, for it is written in 2 Samuel 15:31, **"O LORD, I pray thee, turn the counsel of Ahithophel into foolishness."**

2Sa 15:34, **"...then mayest thou for me defeat the counsel of Ahithophel".**

By the power of the judgement and the authority of the Word of God in Luke 10:19, Psalms 11:6, and Exodus 9:24, I call down a rain of fire mingled with grievous hail; I call down rains of snares and terrors, rain of fires, brimstone, horrible tempests, and the fiery terror of God's divine judgement in the form of thunderclaps and thunder breaks, lightnings and windstorms, and the thick cloud of Almighty God upon all Witches, warlocks, satanists, ritualists, grand masters, ascending masters, Gurus, witch doctors, native doctors, wise men, Avatars, Ascended Masters, mermaids, Sirens, voodoo priests, vicious psychic entities and all other occult agents within the occult centers, regions, zones in the land, sea, air and under the earth, and all the bands of occultic agents and representatives of the Gates of Hell conspiring my death and destruction.

Swallow them up by fire O Lord God of Israel, for it is written in Psalms 21:9, **"Thou shalt make them as a fiery oven in the time of thine anger: the LORD shall swallow them up in his wrath, and the fire shall devour them."**
May these workers of the occult be caught in their own snares and be slain by the evil works of their own hands and become desolate, according to Psalms 34:21, which says, **"Evil shall slay the wicked: and they that hate the righteous shall be desolate."**

By the power of the Holy Spirit, let them be arrested and incarcerated by fiery chains in dark places, and let torment, terror, and dread be their bread of affliction by day and by night, in season and out of season. Let every human agent of witchcraft assigned against me vomit and swallow back their vomit continually without cure, in Jesus Name.

It is written in Psalms 62:3, **"How long will ye imagine mischief against a man? ye shall be slain all of you: as a bowing wall shall ye be, and as a tottering fence."**
Let all astral or terrestrial agents of the Occult who come against me be met with unconditional and incomprehensible disasters of fire from the Lord Jesus.

Agents of darkness fall into your own pits, which you dug for me according to Proverbs 26:27, and let the stone that you rolled against me return upon you.
Let the judgement of Psalms 140:9-10 fall upon them, as it is written, **"As for the head of those that compass me about, let the mischief**

of their own lips cover them. Let burning coals fall upon them: let them be cast into the fire; into deep pits, that they rise not up again."

Therefore, all occult agents who are gathered to conspire against me by divination and incantation, I pray for their sudden destruction before sunrise or sunset this day. By the power of Jesus Christ of Nazareth, all evil plotters working against my destiny and ministry, fall for my sake as it is written in Isaiah 54:15, **"Behold, they shall surely gather together, but not by me: whosoever shall gather together against thee shall fall for thy sake."**
Lord Jesus, let their counsel become their trap, pit, and destruction, according to Psalms 5:10, **"Destroy thou them, O God; let them fall by their own counsel; cast them out in the multitude of their transgressions."**

Any diabolical and satanic decision, taken against and over my life across the astral planes, by the authority of the right hand of Jesus of Nazareth, let these decisions swallow up those who concocted them. Let them not rise, for it is written in Psalms 44:5, **"Through thee will we push down our enemies: through thy name will we tread them under that rise up against us."**

I claim immunity by Isaiah 54:17, which says, **No weapon that is formed against thee shall prosper; and every tongue that shall rise against thee in judgement thou shalt condemn.**
By virtue of the glorified blood of Jesus of Nazareth, the Lamb of God, I condemn every condemnation that is working against my heritage and destiny.
It is written in Psalms 21:11, **"For they intended evil against thee: they imagined a mischievous device, which they are not able to perform."**

29. Prayer Against Spirit Imprisonment In The Shadow Of Captivity

My Lord, God, and Father in Heaven, I bring my life, spirit, soul, and body before Your throne of judgement. Behold my captivity in the astral prison of darkness, where my life is held in the shadows of death and gross darkness.

My sufferings and captivity are before you; now I implore Your divine intervention through Your Son, Jesus of Nazareth.
You said in Your word in Psalms 50:15, **"And call upon Me in the day of trouble; and I will deliver you, and you shall honour Me."**
Your word also says in Romans 10:13, **"For whosoever shall call upon the name of the Lord shall be saved"**. So, by Your covenant and mercy, I call upon Your name for deliverance from every satanic dispute, trap, and captivity that's over my life.

I pray, in every place where my soul is terrified by the darkness of the day and stained with the shadows of death, as described in Job 3:5, that I may be released by the power of God Almighty. By fire I charge against and destroy all powers of darkness that have built walls of darkness and imprisonment around me by demons.
It is said in Job 10:22, **"A land of darkness, as darkness itself; and of the shadow of death, without any order, and where the light is as darkness"**.
But also remember, O El Shaddai, Your word says in Psalm 107:14, **"He brought them out of darkness and the shadow of death,"**

Shine Your light upon me, for it is written in Isaiah 9:2, **"The people that walked in darkness have seen a great light: they that dwell in the land of the shadow of death, upon them hath the light shined."**

It says in Psalms 23:4, **"Yea, though I walk through the valley of the shadow of death, I will fear no evil: for thou** *art* **with me; thy rod and thy staff they comfort me."**
Let the Shadows of Death over my life be destroyed by the Light of Your Pillar of Divine Fire.
As it is written, Jeremiah 17:14, **"Heal me, O LORD, and I shall be healed; save me, and I shall be saved: for thou art my praise."**

Allow me to taste of Your goodness, O Jesus, as it is written in Psalms 34:8, **"O taste and see that the LORD is good: blessed is the man that trusts in him."**
Pull me out from within the doors and the gates of the Shadows of Death mentioned in Psalms 107:18 and Job 38:17; and let not the Gates of Hell and Death prevail against me, in Jesus' name I pray.

I also pray that I am released from any spiritual imprisonment where my soul is incarcerated by brazen gates and iron bars.
It is written in Acts 12:6, **"And when Herod would have brought him forth, the same night Peter was sleeping between two soldiers, bound with two chains: and the keepers before the door kept the prison."**

Wherever my life is held trapped within any land of darkness, within the valley of the shadows of death, within an underground cave, within an astral labyrinth, within a spiritual maze, within a sarcophagus, or a box, a vase, a tree, a coffin, a rock, a catacomb, a pit, a witchcraft coven, or within a spiritual jail cell, a satanic sanctum, or any spiritual incarceration chamber within the forest, desert, water, air, or within an underground astral chamber, and in every place where I am held by darkness as a felon, and am sentenced to witchcraft imprisonment without parole, I call upon the fiery terror of God's divine judgement to shatter to pieces, consume to powder, dissolve and eradicate these prison facilities, and nullify the sentence of my imprisonment, by thunderclaps, thunder breaks, lightnings and wind and firestorms.

In every place where the death hunters and other agents of Hades have cast shadows upon an afflicted area of my life or family bloodline, and wherever I am bound with iron chains and with the spirit of affliction according to Psalm 107:10, look upon my affliction and send Your Angel to rescue me.
Pull me out of any demon pit that I am in, for it is written in Psalms 40:2, **"He brought me up also out of an horrible pit, out of the miry clay, and set my feet upon a rock, and established my goings."**
It is said of you in Genesis 29:32, **"Surely the LORD hath looked upon my affliction."**
By the ransoming blood of Jesus, set me free from the four realms of spiritual imprisonments, the incarceration facility in the second heaven, or the incarceration facility in the water world, or the incarceration facility in the forest world, or from the incarceration facility in the realm of the dead or subterranean world. Deliver me from the prison of the sins of the body, the soul, and the prison of spiritual sins.

I call upon the fervent heat and consuming fire of Adonai Tzevaot, to vaporize the bars of iron and bronze gates that are holding my soul in captivity, in the land of the shadow of death [Isaiah 9:2], in the land of darkness [Job 10:21], in the shadow of death [Job 10:22], in the terrors of the shadow of death [Job 24:17], in the doors of the shadow of death [Job 38:17], in the valley of the shadow of death [Psalms 23:4], in the place of dragons and the shadow of death [Psalms 44:19], in perpetual desolation [Psalms 74:3], in the valley of dry bones [Ezekiel 37:1], in the Valley of desolation, within the Valley of the Shadows of death, or within the realm of perpetual desolation, or within the Valley of dry bones, or within the Valley of desolation, or within any astral prison.
It is written in Psalms 142:7, **"Bring my soul out of prison, that I may**

praise thy name: the righteous shall compass me about; for thou shalt deal bountifully with me."

I call upon Your power and might, O God, and I petition that the Angel of Your presence be deployed to burst the bands asunder and set me free by Your unapproachable light and terrifying fire.
Deliver me not over unto the will of my enemies according to Psalms 27:12, for it is written in Psalms 34:6, **"This poor man cried, and the LORD heard him, and saved him out of all his troubles"**
Now, O Lord, deliver me, for it is written in Jer 17:14, **"Heal me, O LORD, and I shall be healed; save me, and I shall be saved: for thou art my praise."**
According to Psalms 55:1, **"Give ear to my prayer, O God; and hide not thyself from my supplication."**

Your Word says, Oh Lord God, in Acts 12:7, **"And, behold, the angel of the Lord came upon *him,* and a light shined in the prison; and he smote Peter on the side, and raised him up, saying, Arise up quickly. And his chains fell off from *his* hands."**
Vs.10, **"Now after going past a first guard and a second, they came to the iron gate that leads into the city, which opened to them by itself; and after going out, they went on through one street, and then the angel suddenly departed from him."**
Vs.11, **"And when Peter came to himself, he said, "Now I truly understand that the Lord sent His angel and has delivered me."**
Vs. 26, **"And suddenly there was a great earthquake, so that the foundations of the prison were shaken: and immediately all the doors were opened, and everyone's bands were loosed."**

Your word says in Isaiah 61:1, You are anointed to bind up the brokenhearted, to proclaim liberty to the captives, and the opening of the prison to them that are bound; now Holy Spirit of Yah, by Your divine eternal fire, repair my wounds and breaches, deliver me from emotional, psychological, mental, and spiritual captivity, and open the prison for me like you did for Peter in Acts 12:7, 11, 17, and for Paul in Acts 16:26.

It is written in Isaiah 28:21, **"For the LORD shall rise up as in mount Perazim; he shall be wroth as in the valley of Gibeon, that he may do his work, his strange work; and bring to pass his act, his strange act."**

Isaiah 61:2 **To proclaim the acceptable year of the LORD, and the day of vengeance of our God; to comfort all that mourn.**
Vs.3 **To appoint unto them that mourn in Zion, to give unto them beauty for ashes, the oil of joy for mourning, the garment of praise for the spirit of heaviness; that they might be called trees of righteousness, the planting of the LORD, that he might be glorified.**
Vs.4 **And they shall build the old wastes; they shall raise up the former desolations, and they shall repair the waste cities, the desolations of many generations.**
Vs.5 **And strangers shall stand and feed your flocks, and the sons of the aliens shall be your plowmen and your vinedressers.**
Vs.6 **But ye shall be named the Priests of the LORD: men shall call you the Ministers of our God: ye shall eat the riches of the Gentiles, and in their glory shall ye boast yourselves.**
Vs.7 **For your shame ye shall have double; and for confusion they shall rejoice in their portion: therefore, in their land they shall possess the double: everlasting joy shall be unto them.**

By Your supreme and eternal power, oh Lord God, possessor of the heavens and the earth, break the gates of brass, and cut the bars of iron asunder, and set me free from the prison where my soul is held incarcerated by witchcraft and demons. For it is written in Your Word in Isaiah 45:2, **"I will go before thee, and make the crooked places** straight: I will break in pieces the gates of brass and cut in sunder the bars of iron."

Hence, by the authority of the Word of the Almighty God written in Luke 10:19 that says, "Behold, **I give unto you power to tread on serpents and scorpions, and over all the power of the enemy: and nothing shall by any means hurt you,**" I pray and invoke a divine dynamic electrical discharge to manifest and shatter every astral prison facility into pieces and debris.

Let dynamic fires mixed with lightnings and thunders be released from the North, South, East, and West, and destroy the place where I am held in captivity within the spirit world, right now in Jesus' Name.

Let the dark walls of the fortresses of terror and the prison walls of the shadows of death, desolation, and imprisonments within all four worlds of darkness explode to pieces by the invisible force of a terrible windstorm, a terrible firestorm, a terrible earthquake, a terrible tempest, and fire mixed with brimstone and hail.

With the blast of Your nostrils according to Exodus 15:8, cause an electromagnetic explosion to detonate in any place where my soul is held in captivity in the spirit world because of witchcraft.

By the power of the Holy Spirit, let every prison guard securing my captivity in the astral realms burst into flames and be consumed to fine ashes, in the name of Jesus of Nazareth.

All restrictive measurements placed upon my life to retard and mummify my life, let these demonic restrictive measures be restrained and destroyed by fire from Heaven, now in Jesus Name.

Send now Your Angel, O Jesus of Nazareth, and pull me out of this horrible pit, for it is written in Psalms 34:7, **"The angel of the LORD encamps around those who fear Him and delivers them."**

Every demon guardian, set as watchmen over my imprisonment in the spirit realm, just as Peter was set free by the holy Angel of God in Acts 12:7-11, let my Angel set me free now, as my prison chains fall off now, and the prison guards are overthrown by the invisible force of the power of Jesus Christ.

Heavenly Father, in the name of Jesus of Nazareth, by the power of the divine fire of Jesus Christ, I condemn, renounce, revoke, overturn, and overthrow all evil invisible barriers and partitions, and shatter beyond repair every power and altar within the invisible realm that has me under the force of detention and retention.

I ask you to declare the boundaries beyond which the enemy may not come. Cause Your brilliance and holiness to shine around me so that the enemy cannot see.

In the name of Jesus, let every witch and demon operating these monitoring devices be scattered and banished in chains of torments, and let the token of evil against me be frustrated; let the wise men of the occult be turned backward, and their knowledge turn to foolishness, and all diviners be struck with madness, for it is written in Isaiah 44:25, **"That frustrateth the tokens of the liars, and maketh diviners mad; that turneth wise *men* backward, and maketh their knowledge foolish**?

I call the fire of the verdict of the judiciary, blood of Jesus to dispel the verdict of the satanic council, which has given jurisdiction to the astral spirits to work against my life because of sacrifices offered up to the gods against me through witchcraft.

Let their golden bowl be broken, or the pitcher be broken at the fountain, or the wheel be broken at the cistern [Ecc 12:6].

I impede every combat, revolt, snare, plot, and device that is programmed to impeach, impede, manipulate, suppress, oppress, and depress me; let them fail in disgrace, shame, and defeat, in Jesus' name.

Let every occult aquatic weapon and device, cosmic occult weapons and devices, occult weapons of the dead and their devices, occult Pestifera astral weapons and devices, hidden psychic surveillance, mysterious schemes, occult human oppositions and blockages, and sabotage mechanisms be met with resistances of fire and defences of lightning.

It is written in Exodus 15:6, **"Thy right hand, O LORD, is become glorious in power: thy right hand, O LORD, hath dashed in pieces the enemy."**

Genesis 49:18, **"I have waited for thy salvation, O LORD."**

I submit all of you evil, foul spirits, your devices, your asternal and kingdom into the hand of the Almighty God, who rides upon the heavens by His name Yah, for your perpetual destruction and annihilation from my life, and you evil powers, you cannot escape His fiery wrath, for thus says the God in Isaiah 43:13, Yea, before the day was, I am He; and no one delivers out of My hand; I will work, and who can reverse it?

RESTORATIVE ARROWS OF DECREES

- By Your command, Lord Jesus, let my life be restored to me by the fire of the Holy Spirit of Jesus Christ. Amen and Amen.
- O keep my soul and deliver me: let me not be ashamed; for I put my trust in thee. [Psalms 25:20].
- Be pleased, O LORD, to deliver me; O LORD, make haste to help me. [Psalms 40:13].
- Deliver me from mine enemies, O my God: defend me from them that rise up against me" [Psalms 59:1].
- Deliver me from the workers of iniquity and save me from bloody men. [Psalms 59:2].

- Deliver me out of the mire and let me not sink; let me be delivered from them that hate me, and out of the deep waters. [Psalms 69:14].
- Draw nigh unto my soul and redeem it: deliver me because of my enemies. [Psalms 69:18].
- To the chief Musician, A Psalm of David, to bring to remembrance. Make haste, O God, to deliver me; make haste to help me, O LORD. [Psalms 70:1].
- Deliver me in thy righteousness and cause me to escape; incline thine ear unto me and save me. [Psalms 71:2].
- Deliver me, O my God, out of the hand of the wicked, out of the hand of the unrighteous and cruel man. [Psalms 71:4].
- Deliver me from the oppression of man: so will I keep thy precepts. [Psalms 119:134].
- Consider mine affliction and deliver me: for I do not forget thy law. [Psalms 119:153].
- Psalms 119:154, Plead my cause and deliver me: quicken me according to thy word.
- Let my supplication come before thee: deliver me according to thy word. [Psalms 119:170].
- To the chief Musician, A Psalm of David. Deliver me, O LORD, from the evil man: preserve me from the violent man; [Psalms 140:1].
- Attend unto my cry; for I am brought very low: deliver me from my persecutors; for they are stronger than I. [Psalms 142:6].
- Send thine hand from above; rid me, and deliver me out of great waters, from the hand of strange children. [Psalms 144:7].
- Rid me, and deliver me from the hand of strange children, whose mouth speaketh vanity, and their right hand is a right hand of falsehood: [Psalms 144:11].

This I pray in the name of the Father, the Son, and the Holy Spirit, Amen and Amen.

30. Prayer Against Spirits Of Astral Projection

Heavenly Father, Your word commands that in Deuteronomy 18:10-12, **"There shall not be found among you *any one* that maketh his son or his daughter to pass through the fire, *or* that useth divination, *or* an observer of times, or an enchanter, or a witch, or a charmer, or a consulter with familiar spirits, or a wizard, or a necromancer."** Moreover, you said in vs. 12, **"For all that do these things *are* an abomination unto the LORD: and because of these abominations the LORD thy God doth drive them out from before thee."**
Hence, we know that astral projection, which is a practice of witchcraft, is an abomination to you. Moreover, Your word says, **"because of these abominations the LORD thy God doth drive them out from before thee."**

Heavenly Father, by the authority of the Blood, fire, and Spirit of the Living God, with the voice of thunder, I now decree by law that anyone who has or is trying to astral project into my home, surrounding, or family through Kundalini powers, Transcendental meditation, through soul travel or esoteric craft, through the magic of levitation, vanish, production, transformation, transposition, penetration, restoration, escape, teleportation, prediction, alteration, transmutation, or transmigration, let each of these evil powers be confronted, apprehended, and neutralized by advanced defences of lightning, whirlwinds, and uncompromising, unquenchable, and incomprehensible terrifying fire of mass destruction of disastrous proportions.
It is written in 1 John 3:8, **"For this purpose the Son of God was manifested, that he might destroy the works of the devil."**
Acts 17:28, **"For in him we live, and move, and have our being;"** and Eph 2:6 says, **"And hath raised us up together, and made us sit together in heavenly places in Christ Jesus."**

Therefore, by this authority in the Word of God, in the name of Jesus of Nazareth, I call forth a barrier of fire to block every psychic channel that vibrates occult frequencies in order to accommodate astral or soul travel into my home or atmosphere.

I distort the meditation channels of the Mantra sound frequency of the spirit of 'LAM' [Root Chakra], the spirit of 'VAM' [Sacral Chakra], the spirit of 'RAM' [Solar Plexus], the spirit of 'YAM' [Heart Chakra], the spirit of 'HAM' [Throat Chakra], the spirit of 'OM' or 'AUM' [Third Eye Chakra], the spirit of 'OM' or 'AH' [Crown Chakra], and render every agent of darkness incapable of making contact in the astral planes and higher consciousness through these frequencies.

Every being who tries to invade my life and home or space via soul travel or astral projection, I compromise his or her silver cord so that it is in danger of being severed by the power of Jesus Christ.

I barricade my home, my workplace, my family, my [Name wherever you want to barricade] with barriers of electric fire, and permanent walls of reinforced resistance and defences of lightning. It is written in Isaiah 59:19, **"So shall they fear the name of the LORD from the west, and his glory from the rising of the sun. When the enemy shall come in like a flood, the Spirit of the LORD shall lift up a standard against him."**

By the name of Y'ahushua of Nazareth, I pray by the faith that every astral poison and venom of tranquilization and neutralization that these astral projecting entities are carrying in order to vaccinate me, let them poison themselves and be neutralized by their own hands now. In the powerful name of Jesus, I pray, Amen!

31. Prayers Against Evils Attacking Your Child

Heavenly Father, King of the universe, Omnipotent God who is, who was, and who is to come. Hallowed be Your name in all kingdoms of the heavens and the earth, for You are the Most High God; Your name is holy and exalted in all kingdoms, realms, dimensions, and spheres. Lord of hosts, you said in Mark 10:14, **"But when Jesus saw it, he was much displeased, and said unto them, Suffer the little children to come unto me, and forbid them not: for of such is the kingdom of God."** Through the sanctification of my children through the believing parents, I bring my children before Your sapphire Throne in prayer, requesting that you bless my children and deliver them from the holds of the kingdom of darkness. My children/child [CALL THEIR NAMES] belong to the kingdom of God.

I petition you, Lord Jesus, by Your Holy Spirit, that you protect my child/children [CALL THEIR/HIS/HER NAME] and lay Your holy hands upon them, for it is written in Matthew 19:13-15, "Then were there brought unto him little children, that he should put his hands on them and pray."
Destroy all diabolical strategies and satanic traps from the book "Technique Tactics" that are used against them/him/her.
Protect them/him/her from the lowest to the highest level of diabolical assaults projecting from the Book of Grimoire and the Book of the Dead, and destroy every Satanic formula for death and destruction that is sent against them/him/her.
Lord, you have given me authority to fight against the powers of darkness and prevail; and have anointed me with the fire to disarm the powers of darkness on behalf of my child/children.
Right now, by Your Holy Spirit, I stand in the capacity of my parental authority and petition that you clothe me with Your light and fire, so

that I can stand in prayer and warfare for my children this day against the diabolical system of the gates of Hell.

Today, by the jurisdiction of the Blood of the Lamb of God, in the holy name of Elohei Tzeva'ot, and El-Gibbor, I declare war against all the hosts of darkness.

I pray against every working of Satan, and the operation of the prince of darkness and their subordinate spirits, working within the Mephistophelian seals, and the degree of psychic strongholds in the astral world.

By my authority in Christ, by chains of vehement flames of the holiness of Jesus Christ of Nazareth, I bind, disarm, and neutralize every demon of death, demon head-hunter, demon reaper, and all destroyer demons, etc., who are sent to annihilate and kill my child/children physically in any way.

Any of my children who are placed on death row by the kingdom of the Occult and Demons, I deliver this child from death row this minute, by the power of Jesus of Nazareth, and I command Hell to release my child/children from death row now, effective immediately, in the exalted name of Jesus of Nazareth.

I also remove my children's names from the Death register of the Underworld, and I scatter and liquidate by fire all combined elements of astral poisons working together to bring about the specific task and mission of implementing premature death, sudden death, slow death, and death by accident upon my child/children.

I now call upon the fiery lightning of the holy presence of the Lord Jesus to burn out all evil marks, identifications, occult names, sigils, and the date of my children's death that has been placed upon their foreheads, in Jesus' Name.

I withdraw my children's names from every tombstone, gravestone, grave, cemetery, and I pray that any tombstone or headstone in the spirit realm, upon which the name, the date of birth, and the date of death of my child/children are inscribed, by the power of the name of Jesus, I demolish and shatter this gravestone to powder; let it be blown to pieces now!

I invoke the lightning of the invisible destructive fire from Almighty God in Heaven to shatter any coffin into debris that was constructed for any of my children in the astral realm through witchcraft.
I tear to threads any grave clothes tailored specifically for my child/children in the occult realm. I say you are a liar; catch fire and be consumed to ashes now in Jesus' mighty name.
I neutralize every astral poison, astral motion, astral venom, and psychic vibration and sound frequency, and destroy the powers of the elemental spirits. In the name of Jesus, the Christ of Nazareth, may these evil forces backfire in the face of the Grand demon in charge of these attacks. Amen!

All astral poison and venom of tranquilization and neutralization that have neutralized my children, so that they cannot function with precise intellectual capacities, pristine intelligence, and pristine articulation of their expression of morals, self-worth, integrity, knowledge, and love for Jesus, release my children's lives and potential now.

Every subtle psychic manipulation by witchcraft, necromancy, injuring, conjuring, projecting, voodoo herb mixture, incantation, ritual, altar, and every plot, plan, weapon, curse, snare, lair, or any other esoteric craft deployed to destroy any of my children shall be met with incomprehensible destruction by fire and shall be roasted to dry ash, vaporized by fire, and vanished into thin air without a trace. In the mighty name of Jesus.
I neutralize you, Demon of venom, and reclaim the full functionality of my children's faculties—intellectually, spiritually, emotionally, psychologically, mentally, by fire and by the authority of the Blood of

Jesus and the power of the seven horns of the Lamb of God in Revelation 5:6.

By lightnings and thunders of fire wrapped in the glory of the eternal light of Christ, I gather the fragments of my children's souls from every realm, sphere, occult zone, region, center and dimension of the upper darkness and lower darkness, in Jesus' name.
Every crocodilian, reptilian, and serpentine spirit that has swallowed my children in realms and spheres of darkness, despair, and gloom, I release a detonation inside your bowels now, and shatter to bits and pieces the prison holds that are holding my children in realms and spheres of darkness, despair, and gloom.

By the power of the Holy Spirit of Jesus Christ, I take up as my companion the light, lightning and thunder of the presence of Jesus, the King of Kings, and I now enter into all realms where the spirits of my children are trapped, and I declare a divine rescue.
In the name of Jesus of Nazareth, by the God of Noah, Abraham, Moses, Daniel, Job, and Elijah, with fire and force, I burst every iron bar asunder and destroy every bronze gate, and all energy forces that are trapping the spirits of my children within the realm of witchcraft.

I declare wars of fire against all dimensions of demons and Fallen angels, and by the power of Jesus Christ I pull out the spirit of all my Children from within any land of darkness, from within the valley of the shadows of death, from within any underground cave, from any astral labyrinth, from any cemetery, from any spiritual maze, from any catacomb, demonic pit, trench, slum, and from within any spiritual jail cell, desert, water, and air; and from within any underground astral chamber, from any wastelands, barren lands, desolate places, woodlands, wetlands, enchanted forest, monsoon forest, tropical forest, swamp, sacred grove, mangrove, everglades, and from any catacomb, grave, crossroad, fork road, roundabout, metropolitan, megapolitan, town, urban, state, and nation.

I speak with fire to every realm, category, and rank of witchcraft, and I say powers of witchcraft be broken, destroyed, nullified, and banished, and release the spirits of my children now, effective immediately.
I barricade my children with barriers of electric fire, and permanent walls of reinforced resistance and defences of lightning and light.

It is written in Psalm 27:2, **"When the wicked, even mine enemies and my foes, came upon me to eat up my flesh, they stumbled and fell."**
It is written in Psalms 71:13, **"Let them be confounded and consumed that are adversaries to my soul; let them be covered with reproach and dishonour that seek my hurt."**
By the invisible fire of the Almighty God in Heaven, which is mixed with brimstone, tempest, lightning, thunders and hail, I destroy any coffin that was constructed for any of my children in the astral realm through witchcraft, in the name of Jesus. Arrows of slow death, fired into the body of my children, be removed by the power of Jesus.

Demon of failure, setback, and stagnantness retarding the spiritual growth of my children, [call your children's name], be shattered to pieces by holy lightning according to Psalm 18:14.
Arrows of the Almighty God in Psalms 18:14, locate my children's enemies who are working evil against them. Let my children's enemies be scattered and be rendered in grievous shame and disgrace now, in Jesus' name.

Powers of the air feeding on my children's destiny, by the invisible fire of the Almighty God in Heaven, and with brimstone, tempest, lightning, thunders, and hail, I destroy and banish you evil spirits from my children's lives, effective immediately.

Power of the grave, the graveyard, tombstones, and catacombs, created and marked for any of my children, I render your power impotent, frustrated, nullified, barren, ineligible, and useless in the lives of my children, in the name of Jesus.

Any evil poison, concoction, and enchanted substance from the realm of the dead, the aquatic occult kingdom, or any other kingdom of darkness, given to any of my children to eat or drink by psychic travel, through a magic mirror portal, or in a dream; and every demonic creature that was placed inside any of my children through these ingested evil substances, let these astral substances be neutralized and flushed out of my children's bodies and souls. Let these creatures in the belly, spine, sacral region, or any other part of my children's bodies become powerless, impotent, frustrated, barren, illegal, and useless, and be banished by the power of the blood of Jesus and the throne of Jesus Christ.

Any sickness planted in the bodies of my children while sleeping, or through any spiritual food or water, or any point of contact, be flushed out by the blood of Jesus, the power, and the name of Jesus of Nazareth.

I liquidate, dissolve, nullify, and dispel every demonic or satanic alliance, relationship, covenant, connection, and partnership that was made with my children or any of my children through contact, association, or dream, astral soul travel, or through magic mirrors, now in the name of Jesus of Nazareth.

Every witchcraft power that has placed and imprisoned the spirit of my child/children inside a burial tomb, underground chamber, bottle, vase, witch bag, black box, tree, rock, maze, or any other item or realm, I destroy these evil holds and prisons, and by the power of

Jesus Christ, I set the spirits of my children free from all demonic captivities.

I address you demons of captivity, and I now place you into captivity by the blood of Jesus and fire, for it is written, captivity shall go into captivity. You have no power to hold my child or children any longer. Therefore, all you evil forces of captivity by witchcraft, be shattered by lightning and power of Jesus Christ now, in Jesus' name.

No witchcraft curse by the hands of the Secret Cult or Satanic Coven will terminate the lives of my children in the name of Jesus.
Every agent of darkness seeking to drink the blood of my children, I say these evil agents of darkness will drink their own blood by force and stifle in the process, in the name of Jesus.
Death, I rebuke your hands from over my children by the power of the death, burial, and resurrection of Jesus Christ of Nazareth. My children are not your victims, nor are they your candidates; therefore, hand of death, be removed from over my children now, in the name of Jesus of Nazareth.

I retrieve my children's memory, ability, and potential from the chambers of the Marine kingdom and every place where their memory is being held incarcerated. By fire, I also retrieve my children's memory, ability, and potential from the den of thieves and every marketplace of Hell.

I command Fire of the Holy Spirit in the secret places of the mysterious kingdom of darkness, and all storerooms, vessels, chambers, or anything that is holding my children's memory, name, and destiny trapped.
I command these evil forces to melt by the Fire of El-Eliyahu, in Jesus' Name. Let every creature who has stolen or is stealing from my children be roasted by the fire of amber proceeding from the throne

of Jesus Christ. Let terror, fire, and brimstone come upon all evil for my children's sake now, in the name of Jesus of Nazareth.

Any of my children who may have been initiated from the mother's womb or shortly after birth, or growing up, I nullify and denounce this initiation as void, redundant, and useless. I destroy this initiation and the agents of darkness who are responsible for this initiation; let them be burned by the unquenchable holy Fire of Yahuah, El-Shaddai. In Jesus Name.

Blood that was taken from my children for testing, which was used by occultists, witches, grand masters, satanic midwives, and nurses, occult doctors, and laboratory personnel, I plead the verdict of the blood of Jesus into this past reality and destroy every witchcraft placed on my children.

Wherever my children's blood is being held in darkness, let it vanish now in Jesus' name, and the chamber where the blood is held be destroyed by fire beyond recognition, now in Jesus' name.

I also pray that every demon of land, sea, and air; every water, land, and cemetery dragon, every serpent of the waters and dry places, every demonic wild beast and creature who has drunk the blood of our children or child in the hospital, in dream. Or astral projection, or sexual violation in sleep, I command, in the Name of Jesus of Nazareth that these children's haemoglobin, lifeforce, and destiny be vomited up now, and all you evil creatures catch fire and roast to powder now, by the fire of El- Eliyahu, in Y'ahushua's Name.

My daughters *will be* as cornerstones, polished *after* the similitude of a palace: according to "Psalms 144:12, for it is written, "That **our sons *may be* as plants grown up in their youth; *that* our daughters *may be* as cornerstones, polished *after* the similitude of a palace:"**

Wherever I have built a godly and holy altar, cause my children to have an encounter there like Jacob, who had an encounter where Abraham built an altar in Luz.

Let my children be taught the mechanics of things that will build them for future events through the power of Jesus Christ of Nazareth, and give my children divine intelligence.
Lord God, teach my children the dynamics of time and seasons.
Teach my children the dynamics of the Word of God,
Teach my children the dynamics of fervent prayer.
Teach my children the dynamics of economizing.
Teach my children the dynamics of fervency.
Teach my children the dynamics of strong faith.
Teach my children the dynamics of fasting.
Teach my children the dynamics of cultivation.
Teach my children the dynamics of skills.

1. Salvation
Lord, let salvation spring up within my children, that they may obtain the salvation that is in Christ Jesus, with eternal glory (Isaiah 45:8, 2 Timothy 2:10).

2. Growth in Grace
I pray that they may 'grow in the grace and knowledge of our Lord and Savior Jesus Christ (2 Peter 3:18).

3. Love
Grant, Lord, that my children may learn to live a life of love through the Spirit who dwells in them (Ephesians 5:2, Galatians 5:22).

4. Honesty and Integrity
May integrity and honesty be their virtues and their protection, (Psalm 25:21).

5. Self-Control
Father, help my children not to be like many others around them, but let them be alert and self-controlled in all they do" (1 Thessalonians 5:6).

6. A love for God's Word
May my children grow to find Your Word 'more precious than gold, than much pure gold; [and] sweeter than honey, than honey from the honeycomb (Psalm 19:10).

7. Justice
God, help my children to love justice as you do and to 'act justly' in all they do (Psalm 11:7, Micah 6:8).

8. Mercy
May my children always be merciful, just as [their] Father is merciful (Luke 6:36).

9. Respect (for self, others, and authority)
Father, grant that my children may 'show proper respect to everyone,' as Your Word commands (1 Peter 2:17).

10. Strong, biblical self-esteem
Help my children develop a strong self-esteem that is rooted in the realization that they are 'God's workmanship, created in Christ Jesus (Ephesians 2:10, NASB).

11. Faithfulness
Let love and faithfulness never leave [my children],' but bind these twin virtues around their necks and write them on the tablet of their hearts (Proverbs 3:3).

12. Courage
May my children always 'be strong and courageous' in their character and in their actions (Deuteronomy 31:6).

13. Purity
Create in [my children] a pure heart, O God,' and let their purity of heart be shown in their actions (Psalm 51:10).

14. Kindness
Lord, may my children always try to be kind to each other and to everyone else (Ephesians 4:32, 1 Thessalonians 5:15).

15. Generosity
Grant that my children may 'be generous and willing to share [and so] lay up treasure for themselves as a firm foundation for the coming age (1 Timothy 6:18-19).

16. Peace, Peaceability
Father, let my children 'make every effort to do what leads to peace (Romans 14:19).

17. Joy
May my children be filled 'with the joy given by the Holy Spirit (1 Thessalonians 1:6).

18. Perseverance
Lord, teach my children perseverance in all they do, and help them especially to 'run with perseverance the race marked out for [them] (Hebrews 12:1).

19. Humility
God, please cultivate in my children the ability to 'show true humility to everyone (Titus 3:2, Philippians 2:3).

20. Compassion
Lord, please clothe my children with the virtue of compassion (Colossians 3:12).

21. Responsibility
Grant that my children may learn responsibility, 'for each one should carry his own load (Galatians 6:5).

22. Contentment
Father, teach my children 'the secret of being content in any and every situation… through him who gives [them] strength. (Philippians 4:12-13).

23. Faith
I pray that faith will find root and grow in my children's hearts, that by faith they may gain what has been promised to them. (Luke 17:5-6, Hebrews 11:1-40).

24. A Servant's Heart
God, please help my children develop servant hearts, that they may serve wholeheartedly, 'as if serving…the Lord, not people. (Ephesians 6:7).

25. Hope
May the God of hope grant that my children may overflow with hope and hopefulness by the power of the Holy Spirit (Romans 15:13).

26. The Willingness and Ability to Work Hard
Teach my children, Lord, to value work and to work hard at everything they do, 'as working for the Lord (Colossians 3:23).

27. A Passion for God

"Lord, please instill in my children a soul that clings passionately to You" (Psalm 63:8).

28. Self-Discipline
"Father, I pray that my children may develop self-discipline and 'prudent behaviour, doing what is right and just and fair'" (2 Timothy 1:7, Proverbs 1:3).

29. Prayerfulness
"Grant, Lord, that my children's lives may be marked by prayerfulness, that they may learn to 'pray in the Spirit on all occasions with all kinds of prayers and requests'" (Ephesians 6:18).

30. Gratitude
Help my children to live lives that are always 'overflowing with thankfulness,' 'always giving thanks to God the Father for everything, in the name of our Lord Jesus Christ (Colossians 2:7, Ephesians 5:20).

31. A Heart for Missions
"Lord, please help my children to develop a heart for missions, a desire to see Your glory declared among the nations, Your marvellous deeds among all peoples" (Psalm 96:3).

I declare by the jurisdiction of the Blood upon the Mercy Seat, that my children [CALL THEIR NAMES] are a heritage of the LORD: and the fruit of the womb is his reward. Psalms 127:3 I declare by the jurisdiction of the Blood upon the Mercy Seat, that my children [CALL THEIR NAMES] are trained up in the way he/she/they should go: and when [CALL THEIR NAMES] is/are old, he/she/they will not depart from it.

Proverbs 22:6 I will not provoke my children to wrath; but bring them up in the nurture and admonition of the Lord according to Ephesians 6:4. I declare by the jurisdiction of the Blood upon the Mercy Seat, that my children [CALL THEIR NAMES] shall be taught of the LORD; and great shall be the peace of thy children [CALL THEIR NAMES] according to Isaiah 54:13. I declare by the jurisdiction of the Blood upon the Mercy Seat, that my children are obedient to their parents in the Lord: for this is right, according to Ephesians 6:1-4. Proverbs 17:6 - Children's children are the crown of old men; and the glory of children is their fathers.

32. Petition To God For Your Marriage

Prayer for Forgiveness and Healing

Heavenly Father God, I bring my marriage before the Throne of glory, to find grace and healing.

It is you who created a man for a woman and a woman for a man, therefore, by Your divine principle for matrimonial relationship, I petition Your heart and request a court order against the kingdom of darkness who is afflicting my marriage.

Father, we have violated Your law, and breach spiritual laws and principles, therefore, we have made ourselves vulnerable to the attack of the kingdom of darkness.

We have given the enemy legal grounds to afflict our minds and emotions, but father, today I place my Marriage upon Your altar and give it to you as a sacrifice. I place it in Your hands and subject my marriage to Your fire and salt for purification and preservation. Approve my marriage by salt and confirm it by fire and let the savoury return to my marriage.

Bind up our wounded hearts and wash away the pain and hurts that linger. Let Your love fill the voids left by our mistakes.

Heal us from past hurts and guide us towards a future filled with grace and compassion. Teach us to embrace each other with the same mercy You show us every day.

Holy Father, renew our spirits, so we can rebuild our marriage on the foundation of Your unfailing love. In Jesus' name, Amen.

Prayer for Communication

Gracious God, we struggle to communicate with each other in love and understanding. But today I petition Your Council that we be granted the wisdom to choose our words carefully and the patience to listen fully.

Help us to speak with kindness and to hear each other's hearts without judgement. Let our conversations reflect Your peace and grace.

Remove any barriers that hinder our ability to connect deeply and sincerely. Guide us to express ourselves openly and honestly, creating a safe space for our relationship to thrive.

May our dialogue strengthen our bond and bring us closer together. In Your holy name, Amen.

Prayer for Love and Affection

Lord, our hearts yearn for the warmth of love and the tenderness of affection that once filled our marriage.

Ignite the flame that has dimmed, and let our love burn brightly once again. Help us to cherish each other and show our love in meaningful ways every day, restoring the joy and passion that first brought us together. Teach us to love selflessly, as You love us, and to see each other through Your eyes.

May our renewed affection be a testament to Your miraculous power of restoration.

Any sin that is abounding in us, causing our love to wax cold, rekindle our love by the sparks of Your heart.

In Jesus' name, we pray, Amen.

Prayer for Unity and Togetherness

Heavenly Father, we need Your help to bring unity and harmony back into our marriage.

Draw us closer to each other, binding us with Your perfect love. Help us to stand united against the challenges that seek to divide us.

Guide us to support and uplift one another, fostering a deep sense of partnership. Align our paths and dreams so we can walk hand in hand through life's journey.

Strengthen our bond and make us one. May our unity reflect Your divine intention for marriage, bringing glory to Your name. In Jesus' name, Amen.

Prayer for Spiritual Growth

Almighty God, our spiritual journey is meant to be a shared adventure, yet too often we have strayed from You and from each other's side.

Your word says how can two walk together if they are not in agreement. Re-align our steps and keep us on the narrow path that leads to eternal life.

Please draw us closer to You, so we may grow closer to one another. Help us to prioritize our spiritual lives and to nurture our relationship with You.

Guide us in prayer, study, and worship together. Let Your presence be the cornerstone of our home. Teach us to seek Your will in all we do, and to trust in Your plans for our future.

May our spiritual journey bring us peace, wisdom, and a deeper connection. In Your holy name, we pray, Amen.

Prayer for Protection

Defender of the faithful, we live in a world beset by temptations and snares. Shield our marriage from harm, both seen and unseen.

Surround us with Your angels and keep us safe from the temptations that seek to undermine our sacred vows. Help us to recognize and reject anything that seeks to divide us.

Strengthen our resolve to remain faithful and committed to each other. Grant us the wisdom to make choices that honour You and protect our union.

Cover us with Your grace, and let Your love be our refuge and strength. In Jesus' name, we pray, Amen.

Prayer for Gratitude and Appreciation

Gracious Father, we've taken each other for granted. We've focused on the flaws and forgotten all the good things you have bestowed upon our union.
Please open our eyes to see the blessings in our marriage, even in the midst of struggles. Teach us to express our thankfulness for the small and large ways we support and love each other.
May our words and actions reflect a deep appreciation for the gift of our union. Let gratitude replace any bitterness or discontent in our hearts.
Remind us daily of the love we share and the reasons we chose each other. This, we pray in Your Holy name, Amen.

Prayer for Commitment and Dedication

Eternal Father, the vows we exchanged, once vibrant and full of promise, now feel like whispers carried away by the wind.
We confess that we've lost our way. We've allowed hurt and resentment to build walls between us, and the love that once burned brightly has grown dim.
But we refuse to give up, Lord. We remember the joy of our early days, the laughter and dreams we shared.
We recall the promises we made before You and our loved ones – promises to love, cherish, and support each other through thick and thin.
We come before You now, humbled and contrite. Forgive our failures, our moments of selfishness and pride.

Renew our spirits, Almighty Father, and reignite the love that first brought us together. Help us to see each other through Your eyes, with compassion and understanding.

We recommit to our marriage, Lord. Grant us the grace to forgive past injuries, the patience to faithfully navigate our differences, and the strength to love each other, even when it's difficult.
We trust in Your unfailing love, Father, and Your power to heal even the deepest wounds.

We place our marriage in Your hands and pray for Your will to be done in our lives. In Jesus' name, we pray, Amen and Amen.

33. Combat Against Hell For Your Marriage

In the name of Jesus, all astral poison and venom of tranquilization and neutralization that have neutralized my marriage, release my marital joy, fulfilment, and love expressions and passion to express love now, as I neutralize you venom and reclaim the full functionality of my marital life according to the plan of God for marriages.

By the power of the Most High, and the resurrection of Christ, by fire, thunder and lightning, I break from over my marriage the power of Akam, who is the demon over Tuesday, the Queen of the South, the demonic creatures of the forest and cemeteries, the octopus demons, the serpentine spirit, the crocodilian spirit, the reptilian spirit, the spirit of the Gorgons, the powers of the Queen of Beta, the Queen of Shylon, the Queen of Yemunah, the Queen of Delta, the Queen of the Coast, the Tritons, the Trigons, the supreme elemental spirits, supreme Mermaids, the Sirens, the Nymphs, astral poisons, the Demi-gods, Planetary Spirits, Avatars, Grand Masters, Witches, Warlocks, Satanists, Wiccans, Sorcerers, Monitoring spirits, Ascended Masters, Solar Lords, Inter-Planetary Lords, Inter-Galactic Lords, Guardians of Fate and the Cycles of life, dark Principalities, Powers, Rulers of darkness, Legion of the air, Aquatic forces, Subterranean forces, Earth masters and all other forces of the Mephisthophelean seals.

By the power of Jesus, the Christ of Nazareth, and through his holy blood, I banish from my life the Crocodile demon "Lacoste", [a river demon of unnatural marriage], and all other evil spirits that may have entered my marriage to destroy it through enchanted products, covenanted products or products made in the water kingdom, forest kingdom etc.

By the power of Jesus, the Christ of Nazareth, and through his holy blood, I also break and banish from my life every curse and spirit of marital destruction and chaos that came into my marriage to wreak havoc, destruction, separation and divorce through the use and possession of the products of Versace, Channel, Victoria's Secret, hypnotic poison, Hugo Boss, Midnight Rose, Midnight Poison, Scandal, Dhoon Glen Perfume, Flower bomb, Cabello, Georgio Amani, Dolce Gabbana, Sigma Products, Hermes, Uber universal, Carol beauty products, Beauty clear, Clear hair products, Louis Vuitton etc., and all other products used by spirits to destroy marriages.

By the power of Jesus, Son of the Living God, I also break and banish from my life every curse and spirit of marital destruction and chaos, that came into my life through any Love portion, enchanted aromas, magical powders, visual seduction, sensory manipulations, love pendant, enchanted cosmetics, love charm, words or prayers of the law of attraction, goddess of false love, enchanted incenses, witchcraft enchantments concocted with herbs, animal urine, dung, blood of animals or human, or any other paraphernalia.
Any witch and nymph manipulating the happenings and misfortunes surrounding the calamity of my marriage, I call the judgement of Jesus Christ upon you, and I say be rendered mute, maimed, deaf and blind effective immediately, in Jesus name.

By the jurisdiction of the sapphire Throne of my Father God in Heaven and by the power of Jesus, Adonai Tzeva'ot, the Lord of host, I pull my marriage out from every watery prison and kingdom, from any enchanted forest, grave, cemetery, hole, culvert, sacred grove, shrine, altar, cauldron, swamp, mangroves, everglades, and from any trench, drain, drainage pipe, sewer, sewage pipe, waste channel, roadside, under bridge, railroad, valley, mountain ridge, Cave, Labyrinth, and from within any land of darkness, from any spiritual maze, catacomb, pit, crooked place, spiritual crevices, and from any place within the

forest, desert, water, air, and underground occult kingdoms and zones, in the name of Jesus of Nazareth.
In the name of Jesus of Nazareth, I address the powers of darkness by the Blood and Fire of Jesus Christ, and I rebuke the assignments of Hell programmed against my marriage.

All astral poison and venom of tranquilization and neutralization that have neutralized my marriage, and captured my marital joy, fulfilment, peace, financial wealth, sexual fulfilment and love expressions, I demolish the structure and network of witchcraft from my marriage, now in Jesus name.

I stand erected in the authoritative capacity of the blood, water and Spirit of Jesus of Nazareth, and by the authority of the word and name of Yah, I arrest, bind, disarm and banish from my marriage Every power of Asmodeus and his hold, and the chains of marital destruction, every demon of the fly, squirting demon, spirit of filth, and demon of uncleanness, lack of vision, misunderstanding, spirit of confusion, demon of sexual deprivation, demon of anger, bitterness, resentment, unforgiveness, hatred, and desire for revenge, quarrels and lack of affection, or cold affection.

If there be demonic vines, creepers, climbers or moss covering my marriage, if there be any demon spirit defecating, vomiting or spitting on my marriage, if there be any unclean spirit nesting, brooding, settling or lodging upon or within any part of my marriage, and any spirit that has set itself as an evil guardian, spirit guide or totem in my marriage, by the judicial verdict of the power of the Blood of the Lamb of God Almighty,

I banish by fire all you demons in the name of Jesus name.
I stand by the jurisdiction of the Blood upon the Mercy Seat, and I say to the four corners of the heavens above loose my marriage and

release all its glory, splendour and prosperity, effective immediately, in Jesus name.

I say to the four cardinal points, the four sub-cardinal points and the four inter-cardinal points of the Earth, O Earth, loose my marriage and release all its glory, splendour and prosperity, effective immediately, in Jesus name.

I say to the 12 gates of Hell, O gates of darkness, all kingdoms of the Occult, all regions, zones, and realms, loose my marriage and release all its glory, splendour and prosperity, effective immediately, in Jesus name.

In Jesus name, I break every psychic manipulation from over my [Husband/Wife], and block every satanic movement, signal, frequency, channel, code, formular and operation constructed to destroy his/her integrity, vitality, faith, strength, zeal of God, visions etc.

I declare by the fire of the prophetic, according to Song of Solomon 4:4, **"My neck *is* like the tower of David built for an armoury, whereon there hang a thousand bucklers, all shields of mighty men."**
I declare by the fire of the prophetic according to Song of Solomon 4:4, My Husband/Wife's neck *is* like the tower of David built for an armoury, whereon there hang a thousand bucklers, all shields of mighty men.

I declare by the fire of the prophetic, according to Song of Solomon 4:4, My children's necks *are* like the tower of David built for an armoury, whereon there hang a thousand bucklers, all shields of mighty men.

Father God, you said in Your word in Isaiah 40:2, **"Speak comfortably to Jerusalem, and cry unto her that her warfare is accomplished, that her iniquity is pardoned; for she has received of the LORD'S hand double for all her sins."**
You also said in Your word in Isaiah 61:7, **"For your shame you will have double;"**
At this point I am requesting and claiming this double; double grace, double anointing, double victory, double power, double strength and double blessings of all categories, in the name of Y'ahushua HaMashiach.
Heavenly Father, repair and restore my marital wholeness and wellness and give unto us beauty for ashes, the oil of joy for mourning, the garment of praise for the spirit of heaviness; that me and my spouse might be called trees of righteousness, the planting of the LORD, that you might be glorified, according to Isaiah 61:3.
For our shame give us double; and for confusion let us rejoice in our portion: therefore, in our land we shall possess the double: everlasting joy shall be unto us, according to Isaiah 61:7.

Restore to us the years that the locust hath eaten, the cankerworm, and the caterpillar, and the palmerworm, according to Your word in Joel 2:25.
I reclaim the full functionality of my marital life and passion to express love, according to the plan of God for marriages, In Jesus Name.
This I pray in the name of the Father, the Son and the Holy Spirit. Amen and Amen.

34. Prayer When In Trouble

Let my cry for help trigger an emergency alert to accelerate the velocity of mercy for intervention on your behalf. An example is in Psalms_69:17, **"for I am in trouble: hear me speedily,"** Psalms 31:2, **"...deliver me speedily"**, Psalms 38:22, **"Make haste to help me"**, Psalms 70:1, **"Make haste, O God, to deliver me; make haste to help me, O LORD"**.
In Psalms 69:2, **"God, my God, come and save me! These floods of trouble have risen higher and higher. The water is up to my neck! I am sinking into the mud with no place to stand, and I'm about to drown in this storm."**

God of the wind and waters, still the storms that trouble me. Let Your Spirit brood over the surface of the waters, and let Your voice be thereupon.
It is written in Psalms 57:3, **"He shall send from heaven and save me; He rebukes him who would swallow me up. Selah. God shall send forth His mercy and His truth."**

Psalms 57:4, **"My soul is among lions; I lie among those who breathe out fire, the sons of men whose teeth are spears and arrows, and their tongue a sharp sword."**
Psalms 57:5, **"Be exalted, O God, above the heavens; let Your glory be above all the earth."**
Psalms 57:6, **"They have prepared a net for my steps; my soul is bowed down; they have dug a pit before me; into the midst of it they have fallen themselves. Selah."**
Psalms 57:7, **"My heart is fixed, O God, my heart is fixed; I will sing and give praise."**
Psalms 57:8, **"Awake, my glory! Awake, harp and lyre! I myself will awake the dawn."**

Psalms 57:9, "**I will praise You, O LORD, among the people; I will sing of You among the nations,**"

Father, I pray, any plan of the Kingdom of darkness, Witchcraft or Satanism to use me as a "Compensation sacrifice", "Collateral sacrifice" or a "Replacement sacrifice" or "Freewill sacrifice", I destroy this diabolic plan by the Name of the Messiah Jesus and fire of the Holy Spirit, right now.
I will not be a scapegoat, nor a victim of sacrifice unto devils, in Jesus' name.
You are my shield and my buckler, and my strong tower. Do not let me be ashamed, neither let the forces of the secret places of darkness rejoice over me. In every realm and dimension, scatter my enemies and those who trouble me for spite.

Oh Lord, be an enemy to my enemies and an adversary to my adversaries, and judge all situations, for I am the apple of Your eyes.
It is written in Psalms 59:1 **Deliver me from my enemies, O my God; defend me from those who rise up against me.**
Psalms 59:2, "**Deliver me from the workers of evil and save me from bloody men,**"
Psalms 59:3, "**For behold, they lie in wait for my soul; the mighty are gathered against me—not for my transgression, nor for my sin, O LORD.**"
Psalms 59:4, "**Without my fault they run and prepare themselves; awaken to help me, and look upon me.**"
Psalms 59:5, "**And You therefore, O LORD God of hosts, the God of Israel, awake to punish all the nations; show no mercy to any wicked traitors. Selah.**"
Psalms 59:6, "**They return at evening; they snarl like a dog, and prowl about the city.** "
Psalms 59:7, "**Behold, they bellow out with their mouths; swords are in their lips, for they say, "Who hears?"**"

Psalms 59:8, "**But You, O LORD, shall laugh at them; You shall hold all the nations in derision.**"

Psalms 59:9, "**Because of His strength will I wait for You, for God is my strong tower.**"

Father, thank you for Your protection and for defending me from the powers of evil men and spirits. For this I thank you, in Jesus' name.

35. Prayer To Break Ties With Cults, Curses, And Demonic Religion

[Scriptures to Stand Upon: Isaiah 28:14-19; Isaiah 10:27; Numbers 23:23; Matthew 15:13.]

Lord our God, King of the ages, All-powerful and All-mighty who sits between the Cherubim of burning coals, hallowed be Your name in all kingdoms of the heavens and the earth. Heavenly Father, and Most High God, Your name is holy, and You are exalted in all kingdoms, realms, and dimensions. Behold, O Lord Jesus, my battles and captivity are before you. Now, I implore Your divine intervention through Your Holy Spirit. You said in Your Word in **Isaiah 61:1**, **"The Spirit of the Lord GOD *is* upon me; because the LORD hath anointed me to preach good tidings unto the meek; he hath sent me to bind up the brokenhearted, to proclaim liberty to the captives, and the opening of the prison to *them that are* bound;"**

You said in Your word in Psalms 50:15, **"And call upon Me in the day of trouble; and I will deliver you, and you shall honour Me."**

By my authority through Jesus of Nazareth, I now take authoritative commands, and I bring into subjection all spirits of the occult world and all powers of the Mephistophelian seals, the Esoteric sciences and Craft, and over all psychic entities operating under the laws of the fallen Angels of Tartarus and other dimensions, within the four kingdoms of the Air, the kingdom of the waters below, the kingdom of the land, and the kingdom of the subterranean region, and over the four elements of the four cardinal dimensions.

Confession and Renunciation

By the judicial verdict of the power of the Blood of the Lamb of God Almighty, I confess, expose, renounce, rebuke, and forsake my ancestral connection, or my direct and indirect, current and past, conscious and unconscious involvement, spiritual marriage, soul tie, agreement, connection, covenant, truce, alliance, or any secret link and involvement that I may have with the arts of white witchcraft, black witchcraft, blue witchcraft, green witchcraft, and red witchcraft.

I hereby revoke and withdraw my sworn oaths, all confessions, profession of faith, verbal agreements, swearing of allegiance, written contracts, blood signatures, and agreements that I have with Gardnerian witchcraft, Sicilian witchcraft, Dianic witchcraft, Alexandrian witchcraft, Kali witchcraft, Rajo witchcraft, or the Abra Melin witchcraft, or with the Church of Satan, the International Council of White Witches, the Royal Order of White Witches of England, the Church of Wicca, the Research Bureau of the Twilight Zone, the Witchcraft Fraternity of Canada, the Rosicrucian Order, Order of the Templar Knights, Heaven's Gate Cult, Latter Day Saints, Scientology, the Hermetic Order of the Golden Dawn, ceremonial magic, Enochian magic, Christian mysticism, Hermeticism, alchemy, theurgy, and ancient Egyptian paganism, cults Hare Krishna, Jehovah's Witnesses, KKK, Roman Catholic Church, Christian Science, Islam, Freemasonry, Rosicrucianism, Buddhism, Illuminati, Lodge, theosophy, Urantia, unity, Mormonism, Bahaism, Unitarianism; faction, party, schism, heresy, false teaching, religious spirits, control, confusion, deception, error, spirit of Nazi, anti-submissive stubbornness, rebellion, disobedience, self-will, pride, or any other fraternity or secret society.

I confessed, exposed, renounced, rebuked, and forsook my ancestral connection, or my direct and indirect, current and past, conscious and unconscious involvement, spiritual marriage, soul tie, agreement, connection, covenant, truce, alliance, or any secret link and involvement that I have with the evil powers of the books of grimoire, technique, tactic, mysterious witchcraft, sorcery, divination, ESP, hypnosis, fortune-telling, crystal ball, Ouija board, tarot cards, Freemasonry, martial arts, magic, séances, clairvoyance, mediums, psychics, readers, advisors, necromancy, handwriting analysis, astral projection, yoga, metaphysical healing groups, crypt-aesthesia, telepathy, psychokinesis, precognition, psychometry, dowsing, hypnotism, occult movies, occult programs, occult books, occult games, New Age movement, amulets, talismans, ankhs, yin yang, transcendental meditation, familiar spirits, channeling, Santería, General Divination, astrology, and Thoth Tarot, esoteric traditions, Spiritualism, Theosophy, Anthroposophy, New Age, and the left-hand path and right-hand path, and any other branch of occultism.

Let the agreement between me and the temples of the gods of darkness be broken and destroyed in Jesus' name. I hereby revoke and withdraw my sworn oaths, all confessions, professions of faith, verbal agreements, swearing of allegiance, written contracts, blood signatures, and agreements, and marital vows with every psychic spirit of darkness.

I confessed, exposed, renounced, rebuked, and forsook my direct and indirect, current and past, conscious and unconscious involvement, spiritual marriage, soul-tie, agreement, connection, covenant, truce, alliance, or any secret link that I have with the Devas and Devatas (male and female "Guardian Spirits"), witches, warlocks, satanists, ritualists, grand masters, Ascended Masters, ascending masters, Guardian of the Flame, Avatar, brotherhood, sisterhood, Guru, native doctor, wise man, witch doctors, mermaids, Sirens, voodoo priests, or with any other cult organization, vicious psychic entities, and occult agents within the occult zones, regions, centers within the land, sea, air, and underground. It is written in Zephaniah 2:11, **"The LORD *will be* terrible unto them: for he will famish all the gods of the earth; and *men* shall worship him, everyone from his place, *even* all the isles of the heathen."**

- **Taking Authority**

Jesus, Son of Almighty God the Father, I petition you to release Angels of forefront warfare, wielding the most sophisticated divine weapons, and let them declare war, revolt, and destroy all satanic powers of the five Esoteric Seals of darkness that are fighting against my life and are subjecting me to their evil influences by psychic manipulations. It is written in Numbers 23:23, **"Surely *there is* no enchantment against Jacob, neither *is there* any divination against Israel: according to this time it shall be said of Jacob and of Israel, What hath God wrought!"**

By lightning, thunder and fire of Jesus Christ of Nazareth, I renounce, revoke, shatter, and banish from me any demon spirit beast, spirit guide, creature, poison, charm, subtle power, and gift that was placed in my body by ingestion or incision, or entered my soul and body during any trauma or any demonic open door, or an evil dream that has subjected me to become the victim, a prisoner, an object, and subject of the demon of occultism. I call the fiery light of the Garment of El-Shaddai to light up and destroy every one of these occult powers placed in me, and set me free from the secrets of the five Mephistophelian seals of darkness.

It is written in Psalms 97:7, **"Confounded be all they that serve graven images, that boast themselves of idols: worship him, all *ye* gods."**

By the Fire and Blood of Jesus of Nazareth, I loose my life from all occult curses and demons whereby I was initiated before conception, while in the womb, or at the naming ceremony; for it is written in Isaiah 10:27, **"And it shall come to pass in that day, *that* his burden shall be taken away from off thy shoulder, and his yoke from off thy neck, and the yoke shall be destroyed because of the anointing."**

By the Fire and Blood of Jesus of Nazareth I loose my life from all occult curses and demons whereby I was initiated into the occult spirit by handling cursed objects, contact with satanic agents, or living in a cursed home or land. By the Fire and Blood of Jesus of Nazareth I loose my life from all occult curses and demons whereby I was initiated by being born on a satanic altar/shrine; By the Fire and Blood of Jesus of Nazareth I loose my life from all occult curses and demons whereby I was initiated by drinking blood or unholy water; or where I was bathed in blood, sprinkled with blood, anointed with blood. By the Fire and Blood of Jesus of Nazareth I loose my life from all occult curses and demons whereby I was initiated by receiving strange money or cursed gifts; By the Fire and Blood of Jesus of Nazareth I loosed my life from all occult curses and demons whereby I was initiated by my participation in village, compound and township satanic festivals.

I revoke and destroy by the Blood of Jesus every blood and soul-tie covenant attaching me to any satanic agent, and I destroy every evil covenant and initiation made with me through dreams in the Name of Jesus. Therefore, by the lightning, thunder, and fire of Jesus Christ of Nazareth, I renounce, revoke, shatter, and banish from me all strongholds, and I break myself loose from every personal and collective curse and covenant in the Name of Jesus.

By lightning, thunder and fire of Jesus Christ of Nazareth, I renounce, revoke, shatter, and banish from me every wife/husband that was given to me in my dream or by covenant, or as a token of initiation, and I destroy all witchcraft manipulations, curses, locks, and chains that were placed upon my life as a result. This I pray in the name of Jesus the Christ.

By the Fire and Blood of Jesus of Nazareth, bring into subjection and destruction all powers of darkness invading, intruding, lodging, violating, harassing, and tormenting me through occult judicial verdicts and satanic devices such as the Astro-Omnidictator, the

Celestial Mirrors, Astral Gemstones, the Etheric Gemstones, the Animus Third Eye, the Psychic Cameras, and the Astral Televisions. Let them be destroyed by the Fire and Blood of Jesus of Nazareth.

Fire and Blood of Jesus of Nazareth, release me from every covenant, oath, allegiance, and inheritance made for me or by me, consciously or unconsciously, in the Almighty Name of Jesus Christ.

Fire and Blood of Jesus of Nazareth, release me from any family, community, or neighbourhood trait of witchcraft, and every evil planted in my life, let them be uprooted for it is written, Mat 15:13, **"But he answered and said, Every plant, which my heavenly Father hath not planted, shall be rooted up,"** in the Name of the Lord Jesus Christ.

Father, I thank You for making me victorious over all my enemies. From henceforth I will rise in victory and freedom in the liberty of Christ, for it is written in Isaiah 52:2, **"Shake thyself from the dust; arise, *and* sit down, O Jerusalem: loose thyself from the bands of thy neck, O captive daughter of Zion."**

No weapon formed against me as a result of former covenants and curses shall prosper in the name of Jesus. Amen.

36. Prayer Against Witchcraft Altars

My Lord, God, and Father in Heaven, I bring my life, spirit, soul, and body before Your throne of judgement. Behold my captivity in the astral realm of darkness because of evil altars.
My sufferings and captivity are before you; now I implore Your divine intervention through Your Son, Jesus of Nazareth.
Lord, You said in Your word in Psalms 50:15, **"And call upon Me in the day of trouble; and I will deliver you, and you shall honour Me."**

Any witchcraft altar upon which any part of **my integumentary system, skeletal system, muscular system, nervous system, endocrine system, cardiovascular system, lymphatic system, respiratory system, digestive system, urinary system, or my reproductive system is** placed as a ritual for incantation, by warfare of fire, lightning, and faith in Jesus Christ, I command the release of all my organs now. I hereby retrieve my body organs and health from every witchcraft altar and pray for destruction upon these altars with immediate effect.

In the Name of Jesus and by the power of the Spirit of Jesus, I sever, block, and stop every communication, channel, signal, frequency, and intel that is communicated between altars of the land and altars of the waters and the air against my life. Every communication and transmission of evil info between altars against my life, backfire now, in Jesus name. You evil altars, let your communication system jam, and all satanic transmission be interrupted by the fire of the holy Spirit of Jesus. I set your boundaries on fire now, and I neutralize receptions between the altars of the oceans, rivers, lakes, and ponds which are carrying the formula for my destruction.

Every witchcraft altar fighting for my life, roast the demons who constructed you, and bind the occultist who initiated and is servicing you. It is written in Psalm 27:2, **"When the wicked, even mine enemies and my foes, came upon me to eat up my flesh, they stumbled and fell."**

By the power of the Holy Spirit of the Almighty God, I bring under subjection by the blood of Jesus all tribal altars, community altars, ancestral altars, generational altars, and all other evil altars that are connecting me to foreign DNA, demonic bloodlines, tribal ties, ancestral ties, genetic heritage, ancestral lineage, demonic DNA heritage, corrupted genealogies, family alliances, astral links, witchcraft pacts, ancestral gates, ancestral altars, and ancestral iniquities, sins, and abominations.

I invoke and declare the demolition of Destruction, Desolation, Degradation, Annihilation, Liquidation, and Eradication of these witchcraft altars, in Jesus' name.

With hot chains of fire and by force, I bind and bring into captivity and under subjection all forces of darkness working with evil altars, sacrifices, rituals, and incantations against my life.

I call upon the voice of the Lord in Psalm 29, the flood of the Lord in Isaiah 43:19, and the fire hammer of the Word of God in Jeremiah 23:29 against all those altars. They must be destroyed.

Those altars are:
- Any witchcraft spiritual altar in my life, connected to the guardian forces of the four cardinal hemispheres and the four elements: fire, wind, water, and earth.
- Witchcraft altars that have judicial rulings against me in the tribunal of the night.
- Altars that sustain the judicial forces of the four king demons: of the Septentrion, Midi, Orient, and Occident.

- Every stone, soil, tree, memorial, cemetery, teraphim, water, and aerial altar, as well as every sacred grove and high place.

All altars that are used to carry out evil laws, demonic transactions, and agreements against me in the psychic realms, and every evil altar in my life that is charged with diabolic commands from the archdemons of the Winter Solstice, Spring Equinox, Summer Solstice, and Autumn Equinox.

I render every one of these witchcraft altars in operation against my life useless, ineffective, and powerless, irrelevant, inadequate, and incapable of transmitting any incantation and psychic commands to the elemental forces throughout the psychic layers and astral planes against me.
It is written in Psalms 71:13, **"Let them be confounded and consumed that are adversaries to my soul; let them be covered with reproach and dishonour that seek my hurt."**

Any altar that has formed a mutual relationship between the entities of darkness and me, any and every evil altar upon which my fingernail, toenail, my clothes, my hair or hair items, my blood, my semen/sanitary napkin, my photo, my footwear, my sock, my saliva, my sweat or skin tissues, or any other personal item is being held and sacrificed to demon entities, and is being used as a channel and ethereal bridge to access and destroy my life, I call upon the God of Jeshurun, who rides upon the heavens in my help, and in His excellency in the sky [Deut 33:26], and by faith I demolish these altars in the second heaven, land, sea, and underworld.

Any altar built for my life and against my life in order to destroy my destiny by psychic attacks, psychic manipulations, swift and progressive destructions, persistent predicaments, recurring calamities, repetitive failures, blockages, hindrances, disappointments, disgraces, and mutations of afflictions, and every spiritual altar that carries the mandate for my death, annihilation, and clear and present danger, and all altars that have swallowed or are swallowing my glory and eating my destiny, vomiting upon me shame, darkness, disgrace, and poverty, I, by the authority of Jesus Christ of Nazareth and the power of the Holy Spirit, destroy these altars by lightning and thunders and render these evil altars incapable and ineffective in channeling psychic commands into the psychic layers against me, and I render these altars useless and demolished to powder.

By the power of the judgement and the authority of the Word of God in Luke 10:19, Psalms 11:6, and Exodus 9:24, I call down rain of fire, grievous hail; rain of snares and terrors, brimstone, lightnings and thunders from the thick cloud of Almighty God [Exo 19:16], to fall upon and shatter to powder every evil altar in the astral and terrestrial realms, which were built for me by the dark Angels, Guardians, Demi-gods, Astral forces, Planetary Spirits, Prithas, Watchers, Guardians of the Flame, Ascended Masters, Solar Lords, satanic Cherubim, Inter-Planetary Lords, Inter-Galactic Lords, Guardians of Fate and the Cycles of life, dark principalities, powers, rulers of darkness, spiritual wickedness, cosmic forces, aquatic forces, subterranean forces, dwarf demons, minions, cohorts, nymphs, imps, earth masters, avatars, highlanders, mermaids, sirens, and all astral forces of the elemental entities.

Let these evil altars become unusable powders, or be destroyed and banished into oblivion, and all builders and agents of these altars be destroyed, in Jesus name.
It is written in Psalms 11:6, **"Upon the wicked he shall rain snares, fire and brimstone, and a horrible tempest: this shall be the portion of their cup."**

Also, every witchcraft altar operating against my life through the gate of the midday sun, midnight moon, full moon, new moon, waxing moon, and waning moon, or using the gates of any of the seven seas, the five oceans, continental rivers, forests, mountains, or the 12 Zodiac signs, may all of these evil altars explode to pieces by destructive lightnings of thunderclaps, and their stronghold be broken from my life now, in the name of Jesus, Son of the Living God.
It is written in Psalms 18:13, **"The LORD also thundered in the heavens, and the Highest gave his voice; hail stones and coals of fire."**

Let lightning and thunderclaps rattle, explode, and detonate in every place where altars are standing against my life for the destruction of my mind, soul, body, and destiny. Let these witchcraft altars be shattered to pieces by the fire of Yah, and let their molecules be weaponized and become destructive and lethal to the guardians, acolytes, and other occult beings who are utilizing and servicing these witchcraft altars by burning incense within the land, sea, air, and under the earth.

I invoke the power of the judgement of God written in Numbers 16:35 that says, **"Fire also came forth from the LORD and consumed the two hundred and fifty men who were offering the incense."**

Therefore, effective immediately, let electric fire and dynamic thunderclaps from Heaven annihilate, liquidate, dissolve, and eradicate every evil altar that carries the mandate for my destruction by witchcraft and sorceries, and I render the power of these altars built against my life impotent, frustrated, inadequate, incapable, ineffective, nullified, barren, ineligible, and useless perpetually, in the name of Jesus.

All altars of sustaining prayers, hums, chants, mantras against me, I impeach you in the land, sea, and air. Release me and be demolished, effective immediately, in Jesus' name.
Evil altars which speak into the heavens against my destiny and well-being, release me and be demolished in the land, sea, and air, effective immediately, in Jesus' name.

Altar of sudden failure at the edge of a breakthrough, release me and be demolished in the land, sea, and air, effective immediately, in Jesus' name.

By the blood of Jesus, any strange ancestral altar blocking my divine encounter and manifestation, release me and be demolished in the land, sea, and air, effective immediately, in Jesus' name.

All agents of witchcraft who have built altars to roast me, burn, or sacrifice my destiny and life to the demons of Hell, let these agents be placed upon this same altar in my stead, and be roasted there upon by fire.

Any personality or strange thing from these evil altars appearing to me in dreams, sleep-wake moments, in trances, or visions, be demolished in the land, sea, and air, effective immediately, in Jesus' name.

Any strange altar waging war against my progress, advancements, and good results, lose all your battles against me and be demolished in the land, sea, and air, effective immediately, in Jesus' name.
Any negative voice speaking from any evil altar, hear the word of the Lord according to Psalm 29:3-5; be swallowed by the voice of God in Jesus' name.

Any evil altar in my father's house, mother's house, or spousal house, monitoring my progress for evil, be demolished in the land, sea, and air, effective immediately, in Jesus' name.

Territorial, national, or regional altars controlling the affairs of my home or business be demolished in the land, sea, and air effective immediately, in Jesus' name.

Any witchcraft altar sponsoring my life with the spirit of mistakes and errors, be demolished in the land, sea, and air, effective immediately, in Jesus' name.

All evil altars preventing demons from being cast out of my life and body, release me and be demolished and banished in the land, sea, and air, effective immediately, in Jesus' name.

Father, thank you for setting me free from altars of darkness. Now that you have delivered me, I can serve you with no ceremonial attachment to the kingdom of darkness. Thank you, Father, for delivering me from satanic altars. Be exalted, O Lord, in all the Earth, in Jesus' name, Amen and Amen.

37. Prayer Against The Tribunal Of The Night

My God and Father, by the blood of Jesus of Nazareth, I invoke the judicial intervention of Heaven to rule against any and every processing, proceeding, and lawsuit that is set in its course against my life in the tribunal of the night.
"And now, Lord, behold their threatenings: and grant unto thy servants, that with all boldness they may speak thy word," as it is written in Acts 4:29.

By the authority of Jesus Christ and the power of the Holy Spirit of Jesus, I condemn every condemnation laid over my life by the grand juror of the judicial court of the kingdom of darkness, by the attorney general of Hell, by the magistrate of esoteric forces, and by the high Judge of the Devil's kingdom.
Your word says, O Lord, in Psalms 94:21, **"They gather themselves together against the soul of the righteous and condemn the innocent blood"**.

All decisions taken in the courts of darkness against my life by night, let Heaven overrule these evil decisions now.
For it is written in Psalms 109:31, **"For he shall stand at the right hand of the poor, to save him from those that condemn his soul"**.

I pray against every spirit that goes to the courts of hell to accuse my life of error. I renounce and liquidate every court hearing that is held to prosecute me, condemn me, and destroy me by evil judicial councils.

With hot chains of fire and by force, I bind all bailiffs who have served me or are seeking to serve me a court summons from Hell, and I call fire mixed with hail and brimstone from Jesus Christ to chase and roast

these bailiffs and bounty hunters now and consume to ashes every demonic summon, court document, and register or court order from hell.
By the name of Jesus Christ, with hot chains of fire and by force, I bring into subjection to the power of Jesus Christ of Nazareth, every imagination and high thing, every judicial platform, demonic judge, satanic juror, evil bailiffs, occult attorneys, demonic false witnesses, every evil perpetrator, instigator of evil, and every satanic law and order. I invoke upon every occult being functioning in judicial capacities against me the judgement of God written in Numbers 16:35 that says, **"Fire also came forth from the LORD and consumed the two hundred and fifty men who were offering the incense."**

By the power of Jesus, I bring to naught and sever chronic confusion, every witchcraft judicial ruling with false factual premises, and everyone who bears false witness in the tribunal of the night against me.

It is written in Isaiah 50:9, **"Behold, the Lord GOD will help me; who is he that shall condemn me? lo, they all shall wax old as a garment; the moth shall eat them up."**
Any restraint, restriction, and condemnation placed upon my life because of my shortcomings, my sins and iniquities, or the sins and iniquities of my mother's house or father's house, Col 1:14, **"In whom we have redemption through his blood, even the forgiveness of sins:"**

Let these restraints and condemnations be nullified by the jurisdiction of the Blood of Jesus, the Lamb of God Almighty.
It is written, Romans 5:9, **"Much more then, being now justified by His blood, we shall be saved from wrath."**
It is also written in Romans 3:24, **"Being justified freely by his grace through the redemption that is in Christ Jesus:"**

Therefore, by the supremacy of Jesus of Nazareth, I annihilate, liquidate, dissolve, and eradicate every verdict, law, bill, and ruling with the fiery terror of God's divine judgement by the redemption of the blood of Jesus of Nazareth.
Let the Court of the Ancient of Days rise to my help and condemn my accusers in Hell.

Thrones of the Council of Heaven, the Supreme Celestial Court, rise to my help and condemn my accusers in the Kingdom of Darkness.
I say, Court of Petitions and Requests, reject any allegations, accusations, and condemnations that the Devil brings against me.

Throne of Grace, where grace is given to the Saints, rise to my help and condemn my accusers in the Kingdom of Darkness.
Oh, Mercy Seat, where mercy is executed for the Saints, rise to my help and condemn my accusers in the kingdom of Darkness.
Throne of Judgement where judgement is executed for the saints, rise to my help and condemn my accusers in the kingdom of Darkness.

Throne of the Lamb of God, rise to my help and condemn my accusers in the Kingdom of Darkness.
Throne of God the Father, where the Father is seated, rise to my help and condemn my accusers in the kingdom of Darkness.
Court of Accusation where the Devil comes to accuse the Saints, condemn the forthcoming of the Devil within thy chambers.

It is written in Psalms 71:13, **"Let them be confounded and consumed that are adversaries to my soul; let them be covered with reproach and dishonour that seek my hurt."**

38. Prayer To Invoke God's Supernatural Wealth

Lord our God, King of the ages, All-powerful and All-mighty who sits between the Cherubim of burning coals, hallowed be Your name in all kingdoms of the heavens and the earth.
Today I give you praise, honour and glory, as I come boldly before Your Throne of Grace. Heavenly Father You are the Most High God. Your name is holy, and You are exalted in all kingdoms, realms and dimensions and spheres.

I pray in the presence of Your Holy Spirit, that I will shout for joy, and be glad, that you will favour my righteous cause: yea, and let me say continually, let the LORD be magnified, which hath pleasure in the prosperity of his servant. [Psalms 35:27],
You know the desires of my heart and you know my every need before I pray [Mat 6:32]. Not one sparrow falls to the ground without Your knowledge [Mat 10:29]. You clothed the lilies of the field [Mat 6:28-29] and planted the fir trees that all the birds of the air lodge therein.

I say today according to the Psalms 104:17 **"The trees of the LORD are full of sap; the cedars of Lebanon, which he hath planted; Where the birds make their nests:** *as for* **the stork, the fir trees** *are* **her house. The high hills** *are* **a refuge for the wild goats;** *and* **the rocks for the conies."** [Psalms 104:16-18].
Your word says in Mat 6:26, "Behold the fowls of the air: for they sow not, neither do they reap, nor gather into barns; yet your heavenly Father feeds them", and in Mat 10:31 you say, **"Fear ye not therefore, ye are of more value than many sparrows".**

Today I petition by the blood of the Lamb for Your grace and favour of wealth in my life, and that You would expand my influence in many ways. Draw and attract destiny helpers to me and enlarge my borders,

and the parameter of my blessings. You did it for Jabez, now I trust that you will do it for me. It says in Psalms 149:4, **"For the LORD taketh pleasure in his people: he will beautify the meek with salvation."**
I acknowledge you as the great Door Opener and bestower of great blessings of wealth, so that I can give to Your work on earth.

You made Abraham wealthy, and you made Solomon wealthy, and you made Job wealthy, therefore, you can make me wealthy for Your name sake and for the work of Your ministry. Be my exceeding greatness and joy unspeakable that I may be filled with Your glory.
Bestow upon me today supernatural power to gain wealth, and supernatural manifestations of blessings from unexpected places.

Smash through every obstacle, opposition, and resistance that stands in the way of my breakthrough and blessings. I declare in the name of Jesus that I will see the goodness of the Lord in the land of the Living. No weapon formed against me shall prosper and every crooked path be straightened now, in Jesus name!
Lord Jesus, upon the authority of Your word in Exodus 23:25 and Deuteronomy 7:13, I stand erected in the spirit and invoke the authoritative capacity of the Kavod glory, and the fire of the Shekhinah in my mouth, in my prayers, and around me right now. All wealth of the ungodly, I call you forth into my hands by the verdict and jurisdiction of the Word of God in Proverbs 13:22.
With this authority, I curse the demons of miscarriage of my blessing, and the demons of financial infertility, wealth barrenness, poverty and lack, and I now invoke rains of blessings upon my life, in Jesus name.

Lord God Almighty, You said in Psalms 2:8, **"Ask of me, and I shall give you the heathen for your inheritance, and the uttermost parts of the earth for your possession."**

Through the authority of the Altar of divine Flames and the holy Blood of Jesus the Lamb, I loose the financial bands and the gates of treasures, in the heavens and the Earth, and I command the gates of wealth and financial favours to be unlocked unto my life, from the North, South, East and West.

By the grand order of the verdict of the Blood of the New Covenant of Christ, I charge every treasury of finances and wealth in all four corners of the heavens and the earth, to channel into my life a great flow of accumulated finances and wealth, without interruption and delay, effective immediately.

I loose the belly of the heavens and the Earth and command great fountains of wealth to run into my life, and into the life of my children and my children's children.

By the verdict of the Grand Juror of the inner Divine Council of the Celestial kingdom of God, and the Lamb who is without blemish, let all people who do not know me pour into my bosom from every tribe, tongue, nation, age and gender: from the North, South, East and West, according to Luke 6:38 and Deuteronomy 28:6-12.

I command Proverbs 3:10 to come alive and take effect in my life. Hence, I command by the verdict of the eternal flame, let my barns be filled with plenty, and thy presses burst out with new wine. Let my Oils flow without ceasing, and the provisions to sustain my life and family begin to flow like a mighty rushing river, which never fails, effective immediately. By authority in Jesus, let wealth of all categories and financial favours begin to flow into my life and account. Let the Lord be magnified continually.

39. Prayer To Invoke God's Supernatural Blessings

Heavenly, I come to Your presence to humble myself and repent for my sins and iniquities, and those of my ancestors and parents from my mother's house and my father's house, so that the Blood of Christ would remove all allegations against my blessings.

I have seen my blessings being hindered, and I have not been experiencing Your blessings in ways that will confound my adversaries and enemies. Therefore, today through Your Son Jesus of Nazareth, I detest all personal and family transgressions and trespasses, and ask you to remove from me every sin, evil covenant and iniquity that have given demons astral right to capture my blessings in the Land, Sea and Air. By the Judicial Council of Your mercy, judgement and compassion, revive the verdict of the judicial Blood of the Lamb and the Mercy Seat, and acquit me of all allegations, accusations and condemnations, and of all sins, evil and wickedness embedded in me from my youth till now.

"Let them shout for joy, and be glad, that favour my righteous cause: yea, let them say continually, Let the LORD be magnified, which hath pleasure in the prosperity of his servant." [Psalms According to the Words of the Messiah Jesus in Mark 16:17, **"And these signs shall follow them that believe; In my name shall they cast out devils."**

On this authority, by fire I break the backbone of the spirit of delay in my life, effective immediately.

Delay of my financial blessings, material blessings, blessings of clothes, foods, technology, electronic devices, my home and furnishings has come to an end.

By the verdict of the Council of Mount Zion in the sides of the North, the City of the Great King, I now speak forth, decree and declare that the season of delay in my life is hereby terminated effective immediately. I call this wealth out from the hands of the wicked, and out of the hands of my enemies, and command them to be transferred into my hands.

By the authority of Jesus of Nazareth, I created reservoirs to accommodate my blessings of Oils, Corn, grains, wheat, new wine, milk and honey.

I declare by fire, all channels of my blessings that have been blocked from my youth till now are henceforth unblocked.
I call upon the power of Jesus to unclog these channels now, in Jesus Name.

Spirit of the Living God, I welcome You to move like a mighty, rushing wind over my life. Release Your breakthrough anointing to flow through me and propel me forward into my promised land. Give me eyes to see the open doors of favour that others are blind to. Fill me with boldness to seize divinely orchestrated opportunities without hesitation.

It is written in Isaiah 25:6, **"And in this mountain shall Yahuah Tseva'oth make unto all people a feast of fat things, a feast of wines on the lees, of fat things full of marrow, of wines on the lees well refined."**

Blessings that are locked up in my family bloodline, let them begin to gravitate towards me with accelerated velocity now, in Jesus Name.

All Good family blessings that are buried with my ancestors, let these blessings be recovered from the great beyond and be transferred to my life now, That I may become the beneficiary of the family wealth, in Jesus name.

In the name of Jesus of Nazareth, I command the heavens and the earth to be reconfigured and reconditioned now, to accommodate, attract and channel uncommon favours and blessings into my life, from the North, South, East and West, effective immediately.

All my heavenly blessings confiscated in the cosmic net of the second heaven, vibrate at a higher frequency by fire of Jesus Christ, and burn to ashes the powers of hell that are holding you bound in darkness.
In the name of Jesus, the Christ of Nazareth, Let the cosmic nets be burnt to ash, and release my blessings and all answers to my prayers, effective immediately.

All partition, covering, shelter, barricade, satanic interference, astral manipulation, and wall that are keeping the blessings of God from flowing into my life, let these evil powers explode to pieces now and turn to useless powders, in the mighty name of Jesus.

Every evil beast that has swallowed my blessings, I cut the belly of this demonic beast with the sword of the Holy Spirit and retrieve my blessings by fire and by force.

Accumulated blessings from unknown sources, blessings of enormous proportion locate me and answer all my needs now, in Jesus Name.

Whoever is holding my wealth and finances in their hand, let my success become too heavy to hold any longer, and wherever my finances are being held, let it become like a burning fire coal, too hot for the kingdom of darkness to hold any longer.

I will no longer drink from the cup of poverty and lack, and poverty and lack is not my portion and inheritance, neither am I any longer a beneficiary of poverty.

The womb of my destiny will conceive productivity and success financially. I declare I am a conceiver of success, of great and of mighty things, and my paths are successful paths.

Let Money in the North, South, East and West receive ears and hear my voice as I now say, Money come forth and manifest in my life. Become my servant and work for me and answer all things that pertain to my needs and wants, now, effective immediately.

Let wealth run after me and find me, even if I am hiding from wealth.

Let wealth surround me like a wealthy garment, and let my days, weeks, months and years be filled with unexpected accumulation and amount of wealth, to the glory of God the Father.

Let financial prosperity and the prosperity of favour rain upon me like the dew of mount Zion and the dew of Mount Hermon, where the Lord has commanded his blessings.

Father, in the name of the Savior Jesus, through prayer, I build barricades and barriers of incomprehensible protection of fire, and permanent walls and defences of Light around my blessings in the second heaven, or in the hands of the Angels, or wherever my blessings are located within the trajectory leading to my life.

Heavenly Father, in the name of Jesus I petition you for the finances of my household, that you would grace our financial well-being:
- In Luke 12 You say that we should consider the ravens; they neither sow nor reap, they have neither storehouse nor barn,

and yet You feed them. How much more valuable are we than the birds!
- And if God so clothes the grass of the field, which is alive today and tomorrow is thrown into the oven, how much more will You clothe us!
- Therefore, we will diligently observe the Words of this Covenant, in order that we may succeed in everything that we do. (Deut 29:9).
- Deuteronomy 28 gives the promise of blessing as we diligently observe all Your Commandments, that You will set us high above all the nations of the earth; all these blessings shall come upon us and overtake us, as we obey the LORD our God: Blessed shall we be in the city and blessed shall we be in the field.
- Blessed shall be the fruit of our womb, the fruit of our ground, and the fruit of our livestock, both the increase of our cattle and the issue of our flock. Blessed shall be our basket and our kneading bowl. Blessed shall we be when we come in, and blessed shall we be when we go out. The LORD will cause our enemies who rise against us to be defeated before us; they shall come out against us one way and flee before us seven ways.
- The LORD will command His blessing upon us in our barns, and in all that we undertake; He will bless us in the land that the LORD our God is giving us. The LORD will establish us as His Holy people, as He has sworn to us, as we keep the commandments of the LORD our God and walk in His ways.
- All the peoples of the earth shall see that we are called by the Name of the LORD, and they shall be afraid of us. The LORD will make us abound in prosperity, in the fruit of our womb, in the fruit of our livestock, and in the fruit of our ground in the land that the LORD swore to give us.

- The LORD will open for us His rich storehouse, the Heavens, to give the rain of our land in its season and to bless all our undertakings. We will lend to many nations, but we will not borrow. The LORD will make us the head, and not the tail; we shall be only at the top, and not at the bottom. According to Deut 7:20, I ask You LORD to send the hornets against those who are hidden under demonic armour and demonic coverings so that they will be exposed, in Jesus Name!

I love the LORD, because He has heard my voice and my supplications. Because He inclined His ear to me, therefore I will call on Him as long as I live. What shall I return to the LORD for all His bounty to me?
I will lift up the Cup of Salvation and call on the Name of the LORD, I will pay my vows to the LORD in the presence of all His people (Psalm 116).

Now Heavenly Father, I thank You for the countless blessings You have bestowed upon me. I am grateful for Your love, grace, and mercy that surround me each day. Thank You for the gift of life, for my family and friends, and for the opportunities You provide. Your provision and protection are beyond measure, and I am humbled by Your generosity.
Help me to always remember Your goodness and to express my gratitude in all circumstances. May I use the blessings You have given me to bless others and bring glory to Your name.
In Jesus' name I pray, Amen and Amen.

40. Prayer Against Crooked Paths

Heavenly Father, and Most High God, Your name is holy, and You are exalted in all kingdoms, realms and dimensions and spheres. It is through Your power that I was created from the dust, and it is in you that I live, move and have my being.
It is you who knows the end from the beginning because You are the first and the last. Therefore, I come to you to acknowledge my need for Your divine intervention, because of the crooked paths that were set before me.

Father, the kingdom of darkness has broken protocol, violated my rights, overstepped their bounds and has weaponized classified information against my life.
Because of this, my life has been a playground arena and battleground for demons who are destiny hunters, destiny eaters and destiny destroyers, who have also created crooked things and crooked paths in my life.

Now, because of this I cannot reach my destiny in you, nor find my way to the place where you have ordained for me to be, because I have been breached and compromised.

Holy Father, in every terrestrial realm, sub-aquatic region, cosmic world, subterranean world, and in every astral layer, plain, zone, region and kingdom where the creatures of the astral forces of darkness through psychic manipulations have interfere with the path of my destiny, and have created in my paths cracks, erodes, trenches, crooked paths, crooked places, false paths, spiritual crevices, potholes, sinkholes, manholes, drains, a breakage, illusionary paths and hallucinations, I pray that by Your dynamic power, and Your name Elohei Tzevaot you make every crooked thing and crooked path straight, and repair the paths of my life by Your eternal light of fire and love, and solidify and reinforce the ground of the path upon which I tread, and release me from within any devilish occult realm, plane and region of the psychic kingdoms of space, land and water, and destroy all verdict and jurisdiction of Hell.

Holy Spirit I also pray, let the fire of Your judgement judge these evil forces, and break the evil bands asunder by Your divine eternal fire.
As you repair all crooked and broken paths, deliver me from emotional, psychological, mental, and spiritual prisons, and open the gates and bars for me like you did for Peter in Acts 12:7, 11, 17, and for Paul in Acts 16:26.

You said in Your word in Isaiah 45:2, **"I will go before thee, and make the crooked places straight: I will break in pieces the gates of brass, and cut in sunder the bars of iron:"**
O Lord, deliver me by the verdict of the judicial blood of Jesus in whom I have redemption and the forgiveness of sins, according to the riches of His grace; [Eph 1:7, Col 1:14.] Your word says in Isaiah 40:4, **"Every valley shall be exalted, and every mountain and hill shall be made low: and the crooked shall be made straight, and the rough places plain."**

Heavenly Father, let the light of Your word shine brightly in my steps and expose the schemes of the wicked, and destroy every evil planted, all hidden traps, land mines, booby traps, every customized snare, and every organized destruction that is strategically placed in my path by psychic forces who operate at the highest velocity of Astro-metaphysical acceleration.
You said in Your word in Isaiah 42:16, **"And I will bring the blind by a way that they knew not; I will lead them in paths that they have not known: I will make darkness light before them, and crooked**

things straight. These things will I do unto them, and not forsake them."

All those who would seek to make crooked my paths in life, may their plots crumble and fall to naught before they take root. Before they rise, let them fall in disgrace and become victims of their own plots in Jesus' name.

I destroy by lightning, fire, and thunder all camouflaged land mines (booby traps) specifically set in my path.
Let every disguised counsel, plan, desire, expectation, imagination, device, plot, snare, and activity of the seven occult kingdoms against my life be exposed.

All humans who have set a broken path in my life, I forgive them, and Lord, forgive them, and every demon who is responsible for the broken paths set in my life, judge these demons seventy times seven.

All demonic council against me shall fail and all human council against me shall come upon themselves,

Thank you, Yah, for repairing the broken paths in my life by faith, for shining in my path, and for filling me with Your Holy Spirit and peace that surpasses all understanding. Proverbs 4:18, **"But the path of the just *is* as the shining light, that shineth more and more unto the perfect day."**
Thank you for Your boundless love, grace, and protection, and for the victory that you have given to me in Christ Jesus. To you be all the glory, honour, and Might, In Jesus Name Amen.

41. Prayers Against Evil Mountains

Lord, I bring before You every long-standing problem that has become a mountain in my life. I subject all these mountains under Your majesty and sovereignty and seek deliverance from all mountains so that I may go forward into my purpose and destiny that You have set for me on this earth.

Father, my spiritual life is being obstructed, and many other areas of my life are affected because of these mountains.
It is not Your will for mountains to stand in our way, but Father, there are mountains in my way, and I don't know how to deal with them.
Lord, ignite the fire of Your Word upon my heart and increase my faith so that I may walk confidently in Your ways.
Now, Father, with a humble heart, I am seeking Your hand and Spirit so that my faith may be strengthened. I desire to have mountain-moving faith and faith as powerful as a mustard seed.

For you have said, if we [Your people] have faith as a mustard seed, we will say to the mountain, 'be removed and be cast into the sea,' and it will move, and nothing will be impossible for us.
Holy Father, who will receive such faith by Your Spirit? Nevertheless, I request this great faith, so that I can please you and that Your name would be glorified upon the earth through me.
Father, in addition to faith, I request of Your Majesty a new sharp threshing instrument having teeth: that I may thresh the mountains, and beat *them* small according to Your word in Isaiah 41:15-16 where You say, **"Behold, I make you a new sharp threshing instrument, having teeth; you shall thresh the mountains, and beat** *them* **small, and shall make the hills like chaff. You shall winnow them, and the wind shall carry them away, and a tempest shall scatter**

them. And you shall rejoice in the LORD *and* shall glory in the Holy One of Israel."

Therefore, in the name of Jesus, and by the authority of the Word of God in Isaiah 41:15-16, I take up the new sharp threshing instrument having teeth; and I now thresh every mountain of doubt and unbelief.
- Mountain of Fear and Anxiety
- Mountain of Temptation and Sin
- Mountain of afflictions
- Mountain of Discouragement and Despair
- Mountain of Pride and Self-Reliance
- Mountain of mountain of lack

Mountain of [_____Name your mountains___] and every other mountain that stands in my way, and I beat *them* as dust.

According to Isaiah 41:16, **"Thou shalt fan them, and the wind shall carry them away, and the whirlwind shall scatter them: and thou shalt rejoice in the LORD, and shalt glory in the Holy One of Israel."**

Now, I command that the dust of all mountains in my life be carried away in the wind and be scattered by a tempest, In the name of Jesus of Nazareth.

At this time, I am rejoicing in the LORD and I am glorying in the Holy One of Israel.

By the power of God, I challenge every mountain that stands in the way of my marriage, my destiny, my ministry, my career, my business, my purpose, visions and dreams, and right now by the power of El-Shaddai, with faith as a mustard seed, I speak to you mountains in my life and I say, O Mountains, hear the word of the Lord to us in Mat 17:20, **"for verily I say unto you, If ye have faith as a grain of mustard seed, ye shall say unto this mountain, Remove hence to** yonder place; and it shall remove; and nothing shall be impossible unto you."

By the authority of the word of Y'ahushua HaMashiach of Nazareth in Mat 17:20 and Mark 11:23, I say unto you mountain of negative decrees and spoken words, I say unto you mountain of ancestral curses in my life, I say unto you mountain of family calamities, I say unto you mountain of lack, I say unto you mountain of financial barrenness and financial crisis, I say unto you mountain of diseases and ill health, I say unto you mountain of opposition, I say unto you mountain of stagnation, I say unto you mountain of demonic obstruction, I say unto you mountain of hardship, I say unto you mountain of guilt, and I say unto you mountain of fear and procrastination and all other mountains standing before me, hear the command of my faith through the faith of the Son of God in whom I live, move, and have my being; be removed from before me and from my life and be cast into the depths of the sea, effective immediately, in Jesus name.
Whatever I bind or loose here on the Earth will be bound or loosed in Heaven according to [Mat 16:19 and Mat 18:18], but know this, O Mountains, every command I give to you, the power and Word of God compel you, for it is written in Zechariah 4:6, **"Not by might, nor by power, but by my spirit, saith the LORD of hosts."**

According to Zechariah 4:7, I shout, Grace, grace unto it.
In the name of Y'ahushua of Nazareth, Son of the Living God, I say by faith, let every valley be exalted, and every mountain and hill be made low; and the crooked be made straight, and the rough places plain.
Let the glory of the LORD be revealed, so that all flesh can see it together, for the mouth of the LORD hath spoken it according to the Word of God in Isaiah 40:4-5, in Jesus name.

Father, I thank you for saving me and hearing my prayers, and for this I give you thanks and I give you praise in the name of thy holy Child, Jesus. Amen and Amen.

42. Prayer For Mountain-Moving Faith

Heavenly Father, I come before You with a humble heart, seeking Your hand and Spirit that my faith be strengthened. I desire to have mountain-moving faith and faith as powerful as a mustard seed.
For you said, if we [Your people] have faith as a grain of mustard seed, we will say to the mountain, 'be removed and be cast into the sea,' and it will move, and nothing will be impossible for us.

Lord, who will receive such faith by Your Spirit? Nevertheless, I request this great faith so that I can please you and that Your name would be glorified upon the earth.
It is not Your will for mountains to stand in our way, but Father, there are mountains in my way, and I don't know how to deal with them.
Lord, ignite the fire of Your word upon my heart and increase my faith so that I may walk confidently in Your ways and move mountains.
I am requesting that Your Divine Council grant me the kind of faith that can move mountains.
You've promised that nothing will be impossible for me if I believe.
My faith is very low, oh Lord; therefore, I am asking that you strengthen my faith and help me overcome doubts that may arise.
Give me also a faith unshaken by circumstances and challenges, just as you gave the 12 Apostles great faith.
Give me faith to encounter my Burning bush – Exodus 3:3
Exodus 7:20–25
Give me faith that invoke Hailstones – Exodus 9:18–24
Give me faith that I can Cross through a Sea – Exodus 14:21–23
Give me faith to turn Bitter waters to sweet waters – Exodus 15:25.
Give me faith that will cause Water to come from the rock – Exodus 17:5–8
Give me the faith that defeat Armies – Exodus 17:9–13
Give me faith that can cause rods to blossoms – Numbers 17:8

Give me faith that can divide rivers supernaturally – Joshua 3:14–17
Give me faith that can throw down walls like Jericho – Joshua 6:6–20
Give me faith that can cause the Sun and Moon to stand still – Joshua 10:12–14
Give me faith to subdue Lions – Judges 14:5–6
Give me faith to tear altars – 1 Kings 13:5
Give me faith for supernatural increase of foods– 1 Kings 17:12–17
Give me faith to raise the dead– 1 Kings 17:17–23
Give me faith to perform miracles by my mantle – 2 Kings 2:8
Give me faith to heal Waters – 2 Kings 2:20–22
Give me faith to supernaturally supply water – 2 Kings 3:16–20
Give me faith that causes Poisoned food to become harmless – 2 Kings 4:38–41
Give me faith to cure leprosy – 2 Kings 5:10–14
Give me faith to strike with judgement– 2 Kings 5:27
Give me faith that can cause the head of an Axe to float – 2 Kings 6:5–7
Give me faith that can protect me from fiery furnaces – Daniel 3:19–27
Give me faith that delivers me from lions– Daniel 6:16–23
Give me faith that turns Water into wine – John 2:1–11
Give me faith that heal the sons of noblemen – John 4:46–54
Give me faith that causes me to become unseen among mobs– Luke 4:28–30.
Give me faith to heal Demoniacs – Mark 1:23–26
Give me faith to heal the Paralytic– Matthew 9:1–8
Give me faith to heal Impotent men– John 5:1–9
Give me faith that restores the withered hand – Matthew 12:10–13.
Give me faith that heals from palsy – Matthew 8:5–13
Give me faith that quiet the Tempest– Matthew 8:23–27
Give me faith that heals Women of issue of blood – Matthew 9:20–22
Give me faith that causes Blind men to be cured – Matthew 9:27–31

Give me faith for supernatural multiplication of food – Matthew 14:15–21
Give me faith where I walk on troubled water – Matthew 14:25–33.
Give me faith for supernatural money -Matthew 17:24–27
Give me faith to heal the Deaf and dumb– Mark 7:31–37
Give me faith where my shadow heals the sick – Acts 5:15
Give me faith that will bring Special miracles by my hands – Acts 19:11–12
Give me faith that will keep me unharmed by viper's bite – Acts 28:5, in the name of Jesus I pray.

I pull down every stronghold and cast down every imagination and high thing, which exalts itself against the knowledge of God according to 2 Corinthians 10:4-5.

Clothe me with the fiery garment of faith and let my faith manifest as explosions of dynamite in the realm of the spirit.
Council of Yah, I petition you to grant my request for the spirit and gift of faith, so that I can set Your people free from the powers of Satan and the Devil.
Configure my mindset to accommodate great faith. Father, I thank you that you have allowed my prayers to come before you, and by the Blood of Jesus has already answered, in Jesus Name, Amen and Amen.

43. Fighting Against Hell To Keep Your Garment White

My God and Father, I come in Your presence today to petition Your majesty that favour be shown unto me, Your servant, and that You would beautify me with Your salvation.
Because you came to set me free, I receive a clean break and release from all yokes and burdens other than those of Jesus Christ, which are easy and light.

Holy Father, I claim Your righteousness and holiness, and request that I be reclothed in Your presence and glorious light. Today, because of the Blood of Jesus, I declare my freedom to live outside the influence of occult manipulations and control.

I hereby invoke the power and authority of the fire of the garment of the Most High God, and I reclaim my garment of zeal (Isaiah 59:17).
I reclaim my **Garment of Glory (Rev** 4:9).
I reclaim my **Garment of Thanksgiving (Neh 12:27).**
I reclaim my **Garment of Thanks (Rev 4:9),**
I reclaim my **Garment of Praises (2 Ch 29:30)**
I reclaim my **Garment of Salvation** (Isaiah 61:10).
I reclaim my **Garment of Righteousness.**
I reclaim my **Garment of the Songs of Combat (Psalm 68:25).**
I reclaim my **Garment of Consolation.**
I reclaim my **Garment of Sanctification.**
I reclaim my **Garment of Healing.**
I reclaim my **Garment of authority,**
I reclaim my **Garment of Honour** (Rev 4:9),
I reclaim my **Garment of Adoration & Majesty,**
I reclaim my **Garment of Songs of Purity**
I reclaim my **Garment of Songs of Joy,** (Psalms 107:22).

I call upon the fire that burnt in the sacred heart of the Messiah Y'ahushua, and I come before Your altar, Lord God of Israel, and the council of Your holiness, that this day you would rest upon me the government of Your kingdom, for behold I come in the volume of Your Book.
I petition Your Divine Council today that you:
Activate my anointing for great faith.
Activate my anointing for righteousness.
Activate my anointing to serve God.
Activate my anointing for in-depth prayer.
Activate my anointing for prophetic worship.
Activate my anointing for prophetic praise.
Activate my anointing for Apostolic Ministry.
Activate my anointing for healing. Activate my anointing for deliverance.
Activate my anointing for longevity. Activate my anointing to seek Your face and find You.
Activate my anointing to enter Your divine courts.
Let there be a revival of Your tremendous and spectacular power upon my life and activate me and Your church for the end-time revival of Your Glory, O Majestic Elohei, HaKadosh.
Activate my anointing for household revival.
Activate my anointing for territorial revival.
Activate my anointing for national revival.
Activate my anointing for regional revival.
Activate my anointing for international revival.
Activate my anointing for global revival.
I declare that victory is always my potion, and I am clothed with the anointing of victory over the enemies.
I am called a tree of righteousness and the planting of the LORD, Isaiah 61:3.

I am a minister and vessel of His presence, for I stand in the presence of the Lord my Saviour, and I am receiving joy, for it is written in Psalms 16:11: **"In thy presence is fullness of joy; at thy right hand there are pleasures for evermore."**
Psalms 91:1, **"I am dwelling in the secret place of the Most High and I am abiding under the shadow of the Almighty."**

By the activation of my anointing and garments, I now come against and revolt against all powers of Satan and the Devil that are programmed to fight against the maintenance of my garment and my success to sustain the character of holiness, which is the fabric of my celestial garments.

Heavenly Father, I also pray that anything or any power from the kingdoms of Hell that is dirtying or would seek to dirty, stain, or mark my garment, that you now send Your fire, thunder, and lightning to destroy and burn to ashes all satanic contamination and materials deposited in any part of my body, mind, soul, and character, things that are contaminations to my white garment, in the Name of Jesus!

Enemies of my holy garments, I renounce you and your secret snares today, and banish all occult strategies conjured from the book of Technique Tactic, the Book of Grimoires, and the Book of the Dead against me. I cancel by the Blood of Jesus Christ all handwritings and ordinances written against me, condemning me in the tribunal of the night. I command thunders and lightnings of God to strike, uproot, and destroy all covenant tokens made on my behalf by members of the occult.

Every witchcraft item and incantation buried and programmed to fight against me, let the fire of the altar of prayer in Heaven locate these evil items wherever they may be buried and consume them to ashes, in the name of Jesus Christ.

In Jesus Almighty Name, I command the thunder and lightning of God to break into pieces any evil stone that is set in my heart and remove from my heart the stony and hard heart demons.
I decree that I am an individual single person; I am not a twin or triplet, and therefore I disown any form of duplicate representing me in the astral kingdoms or occult worlds.

I cut myself loose from any representation and representative who negotiates and speaks for me in the satanic world for my destruction.

I call upon the God of Heaven and Earth and smash to powder any statue of me in the second heaven, or in any occult zone, occult sphere, occult realm, occult dimension, occult center, occult region.

Every image of me made of cloth, stone, metal, wood, let the fire of El-Eliyahu, the God of Elijah, destroy these false occult images of me, and destroy, cancel, and nullify what they represent.

I banish the demons behind these occult representations of me and destroy anything in the occult kingdom that represents shame, disgrace, and obstruction of my destiny, productivity, and materialization of my wealth and prosperity.

I reverse all satanic arrows of failure that always show up at the edge of my success and breakthrough, and let all curses be changed into blessings, in Jesus' Name,

I wage combats of offensive and defensive confrontations against witchcraft and occult powers of the kingdom of darkness, and I pray and command the disintegration and annihilation of every wicked plan and evil agenda programmed against my white garments and my life in the psychic layers, through psychic commands by incantations of witchcraft, voodoo, and magic spells. May the ground you evil workers tread upon become shaky, unstable, and cave in, and may you be swallowed by openings in the earth. Let all your schemes collapse, your intents be turned to foolishness, in Jesus' precious name.

Psalms 21:11 says, **"For they intended evil against thee: they imagined a mischievous device, which they were not able to perform."**

Father, destroy the powers of the Occult that are continually surrounding me, seeking to corrupt my garments. With defences of lightning, with raging whirlwinds of terrifying fire and with wind barriers of disastrous proportions, protect my life, home and family from the Mephistophelian and esoteric occult forces of Hell.

Through travailing prayer, I build barricades and barriers of incomprehensible resistance, and permanent walls and defences of Light and Fire around my garments, life, home, and family.

For this, I give you thanks and praise and thank you for what you have done today in the name of Jesus of Nazareth. Amen.

44. Restoration Of God's Goodness In Your Life

Father in heaven, you created the heavens and the Earth and all that dwell in them.
You are the God of restoration in all things. You said in Exodus 33:19, **"And he said, I will make all my goodness pass before thee, and I will proclaim the name of the LORD before thee; and will be gracious to whom I will be gracious, and will shew mercy on whom I will shew mercy."**
I bring my petitions before the 7 Altars of Heaven, and I am requesting that my prayers be mixed with the fiery coals and incense from the hands of the 24 Elders and Seraphim this day, in Jesus name.
I request of Your council that you send the seven lamps that burn before the Throne of the Almighty to my aid, and restore Your promises unto me, as you set the seven colours in the rainbow to remember Your covenant.

Father, I make requests for the restoration of all things in my life, that which is spiritual and material, and that which is of the celestial and terrestrial realms. Father God, you said in Your word in Isaiah 40:2, **"Speak comfortably to Jerusalem, and cry unto her that her warfare is accomplished, that her iniquity is pardoned; for she has received of the LORD'S hand double for all her sins."**
You also said in Your word in Isaiah 61:7, **"For your shame you will have double."**

At this point, I am requesting and claiming this double—double grace, double anointing, double victory, double power, double strength, and double blessings of all categories, in the name of Y'ahushua HaMashiach.
Abba Father Yah, it is written in Your word, Lord God, in Isaiah 54:11, **"O thou afflicted, tossed with tempest, and not comforted,**

behold, I will lay thy stones with fair colours, and lay thy foundations with sapphires."

Vs.12, **"And I will make thy windows of agates, and thy gates of carbuncles, and all thy borders of pleasant stones."**

O God of Zion, arise by Your Divine Council and restore unto me my stones that are of fair colours, and restore my foundations of sapphires, my windows of agates, my gates of carbuncles, and all my borders of pleasant stones.

Heavenly Father, I also request of Your holy council that you repair and restore my wholeness and wellness and give unto me beauty for ashes, the oil of joy for mourning, the garment of praise for the spirit of heaviness; that I might be called trees of righteousness, the planting of the LORD, that you might be glorified, according to Isaiah 61:3.

For my shame, give me double; and for confusion, let me rejoice in my portion: therefore, in my land, I shall possess the double: everlasting joy shall be unto me, according to Isaiah 61:7.

By the power of Jesus of Nazareth, I speak to every realm, kingdom, sphere, and dimension and I say, O heavens and the Earth, and all that dwell therein, all principalities, powers, fallen Angels, gods, demi-gods, sirens, and demons, stars, moon, and Sun, hear the word of the Lord and hear my voice and command, for I stand in the presence of the Most High God, in the presence of the holy angels, and in the presence of the Lamb [Rev 14:10].

I say to all of you, restore to me all the years that the locust, the cankerworm, and the caterpillar, and the palmerworm have eaten, effective immediately [Joel 2:25-26], and restore everything that my ancestors did not attain.

I speak into the past of my ancestral lineage, and I say by the authority of Jesus my King, all blessings, graces, family wealth, family virtue, influence, riches, etc., that were supposed to come unto me and did not, come forth now. I invoke a Divine Judicial Order from the Courts of the Almighty God who is the Grand Judge of the Heavens and the Earth, and I say, Heavens and Earth and all universes, restore to me all good and pleasant things in my family bloodline that were meant for me to inherit and did not. Come forth unto me now by fire and be restored into my life as heir to these things, effective immediately.

Let health be restored to me and my household now, for it is written in Jeremiah 30:17 – **"For I will restore health unto thee, and I will heal thee of thy wounds, saith the LORD;"**
Let the joy of salvation be restored to me and my household now, for it is written in Psalms 51:12 - Restore unto me the joy of thy salvation; and uphold me with thy free spirit.

Let double and everlasting joy be restored to me and my household now, for it is written in Isaiah 61:7 - For your shame ye shall have double; and for confusion they shall rejoice in their portion: therefore, in their land they shall possess the double: everlasting joy shall be unto them. May the presence of the Lord bring times of refreshing upon me and my household seven times, effective immediately, for Acts 3:19-21 states, **"Repent ye therefore, and be converted, that your sins may be blotted out, when the times of refreshing shall come from the presence of the Lord;"**

I stand in the presence of the Most High God. I call for the restoration of my life's tendencies, my prophetic grace, my visions for the future, my creativity, my marriage, my holy lifestyle, my godly character, my memory, my strength, my wholeness, and my glory, past, present, and future.

Restore unto me the code to access dimensions of glory that come with Your divine favours. Restore in my life the symphonies and degrees of celestial music that usher in a dimension of fiery glory for refurbishment, restoration, and restitution.

Job 14:8-9, "**Though the root thereof wax old in the earth, and the stock thereof die in the ground; Yet through the scent of water, it will bud and bring forth boughs like a plant**".
Restore to my life the scent of the living waters and the watercourses. Let there be buds of progress, buds of increase in good things, buds of advancement in idea strategies for a better future, buds of wisdom and spirituality etc.

45. To Be Transformed By The Amber Fire Of His Secret Place

O Great God who burns with the light of eternity and is the glorious fire that is lit in every heart, whose Spirit is holy, incline Your ears and hear me.

You sit between the cherubim, and it is Your breath that kindles the coals before you. You hear the prayers of those who trust in Your sovereignty, for You are clothed with the fire of righteousness, beauty, holiness, and justice. Stir Your atmosphere and release the light of Your eternal Flame in my mind for illumination, in my heart for reformation, and in my soul for sanctification.

Great Elohei, summon my spirit to the 10th Heaven, where Your fire burns with extensive brightness. Penetrate my being with the electric love of Your beauty and let the heat of Your presence melt the evil from my heart and soul.
Make everything in my soul and spirit alive to bow to Your majesty and arouse my spirit to stay in Your presence, where the light and the fire are one.

Cause me to behold Your glory until I am formed in the belly of Your majesty and penetrate the most secret place of my heart and recondition the perspective of my love for you.
Holy Father in the highest Heaven, cause me to stay in Your fire until I am consumed, so that I can shine forth the radiance of Your glory.
Turn me into a rod of power, O God, and make me know wisdom in my innermost being.
Lord, I ask that you give me another dose of Your glory, as I bathe in the splendour of Your divine grandeur.

Bring me into Your secret place, and cause me to behold Your life and truth, and to look upon the beauty of the Lord of hosts.

Make me become acquainted with Your glory and fire, and give me a divine encounter with the ministry of the:

Keepers of the Throne,
Keepers of the Realms,
Keepers of the Book of Life
Carriers of the Glory,
Keepers of the Earth,
Chariots of God,
Keepers of the Eternal Flame,
Keepers of the Oil Vials,
Keepers of the Archives,
Keepers of the Gates,
Keepers of the Garments,
Keepers of the Temple,
Keepers of the Courts (outer, inner),
Keepers of Paradise,

Flow into my heart the crystal-clear water from the river of Your heart and transform me into Your image from glory to glory. I request and petition, O Great King, that you wrap me with the rainbow of Your divinity, and place upon me the garment of the fire of Amber.

Let the lightning of Your presence carve and inscribe the law of Your love, peace, mercy, and compassion in my heart, alongside the laws of obedience and undefiled worship unto you.

Remove all things from my heart that look like iniquity, and purify me by Your sanctification.

O light of Glory, translate me into realms of the symphony of Your light, mixed with fire and water, and may I walk upon Your crystal floor of sapphire, for the ground where You are is holy ground.

May I become a minister of Your inner sanctum, so that the fire of this uppermost part of the sanctuary can have its divine way in me, as I subject my life as a stone, as elements of the creation of Your hands.

Let the magnificent heat and the pressure of Your love and presence transform me into a diamond, so that you can mirror the beauty of Your Holy Spirit in my life, heart, mind, and soul.
Unite my soul, body, spirit, heart, and mind with Your Holy Spirit, and keep me within the pillars of fire that burn with the most vehement and beautiful flames, radiating Your splendour and love.

May I come in unity with Your holy Son Jesus and walk with Your Holy Spirit of comfort, in the name of Jesus of Nazareth.
Cause my eyes to behold the mysteries of the realms and channels of Your glorious grace, joy, and goodness, I pray.
Open my ears to hear the symphony of Your heart, and the orchestra of the songs of the Angels of Fire. Knit me to that presence, where my bones are filled with the essence and substance of worship.

Give me grace and favour to glorify you upon the Earth, and vibrate every molecule in my body, every substance of my soul and the essence of my spirit to worship you, serve you and bear fruit, in Jesus" name. For this I give you praise and glory, for thine is the kingdom, the power and the glory for ever and ever, Amen and Amen.

46. Prayer Against Demonic Communication And Monitoring Systems Against Your Life

In the name of the Lord of hosts, I pray by the essence of the divine fire of amber, which burns around the Throne of Yah, that every power of darkness that serves as a monitoring device against my life may fire destroy these powers set in secret places.

By the power of the Holy Spirit, by lightning, thunder, and fire of Jesus Christ of Nazareth, I pray against and destroy all monitoring systems and devices from the land, sea, and air set at my home, on my job, in my neighbourhood, upon my neighbours' properties, upon my friends and family members, on street lamps, street poles, on towers and antennas, and between the regions of the seven seas: the Arctic, North Atlantic, South Atlantic, North Pacific, South Pacific, Indian, and Southern seas, to monitor my life daily.
I pray against and destroy any familiar birds, familiar cats, insects.

I pray against every monitoring device set between boundaries and boundaries within the marine world, the land and air, and every spider web in my home that is used as communication antennas, to transmit signals back and forth between my home and the kingdom of darkness, any astral television, celestial mirror, etheric gemstone, Akashic black stone, astral gemstone, animus third eye, psychic camera or divining mirror, astral telescopes, magnifying glass, astral binocular etc.

I also pray against all wireless communication systems and devices such as the Obelisks, the Eiffel Tower, the Pyramids, gigantic stone or metal statues, or any other megalithic monument within the five continents, etc., that are being used to monitor my life, my going outs and my coming ins, and every secret information about my life that is

of military or political value in the kingdom of Satan and the Devil; may the electrical fire of God destroy all witchcraft and demonic telecommunication lines, active signals, networks, transmissions, messages, and calls, which operate at 12 Midday and 12 Midnight, or any other timeline. Let the fire from Jesus Christ through the Holy Spirit melt the lens of these demonic scopes and optical views and destroy the channel of sight of all these witchcraft, satanic, and diabolic devices.
Evil powers working with the infrastructure of the communication system of darkness, be struck with blindness, deafness, and be crippled by God's judgement and be paralyzed now, In Jesus name.

By the power of the Holy Spirit, by lightning, thunder, and fire of Jesus Christ of Nazareth, I separate the waters from the waters, and I block and render all powerless, incapable, and ineffective all demonic that is transmitting information about my life to the "Witches' Central Tower of Communication." Let communication between the Witches' Central Tower of Communication and the great communication system in the Pandemonium kingdom be destroyed with permanent effect.

47. PRAYER AGAINST THE CURSE OF ABORTION

Heavenly Father, my Lord and my God, I come to you broken-hearted and repentant, filled with regrets for I am ashamed of my actions of abortion, and I am seeking that you cleanse me; wash away the stain of this sin of abortion and deliver me from the hand of Moloch and other bloodthirsty demons.

It is written in Hebrews 4:16, **"Let us therefore come boldly unto the throne of grace, that we may obtain mercy, and find grace to help in time of need"**.
Now I come boldly to Your throne of mercy, seeking Your royal pardon for my sin of abortion.

Your word has condemned it where you said, Thou shalt not kill. You also say in Genesis 9:6, **"Whoso sheddeth man's blood, by man shall his blood be shed: for in the image of God made he man."** Therefore, by Your word my actions are condemned, but it is also written in Ephesians 1:7, **"In whom we have redemption through his blood, the forgiveness of sins, according to the riches of his grace;"**

I repent for my sin, transgressions, and the iniquities of my bloodline that may have opened a door for the spirit of abortion in my life. Every sin of my forefathers that the enemy would be using as a legal right to build legal cases against me, and to sabotage and ruin my destiny through the sins and guilt of shedding innocent blood, I petition by the blood of the Lamb for the intervention of Your judicial blood and the verdict of the holy altar and the mercy seat.
My God, it is said in Nehemiah 9:17, **"But You are a God ready to pardon, gracious and merciful, slow to anger, and of great kindness, and did not forsake them."**

It is also written in Joel 2:13, **"for he is gracious and merciful, slow to anger, and of great kindness, and repenteth him of the evil"**.

So, through Your blood I seek forgiveness, cleansing, deliverance, healing, for it is written in 1 John 1:9. **"If we confess our sins, he is faithful and just to forgive us *our* sins, and to cleanse us from all unrighteousness."**
Out of panic, fear, desperation, and my selfishness, I made the choice to kill an unborn child.

I confess that I could not see how I would live with the shame of having a child out of wedlock, let alone raise a child by myself or with shame. The choice to terminate has now ruined my life as well. But it is written in Psalms 145:8, **"The LORD *is* gracious, and full of compassion; slow to anger, and of great mercy."**
Psalms 51:1, "Have mercy upon me, O God, according to Your lovingkindness; according to the greatness of Your compassion, blot out my transgressions.
Psalms 51:2 **Wash me thoroughly from my iniquity, and cleanse me from my sin.**
Psalms 51:3 **For I acknowledge my transgressions, and my sin is ever before me.**
Psalms 51:4 **Against You, You only, have I sinned, and done evil in Your sight, that You might be justified when You speak and be in the right when You judge.**
Psalms 51:5 **Behold, I was brought forth in iniquity, and in sin did my mother conceive me.**
Psalms 51:6 **Behold, You desire truth in the inward parts; and in the hidden part You shall make me to know wisdom.**
Psalms 51:7 **Purge me with hyssop, and I shall be clean; wash me, and I shall be whiter than snow.**
Psalms 51:8 **Make me to hear joy and gladness that the bones which You have broken may rejoice.**

Psalms 51:9 **Hide Your face from my sins and blot out all my iniquities.**
Psalms 51:10 **Create in me a clean heart, O God, and renew a steadfast spirit within me.**
Psalms 51:11 **Cast me not away from Your presence and take not Your Holy Spirit from me.**
Psalms 51:12 **Restore to me the joy of Your salvation, and let Your free spirit uphold me.**
Psalms 51:13 **Then I will teach transgressors Your ways, and sinners shall turn back to You.**
Psalms 51:14 **Deliver me from the guilt of shedding blood, O God, O God of my salvation, then my tongue shall sing aloud of Your righteousness.**
Psalms 51:15 **O LORD, open my lips, and my mouth shall declare Your praise.**

In the Name of Y'ahushua HaMashiach of Nazareth, and by the jurisdiction of the sacrificial blood of the Lamb of God, I renounce, denounce, revoke, and withdraw any secret sworn oaths that I made with the spirit of death and murder, and I call for a liquidation, dissolvement, nullification, and destruction of any friendship, embargo, contract, alliance, affiliation, connection, link, communication, covenant, and partnership that I have made with Moloch, Hades, and the evil kingdom of blood and death, and I renounce and revoke all allegiance that I have pledged to the demons of blood sacrifices.

I pray against every evil altar that was built in the astral planes through my abortion. I withdraw myself from the spirit of the Ammonites, and loose myself from the planet Saturn, from the sun god and the demon god of time.

Wherever I have placed my womb upon spiritual altars, and have sacrificed my reproductive system to the demon god Moloch, or any other demon god of blood sacrifice, murder, and death, and wherever my womb is locked up, shut up, and ambushed within the terrestrial realm, sub-aquatic region, astral layer, occult plain, zone, region, or kingdom, or is held in a coffin, upon an altar, or in a cemetery, or is hanging in the neck of any demon, or is in the hands of any demon, I retrieve, reclaim, and recover by fire all components of my reproductive system, and the fertility and blessedness of my womb, for it is written in 1Sa 30:8, "**...Shall I go after this troop? Shall I overtake them?**" And He answered him, "**Go! For you shall surely overtake and will without fail recover all.**"

Heavenly Father, by the fire of the Blood upon Your altar and mercy seat, let the jurisdiction and legal ground, doorways and roots of death, darkness, blind witchcraft, and curses in my life be renounced and revoked and their power broken off me, and that you remove any mark of death that was imprinted upon my womb, and remove any tombstone that was placed in my womb.

All demons who came into my body and soul through abortion, be banished from my life! Get out of my body and leave me now! Effective immediately! In the name of the LORD God of hosts, creator of the heavens and the earth.

Heavenly Father, by the power of the Throne of the Lamb of God, by the authority of his scepter of the Lamb of God, by the name of the King of Kings and Lord of lords, I request from Heaven that I be delivered in all realms of Hell from the grip, ordinances, and law of the spirit of Molech, spirits of the Ammonites, spirit of death, destruction, hatred of children, miscarriage, guilt, murder, condemnation, withdrawal, trauma, stress, insomnia, regrets, shame, and all connected spirits, be banished from my life right now.

Let all the demons behind miscarriage, murder, premature termination of fetus, works with adultery, death, destruction, and hatred of children, seduction, treachery, rebellion, betrayal, sedition, vanity, self-promotion, self-exaltation, self-destruction, abuse, offense, criticism, mistreatment, cursing, torment, exploitation, perversion, hurt; sexual abuse (rape, incest, molestation); mental abuse (mind control, domination); physical abuse (beaten, bruised, cruelty) be cast out and banished from my life, and all other demons connected to Abortion; effective immediately, in the name of Jesus of Nazareth and by the verdict of the judicial blood of the Lamb of Yah.

I pray, Father, that you repair and restore my ability to do again the good works in Your kingdom and give unto me beauty for ashes, the oil of joy for mourning, the garment of praise for the spirit of heaviness; that I might be called trees of righteousness, the planting of the LORD, that you might be glorified, according to Isaiah 61:3.

For my shame, *give me* double; and *for* confusion, let me rejoice in my portion: therefore, in my land, I shall possess the double: everlasting joy shall be unto me, according to Isaiah 61:7.

For Men Who Participated

I come to you and confess that I did not rise to defend life and protect the baby and seed that came from my loins. I did not fulfill my role and responsibility as a father that you bestowed upon me but have walked in the imagination and mischief of my heart to murder innocent blood. **"Against thee, thee only, have I sinned, and done this evil in thy sight,"** [Psalms 51:4]

Your word, 1 John 1:9, tells me that if I confess my sins, you will forgive, and that healing follows forgiveness.

Father, I confess my sin in my participation in abortion and ask for Your forgiveness. Take this shame from me and remove my reproach.

Wherever I am spiritually locked up, shut up, ambushed within any of the occult realms of Hell, let me be delivered from the hands of demons.
For my shame, give me double; and for confusion, let me rejoice in my portion: therefore, in my land, I shall possess the double: everlasting joy shall be unto me, according to Isaiah 61:7.

These I pray in the mighty name of Jesus Christ of Nazareth.
I petition by the blood of the Lamb that you rebuild the old, wasted places of my life, that which the kingdom of darkness has devastated, and raise up the foundations of many generations.
Repair the broken path that was made in every area of my life, restore the paths to dwell in, and by this divine process, make me a repairer of the breach and a restorer of paths to dwell in.

48. Prayer Against The Spirit Of Household Destruction

Heavenly Father, King of the ages, Omnipotent Yah who sits between the Cherubim, hallowed be Your name in all kingdoms of the heavens and the earth. Heavenly Father, indeed, You are the Most High God; Your name is holy and exalted in all kingdoms, realms, dimensions, and spheres.

O Lord my God, I come to You in the name of Jesus Christ, my Savior and Protector, in humility and trust, seeking Your sovereignty and divine protection over my household against every psychic force operating in the Order of Terrestrial and Astral Hierarchy.

Holy Father, I petition You to surround my household with the Angels of Your divine presence, and set guard over, around, and under my home, and let Your chariots of mounting angels draw their swords to stand guard against the Mephistophelian forces of the astral planes that threaten my household.

Defend my household from the 'Avatars' and 'Living Grand Masters,' who operate by the 'Inner Esoteric' framework and the Hierarchy of the powers of darkness, within the Astral and Terrestrial dimension.

Bring judgement upon the 400,000 categories of psychic strongholds and entities, set in astral motion against my household. Judge the entities of the 'Inner Esoteric' framework and the Hierarchy of the powers of the Astral and Terrestrial dimension.

You have given me authority to fight against the powers of darkness and prevail, and have anointed me with the fire to disarm the powers of darkness.

Today, in Your holy name, I declare war against household destruction in the name of the Lord.

I call upon the Pillar of Fire by night and the Pillar of Cloud by day, to divide between the satanic operations of the nighttime and the satanic operations of the daytime. Let my household be covered by the rays of Your lightning and fire, O Adonai Tzevaot, the Lord God of hosts.

Every midnight terror, or arrows of the midday gate of the sun, pestilence that walks in darkness and destruction at noon that is set for my household, I call destruction upon these evil forces. Let the forces of the twilight Zone and the Gates of the Dawn who falsify my household blessings and success and increase be banished by the fire of God's holy altar.
Let my household be protected by lightning and fire, by the verdict of the council of the Almighty God, against every mighty vicious spirit being from the third psychic realm of the air.

Let the terror and the dregs of the cup of the fury of Almighty God terrorize all evil guardians of the flame, who would try to launch satanic assaults against my household using various schemes and strategies from the Book of Technique, tactic, Grimoire, and any other Satanic Script containing deadly formulas for destruction.

In the name of Jesus of Nazareth, I call destructive terror and degradation upon all evil forces of combined elements of astral spirits, sustaining a one thousand- and ninety-five-days cycle attack against my household.
In the mighty name of the Messiah Jesus, Son of God, I place every witchcraft operation in my life under the fiery judgement of God written in Deut 18:10-12.

It is written in Psalms 60:12, **"Through God I shall do valiantly: for he it is that shall tread down our enemies."**

Every satanic assault that is launched against my household from any coven, occult zone, region, center, let these be neutralized, as I apply the force of prayer against them.

In the name of Jesus, I call forth an angelic encampment around my household with flames of lightning, and let every evil structure, demonic fortress, witchcraft monument, and cage explode to pieces. Let there be light in my home, and let darkness and its associates be dispelled now, in Jesus" name. For it is written in Psalms 144:6, **"Cast forth lightning, and scatter them: shoot out thine arrows, and destroy them."**

Surround my household, O Lord, with Your mighty warring angels, Your protecting angels, Your mounting angels, Your linking angels, Your ministering angels, and Your angels of wind and fire, and set Your chariots of divine flames round about every member of my household.

Any human or spirit agent of darkness who attempts to infiltrate the peace and safety of my household, let them be electrocuted by the lightning that emanates from Your face. Cover every door and window with the fire of the Holy Spirit, sealing them against any spiritual intrusion, demonic invasion, and nocturnal contaminations. It is written in 2Sa 22:15, **"And he sent out arrows, and scattered them; lightning, and discomfited them."**

Your Word says that no weapon formed against me shall prosper, and I claim that promise over my household.

Therefore, I rebuke any spirits of destruction, chaos, calamity, or harm and disaster that seek to enter my household. By the authority given to me through Jesus Christ, I command every evil force to leave this place immediately and to never return.

It is written in Psalms 71:13, **"Let them be confounded and consumed that are adversaries to my soul; let them be covered with reproach and dishonour that seek my hurt."**
By the authority of my salvation in Jesus Christ, I pray, all evil powers seeking to swallow up my house in chaos, let them swallow themselves instead.
Gates of good opportunities that were shut to my household swing open now, in Jesus name.
Every turbulence in the air that is programmed to fight against the blessings of my household for cycles of 264 days, be neutralized now in Jesus name.

Traps and snares set for my household by ambushment, using tactical procedures by the serpents and scorpions, are smashed to powder and nothingness, in Jesus' name. It is written in Psalm 27:2, **"When the wicked, even mine enemies and my foes, came upon me to eat up my flesh, they stumbled and fell."**

I pray for wisdom to make wise decisions in maintaining and securing my household, and I pray, Lord Jesus, that You strengthen its foundations, both physical and spiritual.
I pray for discernment to recognize any subtle attacks and wisdom to take preventive measures. Fill our hearts with Your love and peace, that we may dwell securely in Your presence.
Father, thank you for listening to me and delivering my household from evil and setting us free, so that we can glorify you in all wisdom. Thank you, Father, for Your protection and faithfulness.

I pray these prayers in no other name but the name of Y'ahushua HaMashiach, for thine is the kingdom, the power, and the glory forever. Amen and Amen.

49. Haunted House/Paranormal Activities [Prayer Against Witchcraft Attack & Demonic Invasion In Your Home]

Heavenly Father, Your word says to resist the Devil, and he will flee from us, so here I am. I plead for Your divine assistance in this matter in order to rid my home of all spiritual intruders and invaders.

Protect my home and destroy all diabolical strategies and satanic traps from the book "Technique Tactics" that are used against me and my family.
Protect us from the lowest to the highest level of diabolical assaults projecting from the Book of Grimoire and destroy every Satanic formula for death and destruction that is sent against me and my family.

In the name of Jesus Christ, my Savior and Protector, I am requesting an activation of Your sovereignty and divine authority upon me now for divine warfare and the power to drive out demons from my home.

Whatever evil power that has subjected my home to demonic intruders and invaders who are haunting my home with paranormal activities of unusual scents, movement of objects, feelings of being touched, feelings of cobwebs in my face or body, strange emotions, light paranormal, strange sounds, apparitions, severe nightmares, physical assault, sudden wakes from sleep, mysterious disappearance of things, unexplainable prints, unexplained temperature changes, feelings of being watched, feelings of someone standing close to me, sudden change in family and animal behavior, auditory hallucinations, visual hallucinations, olfactory hallucinations, gustatory hallucinations, tactile hallucinations, algetic hallucinations, general somatic hallucinations, and strange ambiances of hearing voices of people quarreling, laughing, speaking, whispering, or someone calling my name, right now, by the power of El-Shaddai, I bind and disarm every combined element of psychic and esoteric operation, and I banish all these evil spirits and paranormal activities taking place in this home.

Every cycle of nocturnal and diurnal demonic invasion and intrusion, every witchcraft presence that is attracting pests to my house, and any occult incantation that has summoned the host of the kingdom Animalia in order to enchant and weaponize ants, grasshoppers, beetles, mosquitoes, cockroaches, flies, spiders, termites, bugs, crickets, silverfish, centipedes, millipedes, earwigs, mites, ticks, fleas, sandflies, beetles, moths, slugs, snails, weevils, worms, rats, and even mice as familiar mercenaries to destroy my home, may they be destroyed by fire and be roasted to ashes. Let all invaders, intruders, and unwanted entities be blocked, stopped, and neutralized by the power of Jesus and get out of my home now.

I command all evil operations and activities in this house to come to an abrupt halt and be banished now, in Jesus' name.
I pull down every communication tower of darkness; I block all signals and distort every piece of information that is passing through this place to and from the Kingdom of Satan.

I pray against the games of thrones, powers, principalities, rulers, and all powers of darkness invading, intruding, lodging, violating, harassing, and tormenting my home through the verdict and satanic devices such as the Astro Omn-idictator, the Celestial Mirrors, Astral Gemstones, the Etheric Gemstones, the Animus Third Eye, the Psychic Cameras, and the Astral Televisions through which satanic battles are waged against my home. I overrule, overturn, and overthrow Your juridical rights to be here, in Jesus' name.

I ambush all Satanic cults that are operating in this place, and every Satanic cult that seeks to enter this place by land, sea, or air shall be ambushed by the Angels of the Lord.

All you evil powers subjecting my home to psychic manipulations by the astral forces of the Causal Plane, the Etheric sphere, the eso-terrestrial kingdom of demi-gods, or subjecting my home to the manipulation and traps set by the Yandavas, the Devas and Devatas [male and female "Guardian Spirits from the first kingdom of air], and also all you evil powers placing my home under the manipulation of the Earth masters, the supreme elementals - the Gomes, or the entities from the marine kingdoms, I block and stop your communication, channel, signal, frequency, and access to my home. I jam your communication channels and satanic transmissions and interrupt them by the fire of the Holy Spirit of Jesus.

In the Name of Jesus of Nazareth, by flames of lightning and thunder, I bind with chains of fire and fetters of hot iron, heated by the fire of the Holy Spirit of Jesus every dragon and serpent circling and sniffing around my home. All you flying serpents fall to the ground in heavy chains and be tormented by the unbearable terror of God Almighty.

I take my home by force, and by the force of the power of Jesus of Nazareth, I banish from my home all subterranean entities, shadow hunters, shadow creepers, black shadows, astral meta-physical projecting spirits, dwarfs and miniature demons, Monera demons, Protista demons, Fungi demons, Plantae demons, Animalia demons, demonic insects, crawlers, wrigglers, spectral spirits, hybrid and crossbred demons, demonic reptiles, amphibians, genies, flying creatures, forest spirits, nature and elemental spirits, fresh and saltwater demons, sirens, nymphs and mermaids, who are hovering over my roof, crawling from the underground, surrounding my dwelling place, and occupying my home.

I, through Jesus of Nazareth, tear down every demonic stronghold established in my home, and I destroy all legal grounds, astral rights, and demonic access established in my home because of ethereal bridges due to current or past sins, iniquities, abominations, past or present use of the Ouija board, witchcraft, necromancy, occultic alphabets, white witchcraft paraphernalia, occult arrangement of letters, or through a past ritual, conjuring of spirits, a witchcraft prayer, evil chant, demonic invocation, worship of false gods and demons, drawing of magic circles, veneration of relics, conjured curses, erected shrines, satanic worship, through sigils and esoteric symbols, or through the burying of human corpses or remains on this land, through the planting of witchcraft items in the ground of this land, or by any subtle incantation in the four corners of this compound, or through any past evil which took place in this house or upon this land such as murder, homicide, suicide, genocide, torture, slavery, unlawful imprisonment, rape, practice of divination, or horrible and terrifying death.

By the power of the Holy Spirit, in the name of Jesus of Nazareth, and by the three witnesses on earth: the water, the blood, and the Spirit, I banish by fire all these evil entities and doorways established in my home, every ghost of the dead, poltergeist, and all other menacing and malevolent spirits.

I barricade my home with reinforced barriers of incomprehensible electric fire and permanent walls of enforced and adamant resistance and defences of lightning.
It is written in Psalms 18:13, **"The LORD also thundered in the heavens, and the Highest gave his voice; hail stones and coals of fire."**

Let hailstones, coals of fire, lightning, and thunderclaps come upon all evil spirits in my home, and let there be an explosion and detonation in every place where you evil spirits are lodging in this home.

By the power of the Holy Spirit of Jesus, I destroy these open channels and doorways, every loophole, and freeway portal that have been open into my home, giving access to unclean spirits, making my home vulnerable and open to all manner of demonic influence and manipulation.

In the Name of Jesus of Nazareth, by flames of lightning and thunder, with chains of fire and fetters of hot iron heated by the fire of the Holy Spirit of Jesus, I bind and disarm every one of you evil spirits that are haunting me, and every combined element of psychic and esoteric powers and astral poisons, I banish you evil spirits and paranormal activities into places of great torment and destruction, and I render you powerless, defenceless, ineffective and useless.

Hence, by the authority of Jesus Christ of Nazareth and the power of the Holy Spirit, I render useless, powerless, and ineffective any incantation and psychic commands within the psychic layers against my home, and hereby render all demonic and witchcraft access and jurisdiction to my home broken with immediate effect, in the mighty name of Jesus of Nazareth.

Home Submerged Under Spiritual Water

Wherever and by whatever aquatic power my home is submerged underwater spiritually, or placed in a watery trench, or caught in the tides of spiritual rip currents, or covered with enchanted seaweeds, demonic sargassum, or any other form of algae by witchcraft, and wherever my home is subjected to water demonic manipulations, or is ambushed by any of the five occult zones of the marine kingdom:

the zone Lumani, Banni, Lemuria, Gamma, and the occult realm of Atlantis, I command my house to surface and be founded upon dry land now, and every watery environment surrounding my home, dry up now, by the power of Jesus Christ.

I separate the waters from the waters, and I neutralize all demonically charged turbulent waters, and destroy every and any water occult system or demonic substance that is covering my home and is programmed to sabotage its light, its peace, and its safety.

Any altar that has formed a mutual relationship between the entities of the waters and my home, and every power of the waters that has ambushed and claimed my home as a property of the kingdom of darkness, because of an evil embargo, link, covenant, tie, contract, relationship, alliance, agreement by words, blood, handwriting, signature, ancestral truce, let all these astral and legal rights be nullified and condemned by the Blood of Jesus, and let my home be set free from the power of every dark covenant of the waters, in the exalted name of Jesus of Nazareth.

Any astral poison, aquatic magic, and blue magic under the command of the Queen of Beta, the queen of the Coast, the Queen of Shylon, the Queen of Yemunah or the Queen of Delta, projected to my home for vicious psychic attacks and manipulations, swift and progressive destructions, persistent predicaments, recurring calamities, repetitive failures, blockages, hindrances, disappointments, marriage dismantlement, disgraces, and mutation of afflictions, shame, disgrace, and backwardness, and a mandate for my death, annihilation, madness, and destruction of my joy, peace, finances, health, and success, I call upon the Voice of the Lord in Psalms 29:3 to neutralize these water occult powers and destroy these psychic manipulations.

I also call upon the Lord God in Psalms 18:8 to breathe smoke out of His nostrils and devouring fire out of His mouth upon these evil powers of oceanic witchcraft.

All you water nymphs, sirens, gods and goddesses, kings and queens, princes and princesses, all marine creatures, tritons, mermaids, sirens, and all other forms of aquatic elemental spirits, water dragons and serpents, and all you aquatic troops, and members of the water dynasties within the different zones wielding tridents or other aquatic weapons and devices of captivity, torture and calamities, and all squads of the naval forces of darkness, working and conspiring and devising evil and destruction against my life, my destiny and my home in the water occult world, in the rivers, lakes and seas, be burned and consumed by the electric fire and dynamic thunderclaps from Heaven, and let all your astral poisons from the supreme elementals and the astral forces become useless, ineffective, powerless, and their force and velocity dissolved and come to naught, effective immediately, by the God of Abraham, Isaac, and Jacob.

In Jesus' Name, let the Angels of the God of the Heavens and the Earth arrest these evil spirits with hot chains of fire and shackles of brimstone, and bring all water occult powers into captivity and under subjection to the Lordship of Jesus the Messiah.

By the Holy Spirit, let electric fire and dynamic thunderbolts and thunderclaps rain terror of lightning storms from Heaven upon all forces of the dark waters working with the enigma of water, sound vibrations and frequencies, evil altars, sacrifices, rituals, and incantations within the seven seas against my life.

Every demonic aquatic spirit and their weapons that are carrying the mandate for my destruction by witchcraft and sorceries, I render the power of these water entities sent against my life and home impotent, frustrated, inadequate, incapable, ineffective, nullified, barren, ineligible, and useless perpetually, in the name of Jesus.

By the judicial verdict of the power of the Blood of the Lamb of God Almighty, these astral poisons, psychic spirits, and astral commands within the psychic layers of the Banwa kingdom are now disqualified and rendered useless, powerless, and ineffective against my life, and all demonic jurisdiction to my home; I hereby command you to be broken now with immediate effect, in the name of Jesus of Nazareth.

Home Trapped In An Enchanted Forest Kingdom

Wherever and by whatever forest witchcraft and demonic power my home is placed within an enchanted forest, monsoon forest, tropical forest, in a swamp, in a woodland, within a sacred grove, among mangroves, in the Everglades, on the forest floor, or in a crossroad or a fork road within the forest in the spiritual realm, I, by the power of Jesus the Christ of Nazareth, command my house to be pulled out of any demonic forest world.

In any way and in whatever forest realm my home is covered by enchanted vines, shrubs, sticks, twigs, herbs, trees, creepers, climbers, grass, bamboo, thistles, weeds, reeds, mushrooms, and moss in the spirit realm, I call upon the fire of El-Eliyahu to descend upon this pestiferous habitat, burn it to ashes, and set my home free from all evil.

All you forest demonic powers afflicting and destroying my home and programmed to sabotage its light, its peace, and its safety, I subject you to the judgement of the Blood of the Lamb of God, Jesus of Nazareth.

By the power invested in me by the Blood of Jesus, the Spirit of Jesus, and the Name of Jesus Christ of Nazareth, I pray and call down holy consuming fire and lightning from the Lord God of the Heavens and the Earth, to fall upon and banish from my life and home all forest witchcraft within, under, above, and around my home, and to banish from my home any spirit of the Hamadryads demons (tree Nymphs), the Oreads demons (nymphs of mountains), the Meliads demons (nymphs of ash trees), the Leimoniads demons (meadow nymphs), and spirits of the dragons, spirits of familiar animals and animal spirit guides, dwarves, elves, fae, giants, gnomes, satyrs, goblins, orcs, trolls, leprechauns, halflings, centaurs, minotaurs, fairies, unicorns, or the spirit of the Dryads demons (Forest Nymphs), spirits of the Amazon forest, spirits of the Everglades, demons of the Himalaya Mountains, forces of the Forest of Surpan, or the spirit of Huldra, Leshy, the Moss Folks, and also the Wood Wives; let these forest entities be consumed by the holy consuming fire and lightning from the Lord God of the Heavens and the Earth. Let them be destroyed now.

Any forest or tree altar that has formed a mutual relationship between the entities of the forest and my home, and every power of the forest that has ambushed and claimed my home as a property of the kingdom of darkness, because of an evil embargo, link, covenant, tie, contract, relationship, alliance, agreement by words, blood, handwriting, signature, ancestral truce, ancestral totem, let all these astral and legal rights be nullified and condemned by the Blood of Jesus, and let my home be set free from the power of every dark covenant of the Pestifera world of witchcraft, in the exalted name of Jesus of Nazareth.

In Jesus' Name, let the Angels of the God of the Heavens and the Earth arrest all evil forest spirits with hot chains of fire and shackles of brimstone, and bring all forest occult powers into captivity and under subjection to the Lordship of Jesus the Messiah.

By the Holy Spirit, let electric fire and dynamic thunderclaps rain terror of lightning storms from Heaven upon all demonic forest spirits and their weapons that are carrying the mandate for my destruction by

witchcraft and sorceries, and all forces of the dark forest who are weaponizing the enigma of nature, sound vibrations and frequencies, evil altars, sacrifices, rituals, and incantations against my life.
I render the power of these forest entities sent against my life and home impotent, frustrated, inadequate, incapable, ineffective, nullified, barren, ineligible, and useless, perpetually, in the name of Jesus.

By the judicial verdict of the power of the Blood of the Lamb of God Almighty, these astral poisons, psychic spirits, and astral commands within the psychic layers of the forest kingdom are now disqualified and rendered useless, powerless, and ineffective against my life, and all demonic jurisdiction to my home; I hereby command you to be broken now with immediate effect, in the name of Jesus of Nazareth.
Father, thank you for listening to me and delivering me from evil. I pray these prayers in no other name but the name of Y'ahushua HaMashiach, for thine is the kingdom, the power, and the glory forever, Amen and Amen.

50. Prayer To Liberate Your Property From Being A Ground For Satanic Secret Operations

(To be Prayed by members of the household. Pour anointing oil in the four corners of the premises, then start your prayer).

By the Power of the Almighty God of Israel, we possess this territorial land and all its access points. We charge against all operations that are in motion in this place. We charge against every aerial transport used for satanic transmission, every negative charge, demonic deposits, and occult transactions. We charge against every satanic financial transaction, spiritual human trafficking, drug trafficking, and deployment of secret agents that are taking place in this place in the spirit realm.

Everything that is buried or set up in this place that is a point of contact or a transmitter of satanic powers, we charge against you right now with the fire of El-Eliyahu (the God of Elijah). As we march upon this ground, we pray for amplification of the sounds of our footsteps, and may our footsteps become roaring thunderstorms in the kingdom of darkness.

Let our footsteps cause earthquakes and destruction in the kingdom of Satan that is established in this place. We pull down every communication tower of darkness, we block all signals and distort every piece of information that is passing through this place to and from the kingdom of Satan. Fire of God Most High, charged against the elements of darkness in this place; Blood of Yahushua, be deployed against every strongman that is in this place.

On this property, we disarm every strong man and his army, and render them shieldless, defenseless, weaponless, impotent, useless, and clueless, in the Name of Yahushua. We ambush all Satanic cults that are operating in this place; and every satanic cult that seeks to enter this place by land, sea, or air shall be ambushed by the Angels of the Lord. Let the witches, warlocks, Satanists, grand masters, avatars, and other occult practitioners be consumed and defeated by the works of their own hands in this place.

Let their works backfire upon themselves, and every trap and snare that they set, let them be caught in it. All demonic dwarfs, demonic giants, demonic beasts and creatures, demonic plants, werewolves and vampires, creatures of the night and day, avatars and hybrid beings, freemasons, and mutants; let them all be burned with holy fire from the Most Holy God of Heaven upon entry into this place.

Let all satanic and witchcraft attempts to enter or operate in this place end in disaster, confusion, and death. In Jesus' Name. We charge against all satanic coffins that are used as transport vehicles in this place. We expose them for what they are, and we call down fire upon them. Let the Blood of Jesus neutralize all blood covenants that are sprinkled in this place and upon this ground. Every power of the Pandemonium kingdom that is affecting this place; every power of the throne of the Queen of Heaven and the Queen of Hell that is influencing this place; every power of the Queen and King of the Sea that is dominating over this place; by the authority of the Blood of the holy Lamb of God, Yahushua the Son of Yah, we command you to be destroyed and shattered NOW!

I barricade my property with reinforced barriers of incomprehensible electric fire, and permanent walls of enforced and adamant resistance and defences of lightning. These things we command by the authority of the name of the Living God and His Son Yahushua Ha-Mashiach. AMEN.

51. Prayers Against Demons That Haunt You

Heavenly Father, who sits within the 10th dimension of Heaven enthroned between the Cherubim, hallowed be Your Name as you have made the Heavens Your dwelling place and the earth Your footstool, and Your will is being done on the earth as it is in Heaven. I approach Your throne of Grace to find mercy and to find grace to help me in this time of need.

My life is haunted and ambushed by various astral poisons of the combined elements of the psychic operations of darkness because of unidentified doorways, links, covenants, past sins, and jurisdictions coming from my mother's house, my father's house, and my own personal life.

I am helpless in this situation, but You are my helper, for it is written in Psalms 30:10, **"Hear, O LORD, and have mercy upon me: LORD, be thou my helper."**
It is also written in Psalms 121:2, **"My help cometh from the LORD, which made heaven and earth."**

In the name of Jesus of Nazareth, I now stand erect in the authority of the Blood of Jesus of Nazareth, and I revolt against any curse that has been propelled into the "psychic layers," giving psychic judicial commands to the "Elemental Spirits, to haunt my life with diurnal and nocturnal terrors, dreads, restlessness, intimidations, fear of death, fright, fear of man, fear of spirits, general phobia, torment, harassment, and affliction by hypnagogic hallucinations [falling asleep] or by hypnopompic hallucinations [waking up in the morning], or by diurnal or nocturnal paranormal afflictions by auditory hallucination, visual hallucination, olfactory hallucination, gustatory hallucination, tactile hallucination, algesic hallucination, general somatic hallucination.

I confessed and asked for pardon for my sins in every area where I have physically or spiritually, consciously or unconsciously, directly or indirectly participated in witchcraft rituals, ceremonies, initiation, necromancy, occult alphabets, usage of white witchcraft paraphernalia, occult arrangement of letters, conjuring of spirits, witchcraft prayers, evil chants, demonic invocation, worship of false gods and idols, drawing of magic circles, veneration of relics, prayers to the dead, veneration of the dead, the use of the Ouija board, the Charlie Charlie Challenge Game, Tarot card reading, palm reading, or the horoscope.

I also confessed my sins in every area where I have physically or spiritually, consciously or unconsciously, directly or indirectly participated in conjuring curses, erecting shrines, satanic worship, drawing demon sigils and esoteric symbols, seeking after diviners, soothsayers, fortune tellers, necromancers, and every alliance and covenant that I made with the kingdom of darkness by giving my money, my body, my soul, and my mind over to demons through these current or past sins, iniquities, and abominations.

You demon of Hallucination, personal paranormal activity, demonic torment, psychosis, epilepsy, schizophrenia, dissociative identity disorder, identity fragments, and all other demonic entities that are stalking, haunting, and demonizing me because of my contact with a cursed human corpse or remains, my visit to a haunted property or cemetery, or my exposure to a demonically charged atmosphere because of an ancient murder, homicide, suicide, genocide, torture, slavery, unlawful imprisonment, rape, witchcraft, practice of divination, trauma, or because of a horrible and terrifying death; I, by the power of Jesus of Nazareth, renounce these evils that have befallen me.

I separate myself from all demons of the elements, demons of torment and terror of the nighttime and the daytime, and I renounce every evil spirit of the twilight zone and the gate of the dawn of evil that is haunting my life.

Every psychic entity and elemental force assigned under the velocity of the 5 esoteric seals of psychic manipulations, under the satanic order of the queen of heaven, the queen of the south, the Queen of Beta, the Queen of Shylon, the Queen of Yemunah, the Queen of Delta, the Queen of the Coast, the gods of the Titans, the Olympian gods, the king demons of the four elements, the evil guardians of the cardinal points, the Mermaids, the Sirens or the Nymphs, or whatever evil power that has subjected me to become a lab rat and subject for occult and witchcraft experiments, and every evil spirit haunting my life wherever I go, making me a victim of paranormal activities, where I hear voices in my ears of people quarrelling, laughing, speaking, whispering, or someone calling my name, or where I am physically being touched, sexually being violated, feelings of cobwebs in my face or body, having strange emotions, seeing apparitions, having severe nightmares, receiving mysterious scratches and marks while in sleep, sudden awakening from sleep and perceiving unusual scents, right now, by the power of ElShaddai, in the Name of Jesus of Nazareth, by flames of lightning and thunder, with hot chains of seraphic fire and fetters of hot iron heated by the fire of the Holy Spirit of Jesus, I strategically bind hands and feet and disarm all of you evil spirits that are haunting me.

I revolt with lightning and thunders of the amber fire of Jesus Christ, and I banish from my life all these combined elements of psychic and esoteric powers, astral poisons, and paranormal activities into places of oblivion and destruction; I render you powerless, defenseless, ineffective, and useless, in Jesus' name.

Through the death, burial, and resurrection of Jesus of Nazareth, I invoke the heavy artillery of destruction to judge, banish, and destroy the power and essence of all demi-gods, all powers of the astral forces, planetary spirits, avatars, grand masters, witches, warlocks, satanists, wiccans, freemasons, sorcerers, watchers, guardians of the flame, ascended masters, solar lords, interplanetary lords, intergalactic lords, guardians of fate and the cycles of life, dark principalities, powers, rulers of darkness, legions of the air, aquatic forces, subterranean forces, Earth masters, highlanders, mermaids, sirens, and the elemental spirits that are haunting me.

In the mighty name of Jesus of Nazareth, I renounce, condemn, and revoke all these evil psychic commands and telepathic channels of destruction formed against me. I tear down every demonic stronghold established in my life, and I destroy all legal grounds and astral rights that give these evil spirits jurisdiction to haunt my life with terror and calamity.
Every cycle of nocturnal and diurnal demonic harassment by pests and insects, let it be broken, and the demons attacking me be destroyed by fire and roasted to ashes.

I command all evil operations and activities following me to come to an abrupt halt and be banished now.
I call upon the Name of Yahushua HaMashiach of Nazareth, and the fire of the Holy Spirit of Christ and the holy Blood of the Lamb of God according to Revelation 12:11, and I claim freedom from the grip of every evil spirit haunting and controlling the faculties of my six senses.

Wherever I have participated physically or spiritually, consciously or unconsciously, directly or indirectly in any blood-drinking ceremony, blood initiation, signature agreement, ancestral worship, witchcraft meeting, occult ritual, or where I have been physically or spiritually, consciously or unconsciously, directly or indirectly initiated into conscious or subconscious witchcraft, Father in Heaven, I ask for Your utmost forgiveness, and I renounce and revoke all repercussions sent upon me because of the occult foods, demonic substances, and blood I have subconsciously ingested in dreams, or in the physical realms.

I renounce any association with demons in dreams and the error of violating Your word in Deuteronomy 12:23 and Leviticus 17:10.

In the Name of Yahushua HaMashiach of Nazareth, I renounce every spiritual chain that is binding me and holding me trapped within the land of darkness, within the valley of the shadows of death, within an underground cave, within an astral labyrinth, within a spiritual maze, or any spiritual incarceration chamber within the forest, desert, water, air, or within any underground astral chamber, or within any other domain of the kingdom of darkness.

By the power of the Lord, I claim freedom and therefore renounce every foul spirit - demonic snakes, newts, spiders, cobwebs, demonic flies, grasshoppers, demonic rodents, land creatures, foul birds, monkey spirits, octopus spirits, leeches, flying and creeping insects, and all other mysterious creatures from the water, land, and air kingdom of Hell placed upon and inside my body as spirit guides, watchers, and tormentors. I renounce and destroy the way of the serpents and the channels by which every other foul spirit is constricting, tormenting, haunting, and afflicting me in the areas of my body, mind, and soul.

52. Prayers Against Curses Of Infirmities

In the name of the God of Abraham, Isaac, and Israel, I approach the throne of grace to obtain mercy and help from the golden altar of Heaven through the blood of the Lamb of God.
Father, in Jesus' name, I implore the judicial authority of Your throne of sapphire and flames, and I summon a "Holy Rebuke" from the courtroom and Divine Council in Heaven against all spirits of infirmity that have imprisoned me or set themselves upon me to afflict me through ancient astral rights, legal ground, and ethereal bridges.

Your word says You sent forth Your word and healed our diseases; therefore, I stand erect in the authoritative capacity of the blood, water, and Spirit of Jesus of Nazareth, and by the authority of Your word and name, O Yah, I address every infirmity by inheritance, paternal, genealogical, traits, ethnic, racial, family line, bloodline, roots, family tree, ancestral, and hereditary curses that are the result of the sins of the fathers (Jeremiah 32:18), especially witchcraft, occultism, perversion, and idolatry. I call upon the judicial blood of Jesus to acquit me from these evil allegations, accusations, condemnations, and strongholds by which the spirit of infirmity has set itself in my body.
By the stronghold of confidence in Christ Jesus, I pray against every curse of infirmity, stronghold, and affliction of various diseases, illnesses, or recurring illness, pains, and stubborn aches afflicting my life by the forces of the psychic entity of the four elements.
I pray against all water sirens revealing the enigma of water in order to use water as a point of mystery for accessing the evil powers of the aquatic world against my health.
I also pray against all nature, sirens revealing the enigma of nature in order to use nature as a point of mystery for accessing the divine powers of the Pestifera world against my health.

By the Throne of El-Shaddai, and by the authority of the Word of the Almighty, I bind with hot chains of holy fire, and call forth the lightning of the eternal fire of the presence of Elshaddai to bring into subjection under bondage, and banish from my life every demon of infirmity standing behind Laboratory Engineered Viruses, Demonic Arrows of Diseases and Viruses, natural diseases and viruses, every astral spirit, all supreme elementals and their subordinate elemental forces, all psychic entities, mermaids, sirens, wandering spirits, familiar spirits, nymphs, spirits of the death hunters, stings of death, or any other psychic entity or agent of darkness that has placed a sigil or mark upon my forehead or in the palm of my hand.

Father in Heaven, You said in Jeremiah 29:11, **"For I know the thoughts that I think toward you, saith the LORD, thoughts of peace, and not of evil, to give you an expected end."**
My expected end is to be in good health and prosper in my health and other areas; therefore, by Your will and word, I declare I am not a candidate for any life-threatening condition. Nothing illegal shall dwell in my mortal body because by Your stripes I am healed [Isaiah 53:5], and my body is also reserved for the Spirit of God.

By the power of the God of Elijah who answers by fire [2 Kings 1:10, 1 Kings 18:24], I command fire to dry up, consume, and eradicate all risk factors of pulmonary embolism, blood clots, and also cardiovascular, respiratory, digestive, psychological, circulatory, lymphatic, skeletal, nervous, integumentary, endocrine, urinary, mental, dermatological, and neurological conditions, diseases, and potential failures; this I pray in Jesus' name.

By the power of Jesus, I invoke a Judiciary Court Order from the Judicial Council, the Mercy seat, and the Blood of the Lamb of God against any terminal illness in my body, that any terminal illness that exists in my

body would be perpetually eradicated and dissolved without a trace, scar, or evidence of existence, effective immediately, in Jesus name.
I invoke a Divine Judicial Order from the Courts of the Divine Council of the Almighty God, who is the Grand Judge of the Heavens and the Earth, and I command by this Divine Judicial Order that my body be healed from any blood clot and blood clotting condition, and cardiovascular, respiratory, digestive, psychological, circulatory, lymphatic, skeletal, nervous, integumentary, endocrine, urinary, mental, dermatological, and neurological failure, temporary illness, and permanent infirmity.

Pray Against Blood Clot Conditions

I invoke a Judiciary Court Order from the Judicial Council, the Mercy seat, and the Blood of the Lamb of God, and I condemn, revolt against, and reject blood clots in my body, and if there are any undiscovered or existing pulmonary embolisms, conditions for coronary thrombosis, or deep vein thrombosis in my body, let these blood clots be vaporized by the blood of Jesus of Nazareth.
Lord, I ask that the fervent heat of the fire of Your love, kindness, and tender mercies would melt out any clot within my body now, in Jesus name.
I pray against all factors of blood clotting: coagulopathy, cancer, obesity, smoking, chronic inflammatory diseases, atherosclerosis, existing medical conditions, hormone replacement therapy, prolonged sitting, reduced blood flow, surgery, etc., and I pray that You will deliver me, O Lord, my Savior and King.
I summon a judicial order from the mercy seat that is covered with the Blood of the Lamb of God, and I invoke the verdict of the wounds, the blood, and the water from the side of Christ, and I rebuke and eradicate cancer or potential cancer, diabetes, high blood pressure, and high cholesterol, and curse these to the root and command them to die, in Jesus name.

Family history

Any hereditary blood clotting condition that has been passed down to me, which is currently affecting my life and health, I invoke a Judicial Order from the Courtroom of the Mercy Seat that is covered with the Blood of the Lamb of God, and I command fire and the Blood of Jesus to revoke the council of ancestral blood clotting, all its factors and effects in my life, and that I be healed from this family genetic sickness of blood clotting, effective immediately.

Medications

Any medication, including birth control pills and certain other treatments, that places me at an increased risk of developing blood clots, I invoke a judicial order from the mercy seat that is covered with the Blood of the Lamb of God, and I command fire to dry up, consume, and eradicate the negative effects of these medications and the effect of causing blood clots.

Vitamin deficiencies

Any deficiency in B6, B12, or folate which increases my risk of developing blood clots, blood clotting disorders, an imbalance of procoagulant and anticoagulant factors in my blood, which also leads to a clotting disorder, I summon mercy from the Judicial Council of Heaven, and request that my virtue be restored, and all vitamins and minerals be regulated and balanced in my body, effective immediately, In Jesus name.

I submit the symptoms to the altars of God in Heaven.
- Sudden shortness of breath
- Chest pain,
- Pain when coughing or breathing deeply.

- Coughing up blood or bloody mucus.
- Rapid breathing or wheezing.
- Increased heart rate
- Dizziness, lightheadedness, and fainting.
- Low blood pressure
- Anxiety and all other symptoms of pulmonary embolism, or blood clots, upon the altar of God's mercy and covenantal healing.

Let any infirmity sent into my body through occult sound vibrations, frequencies, psychic commands, or through various incantation techniques and through the enigma of water, forest, land, and air be pulled out and cleaved unto those who sent this sickness by witchcraft.

I call for the holy fire of Yah, and the blood of the Lamb of God that was sprinkled upon the mercy seat to intervene and erase every mark of infirmity that was placed upon my forehead, hand, or any other part of my body by demonic spirits.
Great Father, I petition You to touch me with that same power that raised Christ from the dead, and by this quicken my mortal body.

You, O Lord, have created me from nothing, and You can certainly recreate my body, organs, tendons, nerves, sinews, muscles, blood vessels, and blood organelles.
Fill me with the healing power of Your spirit and cast out anything that should not be in me.

Repair what is damaged, root out all unproductive cells, open any blocked arteries or veins, and rebuild any damaged areas.
Remove all inflammation and cleanse out any infections.
Let the warmth of Your healing love pass through my body to renew all unhealthy areas, so that my body will function the way You created

it to function. Restore me to full health in mind and body so that I may serve You for the rest of my life.

Therefore, I pray O Most High God, if my health is tied to any green tree, or is hidden under any stone, or is buried beneath the foot of any mountain or hill, or is captured beneath a river, sea, or any body of water, by the power of Jesus of Nazareth and the power of the Holy Spirit, let my health be released and the occult place where my health has been incarcerated be burned to the ground.

I revoke all water and forest witchcraft incantations done over my body, and through Jesus the Christ, I destroy all witchcraft from over my health.

I now invoke a Divine Judicial Order from the Courts of the Almighty God who is the Grand Judge of the Heavens and the Earth, and I command by this Divine Judicial Order that there be an immediate release of my health and organs from any witchcraft coven, witchcraft altar, black box, vase, bottle, magic pot, magic basin, chamber, or from the forest where my health or organs may be locked up by witchcraft powers, or from any cauldron where my health or organs are being boiled by witchcraft, or from the pendant in the necklace of any demon, and from the powers of the enigma of the waters; the sea, the river, the lake, the pond, the streams, the pools of water, the swamp, the marshes, and the waterfall, effective immediately, in Jesus' name.

Send Your Angels, O Lord, to recover my health and organs from darkness. Psalms 103:20, **"Bless the Lord, ye his angels, that excel in strength"**.
By the power of the Holy Spirit of Jesus, I revoke all witchcraft incantations done over my body, and I destroy any witchcraft hex and cage that are over my health, and I retrieve by fire my health and

organs from the Gates of Hell; I smash to pieces every pendant, cauldron, black box, vase, bottle, or any other vessel in which my health is trapped.

Every realm and astral plane receiving psychic commands through the vibration of witchcraft, incantations, sins, and family iniquities in order to sustain various cycles of invasion and manipulation of my health; may the terror of God Almighty bring judgement upon these evil powers.

Every evil power of the full moon, new moon, waxing moon, waning moon, season, star, planet, weather pattern, and planetary alignment that is charged with psychic commands from the astral layers to control sickness in my body.

Every warfare that is waged over my body and health by demons, let the inner system of defence of my spirit, soul, and body prevent the entry of unwanted substances and reject all demonic invaders who seek to forge an uninvited and unauthorized entry into my body.

Effective immediately, by the Wounds of the body of Jesus the Messiah of Nazareth, and by the blood and water of His side, I disarm and cancel every impending organ failure, organ disease, or sickness cycle continuum that is mandated through psychic commands to rule in my body. Wherever my body is subjected to the velocity of Five Esoteric Seals of the occult, let my body be delivered by Jesus of Nazareth.

Father, Great Healer, I want to thank you this day for taking the time to heal and deliver me from all evil. Seal my healing and health in Your holy name, as You are exalted in all the Earth.
Be glorified for the victory You have given to me today in Jesus' name, Amen and Amen.

53. Prayers Against Curses Of Failures

Heavenly Father, I come before You today, seeking Your divine intervention against the curse of failure in my life. I acknowledge that You are the Almighty, and there is nothing too difficult for You.

Lord, I pray by the power of the Holy Spirit in the name of Jesus of Nazareth against every curse, hex, and cage placed upon my life.

I pray against every mark of failure placed upon my forehead or in the palm of my hand. Wherever my life was placed in a knot by witchcraft, or a knot was placed in a rope to represent my life as a knotted life and failure, by the power of the redemptive blood of Jesus of Nazareth, let my life be unknotted now, and every knotted rope that represents my failure catch fire and turn to ash, in Jesus Name.

I break the power of influence coming from the channels of psychic manipulation, and I render every demon of failure and disappointment powerless, ineffective, useless, and barren in its ability to ruin my life.

Every dangerous power of diverse esoteric crafts, manipulations, and weapons, systems, and techniques which any human occult agent, demon, or spirit is using to destroy my life through continual and repetitive failures, I call for the power of the fire of the Holy Spirit to descend in the space between spaces, within every crevice in the cosmic cracks, portals, elevated realms, upper dimensions of the cosmic layers, and lower regions of darkness, to destroy these evil armed forces.

I revoke the verdict of any and every tribunal of the night that was held against me within any of the occult zones, occult regions, or occult centers, or within the cosmic planes and psychic layers to build strongholds over my life to fail.

Every power within the invisible level that has spiritually plunged me into a detention camp of witches and wizards for continual failure in all that I do, by the power of Jesus' resurrection from the dead, I call upon the wings of the wind of God to deliver me from spiritual enslavement and pull me out of the snare and lair of darkness.

I revolt by my liberty in the Blood of Jesus and by the power of his salvation against every degree of stronghold, operating under the velocity of the five Mephistophelian occult seals, which are mandated to fight against my destiny.
I detach every enforced link that is built to hold me bound under the curse of the failure continuum, and by the power of the Messiah Jesus of Nazareth, I break that pattern and cycle from my life, effective immediately.

I will no longer drink from the cup of failure, and failure is not my portion and inheritance; neither am I any longer a beneficiary of failure. My destiny is a womb of productivity and success. I declare I am a success conceiver of great and mighty things, and my paths are successful paths.

No weapon formed against me shall prosper, for greater is he who is in me than he who is in the world. Hence as it is written in Psalms 18:3, **"I will call upon the LORD, who is worthy to be praised; so shall I be saved from mine enemies."**
Psalms 23:5, **"You prepare a table for me in the presence of my enemies. You anoint my head with oil; my cup runs over."**
Psalms 2:8, **"Ask of me, and I shall give thee the heathen for thine inheritance, and the uttermost parts of the earth for thy possession."**

Therefore, I possess my rightful possession. Whoever is holding my success in their hand, let my success become like a burning fire coal, too hot to hold any longer.

Blood of Jesus and fire of the judicial altar of God Almighty, remove all generational curses or negative patterns of failure that have hindered my progress all these years.

Let every agent of the Twilight Zone, the gates of the dawn, all agents of the upper darkness, and the lower darkness be destroyed by consuming fire from Heaven's gate.

I declare that I am more than a conqueror through Christ who strengthens me. I trust in Your promises and believe that You have a plan for my life, a plan to prosper me and not to harm me, to give me an expected end of success, righteousness, peace, and joy in the Holy Spirit.

Thank you, Lord, for Your unfailing love and support. I place my trust in You and look forward to the victories that lie ahead.

In Jesus' mighty name, I pray, Amen and Amen.

54. Warfare Against The Spirit Of Abandonment & Rejection

Abba Father, I come before You today, feeling the weight of abandonment and rejection. I petition by the blood of the Lamb for Your divine presence to fill my heart and mind, bringing comfort and inner peace within the chambers of my soul, mind, and heart.

Lord, I pray, surround me with Your love and let me feel Your comforting embrace. Heal the wounds of abandonment and rejection that have left me feeling isolated, neglected, and orphaned. It is written in Psalms 27:10, **"When my father and my mother forsake me, then the LORD will take me up"**.
I implore Your divine intervention against the spirit of rejection and abandonment that has been programmed to be my oppressor and mystery of affliction. I acknowledge that You are the Almighty, and there is nothing too difficult for You. I petition by the blood of the Lamb for Your yoke-breaking power and eternal love and warmth to fill me and overcome every feeling of rejection and unworthiness that has been structured around my life. 1 Peter 5:7 says, **"Casting all your care upon him; for he careth for you"**.

Every demonic manipulation, degradation, and astral contamination that has become a stronghold upon my life through rejection and abandonment, and every spirit of rejection and abandonment that I have acquired from my mother's house or my father's house, that is currently speaking into my life, O God, let these psychic poisons be neutralized and banished from my life and family foundation. Let these evil spirits be tormented with fire and brimstone in the presence of the holy angels, and in the presence of the Lamb. [Rev 14:10]

I pray against every degree of psychic manipulation that has restrained, corrupted, disorganized, decharacterized, and reconfigured my life in a negative way.

I break the backbone of the spirit of trauma that has latched itself to me through my past experiences with fear, loneliness, and abandonment. I break all taproots of rejection, including fear of rejection, self-rejection, fear of abandonment, isolation, orphan spirits, and all unforgiveness and unworthiness that came as a result of these traumas.

I block and stop every psychic command that carries the mandate to sabotage my future and destiny because of abandonment and rejection.
By fire of the Word of God, I charge against every demon spirit of the elementals who have plunged me into deep pits of despair where I am imprisoned within chambers of the realm of the shadows of death and darkness.

Wherever my soul was taken captive by dwarf demons, or any other psychic spirit to a valley of darkness, Cave of Terror, Labyrinth of Illusions, horrible pit, or is held within many waters, a prison facility, or is placed to wander in empty barren land in the spirit realm, I call for a judicial verdict from Heaven to overthrow any judicial law that was set over my life by darkness. Let God arise and let His Angels from Heaven intervene.

Blood of Jesus, arise against the highest council of darkness and condemn their verdict to destroy me through rejection and abandonment. In every way I was rejected, placed in an orphanage, or disliked by my parents or caretaker, mistreated and abandoned, I call upon the God of Moses who parted the Red Sea, the God of Elijah who sent fire from heaven, the God of Paul who wrought great miracles by the hands of Paul to rise for my defence and deliverance and make haste to help me by the divine intervention of the holy council of the divine presence of the Godhead.

Let the mighty rushing wind and fire fight for me to liberate my soul from the prison of abandonment and rejection; and let the chains of rejection and abandonment that have bound me these years with heavy weights of spiritual slavery be broken from my life by the power of Jesus Christ.

By the power of Jesus Christ, I challenge and confront with fire and the Blood of Jesus of Nazareth, every power that has been and is still contributing to the predicament, calamities, and afflictions in my life. May the Order of the holy Council of God Almighty condemn every condemnation of Hell and rebuke every rebuke of darkness that is sitting upon my life and destiny.
Right now, I shake off the beast in the fire, and I smash every monument that represents my emotional and mental fragmentation, shame, disgrace, and humiliation in the second heaven, the sea, the cemetery, or in the forest, and on land. I retrieve my destiny from the hand of rejection and abandonment, and from the hold of every foul bird, and command my life to be rearranged and fall in alignment with the divine order of God the King; in Jesus' name, I pray, Amen and Amen.

55. Prayers Against Curses Of Fear

Heavenly Father, in the name of Jesus the Messiah, I stand before You in repentance for any psychic gate I have opened in my life through the propensities of the flesh or any door I have opened to give jurisdiction to unclean spirits of fear. I repent for allowing the terror of fear to rule over me through factors I can see and cannot see; You are my strong confidence in all things.

I come boldly before Your Throne of Grace, seeking Your divine intervention against the curse of fear that is tormenting me, for Your word says fear has torment, but it is also written perfect love casts out all fear [1 John 4:18].

Any legal rights I have created that became a platform for the demonic manipulation and terrors of fear, I subject them to the judgement of the blood of Jesus.
Oh God Most High, grant me at this very moment the fire of power and authority through Jesus the Christ, as I take a stand right now to overpower every evil spirit of fear.
Not, I address any and every spirit of fear, dread, and terror that is holding my life under the grip of terror by night and by day. It is written in Isaiah 41:10, **"Fear thou not; for I am with thee: be not dismayed; for I am thy God: I will strengthen thee; yea, I will help thee; yea, I will uphold thee with the right hand of my righteousness"**.

Therefore, I speak under the authority of the blood of Jesus of Nazareth. All vicious power of diverse esoteric crafts, manipulations, systems, techniques, and weapons of fear, which any human occult agent, or demon or spirit is using to cripple and torment me with various categories of fears, I call upon the power of the fire of the Holy

Spirit to descend in the space between spaces, within every crevice in the cosmic cracks, portals, elevated realms, upper dimensions of the cosmic layers, and lower regions of darkness, to destroy these evil armed forces that have ambushed my life with terrors of fear.

By the Holy Spirit, I release my soul from the grip of the shadows and the valley of fear and death. It is written in Psalms 23:4, **"Yea, though I walk through the valley of the shadow of death, I will fear no evil."**

Every power within the invisible layers which has spiritually plunged me into a detention camp of the spirit of fear, dread, and terror, so that I would continually live in torment and fright, right now by the power of the Holy Spirit, in the name of Jesus of Nazareth, and by the three witnesses on earth; the water, the blood, and the Spirit, I banish by fire all these evil entities of fear and doorways of terror established in my life. For it is written, Psalms 34:4, **"I sought the LORD, and he heard me, and delivered me from all my fears."**

Through Jesus, I break the power of psychic manipulations and influences coming from any of the psychic layers of the elemental entities of fear and terror, and I render every demon of fear and psychological torture powerless against me. According to Rev 14:10, be tormented with fire and brimstone in the presence of the holy angels, and in the presence of the Lamb.

Every power of fear manipulation that is causing me to walk as a coward, every episode of psychosis where my thoughts and perceptions are disrupted by fear, any spirit that causes me to be always hiding, always scared, always terrified, always running away, always suspicious, and every spirit that causes me to walk in paranoia, lack of confidence, easily frightened, powerless in confrontations, ineffective in applying boldness, useless in offensive warfare, and barren in my victory against evil spirits, by the Blood of Jesus and the fire of the judicial altar of God Almighty, I break this curse of fear and terror that has hindered my life and peace all these years.

By the faith of the Son of God, I say to the 12 gates of Hell, I will not be terrified by terror and fear. Thus says the Lord to us in Romans 8:15, **"For ye have not received the spirit of bondage again to fear; but ye have received the Spirit of adoption, whereby we cry, Abba, Father."**

It is written, Provers 3:25-26, **"Be not afraid of sudden fear, neither of the desolation of the wicked, when it cometh."**
"For the LORD shall be thy confidence and shall keep thy foot from being taken."

Hence, on this authority, I command terror to be terrified, and I strike fear with fear, and dread and terror.
Also, thus says the Lord to us in Psalms 91:5, **"You shall not be afraid for the terror by night;** *nor* **for the arrow** *that* **flies by day;"**
"*Nor* **for the pestilence** *that* **walks in darkness;** *nor* **for the destruction** *that* **wastes at noonday."**
"A thousand shall fall at your side, and ten thousand at your right hand; *but* **it shall not come nigh you."**
With the velocity and charge of the dynamic firepower of Jesus, I release an electrical discharge by the Holy Spirit to detonate in the camps of darkness responsible for tormenting me with fear and terror, and I ravage and plunder the camp of Satan wherever my assets, successes, inheritance, goals, and destinies have been locked up because of my walk in fear. Let fear release me now, and let the occult kingdom of demons release my assets, inheritance, and blessings that are rightfully mine.

By the Blood of Jesus, I revolt against every degree of the stronghold of fear, operating in my life under the velocity of the five Mephistophelian occult seals.

I detach every enforced link that is built to hold me bound under deep and terrifying fear, and by the power of the Messiah Jesus of Nazareth, I break that cycle and pattern of continual fear in my life. I revolt against every revolving force that subjects me to animal phobias, natural environment phobias, situational phobias, and torment by primal fear, irrational fear, rational fear, and terrors of the nighttime and daytime. Let the fear of me be upon all living things upon the face of the earth, for it is written in Genesis 9:2, **"And the fear of you and the dread of you shall be upon every beast of the earth, and upon every fowl of the air, upon all that moveth *upon* the earth, and upon all the fishes of the sea; into your hand are they delivered."**

Wherever my life was placed in a knot by fear, or in a pit of withdrawal, uncertainty, and wherever I was crippled and disarmed because of the spirit of fear, by the power of the Holy Spirit in the name of Jesus of Nazareth, let my life be unknotted now, and every fear factor that is being manipulated and modified to be a chain around me, a shackle on my members, and a cloak of mental torment, let these evil powers be destroyed and banished from me.

Blood of Jesus, arise against the highest council of darkness and condemn their verdict to destroy me by fear, torment, mental and psychological disturbances, and every manner of phobia.
Fire of El-Eliyahu, descend for my sake, and let every psychic command given to the elemental demons for my destruction be destroyed.

No weapon formed against me shall prosper, for greater is he who is in me than he who is in the world. Hence it is written in Psalms 18:3,

"I will call upon the LORD, who is worthy to be praised: so, shall I be saved from mine enemies."

Hence, it is written in:

John 14:27, "Peace I leave with you; my peace I give you. I do not give to you as the world gives. Do not let your hearts be troubled and do not be afraid."

Isaiah 41:10, "Fear not, for I am with you; Be not dismayed, for I am your God. I will strengthen you, Yes, I will help you, I will uphold you with My righteous right hand."

Philippians 4:6-7, "Do not be anxious about anything, but in every situation, by prayer and petition, with thanksgiving, present your requests to God. And the peace of God, which transcends all understanding, will guard your hearts and your minds in Christ Jesus."

Deuteronomy 31:8, "The Lord himself goes before you and will be with you; he will never leave you nor forsake you. Do not be afraid; do not be discouraged."

Psalm 27:1, "The LORD is my light and my salvation – so why should I be afraid? The LORD is my fortress, protecting me from danger, so why should I tremble?"

Exodus 14:13, "And Moses said to the people, 'Fear not, stand firm, and see the salvation of the Lord, which he will work for you today."

Joshua 1:9, "Have I not commanded you? Be strong and courageous. Do not be frightened, and do not be dismayed, for the Lord your God is with you wherever you go."

Isaiah 41:13, "For I am the LORD your God who takes hold of your right hand and says to you, Do not fear; I will help you."

1 Peter 5:7, "Cast all your cares upon him because he cares for you."

2 Timothy 1:7, "For God has not given us a spirit of fear, but of power and of love and of a sound mind."

Psalms 34:4, "I sought the Lord, and he answered me; he delivered me from all my fears."

56. Prayer Against Past Hurts And Pains

Oh Lord Yah, my soul and emotions are open before You. From my youth up, I have been abused, criticized, and frustrated by the words and actions of my friends, my family, and foes.
Let Your heart not turn away from me, O Lord, but look upon me with Your eyes of deliverance. Forgive all those who hurt me as I forgive them also.

I will not allow my heart to see them as filth, nor will I hold grudges against them, but I release them and all negative energies they have projected against me. Turn the bad things that they have done to me into a weapon against the devil and turn all hurts and pain into vigorous boldness and forwardness, where I will stand and love my enemies with perfect love.
Father, erase all emotions that have developed negatively because of the pain that I have carried. I also pray that all my actions that have been negatively modified and mutated because of these hurts and pains, O Lord, eradicate these evil works in Jesus' name.

Let Your comfort soothe me so I will know how to treat all men. Your word says all things work together for good to those who love Christ.

In the name of El-Shaddai, creator of the heavens and the earth, I also renounce all demons that have entered me because of these hurts and pains. Every demon that is using and manipulating my past and current hurts and pains for the evil plan to destroy my life, I bind them right now with the chains of the Holy Spirit in Jesus the Messiah's name.
Every demon that has robbed me of my happiness, emotional bliss, and stability, the Lord God of hosts rebuke you foul spirits, and I command the release of my stolen emotional benefits; be tormented

with fire and brimstone in the presence of the holy angels and in the presence of the Lamb. [Rev 14:10]

By Jesus, I renounce and cast into dry deserts all demons that are feasting on my hurt and pain.

Every resistance, attitude, thought pattern, protectiveness, and carefulness that is not of God, that which I have developed because of the hurt, I renounce it now in Jesus' name.

I break the backbone of the spirit of trauma and hurt that has latched itself to me through my past experiences with fear, loneliness, and abandonment. I break all taproots of hurt, including fear of rejection, self-rejection, fear of abandonment, isolation, orphan spirits, and all unforgiveness and unworthiness that came as a result of these traumas.

I break every chain of hurt and pain that is binding around my neck, feet, hands, and waist. Let the fervent heat of the fire of the Lord Y'ahushua, whose eyes are like flames of fire, whose voice is as many waters, melt the chains from my soul and mind.

I retrieve my mind, thoughts, and emotions from the world of darkness and captivity, and I say, let there be light now, in Jesus' name.

I destroy all scavenging demons who are seeking to scavenge my past in order to bring up the past and buried things to recreate my emotional state of these past events; let them be banished under chains of fire now, in Jesus' name.

Every demon feeding on the energy of my hurts and pain, I bind you to a pole and cast you into deserted places. Let the sun, the screech owl, the serpents, and the satyr be your tormentors and starve to death now, in Jesus' name.

Most High God, You said in Your word in Isaiah 40:2, **"Speak comfortably to Jerusalem, and cry unto her that her warfare is**

accomplished, that her iniquity is pardoned; for she has received of the LORD's hand double for all her sins."
You also said in Your words in Isaiah 61:7, **"For your shame, you will have double."**

At this point, I am requesting and claiming this double—double grace, double anointing, double victory, double power, double strength, and double blessings of all categories in the name of Y'ahushua HaMashiach.

Heavenly Father, repair and restore my wholeness and wellness and give unto me beauty for ashes, the oil of joy for mourning, the garment of praise for the spirit of heaviness; that I might be called trees of righteousness, the planting of the LORD, that You might be glorified according to Isaiah 61:3.
For my shame, give me double; and for confusion, let me rejoice in my portion: therefore, in my land, I shall possess the double; everlasting joy shall be unto me according to Isaiah 61:7.

Restore to me the years that the locust hath eaten, the cankerworm, and the caterpillar, and the palmerworm, according to Your word in Joel 2:25.
I am free, for it is written, those whom the Lord makes free shall be free indeed.

57. Prayers Against The Spirit Of Abnormality

Heavenly Father, I come boldly before Your Throne of Grace, seeking Your divine intervention against the curse of abnormality and strange maledictions, weird, unnatural, odd, unusual, irregular, awkward, bizarre, twisted, unhealthy, and distorted, and all perplexing things that have become a part of my daily life.

I acknowledge that You are El-Shaddai; therefore, give me power to overthrow the forces of darkness, for You said in Your word, in Jeremiah 32:27, **"Behold, I am the LORD, the God of all flesh: is there anything too hard for Me?"**
Today, I stand against the forces of darkness and all turbulent situations that are haunting me, and with the authority of God, I denounce and defy all operations of the darkness as they pertain to the strange things that manifest through witchcraft and psychic manipulation in my life.
I revolt against every degree of stronghold, operating with the acceleration of the power of the occult seals, the pentagram, the sigils of demons and fallen angels, and all psychic commands fighting my life with unnatural and strange manifestations and situations.

By the power of the Holy Spirit, in the name of Jesus of Nazareth, I banish by fire all these evil entities and doorways that have opened in my home and life to demons of strangeness and irregularities. I detach myself from every enforced chain of affliction and occurrences of abnormality.
Hence, I say, strange fires in my life, be quenched now by the power of the Messiah, Jesus of Nazareth. I break that pattern and cycle of abnormal situations and happenings in my life.
Evil powers that are causing my own to always be different from others in a weird, unnatural, bizarre, odd, unusual, and irregular way,

be tormented with fire and brimstone in the presence of the holy angels and in the presence of the Lamb [Rev 14:10].

Cycles of abnormalities in my finances, be arrested by the fire of the Holy Spirit and by the power of the Messiah, Jesus of Nazareth, effective immediately.
Unnatural and abnormal behaviors in my character, die now by the power of the redeeming blood of Jesus in the name of the Messiah Jesus of Nazareth.
Brood of psychic forces manipulating my friends, coworkers, and family members to manifest weird and odd treatments toward me, be neutralized and self-destruct now, by the power of the Messiah Jesus of Nazareth.

Demons of abnormalities—weird, unnatural, odd, irregular, awkward, bizarre, perverted, twisted, unhealthy, distorted, and malformed—are tormented with fire and brimstone in the presence of the holy angels and in the presence of the Lamb, according to Rev. 14:10.
I call forth into normality and regularity all things in my life, and I call into divine order and alignment all operations, happenings, and occurrences in my life. Let everything that befalls me carry the mandate for my advancement, increase in good things, prosperity, and blessings.

Let the heavens and earth be rearranged and put back into order in order to accommodate my blessings and success, all in Jesus' name. To God be all the glory and honour and praise, now and forever, Amen and Amen.

58. Prayers Against The Spirit Of Abuse

Heavenly Father, I seek the intervention of Your Eternal Council, requesting that Your fire will render Your judgement against every agent of darkness for my sake, who has stolen, killed, and destroyed my life in many ways through abuse, hurts, and pains.

I have been a victim of abusive and violent behaviors which have greatly injured my life, destiny, and inflicted damage on the purposes of God in my life.

Oh Lord God of Israel, from my youth up I have been a victim of suppression, depression, oppression, guilt, shame, humiliation, disgrace, withdrawal, hurt, wounds, victimization, offense, mistreatment, cursing, torment, exploitation, perversion, mind control, domination, and cruelty.

I have been beaten, bruised, bullied, criticized, frustrated, and abused emotionally, mentally, physically, psychologically, and sexually by the words and brutal actions of my friends, my family, and foes. Let Your heart not turn away from me, O Lord, but look upon me with Your eyes of compassion and deliverance. It is written in Genesis 29:32, **"Surely the LORD hath looked upon my affliction."** Forgive all those who hurt me as I forgive them also.

But at this moment, Abba Father, I repent for my sins, transgressions, and the iniquities of my bloodline that may have opened a door for the spirit of abuse in my life. Every sin of my forefathers that the enemy would be using as a legal right to build legal cases against me and to sabotage and ruin my destiny, I petition by the blood of the Lamb that the justifying blood of Jesus would wash them away.

I petition by the blood of Christ that every legal right the spirit of abuse is using as a gate to afflict me be revoked, effective immediately, in Jesus' glorious name.

Abba Yah, who are in Heaven, let all hurt and abuse they have done to me serve to my advantage and become a weapon that will equip me to fight against the kingdom of darkness and turn all hurts and pain into vigorous boldness and forwardness, where I will stand and love my enemies with a perfect love. Your word says all things work together for good to those who love Christ.

Erase all my emotions that have developed negatively because of these pains of being abused, and all my actions that have been negatively modified and mutated because of these hurts and pain; eradicate them, O Lord Jesus, my Saviour. Let the dark fortresses and demonic strongholds built around and over my life be destroyed.

Let Your comfort embrace me, so I will know how to treat all humans and comfort them with love and compassion.

In the name of El-Shaddai, creator of the heavens and the earth, I renounce all demons of unforgiveness, bitterness, rage, murder, violence, hatred, anger, resentment, and fear, which came into my life because of the spirits of abuse.

Every demon that is using and manipulating my past and current hurts and pain for the evil plan to destroy my life, I bind them right now with the chains of the Holy Spirit in Jesus the Messiah's name. Every demon that has robbed me of my happiness and emotional bliss and stability; the Lord God of hosts rebukes you foul spirits, and I command the release of my stolen emotional benefits.

Wherever I am bound with iron chains and with the spirit of affliction according to Psalm 107:10, wherever my life is held trapped within any land of darkness, within the valley of the shadows of death, within an underground cave, within an astral labyrinth, within a spiritual maze, a catacomb, a pit, within a spiritual jail cell, or any spiritual incarceration chamber within the forest, desert, water, air, and in every place where I am held by darkness as a victim of abuse, trauma, and despair, look upon my affliction and send Your Angel to rescue me. Pull me out from any demonic pit that I am in, for it is written in Psalms 40:2, **"He brought me up also out of a horrible pit, out of the miry clay, and set my feet upon a rock, and established my goings."**

I call upon the fiery terror of God's divine judgement to shatter to pieces, consume to powder, dissolve, and eradicate these prison facilities, and nullify the sentence of my imprisonment by thunderclaps, lightnings, and wind and firestorms.

By Your supreme and eternal power, oh Lord God, possessor of the heavens and the earth, break the gates of brass, and cut the bars of iron asunder, and set me free from the prison where my soul is held incarcerated because of the trauma of abuse, hurts, and pains. For it is written in Your Word in Isaiah 45:2, **"I will go before thee, and make the crooked places straight: I will break in pieces the gates of brass and cut in sunder the bars of iron."**
Hence, by the authority of the Word of the Almighty God written in Luke 10:19 that says, **"behold, I give unto you power to tread on serpents and scorpions, and over all the power of the enemy: and nothing shall by any means hurt you."**
I pray and invoke a divine dynamic electrical discharge to manifest and shatter to pieces and debris every astral prison holding me shut in because of abuse.

Let dynamic fires mixed with lightnings and thunders be released from the North, South, East, and West, and destroy the place where I am held in captivity within the spirit world, right now in Jesus Name.

59. Prayers Against The Spirit Of Anger

Heavenly Father, I come before Your throne of grace through the judicial and redeeming blood of Jesus. I recognize and acknowledge that I am a prisoner of anger and rage, which have greatly injured my life and my relationship with others, compromised my destiny, and inflicted damage on the purposes of God in my life.

Abba Father, Your word says in Pro 29:22, **"An angry man stirreth up strife, and a furious man aboundeth in transgression."**
I repent for my sin, transgressions, and the iniquities of anger associated with my bloodline that may have opened a door for the spirit of anger in my life. Every sin of anger from my mother's house or from my father's house that the enemy is using as a legal right to build legal cases against me and to sabotage and ruin my destiny, let the fire that is in Your blood burn out this evil of anger. Let all traps of anger mandated to oppress, depress, and confiscate my blessings in the cosmic nets be destroyed now, by the velocity of the fire of the altar mentioned in Revelation chapter 8.

Erase the mark of anger (ancestral or personal) from my forehead and DNA that has caused me to develop angry emotions towards others for no apparent reason or for simple reasons, and the cloak of wrath that has clothed me with anger tantrums and outbursts.
Because of this anger issue and stronghold, all my actions have been negatively modified and mutated; therefore, I pray that you eradicate them, O Lord Jesus, my Saviour. Let the dark fortresses and demonic strongholds built around and over my life because of anger be destroyed.
Let Your peace, calmness, and pleasant personality be my character in communicating with others throughout various situations.

I will not deal foolishly because of my nature to get angry easily (Proverbs 14:17).

In Jesus' name, I will no longer be an angry and furious person (Proverbs 22:24); therefore, I will make friends with others, in Jesus' name.

In the name of El-Shaddai, creator of the heavens and the earth, I call out to all you demons associated with the spirit of anger. I renounce and rebuke all demons of anger, animosity, murder, vandalism, choler, fury, spite, temper, indignation, wrath, revenge, outrage, outburst, hostility, enmity, foolishness, contention, hatred, retaliation, strife, resentment, bitterness, unforgiveness, gall, and all other spirits that have entered my life because of these anger tantrums.

Every demon that is using and manipulating me through anger, I bind right now with the chains of the Holy Spirit in Jesus the Messiah's name. Every demon that has robbed me of relationships, good opportunities, open doors, destiny helpers, and has caused me to lose friends, destroy others, sabotage my blessings, and condemn good doors of success, the Lord God of hosts rebukes you foul spirits, and I command the release of my life.
Every form of anger and connective spirits lodging in my belly and liver, I command you, spirit of anger, to get out of my bosom (Ecclesiastes 7:9), by fire, now, in Jesus' name, for it is written, Ecclesiastes 7:9, **"Be not hasty in thy spirit to be angry."**

I come against the spirit of Cain, and I destroy every idol that was built in my life to represent the worship of the god of anger.

Anger, I speak to you in the name of Jesus Christ; you will not cause me to lose my blessings.

Every demon using anger to block my blessings in the second heaven, I block these aerial demons now, in Jesus' name.
I set fire to every territorial border where ambushment is being set up against me because of anger.
Every blessing the spirit of anger has swallowed at sundown because of wrath, I cut the belly of the beast asunder, and I retrieve my blessings in Jesus' name.

Wherever the Sun went down on my wrath because of anger, I overthrow you, demon of condemnation in the nighttime, and I declare that I am justified in Christ.
Wherever I am bound with iron chains by the spirit of anger, rage, and hostility according to Psalm 107:10, and wherever my life is held trapped within any land of the shadows of death and darkness, within an astral labyrinth, within a spiritual maze, a pit, a spiritual jail cell, or any spiritual incarceration chamber within the forest, desert, water, air, and subterranean astral chamber or cave of imprisonment, or in any place where I am held by darkness as a victim, look upon my affliction and send Your Angel to rescue me. Pull me out from any demonic pit that I am in, for it is written in Psalms 40:2, **"He brought me up also out of a horrible pit, out of the miry clay, and set my feet upon a rock, and established my goings."**

I call upon the fiery terror of God's divine judgement to shatter to pieces, consume to powder, dissolve, and eradicate these prison facilities, and nullify the sentence of my imprisonment by thunder, lightnings, wind, and firestorms.
By Your supreme and eternal power, oh Lord God, possessor of the heavens and the earth, break the gates of brass, and cut the bars of iron asunder, and set me free from the prison where my soul is held incarcerated because of anger and wrath within me. For it is written in Your Word in Isaiah 45:2, **"I will go before thee, and make the**

crooked places straight: I will break in pieces the gates of brass, and cut in sunder the bars of iron."

I decree that the sun will not go down on my wrath, in Jesus' name.

60. Prayer For Your Unborn Baby

Father, God of Israel, You are the Creator of the heavens and the earth! You have created the baby in my womb. You formed this child's inward parts; You did knit her in my womb. (Psalms 139:13)

Because You choose to give the Breath of Life to my baby, this baby shall live and not die, regardless of the assaults, attacks, and warfare that are waged against this baby by the kingdom of Satan. No weapon formed against my unborn baby shall prosper, and every weapon from the Mephistophelian world, and all powers from the 12 gates of Hell under the five esoteric occult seals are hereby liquidated, eradicated, annihilated, and destroyed beyond repair and recognition.

Father, supply all my baby's basic needs for proper foetal growth, and let all substances essential for normal growth be supplied with no deficiency. This child in my womb shall come to full maturity and full term with no complications, because complications are far from my womb and unborn baby. No evil, plague, or curse shall befall my unborn baby or come near me, neither shall any plague come near my dwelling.

By the highest authority of the highest Heaven, and by the power of His Name Yah, I build barricades and barriers of incomprehensible resistance against every evil spirit, and I call forth permanent walls and defences of Light and electric Fire around my womb, and around my unborn baby, effective immediately.
Every subtle psychic manipulation by witchcraft, necromancy, injuring, conjuring, projecting, voodoo herb mixture, incantation, ritual, altar, and every plot, plan, weapon, curse, snare, lair, or any other esoteric craft deployed to destroy the unborn baby in my womb

shall be met with incomprehensible destruction by fire and shall be roasted to dry ash, vaporized by fire, and vanished into thin air without a trace. In the mighty name of Jesus.

All evil powers of the kingdom of Hell orchestrated against me and my unborn baby; I sabotage their evil plans while still in discussion, I scatter their forces before they are formed, I abort their ideas of attack and manipulation before they are conceived; and may their strategies of attack start and end in confusion. Before they rise, let them fall and crumble in shame, defeat, and disgrace, and become victims of their own plots and evil devices, in Jesus' name.

I destroy and banish by lightning, fire, and thunder all secret landmines and booby traps that are specifically set against my pregnancy.

Let every secret counsel, plan, desire, expectation, imagination, device, plot, and snare of the 7 Occult kingdoms formed against my life and the life of my unborn baby be destroyed beyond comprehension now, in Jesus' name.

Through Jesus the Messiah, and by the power of the Holy Spirit, I render all spiritual forces of the kingdom of Hell programmed against me and against my unborn child impotent, frustrated, inadequate, incapable, barren, void, liquidated, ineffective, nullified, ineligible, and useless in the name of Jesus.

All you occult kingdoms of the land, the sea, and the air, I notify you that all your efforts to harm, manipulate, or destroy my unborn child have already failed miserably, by the power of the Holy Spirit and the fire of the highest altar in Heaven, in Jesus' name.

There will be no trauma to my baby, nor will there be any sabotage or ambushment of this child's mental, emotional, or spiritual life.

This child in my womb is made for signs and wonders. For it is written in Isaiah 8:18, **"Behold, I and the children whom the LORD hath given me** *are* **for signs and for wonders in Israel from the LORD of hosts, which dwelleth in mount Zion"**.
This baby in my womb shall be an oracle of God's word to the nations, tribes, and tongues.
This child in my womb has inbuilt wisdom and has divine intelligence to articulate sophisticated knowledge and knowledge.

This baby in my womb belongs to the Lord Jesus and is a priest unto God, a servant of Jesus, a messenger of the Lord, and a steward of good works.
Let the Spirit of excellence be found in this child in my womb, and let this child be filled with the Spirit of the Lord from the womb.

I pray by fire that my baby in my womb will not be bound to any stage of underdevelopment and will not be an underachiever after birth.
Heavenly Father, I pray that any family curse, sin, or iniquity that has caused certain negative family traits to be embedded in the child's DNA, character, and personality, let the fire of the Altar of God Almighty burn and purge out these things from my baby.

Every transfer of family evil and wickedness that has passed from me to this baby via the umbilical cord, or through the testicular gate of the father, let this wickedness be burnt out and all sins be purged from my baby. Reconnect the dendrites for new godly pathways in my baby's brain.
Let no physical, mental, or psychological damage be done to this baby during the months of pregnancy due to lack of nutrition, spirit of alcohol, spirit of drugs, spirit of smoking, spirit of sexual perversion, or evil covenants in the bloodline from the mother's house and the father's house.

I also petition You, Father, to cleanse my unborn baby from all negative and damaging thought patterns, perceptions of life in general, of himself, and of others, as well as of who You are, and protect this child from the spirit of identity crisis and gender dysphoria (gender identity disorder].

Remove all ungodly barriers between the needed neurons and break any ungodly seals over certain areas of my baby's brain, in Jesus' name. Destroy every ungodly, unhealthy type of neurotransmitter and other chemicals/hormones that would cause negative changes in thought patterns, tantrums, anger, aggression, or depression in my baby.

I pray that every unhealthy demand by the receptors will be removed, that the shape and sensitivity of all receptors will change according to Your supply of love, in Jesus' name.
Father God, we petition You, according to Your Word in Isaiah 61, that my baby's mind, and the eyes of this child's understanding and spiritual ears will be open to recognize, see, and hear Your voice, see Your glory, and receive and know the truth. It is written, **"Lo, children are a heritage of the LORD: and the fruit of the womb is his reward".** Psalms 127:3.
"And all thy children shall be taught of the LORD; and great shall be the peace of thy children". Isaiah 54:13.
Therefore, let my baby after birth be enabled to receive Your love, acceptance, nurture, etc. We pray that there will be an early unlocking of this baby's potential, gifts, insight, and intelligence, and that he or she will identify with Your opinion all the time.

For this, I give You thanks and praise in the name of Your Son Jesus, my Saviour, Amen and Amen.

61. Prayer Against Venom Of Neutralization

Heavenly father, in the name of Jesus, I come to You through the blood of the Lamb which gives me access to Your throne of Grace by the Holy Spirit, and I petition You for my spiritual well-being according to Deuteronomy. 10 and 11. It is written in Deuteronomy 10:16, **"Circumcise therefore the foreskin of your heart, and be no more stiff-necked."**
According to Your requirement I should only fear You, O LORD our God, to walk in ALL Your ways, to love You, with all my heart, mind, soul and might.

By the blood of the Lamb, I petition You to circumcise my heart, deliver me from the hand of evil spirits that are manipulating my character and attitude through the corruption of my heart and mind. It is written in Psalms 35:10, **"All my bones shall say, Yahuah, who is like unto you, which deliver the poor from him that is too strong for him, yea, the poor and the needy from him that spoils him?"**
Acts 4:29, **"And now, Lord, behold their threatenings: and grant unto thy servants, that with all boldness they may speak thy word,"**

I pray against the vaccine and venom of tranquilization and neutralization that is injected into me by the Demon Venom, and by every other demon which carries venom in order to neutralize humans.
Through Jesus of Nazareth, let every astral poison and the venom of tranquilization and neutralization be neutralized and lose all substance of power and effectiveness against me.
Let God arise for my sake and let the enemies be scattered. Demons within the cracks of the earth, crevices of the cosmic realm, and within potholes in the cemeteries sniffing, snitching and plotting my

destruction, let them be roasted by fiery coals from the holy altar of the Almighty God.

Every evil spirit seeking to give me a hardened heart through the deceitfulness of sin, and an evil heart of unbelief to depart from the living God, I now draw from the blood of Jesus and claim immunity to withstand these assaults of the forces of cosmological verdict of the Inner Esoteric framework of Satan.

Exodus 15:11, **"Who is like unto you, O Yahuah, among the elohim? Who is like you, glorious in holiness, fearful in praises, doing wonders?"**

Deuteronomy 33:29, **"Happy are you, O Yashar 'El: who is like unto you, O people saved by Yahuah, the shield of your help, and who is the sword of your excellency! and your enemies shall be found liars unto you; and you shall tread upon their high places."**

Through Jesus of Nazareth, I call forth into the light of Jesus Christ all satanic powers, and I declare war, and revolt against, neutralize, destroy and banish from my liver, my heart, my throat, my ears, my mouth, my kidney, my spine, my spleen, my genital, my belly and my forehead every astral poison and all venom of tranquilization and neutralization mentioned in 2Timothy 3:2 -7, the venom of lovers of selves, venom of covetousness, venom of boasters, venom of proudness, venom of blasphemy, venom of disobedient to parents, venom of unthankfulness, venom of unholiness, venom of no natural affection, venom of truce breaking, venom of false accuser, venom of incontinent, venom of fierceness, venom of despiser of those that are good, venom of traitor, venom of headiness, venom of high-mindedness, venom of lovers of pleasures more than lovers of God; venom of a form of godliness, venom of divers lusts, venom of ever learning, and never able to come to the knowledge of the truth, and all other psychic entity in my life operating under the First Esoteric

Seal 333, within the five Mephistophelian Occult system and stronghold.

Through Jesus of Nazareth, let every astral poison and venom of tranquilization and neutralization that has reconfigured, reprogrammed and neutralized my prayer life, be neutralized and lose all substance of power and effectiveness against me, effective immediately.

I also call forth into the light of Jesus Christ all satanic powers, and I declare war, and revolt against, neutralize, destroy and banish from my liver, my heart, my throat, my ears, my mouth, my kidney, my spine, my spleen, my genital, my belly and my forehead every astral poison and all venom of tranquilization and neutralization mentioned in Romans 1:29-31; the venom of all unrighteousness, venom of fornication, venom of wickedness, venom of covetousness, venom of maliciousness; venom of envy, venom of murder, venom of debate, venom of deceit, venom of malignity; venom of whisperer, venom of backbiting, venom of haters of God, venom of despitefulness, venom of proudness, venom of boasters, venom of inventors of evil things, venom of disobedient to parents, venom of no understanding, venom of covenant breaker, venom of no natural affection, venom of implacable, venom of unmerciful, and all other psychic entity in my life operating under the First Esoteric Seal 333, within the five Mephistophelian Occult system and stronghold.

O Lord God of the Heavens and Earth, I pray against the Guardians of fate and the cycles of life, dark principalities, powers, rulers of darkness, legions of the air, aquatic forces, subterranean forces, earth masters, mermaids, sirens, the elemental spirits and all other demons who have formed artilleries of destruction, calamities, and systems of evil operations against my life through the subtle psychic manipulations, let these evil spirits be tormented with fire and brimstone in the presence of the holy angels, and in the presence of the Lamb. [Rev 14:10].

All astral poison and venom of tranquilization and neutralization that have neutralized my life, so that I cannot function with precise intellectual capacities, pristine intelligence, pristine articulation of my expression of morals, self-worth, integrity, knowledge and love for Jesus, release my life and potential now.

I neutralize you Demon of venom and reclaim the full functionality of my faculties, intellectually, spiritually, emotionally, psychologically, mentally, by fire and by the authority of the Blood of Jesus and the power of the 7 horns of the Lamb of God in Revelation 5:6
By lightnings and thunders of fire wrapped with the glory of the eternal light of Christ, I gather the fragments of my members from every realm, sphere, occult zone, region, centre and dimension of the upper darkness and lower darkness, In Jesus Name.

Every black heart demon specifically assigned to give me a black heart and hard heart of stone and pride under the stronghold of Occult Seal 333, be banished now, in Jesus Name.

All astral poison and venom of tranquilization and neutralization that have neutralized my prayer life, release my prayer life and potential now, as I neutralize you venom and reclaim the full functionality of my prayer life, In Jesus Name.

All astral poison and venom of tranquilization and neutralization that have neutralized my ability to resist temptation and sin, release my will, strength and resistance against sin now, as I neutralize you venom and reclaim the full functionality of my strength, will and power to resist the devil, In Jesus Name.

All astral poison and venom of tranquilization and neutralization that have neutralized my marriage, release my marital joy, fulfilment, and love expressions and passion to express love now, as I neutralize you venom and reclaim the full functionality of my marital life according to the plan of God for marriages, In Jesus Name.

All astral poison and venom of tranquilization and neutralization that have neutralized my household, so that they would not express love, gratitude, thankfulness, fellowship, unity, and care amongst themselves, release my family household, you foul spirits. I neutralize you demons of venoms, and I reclaim the full love family functionality of my household, In Jesus Name.

Through Jesus of Nazareth, let every astral poison and venom of tranquilization and neutralization that is programmed to force me into backsliding be neutralized and lose all substance of power and effectiveness against me, effective immediately.
Father, I thank you for delivering me today by grace through faith, and for this victory through Your Son Jesus, and I am walking in this victory.

62. Prayer To Deliver From Fragmented Soul

Father, You who is worthy of all praise and adoration. Worthy is the Lamb that was slain to receive power, and riches, and wisdom, and strength, and honour, and glory, and blessing.
Lord God, by the blood of the Lamb and in the name of Jesus Christ, I make petitions today, and I ask You to deploy Your holy angels to gather up the fragments of my soul from every Realm, Dimension, Zone, Region and Centre of the Occultic world and restore them to their rightful place in me (Psalm 7:2, 23:3).

I am aware that my soul has become fragmented due to life's challenges, hurts, and horrific experiences, sexual immorality, fornication, soul-ties, trauma, abuse, war, conflict, terror and great fear.

I call upon You Lord Jesus of Nazareth, and I call upon divine intervention to gather those scattered pieces of my soul and bring healing. I acknowledge that I feel disconnected from my own thoughts, body, soul, my mind, my emotions, my environment.
I am experiencing dissociation, depression, fatigue, loss of trail of thoughts and anxiety, and have developed unhealthy coping mechanisms to deal with these issues.
Retrieve my fragmented soul and send the fire and the balm of the stripes of Jesus the Lamb of God and address my inner wounds.
Psalms 143:7, **"Hear me speedily, O LORD: my spirit failed: hide not thy face from me, lest I be like unto them that go down into the pit."**
Psalms 143:8, **"Cause me to hear thy lovingkindness in the morning; for in thee do I trust: cause me to know the way wherein I should walk; for I lift up my soul unto thee."**

Psalms 143:9, **"Deliver me, O LORD, from mine enemies: I flee unto thee to hide me."**

Every fragmentation of my soul which took place because of sexual immorality, fornication, soul ties, trauma, abuse, war, conflict, terror, and great fear, I pray for healing for my soul, for it is written in Psalms 23, **"He restoreth my Soul."**
I renounce false comfort and break ungodly soul ties formed between me and any demon binding me to my past and holding any part of my life captive thereby.

I renounce any false sources of comfort (addictions, distractions, etc.) and invite God's true comfort into my life.
I break any ungodly soul tie that may be binding me to the past. I renounce and revoke the satanic and diabolical verdict and law of Hell that sustains this evil operation.
Genesis 2:7, **"And the LORD God formed man of the dust of the ground and breathed into his nostrils the breath of life; and man became a living soul."**
Proverbs 10:3, **"The LORD will not suffer the soul of the righteous to famish: but he casted away the substance of the wicked."**

By lightnings and thunders of fire wrapped with the glory of the eternal light of Christ, every place where fragments of my soul and mind are scattered and are being held captive within the zones, regions, and centres of the realms of the dead, the air, the forest, the land, and in the different levels of the shadows of death, I gather the fragments of my members from every realm, sphere, occult zone, region, center and dimension of the upper darkness and lower darkness, in Jesus' Name.

I call upon the God of my salvation to draw every fragment of my soul out from these places and condemn the path, the guardians, and the gates of these evil dimensions.

Give unto me beauty for ashes, the oil of joy for mourning, the garment of praise for the spirit of heaviness; that I might be called trees of righteousness, the planting of the LORD, that You might be glorified, according to Isaiah 61:3.

For my shame, *give me* double; and *for* confusion, let me rejoice in my portion: therefore, in my land I shall possess the double: everlasting joy shall be unto me according to Isaiah 61:7.

Thank You, Yah, for restoring my soul from fragmentation by faith, and for filling me with Your Holy Spirit and Your peace that surpasses all understanding.

To You be all the glory, honour, and Mighty, In Jesus Name Amen.

63. Destroying Witchcraft Fortresses From Your Mind And Thoughts

Holy Father, I know that the transformation of my life can only come by the renewing of my mind, as my thoughts are renewed. The first battleground that determines my victory or defeat is the mind. Hence, the first ground of confrontation and forefront warfare is in my mind. Your word says, Romans 12:2, **"And be not conformed to this world: but be ye transformed by the renewing of your mind, that ye may prove what *is* that good, and acceptable, and perfect, will of God."**

Our God and King, Your name is holy in all kingdoms of the heavens and the earth, in all realms, dimensions, and spheres.
You who sit between the Cherubim rule in the affairs of men, because You are the Most High God, but You are also my father.
It is written in Your word in Romans 8:6, **"For to be carnally minded *is* death; but to be spiritually minded *is* life and peace."** Romans 8:7, also says, **"Because the carnal mind *is* enmity against God: for it is not subject to the law of God, neither indeed can be."**

Lord, I acknowledge that my mind is not clean before You.
Like the Apostle Paul, I see another law in my members, warring against the law of my mind, and bringing me into captivity to the law of sin that is in my members. [Romans 7:23].
But Your Word has commanded us to bring our thoughts into captivity and under subjection to the obedience of Christ.
Hence, today I place my mind and thoughts upon Your holy altar, and I petition by the blood of the Lamb for Your divine intervention, that You would transform my mind, my thinking system, and my paradigm, so that I can fulfill Your divine will for my life.
Your word says in Psalm 94:11, **"The LORD knows the thoughts of man, that they *are* vanity."**

Father, I humbly acknowledge that my thoughts are vanities and are unclean continually, full of evil and foul contemplations. My focus has been diverted to perverted thinking, and carnalities have invaded my mind and thoughts. These evil thoughts have corrupted my attitude, personality, and character towards the Word of God, towards others, and towards God the Father. Hence, I call upon Your purifying fire to purge my mind.

Heavenly Father, You commanded that we should allow the mind which was in Christ to be also in us. [Pup 2:5], but I cannot do it by myself; You promised to put Your word in our hearts and minds.
Cleanse my mind with a strong purging and remove all unclean thoughts.
It is written in Hebrews 12:3, **"For consider him that endured such contradiction of sinners against himself, lest ye be wearied and faint in your minds."**
Do not allow me to faint in my mind because Your word says to us in Colossians 1:21, **"And you, that were sometime alienated and enemies in** *your* **mind by wicked works, yet now has he reconciled."**
Because I am reconciled, please present me blameless according to Colossians 1:22, which says, **"In the body of his flesh through death, to present you holy and unblameable and unreproveable in his sight:"**

Let Your blood and fire deliver my mind from the hold of the kingdom of sin and death. Romans 8:6, **"For to be carnally minded** *is* **death; but it also says to be spiritually minded** *is* **life and peace," [Romans 8:6]**. Let the life and peace of Your light and life fill my heart today so that I can please You.
Let the council of the blood of the new covenant destroy all planted evil that is in my mind and thoughts. All degrading thoughts,

perverted thoughts, thoughts of evil plots, revenge, manipulations, rebellion, carnal proclivities, seeds of wickedness, wicked imaginations, and every imagination of the thoughts of my heart *which are* only evil continually, [Gen 6:5]. Cleanse by the fire of Your blood.
O Lord, Your word says in Psalms 10:4, **"The wicked, through the pride of his countenance, will not seek** *after God:* **God** *is* **not in all his thoughts."**

Remove pride from my heart and mind, and reconfigure and recondition my thoughts and the imagination of my heart.
Create in me a clean heart, O God; and renew a right spirit within me, according to Psalms 51:10.

Today, in the name of Elohei Tzevaot, by fire, lightnings, and holy thunders, I declare war against the Devil's war.
Satan, Lucifer, and you Devil, and all hosts of the kingdom of darkness, we have been commanded by Yah to forsake our wicked ways and renew our minds, as it is written in Isaiah 55:7, **"Let the wicked forsake his way, and the unrighteous man his thoughts: and let him return unto the LORD, and he will have mercy upon him; and to our God, for he will abundantly pardon."**
It is also written in Ephesians 4:23, **"And be renewed in the spirit of your mind;"**

Today, I forsake my ways and my evil thoughts; I have returned unto the LORD my God, and He will have mercy upon me.
Hear me, all you hosts of the kingdom of darkness, the Lord Y'ahushua of Nazareth has given me authority in Luke 10:19, where He says, **"behold, I give unto you power to tread on serpents and scorpions, and over all the power of the enemy: and nothing shall by any means hurt you."**

Therefore, today I wage warfare against the law of sin that is in my members, and the evil laws of my mind, and bring into captivity all evil thoughts and demons.

Hence, by the standard of the authority of the Word of the Almighty God, I take authority over all demonic operations in my mind and thoughts, and I invoke divine Angelic interventions against the demonic forces of carnal thoughts and a carnal mind.

I pray, let dynamic fires, lightning, and thunders shatter every astral prison facility where my mind is held in captivity by the demonic spirit of evil thoughts and wicked imaginations.

I ambush every demonic ambushment that has ambushed my mind and thoughts, and command by fire that my thought-life, mind, and thinking system be released from all satanic holds of darkness, effective immediately.

By Jesus the Messiah, I pray, let every evil fortress that has been constructed around my mind, and let every evil tower that has been mounted up in my mind, self-destruct now, in Jesus' name.

The Holy Spirit of Wisdom commanded us in Proverbs 6:5, and says, **"Deliver thyself as a roe from the hand *of the hunter,* and as a bird from the hand of the fowler."**

Also, thus says the Lord to us in Zechariah 2:7, **"Deliver thyself, O Zion, that dwellest *with* the daughter of Babylon."**

Therefore, by this power of the command of El-Shaddai, the Lord of Armies, I break in pieces every prison bar of iron and gate of bronze, and all demonic imprisonment where my soul is held in captivity by Satan or the Devil, and I release and deliver myself from the demonic degrees and strongholds coming from the North, South, East, and West, and destroy the place where I am held in captivity within the spirit world, and also block every invasion of my thoughts, thinking, and reasoning right now, effective immediately, in Jesus Name.

Now by faith, I release a dynamic electrical discharge and detonation of fire from the Altar of Heaven upon all demons in my mind and thoughts, and I command the immediate disarming and degradation, eradication, destruction, annihilation, and banishment of all maggot demons, demonic flies, spirit of Baalzebub, monkey demons, worm demons, fungi, insects, crawlers, wrigglers, evil seeds, demonic eggs, demonic larvae, doorways of evil, and all wickedness established in my thoughts, in my mind, over my mind, and upon my head.

In Jesus' exalted name, all of you demons of evil thoughts and carnal minds, be gone from me. The power of Jesus Christ of Nazareth compels you; the authority of the Blood of Christ commands you. Get out of my head and go now! In Jesus Name.

By the power of the Holy Spirit, and the faith of Jesus of Nazareth, and by the three that bear witness on earth: the Water, the Blood, and the Spirit, I destroy the power, jurisdiction, and velocity of all you guardians of fate and the cycles of life, principalities, powers, transformers of minds, Astro-Omnidictator, demi-god, god, goddesses, siren, Earth master, psychic force, planetary spirit, Python, watcher, guardians of the flame, solar lords, inter-planetary lords, inter-galactic lords, supreme elementals, mermaids, and all you evil forces that are over my mind and have built evil strongholds, garrisons, sanctuaries, and shrines in and around my mind, brain, and principles of thoughts.

Let all you evil spirits that have taken over my thinking system, reasoning, understanding, and the mental integrity of a pure mind be gone from my conscience and mind by fire; get out of my life right now and be gone, effective immediately.
Satan, the power of Jesus Christ of Nazareth commands you; the authority of the Blood of Christ commands you.

Through the Holy Spirit, in the name of Jesus of Nazareth, I call forth the seraphic fire of the burning coals from between the holy altar to manifest like a dynamic and raging fire and burn out from my mind all filthy thoughts, wrong emotions, wicked proclivities, evil intentions, evil inclinations, atrocities, evil thoughts, and all wicked and unclean imaginations planted in my mind through dreams, filthy materials, corrupt communications, videos, audios, sense of touch, and sense of taste, which have taken the form of maggots or bred maggots or other forms of creatures in and around my mind, upon my head, or in my thoughts.

Every spiral snake coiled around my mind; I place a hook in your jaw and bind your head to your tail and cast you into the fire of the presence of the Holy Spirit of Jesus, as in Acts 28:5, for it is written in Psalm 119:113, **"I hate *vain* thoughts."**

All agents and powers of darkness, take up your devices, deposits, baggage, manipulation, and evil things from my mind and thoughts and disappear from my life; be gone from me now and get out of my life, now in Jesus' name.

Let every mind suppression, depression, oppression, guilt, exploitation, perversion, mind control, and domination be banished from my brain and heart now, in the name of Jesus the Messiah.

The Lord is saying to us in Proverbs 16:3, "**Commit thy works unto the LORD, and thy thoughts shall be established.**" Therefore, I commit my works unto God Almighty; now, let my thoughts be established in Christ, my Lord.

Lord Jesus, set my mind and cause it to be stayed on You, and keep me in perfect peace, and build protections of righteousness in my mind, for it says in Isaiah 26:3, **"You will keep *him* in perfect peace, whose mind *is* stayed on You; because he trusts in You."**

I say, as in Psalm 119:113, **"I hate *vain* thoughts; but thy law do I love."** I decree with a tongue of fire that I am delivered from the curse and stronghold of an evil and carnal mind because it is written in Colossians 1:22, concerning me saying, **"In the body of his flesh through death, to present you holy and unblameable and unreproveable in his sight:"**

Defend my mind, Lord Jesus, from all evil beings and creatures who operate under the 'Inner Esoteric' framework and the Hierarchy of the powers of darkness within the Astral and Terrestrial dimension. Please present me holy, unblameable, and unreproveable in Your precious sight; in the name of Jesus, I pray…Amen and Amen.

64. Prayer For Repairing The Breach Made In Your Life.

Heavenly Father and Most High God, Your name is holy, and You are exalted in all kingdoms, realms, and dimensions. It is through Your power that I was created from the dust, and it is in You that I live, move, and have my being.
It is You who knows the end from the beginning because You are the Most High God. Therefore, I come to You to acknowledge my need for Your divine intervention because of the breach that was set in my life.

My life has been a project, a monopoly, and a playground for demons of affliction who have set a breach in my life.
Because of this, I cannot fully function in the work of God because I have been breached and compromised.

Holy Father, I pray in every terrestrial realm, sub-aquatic region, cosmic world, subterranean world, and in every astral layer, plain, zone, region, and kingdom where the kingdom of darkness, by psychic manipulations, has reduced me to a doormat, a victim, a prisoner of affliction, a lab rat, a test subject, a candidate, a secret initiate of darkness, and where I have been a monopoly and playground for serpentine spirits and other evil creatures of the astral forces, who have set in my life spiritual crevices, breaches, cracks, tears, a rending asunder, a breakage, leakage, and trenches in my ministry, my mind, my emotions, my character, in my spiritual growth, in my understanding, in my perception, my dreams, my destiny, and future; and in every place where I have been breached, ambushed, and trapped with broken trust, a broken emotional system, a torn personality, and a broken life, by psychic forces who operate at the highest velocity of Astro-metaphysical acceleration, I now invoke the power of Elohei Tzevaot to destroy all these evil strongholds, spirits, entities, agents, and realms, and release me from within every realm, plane, and region of the psychic kingdoms of space, land, and water, and destroy all verdicts and jurisdictions of Hell from over my life.

Heavenly Father, I call upon Your eternal light of fire and love, and Your restorative flames and power of repair, to descend and repair me in every component of my life where humans and demons have made a breach. Repair every spiritual crevice, tear, breakage, leakage, trench, broken trust, broken emotional system, torn personality, broken life, broken mental stability, and every breach that was made. Reconfigure my life wherever I was emotionally, psychologically, mentally, and spiritually dismembered and tampered with.

O Lord, deliver me by the verdict of the judicial blood of Jesus, in whom I have redemption and the forgiveness of sins, according to the riches of His grace; [Eph 1:7, Col 1:14.]
Your word says in Isaiah 58:12, **"And *they that shall be* of thee shall build the old waste places: thou shalt raise up the foundations of many generations; and thou shalt be called, The repairer of the breach, The restorer of paths to dwell in."**
My Father and my God, in the authority of Your word in Matthew 7:8 that says, **"For everyone that asks receives; and he that seeks finds; and to him that knocks it shall be opened."**
I petition by the blood of the Lamb that You rebuild the old wasted places of my life, that which the kingdom of darkness has devastated, and raise up the foundations of many generations.
Repair the breach that was made in every area of my life, restore the paths to dwell in, and by this divine process, make me a repairer of the breach and a restorer of the paths to dwell in.

Your word says in Isaiah 61:1, You are anointed to bind up the broken-hearted, to proclaim liberty to the captives, and to open the prison to them that are bound. Now, Holy Spirit of Yah, by Your divine eternal fire, as You repair my wounds and breaches, deliver me from emotional, psychological, mental, and spiritual captivity, and open the prison for me like You did for Peter in Acts 12:7, 11, 17, and for Paul in Acts 16:26.

All those who have set a breach in my life, I forgive them, and Lord, forgive them, and every demon who is responsible for the breaches set in my life, judge these demons seventy times seven.

Repair and restore my ability to do again the good works in Your kingdom and give unto me beauty for ashes, the oil of joy for mourning, the garment of praise for the spirit of heaviness; that I might be called trees of righteousness, the planting of the LORD, that You might be glorified, according to Isaiah 61:3.

For my shame *give me* double; and *for* confusion, let me rejoice in my portion: therefore, in my land I shall possess the double: everlasting joy shall be unto me, according to Isaiah 61:7.

All these prayers I pray in the holy name of Y'ahushua

Thank you, Yah, for repairing the breaches in my life by faith, and for filling me with Your Holy Spirit and peace that surpasses all understanding.

Thank you for Your boundless love, grace, and protection, and for the victory that You have given to me in Christ Jesus. To You be all the glory, honour, and Mighty, In Jesus Name Amen.

65. Prayers Against The Spirit Of Mind Wandering & Daydreaming

Heavenly Father, my shelter and fortress, I come before You by faith, through the Blood of Jesus and by Your Holy Spirit, and I declare Your sovereignty over my situation of mind-wandering.

Lord, Your word says that we should be sober and vigilant and think of godly, righteous things. But the kingdom of darkness has infiltrated my mind, in the name of Jesus.
Lord, I come before You as a wanderer, often straying from the path You have set for us and straying in my thoughts. Heavenly Father, You are the God of all wisdom and truth, the shepherd of my soul. I petition by the blood of the Lamb for Your guidance and strength to find our way back to where I should be and refocus on you and the things that are important.
Set guards of fire to keep me from wandering off the path of righteousness and holiness, and to remember who I am in Christ.
Teach me to trust in Your plan and to find peace in Your presence and the fullness of joy. Therefore, let Your joy be my strength.

Grant me the wisdom to see what's going on in my surroundings and the ability to stay focused and vigilant.
It is written in Luke 10:17, **"And the seventy returned again with joy, saying, Lord, even the devils are subject to us through thy name."**

Therefore, I command by the voice of thunder and fire that ALL demons, sirens, demigods, astral powers, and evil dark angels of the land, sea, air, and underground be subjected to me now, effective immediately, for the Lord Jesus says to us in Luke 10:19, **"Behold, I give unto you power to tread on serpents and scorpions, and over all** the power of the enemy: and nothing shall by any means hurt you."

Therefore, in the Name of Y'ahushua HaMashiach of Nazareth, by the power of the judgement and the authority of the Word of God in Luke 10:19, Psalms 11:6 and Exodus 9:24, I cast out from my life every spirit of poor attentional control, short attention span, spirit of lack of focus, spirit of distraction, spirit of laziness, spirit of lethargy, spirit of unproductiveness, demon of fantasy, demon of unreality.

I also cast ouarefrom my life every demon of retention, demon of schizophrenia, demon of withdrawal, demon of denial, demon of self-seclusion, demon of worry, demon of self-seeking attention, demon of deprivation of inner peace, love and security, and I banish any demon of scattered mind and thoughts that is snatching me away from the realm of full consciousness to a place of an aimless wanderer.
In like manner, by the name of El-Shaddai, creator of the heavens and the earth, by the power of the Holy Spirit/

I banish from my life and awareness every imaginary creativity, demonically induced emotional processing stimuli, and demons of escape from reality, and all spirits who are seducing me and reducing me into guilty-dysphoric daydreaming, obsessive thoughts, guilt, or anxiety dreamlike scenes, negative and destructive daydreaming that are controlling, afflicting, and affecting my life negatively, and are seeking to divert my purpose, thought, mind, and path. Let all signals to my brain be broken permanently, now in Jesus' name.

I charge against, rebuke, destroy, and banish the power of all demons of wandering (Jeremiah 48:12), demon of roaming, homeless, rejection, outcast, poverty, and the spirit of the vagabonds (Psalm

109:10); I rebuke these spirits in Jesus' name and command them to leave my mind and body now.

By the fire of the Holy Spirit, in Jesus' Name, and the jurisdiction of the Blood and Word of God, I address all spirits that are swaying me or would seek to sway me in psychological and mental channels of worries or unresolved issues or are drawing me into mental places where I am continually entering an imaginary world, astral plane, with replays, fantasies and imaginary scenes.

By the power of Jesus the Christ of Nazareth, Son of the Living God, let these demons be gone from me, and be banished into exile in oblivion and barren unknown places of no return, now, In Jesus Name.
I pray that every path, channel, realm, and phase where my mind and awareness are swallowed by imagery, fantasy dream worlds, and imaginary realities be cut off from me, effective immediately, in Jesus' name.

I pray that every demon that would seek to blend or is blending elements of my imagination and perception to create mental scenarios or imaginary worlds, I arrest, bind, and banish these demons from my life, and send them into oblivion and chaos.

All elemental spirits use psychic manipulation to create vivid mental images and scenarios that can feel almost as real and give me a sense of euphoria, false joy, excitement, hope, and purpose. I dissolve these evil subtle manipulations and banish all demons responsible for these evil works in my mind by the name of El-Shaddai, creator of the heavens and the earth, by the power of the Holy Spirit.

66. Prayers Against The Spirit Of Bitterness, Hatred, & Unforgiveness.

Lord God of the Heavens and the Earth, I come before Your throne of grace through the Holy Spirit and the judicial and redeeming blood of Jesus.

Heavenly Father, I seek the intervention of Your Eternal Council, requesting that Your fire will render Your judgement against every agent of darkness for my sake, who has robbed, confiscated, and destroyed my life in whatever way because of unforgiveness and bitterness.

Ephesians 4:31 says, **"Let all bitterness and indignation and wrath and clamour and evil speaking be removed from you, together with all malice;"**

Ephesians 4:32, **"And be kind and tenderhearted toward one another, forgiving one another, even as God has also in Christ forgiven you."**

LORD Jesus, (name the offender) deeply hurt me by (describing what was done to you). I am still very hurt and wounded, and I am having difficulty forgiving (name the offender).

I acknowledge that in myself, I do not want to forgive (name the offender), and I am angry and I feel hatred, bitterness, unforgiveness, and resentment towards (name the offender), but anger, bitterness, resentment, hatred, unforgiveness, and desires for revenge are interfering with my healing, ministry, health, and relationship with You and others, and have interrupted my prayer life, true worship, and sincere praise.

However, Your word says that we must forgive if we desire our heavenly Father to forgive us for our trespasses, and that we must overcome evil with good. Col 3:13 says, **"Forbearing one another, and forgiving one another, if any man has a quarrel against any; even as Christ forgave you, so also do ye."**

I now confess that I have harboured anger, bitterness, resentment, unforgiveness, hatred, and desire for revenge toward (name the offender). I petition by the blood of the Lamb for Your forgiveness as I renounce these sins and iniquities. 1 John 1:9 - If we confess our sins, He is faithful and just and will forgive us our sins and purify us from all unrighteousness.

I am willing to forgive and release (name the offender); therefore, I acknowledge that I cannot change my own heart and mind, so I ask You to give me Your Heart, Your Mind, Your Truth, and Your Compassion, with the spirit of Humility and Forgiveness regarding this situation. Psalm 51:10, **"Create in me a clean heart, O God; and renew a right spirit within me."**

To Forgive a Friend

Dear God, I bring before You a friend who has caused me pain and hurt. It is difficult to carry this burden of anger and resentment in my heart.
Lord, I choose to forgive them for the hurt they've caused me. I release the bitterness and anger, knowing that forgiveness is a gift I give to myself as well. Help me to find understanding and compassion for their actions. May Your love guide both of us toward reconciliation and healing. Grant us the wisdom to rebuild our friendship with love and trust. In Jesus' name, I pray.

Forgiving Family Who Have Caused Pain

Heavenly Father, I lift up my family members who have caused me pain and heartache. Help me to find it in my heart to forgive them, even as I acknowledge the hurt they've caused. May Your healing touch mend the brokenness within our family and bring us closer together. In Jesus' name, I pray.

LORD Jesus, I ask You to wash me with Your Blood, cleanse me, and set me free from all harboured anger, bitterness, resentment, unforgiveness, hatred, and desire for revenge towards (name the offender), and hence I stand in Your authority and rebuke all foul spirits of the air who are manipulating my emotions and desires.

By the authority given in the name of Jesus of Nazareth, and by the power of His Spirit and Blood, I call upon the blast of God's nostrils and the voice of the Lord mentioned in Psalms 29 to demolish all spiritual strongholds and demonic fortresses built around my life through anger, bitterness, resentment, unforgiveness, hatred, and desire for revenge.

By the Right Hand of the Lord God and by the power of Jesus, Messiah of Nazareth, Son of the Living God, with chains of fire and shackles of brimstone I strategically bind the neck, the hands, and the feet of all you psychic entities of the four elements and your operations, which are set in astral motion within the psychic layers against my life.

Through Jesus, I bind, disarm, banish, and destroy all foul powers sent against and into my life by the kingdom of the queen of heaven, the queen of the south, the Queen of Beta, the Queen of Shylon, the Queen of Yemunah, the Queen of Delta, the Queen of the Coast, the gods of the Titans, the tritons, and all entities using psychic manipulations of the 5 esoteric seals to vandalize my life through astral rights given by anger, bitterness, resentment, unforgiveness, hatred, and desire for revenge.

Every demon of the fly, squirting demon, spirit of filth, and demon of uncleanness that is associated with or connected to built-in anger, bitterness, resentment, unforgiveness, hatred, and desire for revenge in my life, and any evil power covering, invading, ambushing, terrorizing, and demonizing my life because of anger, rage, bitterness, resentment, unforgiveness, hatred, and such like, and if there are demonic vines, creepers, climbers, or moss covering my life and destiny, if there be any demon spirit defecating, vomiting, or spitting upon me, if there be any unclean spirit nesting, brooding, settling, or lodging upon or within any part of my body, and any spirit that has set itself as an evil guardian to any of the psychic gates of my body, by the judicial verdict of the power of the Blood of the Lamb of God Almighty, in Jesus' name, I call forth the judgement of a holy firestorm and disastrous flame, to overpower, destroy, and consume to ashes all these evil spirits in my life and upon me.

In Jesus' name, I also call forth the judgement of a holy firestorm and disastrous flame, to overpower, destroy, and consume to ashes all astral poisons, psychic spirits, and astral commands within the psychic layers of the forest kingdom, desert kingdom, water kingdom, air kingdom, and subterranean kingdom that came into my life and body through anger, bitterness, resentment, unforgiveness, hatred, and thirst for revenge.

All you evil spirits operating through the carnal propensities of anger and associated negative emotions and thoughts, I, by Jesus, declare you demons disqualified and rendered useless, powerless, and ineffective against my life, and your jurisdiction over my body and life is now broken, effective immediately, in the name of Jesus of Nazareth.

Father, all these I pray in no other name but Your holy name and the name of Your Son Y'ahushua. Thank You for setting me free, for it is written in John 8:36, **"If the Son therefore shall make you free, ye shall be free indeed."**

67. Prayers Against The Spirit Of Oppression

Lord God of the Heavens and the Earth, I come before Your throne of grace through the Holy Spirit and the judicial and redeeming blood of Jesus. My life is continually oppressed, and it has greatly caused sorrows, sadness, and pain in my life, and has compromised my judgements and decision-making and uprightness and retarded the purposes of God in my life. Your word says, "for I glory in my tribulations," and 2 Corinthians 4:17 says, **"For our light affliction, which is but for a moment, worketh for us a far more exceeding and eternal weight of glory."**

However, I am not just going through fiery trials, but I am oppressed by an iron fist, and everywhere I turn, oppression follows me. Psalms 54:3 For **strangers are risen up against me, and oppressors seek after my soul: they have not set God before them. Selah.**

Bow the heavens, O Lord, and let the realm of Angels, the universe, and the Earth be conditioned to accommodate my deliverance and help; rescue me from my oppressors, Lord Jesus, for Your glory. You said in Exodus 3:9, **"Now therefore, behold, the cry of the children of Israel has come unto me: and I have also seen the oppression wherewith the Egyptians oppress them."**
Your word also says in Ephesians 2:10 that we are Your workmanship, created in Christ Jesus unto good works, which God hath before ordained that we should walk in them.
Deliver my soul from the spirit of Pharaoh, and from the oppression of the hands of the kingdom of the queen of heaven, the queen of the south, the Queen of Beta, the Queen of Shylon, the Queen of Yemunah, the Queen of Delta, the Queen of the Coast, the god Hades, and all entities using psychic manipulations of the 5 esoteric seals to sit upon my life with heavy oppression. Judge my oppressors

according to Your word in Psalms 72:4, **"He shall judge the poor of the people, he shall save the children of the needy and shall break in pieces the oppressor."**

Also, it says in Isaiah 54:14, **"In righteousness shalt thou be established: thou shalt be far from oppression; for thou shalt not fear: and from terror; for it shall not come near thee."**
Right now, by the dynamic power of the Lord Jesus of Nazareth, in the exalted name of Jesus Christ, with thunderbolts of the eternal flames of heaven, and lightnings of fire, I destroy the power, hold and jurisdiction all elemental demons operating under psychic commands as spirits of oppression in my life, and I banish from my life every combined element of psychic and esoteric powers, astral poisons, and psychic forces of the Demi-gods, Planetary Spirits, Avatars, Grand Masters, Witches, Warlocks, Satanists, Wiccans, Sorcerers, Watchers, Guardians of the Flame, Ascended Masters, Solar Lords, Inter-Planetary Lords, Inter-Galactic Lords, Guardians of Fate and the Cycles of life, dark Principalities, Powers, Rulers of darkness, Legion of the air, Aquatic forces, Subterranean forces, Earth masters, Highlanders, Sirens, the Elemental spirits, the queen of the South, the king of the North, goddess of the East, the king of the West, the supreme elementals, and the Huna and Huni - supreme mermaids of the lesser mermaids of the waters who have set themselves to brutally and oppress me.

All evil powers of human and spirit agents that have subjected me to become a victim of continual oppression, calamities, and victimization, I call forth the pillar of cloud by day to frustrate every agent of oppression, and I call forth the pillar of fire by night to oppress my oppressors and frustrate oppression. I call down the ten plagues to torment them severely for many seasons.

Let their terror become terrified with terror, let their oppression be oppressed, and let captivity that has laid upon me go into captivity, in the name of Jesus of Nazareth. Let my oppressors go into depression and self-destruct by the thunder and lightning of fire of Jesus Christ. I deconstruct every fortress of oppression built around me. I oppress oppression, and I distress the spirit of distress, and I dismantle all astral manipulation that is working to liquidate my effort to stand in strength.

Let the verdict from heaven be rendered in my favour, and let my oppressors flee.
According to the Word of God, it is written, Psalms 62:3, **"How long will ye imagine mischief against a man? ye shall be slain all of you: as a bowing wall** *shall ye be, and as* **a tottering fence."**
Psalms 18:6, In my distress I called upon the LORD, and cried unto my God: he heard my voice out of his temple, and my cry came before him, even into his ears.
Psalms 18:7, "**Then the earth shook and trembled; the foundations also of the hills moved and were shaken, because he was wroth."**
Psalms 18:8, "**There went up a smoke out of his nostrils, and fire out of his mouth devoured; coals were kindled by it.**
Psalms 18:9, "**He bowed the heavens also and came down; and darkness was under his feet."**

Thank you, Holy Spirit, for breaking the backbone of my oppressors and setting me free, in Jesus' name Amen.

68. Prayers Against The Spirit Of Contention And Discord

Lord God of the Heavens and the Earth, I come before Your throne of grace through the Holy Spirit and the judicial and redeeming blood of Jesus.

Heavenly Father, I seek the intervention of Your Eternal Council, requesting that Your fire will render Your judgement against every agent of darkness for my sake, who has robbed, confiscated, and destroyed my life in whatever way because of contention, strife, division, fighting, discord, and confusion.
LORD Jesus, contention, arguments, and strife have clothed me with the shame and embarrassment of being an argumentative and strifeful person, which have left those who are close to me hurt, wounded, and offended; even those who are unknown to me.

Father, I am struggling with the spirit of contention and discord, but I want peace to flow in my character, personality, and mannerisms. Your word says in Ephesians 4:32, **"And be kind and tenderhearted toward one another, forgiving one another, even as God has also in Christ forgiven you."**
I acknowledge that in myself, the character and spirit of social, household, and family contentions, arguments, strife, division, fighting, discord, and confusion are interfering with my destiny helpers, ministry, and health, and have become a hindrance to Your working in and around my life.

Powers of the Air, and psychic forces across the astral plains operating in my life by contention, argument, strife, division, fighting, and confusion, come into order now. I bring the Divider demon Saint-François, and all you demons of contention, division, and discord into subjection and pull down all your establishments, imaginations, and high things that exalt themselves against the knowledge of God.

By the name of Jesus of Nazareth, the power of the Holy Spirit, and by the judicial blood of Jesus the Lamb of God, I dissolve and dismantle the law of 'metaphysical homogeneity' operating against my life, and I disarm, neutralize, diffuse, banish, and destroy all direct or indirect manipulation, psychic attack, and projectiles sent against and into my life by any rogue demon, squirting demon, spirit of ferocious beasts, and demon of bad character, under the astral command and mandate to divide and cause discord and confusion through me.

By the Right Hand of the Lord God and by the power of Jesus, Son of the Living God, with chains of fire and shackles of brimstone, I strategically bind the neck, the hands, and the feet of all demons of discord, contention, and division operating in my life, and I say go into banishment, all you psychic entities of contention, for it is written in Eph 4:31, **"Let all bitterness and indignation, and wrath, and clamour, and evil speaking be removed from you, together with all malice."**

I nullify and neutralize your destructive operations, which are set in astral motions within the psychic layers against my life through doorways of contention, argument, strife, division, fighting, discord, confusions.

Through Jesus of Nazareth and the power of the Holy Spirit, I destroy every lair and bait where I have become a victim of the lesser spirits and elemental forces of the air, water, land, and subterranean worlds.

All elemental spirits which come through besetting sins of contention, argument, strife, division, fighting, discord, confusions, I break your backbone and neck now, for it is written, blessed are the peacemakers, for they shall be called the children of God.

Therefore, let the judicial verdict of the power of the Blood of the Lamb of God Almighty, in Jesus' name, declare the judgement of a holy firestorm and disastrous flame, to overpower, destroy, and consume to ashes all you evil spirits of discord, contention, argument, strife, and disagreement by which I am being controlled and manipulated, effective immediately.

69. Prayers Against The Demons Of Addiction & Bad Habits

Heavenly Father, I seek the intervention of Your Eternal Council, requesting that You set me free from the addiction and bad habit (name *bad habit or addiction)* that has been a stronghold in my life and has robbed, confiscated, and destroyed my life, and has tampered with my spiritual growth in Christ.

Oh Lord God of Israel, from my youth up I have been a victim of this habit and addiction of [name bad habit and addiction], a victim of oppression, guilt, shame, humiliation, disgrace, withdrawal, victimization, torment, exploitation, perversion, and mental corruption.
But at this moment, Abba Father, I revolt against these strongholds.

I repent for my sin, transgressions, and the iniquities of my bloodline that may have opened a door for the spirit of obsessive-compulsive behaviors in my life. Every sin of my forefathers that the enemy is using as a legal right to build legal cases against me and to sabotage and ruin my destiny, I ask that the justifying blood of Jesus would wash them away. I petition by the blood of the Lamb that every legal right the spirit of abuse is holding unto is hereby revoked, in Jesus' glorious name.

I pray against every elemental spirit behind the bad habits and addictions of [name the addiction/s] that are embedded in the cornerstone and layers of my family's foundation.
I have been a victim of addiction, compulsive behaviors, obsession, and bad habits, which have greatly injured my life, destiny, and inflicted damage on the purposes of God in my life.

Right now, I pray against every stronghold that has been built around my life, and in every place where my soul is held in astral prisons of this bad habit, may I be delivered. It is written in Genesis 29:32, **"Surely the LORD hath looked upon my affliction."**

Every bad habit, compulsive behavior, obsession, addiction, and repetitive sin that has become a weapon and device of combat in the hands of the demons, to torment and destroy my life on earth, I pray against these and subject them to the blood of Jesus for destruction.

Demon of calamities, disaster, and chaos that follows oppression in my life, I deconstruct you foul spirits by fire now, and every satanic ambushment, psychic manipulation, and stronghold of the spirit of carnal addiction, I revoke, destroy, and banish from my life, by the power of Jesus.

Every habit, compulsive behavior, obsession, which has attracted various demons to my home and surroundings and has created a lodging and nesting place in my life to brood, and has created a fort for combat, to inflict and afflict me and combat my angels, let fire from Heaven descend and destroy the evil foundation, judicial grounds, legal rights, and powers of all demonic entities involved in this evil construction of addiction.

In the mighty name of Jesus of Nazareth, I renounce, condemn, and revoke all these evil psychic commands and telepathic channels of destruction formed against me through the addiction of [name addiction]. I tear down every demonic stronghold established in my life, and I destroy all legal grounds and astral rights that give these evil spirits jurisdiction to haunt my life with terror and calamity.

Every one of these habits and repetitive sins that are being used as weapons in the chamber of incarceration to afflict me, I call upon the God and Father of our Lord Jesus to send angels to my aid and destroy these operations of addictive bondage and all demons of my imprisonment.

Wherever I am bound with iron chains and with the spirit of affliction according to Psalm 107:10, wherever my life is held behind astral iron bars and bronze gates because of the addictions, compulsive behaviors, obsessions, and bad habits of [name the addictions and habits], or trapped within any land of darkness, within the valley of the shadows of death, within an underground cave, within an astral labyrinth, within a spiritual maze, a catacomb, a pit, within a spiritual jail cell, or any spiritual incarceration chamber within the forest, desert, water, air, or within an underground astral chamber of the shadows of death or in any place where I am held by darkness because of the addiction and bad habit of [name the addictions and habits], I call for the charged Angel of rescue to rescue me now. Let me be pulled out of any demonic pit that I am in, for it is written in Psalms 40:2, **"He brought me up also out of a horrible pit, out of the miry clay, and set my feet upon a rock, and established my goings."**

Effective immediately, in Jesus' name, I bind, disturb, banish, and destroy every direct or indirect manipulation and 52-day cycle of psychic attack against me, from the land, sea, and air. This includes attacks through forked roads, crossroads, roundabouts, and other points of confrontation, via the law of metaphysical homogeneity. By the fire of the Holy Spirit, lightning, thunder, and the judicial blood of Jesus, I command this.

I also reverse any astral exchange, displacement, and replacement of my items, such as my Christian garments, my glory, my beauty, my character, my job, my career, my destiny, my happiness, my contentment, my success, my fulfillment, my anointing, and my potential marriage (if unmarried), and all other assets that have taken place because of my submission to the addiction and bad habit of (name addiction and bad habit).

All astral poison set to fight me for a 1,095-day cycle, or The Seven Cycles of Attack fighting against me through pornography, seeking to subject me to zero point, you have failed terribly by the laws of Heaven, in Jesus' name.

Every evil power of addiction, compulsive behaviors, obsession, bad habits, and repetitive sins that have reprogrammed, reconditioned, and reconfigured my soul, mind, character, personality, ways, desires, and mannerisms, let these powers be neutralized now, and the negative effects begin to fade away as my soul receives healing now, in Jesus' name.

The patterns and cycles of compulsive behaviors and obsession be broken now, and let my deliverance be permanent.

Father, I thank You for Your mercy upon me and intervention by Your love, mercy, and compassion.

Thank You for delivering me from this evil spirit of addiction, compulsive behaviors, obsession, and bad habits, and let my seal unto the day of redemption remain, according to Ephesians 4:30, and keep me in the will of Your Holy Spirit, now and forever, world without end. Amen and Amen.

70. Prayer Against The Spirit Of Suicide

Father God, my very Source of Life, I declare that You are the Covenant Keeping God, the Creator of the Heavens and the Earth. I acknowledge that You and You alone have given me the gift of life at the time of conception (Gen. 2:7).

Father, I now place my life—past, present, and future—into Your hands! My life belongs to You, and I petition You to redeem back every second, minute, day, season, and year of my life. I counter-petition Satan for my life, for it is written in Psalms 118:17, **"I shall not die, but live, and declare the works of the LORD."**

By the name of the Lord Tzevaot and the fire of the Spirit of the Lord by whom I stand in the blood of Jesus of Nazareth, and by the authority of the scepter and the crown of the King of Kings and Lord of Lords, let brimstone, a horrible tempest, terror, lightnings, destructive fire, and thunders from the LORD God of the heavens and the earth, rain down upon and against and destroy every high altar of witchcraft, sorcery, and satanism that is programmed against me to commit suicide.

Let Heaven and the earthly creation of God fight against and banish every form of esoteric crafts and psychic manipulations, triggers, formulas, and codes of suicide that are set, assigned, and programmed for my annihilation, death, and destruction.

Any demonic program, spell, hex, psychic command, channel, occult sound frequency, and vibration of the curse of suicide that is set, programmed, and brooding upon me that is triggered by a certain position or phase of the waning moon, the waxing moon, the full moon, the new moon, and midnight moon, or by the position of the wheel of the Sun, by the midday sun, the constellation, the midnight moon, the blood moon, the blue moon, planetary alignment, the zodiac, the axis of the earth, weather patterns, or is programmed and triggered by certain times, days, and dates within a certain Solstice or Equinox, or is programmed and triggered by certain words, movies, songs, sound waves, electric waves, and magnetic waves, sound frequency, or is programmed and triggered by salt water, river water, the presence of a certain person or people, situation, food, animal, symbol, or colour; let these triggers, activators be neutralized and have no effect in the realm and art of witchcraft.

I also pray against all programs, Astro-Omnidictator, laws of metaphysical homogeneity, spells, hexes, psychic commands, occult sound frequency, vibration, and the curse of suicide upon my life, that they be bound, condemned, annihilated, liquidated, dissolved, eradicated, and rendered impotent, useless, and clueless, effective immediately.

By the electric fire and dynamic thunderbolts of Yah, the God of Heaven, let fiery destruction eradicate, dissolve, nullify, and cancel every verdict, sentence, and astral command set in psychic motions for my premature death, sudden death, death by my own hands, construction of evil altars of the spirit of murder, suicide, bloodbath, blood splash, and bloodshed, sacrifice, violence, tragedy, legal grounds, ethereal bridges, and astral rights which were built in my life due to murder, miscarriages, suicide, bloodshed, violence, and abortions in my family bloodline, from my mother's house or my father's house.
Let my LORD, the God of heaven and the earth, rain down fire, brimstone, tempest, and terror and destroy the powers of these evil spirits of death, suicidal episodes, cycles, syndromes, demonic rays, altars, and strongholds of occult agents of the kingdom of darkness who are assigned to destroy me by suicide. Destroy them by Your

judgement oh Lord and give all these categories of demons and agents of Hell the portion of their cup, for it is written in Psalms 11:6, **"Upon the wicked he shall rain snares, fire and brimstone, and a horrible tempest: this shall be the portion of their cup."**

In Jesus' Name, with the fire of the Holy Spirit, I release my future from Satan's call to death and deactivate all astral bombs planted in my future, and unset all landmines planted in my path for sudden or progressive destruction.
Therefore, every evil power that has dispelled my life and proclaimed a death sentence over me using the gate of my birth date, age, name, personal item, or through the gate of a friendship, soul tie, covenant, gift, circumstance, etc., through Jesus Christ I condemn, dissolve, and dismantle these evil powers together with the law of 'metaphysical homogeneity operating against my life, and I disarm, neutralize, diffuse, banish, and destroy the demon of death sentence and the demon of self-destruction, and every rogue demon, squirting demon, spirit of ferocious beasts, and demon of the seven seas, the five oceans, continental rivers, the upper firmament, forest, mountains, volcano openings, the cemetery, and all direct or indirect manipulation, psychic attack, and projectiles sent against and into my life by these evil spirits that carry astral commands and mandates to destroy me.
In Jesus' name, I dismantle the minutes, hours, seconds, days, and months that are weaponized against me. I decommission the gatekeepers of death, hell, and the grave.

I sever every legal tie that I have with the grave, the underworld, and the gates of Hell, and I sever every legal tie between my life and the death bounty hunters, the death hunters, the sting of death, and the death reapers. Let their trident and sickle be destroyed from the hands of these demons.

I pray the fire of the Holy Spirit through Jesus Christ to surround me now and let the hit list of death carrying my name be consumed by fire to ashes, and let the register of the butchery of the Devil, upon which my name is written for execution, burn to ashes now.

I now call upon the Lord Jesus to remove all evil marks, identifications, occult names, sigils, and the date of my death that are placed upon my forehead, in Jesus' name.
I withdraw my name from every tombstone, gravestone, grave, cemetery, and tear to threads every graveclothes tailored for me, and the agent who has dug a pit for my burial, let this evil worker of darkness be buried in the pit he or she has dug. Therefore, I rise like a phoenix and remove myself from the hand of death, and from the snares and holds of all demonic creatures who are using the elements of creation and nature against me.

Thank you for delivering me from this evil spirit of suicide and letting my seal unto the day of redemption remain, according to Ephesians 4:30, and keeping me in the will of Your Spirit, now and forever, world without end. Amen.

71. Prayers Against The Spirit Of Backsliding.

Father God, most holy, hallowed be Your name in all kingdoms, spheres, realms, dimensions.
I declare Your Majesty and Sovereignty that You are the Covenant-Keeping God, the Creator of the heavens and the earth.
I acknowledge that You and You alone have given me the gift of life, both physical and spiritual.

Father, I petition You before Your Throne of Grace that You will reveal to me Your perfect will; therefore, keep me by Your truth, so that I will not become a prey of the demon of backsliding. Eph 4:30, **"And grieve not the holy Spirit of God, whereby ye are sealed unto the day of redemption."** But it is written in Psalms 27:4, **"One thing I have desired from the LORD, that I will seek after: that I may dwell in the house of the LORD all the days of my life, to behold the beauty of the LORD and to inquire in His temple,"**

Demons are seeking to pull me down from my walk of faith; in Christ, you are a liar. Be banished in chains of unbearable terror now, in Jesus' name.
It is commanded in Hebrews 3:12, **"Take heed, brethren, lest there be in any of you an evil heart of unbelief, in departing from the living God."** Therefore, I say to the kingdom of evil spirits of backsliding, I will not depart from the Living God through unbelief in my heart.
By my authority through Jesus of Nazareth, I now take authoritative commands over all spirits of the four kingdoms of the Air, the kingdom of the waters below, the kingdom of the Land, and the kingdom of the subterranean region, and over the four elements of the four cardinal dimensions, and I demand the release of my faith in Christ, my mindset, my character, my zeal, my prayer life, and my joy and

excitement in serving Jesus the Christ. 2 Timothy 3:14, **"But as for you, continue in the things that you did learn and were assured of, knowing from whom you have learned them."**

I renounce all demons of backsliding and denial of the household of faith, and every evil spirit that has caused me to withdraw my profession of faith in Jesus. For it is written in Deuteronomy 4:9, **"Only take heed to yourself, and diligently keep yourself, lest you forget the things your eyes have seen, and lest they depart from your heart all the days of your life. And teach them to your children and your grandchildren."**

Let Your glory, O God, in my life fight for me by fire and disarm every nocturnal and diurnal force assigned to my spiritual destruction.
For You said in Isaiah 41:10, **"Fear thou not; for I am with thee: be not dismayed; for I am thy God: I will strengthen thee; yea, I will help thee; yea, I will uphold thee with the right hand of my righteousness."**
I will not be a backsliding heifer, for it is written that those who put their hands to the plow and turn back are not fit for the kingdom of God.
Luke 9:62, **"But Jesus said to him, "No one, having put his hand to the plow, and looking back, is fit for the kingdom of God."**

I will not look back, but I will endure to the end and be saved. I am not of those who draw back unto perdition according to Hebrews 10:38, **"but if any man draws back, my soul shall have no pleasure in him."**
Hebrews 10:39, **"But we are not of them who draw back unto perdition; but of them that believe to the saving of the soul."**

Let my life be pulled out from the clutches of psychic manipulations and be healed from the wounds of the arrows of backsliding and the fiery darts of perdition. Jeremiah 3:22, **"Return, ye backsliding children, and I will heal your backslidings."**

I pray for the restoration of my faith, heart, desire, and zeal by Your Holy Spirit. I petition You, Father, that You restore my life back to the sheepfold, for You are my restorer and revival. I am bought with a price and purchased with the blood of Jesus, the Lamb of God; therefore, let all legal rights the enemy has to draw me away from Christ be overthrown by the verdict of Your blood.
2Chronicles 30:9, **"For if ye turn again unto the LORD, your brethren and your children shall find compassion before them that lead them captive, so that they shall come again into this land: for the LORD your God is gracious and merciful, and will not turn away His face from you, if ye return unto Him."**
Through Jesus of Nazareth, let every astral poison and venom of tranquilization and neutralization that is programmed to force me into backsliding be neutralized and lose all substance of power and effectiveness against me, effective immediately.

Let God arise for my sake and let the enemies be scattered. Demons within the cracks of the earth, crevices of the cosmic realm, and within potholes in the cemeteries sniffing, snitching, and plotting my destruction, let them be roasted by fiery coals from the holy altar of the Almighty God.

Every evil spirit seeking to give me a hardened heart through the deceitfulness of sin, and an evil heart of unbelief to depart from the living God, I now draw from the blood of Jesus and claim immunity to withstand these assaults of the forces of the cosmological verdict of the Inner Esoteric framework of Satan, for it is written in Hebrews 3:12–13, **"Beware, brethren, lest there be in any of you an evil heart of unbelief in departing from the living God; but exhort one** another daily, while it is called Today," lest any of you be hardened through the deceitfulness of sin."

I renounce, block, and stop every astral attack programmed against me in the psychic layers by the elemental demons, the black-hearted demons, and the icy-hearted demons.

I declare by the verdict of the Blood by which I was purchased, I am more than a conqueror and I overcome every demon fighting for my salvation within the Mephistophelian kingdom of Hell.

Thank You, Abba Father, for delivering me from this evil spirit of backsliding, and let my seal remain, and keep me in the will of Your Spirit, now and forever, world without end, Amen and Amen.

72. Prayers Against The Spirit Of Camouflage & Disguise

Father, I petition You before Your Throne of Grace, imploring Your judicial and divine assistance, for behold the kingdom of darkness has set secret and stealth operations against me using subtle esoteric crafts and manipulations. I beseech You, Lord, to expose the hidden traps and destructive plans. Psalm 119:105, **"Thy Word is a lamp unto my feet, and a light unto my path."**

Reveal and expose the stealth operation and secret tactic that ensnared the 7 kingdoms of darkness against my life.
By the power of ElShaddai, in the Name of Jesus of Nazareth, let every camouflaged and disguised counsel, plan, desire, expectation, imagination, device, plot, snare, and activity of the 7 Occult kingdoms against my life be exposed and come to the light of my awareness and discernment.
For it is written in Daniel 2:20, "**…Blessed be the name of God forever and ever: for wisdom and might are His."**
Daniels 2:21, **"And he changeth the times and the seasons: he removeth kings, and setteth up kings: he giveth wisdom unto the wise, and knowledge to them that know understanding:"**
Daniel 2:22 **He revealeth the deep and secret things: he knoweth what is in the darkness, and the light dwelleth with him.**
Daniel 2:23, "**I thank thee, and praise thee, O thou God of my fathers, who hast given me wisdom and might, and hast made known unto me now what we desired of thee: for thou hast now made known unto us the king's matter."**

Make known to me anything intended to cause me harm or take me off the path You have set before me. I pray for the light of Your truth to expose the darkness and for the power of

Your Spirit to protect me from any evil attempts. It is written that the entrance of Your word gives light (Psalm 119:130).
Let the light of Your word shine brightly in my steps and consume every evil planted and every set of destruction that is strategically placed on the ground for me.

It is written in Psalms 27:2, **"When the wicked, my enemies and my foes, came upon me to eat up my flesh, they stumbled and fell."**
Lord Jesus, destroy the powers of the occult that are surrounding me, seeking to devour and eat me up.
By your judgement oh Lord, give all these categories of demons and agents of Hell the portion of their cup, for it is written in Psalms 11:6, **"Upon the wicked he shall rain snares, fire and brimstone, and a horrible tempest: this shall be the portion of their cup."**

Therefore, by the power and name of El-Shaddai, with hot chains of seraphic fire and fetters of hot iron heated by the fire of amber, I strategically bind the neck, the hands, and the feet of all evil lurking in secret places.

In the Name of Jesus of Nazareth, I take authoritative commands over all spirits of camouflage, disguise, cloak, conceal, cover up, deceive, hide; mask, masquerade, stealth, veil, smoke screen, blind, and chameleon spirits from the four kingdoms of the Air, the kingdom of the waters, the kingdom of the Land, and the kingdom of the subterranean region, who are secretly working against my life for my destruction.
O Lord God of the Heavens and the Earth, nullify all legal rights the enemy has to draw me into the Devil's lair and by the judicial blood of

Jesus the Lamb of God, dissolve and dismantle the law of 'metaphysical homogeneity,' and disarm, neutralize, and diffuse every direct or indirect manipulation against me, psychic attack, and projectile coming from the astral layers.

Uncover the hidden traps, O God, and expose the schemes of the wicked. May their plots crumble and fall to naught before they take root. Before they rise, let them fall in disgrace and become victims of their own plots in Jesus' name.
I destroy, by lightning, fire, and thunder, all camouflaged landmines and booby traps specifically set in my path.

Let every disguised counsel, plan, desire, expectation, imagination, device, plot, snare, and activity of the seven Occult kingdoms against my life be exposed and come to the light of my awareness and discernment.
I pray for the disintegration of every wicked plan and evil agenda. May the ground they tread become shaky, their schemes collapse, and their intents be turned to foolishness, in Jesus' precious name.

Psalms 21:11, **"For they intended evil against thee: they imagined a mischievous device, which they were not able to perform."**
I pray for confusion to enter the camps of the wicked, let their communication be disrupted, and their plans be scattered to the winds. As Your word says in Proverbs 26:27, **"Whoso diggeth a pit shall fall therein: and he that rolleth a stone, it will return upon him."**
May this be the portion of those who plot evil against me, in the Name of Jesus of Nazareth.

By the Lord God of Israel, I destroy every camouflage power and all astral and metaphysical forces that operate at the highest velocity of astro-metaphysical acceleration, combating against my life through disguised cycles of psychic manipulation, through the cosmological verdict, and through metaphysical intercourse.

Let all subtle manipulations, camouflage powers of darkness, disguised arrows of calamities, and plots of death be rendered powerless, defenceless, weaponless, unrectified, ineffective, and useless against me, as I now tear down and destroy your rays, altars, fortitude, and powers, in the mighty name of Jesus of Nazareth.

73. Prayers Against The Spirit Of Nightmare

Dear Heavenly Father, my shelter and fortress, I come to You by faith. I declare Your sovereignty over my sleep. It is Your word that says, in Proverbs 3:24, **"When you lie down, you shall not be afraid; yea, you shall lie down, and your sleep shall be sweet."**
As your word said, my sleep shall be sweet. But, Lord, not only my sleep, but my dreams also. It is written in Pro 3:26, "For the LORD shall be thy confidence, and shall keep thy foot from being taken."

In the name of Jesus, I pray against the invasion and ambushment of my dreams. Father, the workers of the craft of Putani-Vigra and the other diabolical and satanic workers of darkness are manipulating my dreams and subconscious in order to deceive me. Your word says in Col 3:3, "my **life has been hid together with Christ in God."**

By the authority of Almighty God in me, I take authoritative measures and stand in revolt against every foul spirit of the mind. By the power of the resurrected Savior Jesus of Nazareth, through the Holy Spirit, I bind the hands, neck, and feet of these demons, and tranquilize and banish the astral poison of the occult art of Putani-Vigra, spirit of the Mares, [Nightmares and Daymares], and every demon monster, incubus, succubus, phantom, spirit of fear of night, spirit of fear of the dark, and the demons of the terror of the night (Psalms 91:5).
I also banish from my mind, subconsciousness, and sleep the demons of all bad dreams. This includes combined elements, dream confusion, forgettable, undistinguishable, wet, troubled, fearful, combined, confusing, and forgettable dreams. In like manner, let all Sirens, mermaids, dream catchers, predators of dreams, psychic manipulators, eaters of dreams, dream corruptions, and other nocturnal and diurnal creatures that are invading, troubling,

manipulating, and influencing my dreams be chased, haunted, and tormented by the fire and blood of Jesus of Nazareth.

For thus saith the Lord to me in His word in Psalms 91:13, **"Thou shalt tread upon the lion and adder: the young lion and the dragon shalt thou trample under feet."**

You foul spirits, you have no jurisdiction to enter, manipulate, invade, or ambush my dreams, nor usurp any powers over my life because your jurisdiction is broken by my Angelic escorts and protection. Thus says the word of the Lord to me in Psalms 91:11, **"For he shall give his angels charge over thee, to keep thee in all thy ways."** Hence, I am under the charge of the Angels of the Lord.

I now sentence to imprisonment under God's judicial Blood of the New Covenant all astral powers and Elemental entities that disguise themselves as masquerades and fearful elements in my dreams. For it is written in Psalms 91:5, I shall not be afraid of the terror by night; nor of the pestilence that walketh in darkness; Psalms 91:6.

I destroy the power of all astral and metaphysical forces that operate at the highest velocity of astro-metaphysical acceleration in the occult world, and I invoke angelic combat against all cycles of psychic dream manipulations taking place in my sleep.
Luke 10:19, **"Behold, I give unto you power to tread on serpents and scorpions, and over all the power of the enemy: and nothing shall by any means hurt you."**

Every law of metaphysical homogeneity and metaphysical intercourse, sustaining the operation of dream manipulations and psychic entities in order to create catastrophes of chaos and calamity in my marriage, finance, education, job, travel, etc., or even strike me with sickness, contamination, or death, I neutralize, nullify, and liquidate these evil laws, programs, and hidden agendas of the land, sea, air, and underground, and I scatter by holy fire all combined forces of witchcraft which incorporate demons of incubus and succubus to suck my blood in dreams; for according to Psalms 91:3.

It is written in Psalms 4:8, **"I will both lay me down in peace, and sleep: for thou, LORD, only makest me dwell in safety."**

I decree that my dreams are blessed, and they are fortified by the Blood of Jesus. I claim clarity of dreams, good dreams, and dreams with meanings, edifying messages, prophetic insights, and meaningful elements in my dreams just as Joseph did in Matthew 1:20-2, as Joseph the son of Jacob did in Genesis 37:6-7, as Solomon did in 1 Kings 3:5, etc. In Jesus' mighty name.

I procure the benefit of sweet sleep, and I lay claim to the health benefits, mental wellness, and spiritual intelligence that come with sweet sleep given by the Lord God. I claim songs in the night from God, my Maker, according to Job 35:10.

It is also written concerning me in Pro 6:22, **"When thou goest, it shall lead thee; when thou sleepest, it shall keep thee; and *when thou awakest, it shall talk with thee.*"**

74. Prayers Against The Spirit Of The Occult

Dear Heavenly Father, our shelter and fortress, I come before You by faith, declaring Your sovereignty over all my situations.

I am confronted with the evil works of the diabolical and satanic armies and workers of darkness, but Your word says in Colossians 3:3, **"my life has been hid together with Christ in God."**

In the face of these adversarial attempts, we proclaim Your Word which says, **"No weapon formed against you shall prosper, and every tongue which rises against you in judgement You shall condemn,"** [Isaiah 54:17]. We fervently pray against every evil work, decreeing it null and void in Jesus' mighty name.

I beseech You, Lord, to protect me, my ministry, and destiny from the powers of the occult. Psalm 119:105, **"Thy Word is a lamp unto my feet, and a light unto my path."**
By the spirit of prophecy and discernment, make known to me all forthcoming movements of occultism projected and assigned against me. It is written that the entrance of thy word gives light [Psalm 119:130].

By my authority through Jesus of Nazareth, I now take authoritative command over all spirits of the occult world, and bring into subjection all powers of the Mephistophelian Seals, the esoteric sciences and craft, and over all psychic entities operating under the laws of the fallen Angels of Tartarus, and in other dimensions, within the four kingdoms of the Air, the kingdom of the waters below, the kingdom of land, and the kingdom of the subterranean region, and over the four elements of the four cardinal dimensions.

I renounce every spiritual marriage, soul tie, connection, covenant, truce, alliance, or any secret link that I have with occult spirits through direct, indirect, or unconscious participation.

I call to the fiery light of the Garment of El-Shaddai every occult power under the five Mephistophelian seals of darkness, and by the name of Y'ahushua of Nazareth, I destroy from over my life the evil powers of the books of grimoire, technique, tactic, mysterious witchcraft, sorcery, divination, ESP, hypnosis, fortune-telling, crystal ball, Ouija board, tarot cards, Freemasonry, martial arts, magic, séances, clairvoyance, mediums, psychics, readers, advisors, necromancy, handwriting analysis, astrology, yoga, metaphysical healing groups, hypnotism, occult movies, occult programs, occult books, occult games, amulets, talismans, ankhs, yin yang, Eastern religions, transcendental meditation, familiar spirits, channeling, Santería, New Age movement, and any other branch of occultism, time magic, space magic, life and/or nature magic, death magic/necromancy, order and chaos magic, creation and destruction magic, warding, divination magic, prophecies, holy magic, dream magic, resurrection magic, summoning, banishing, mind magic, barrier magic, healing magic.

Jesus, Son of Almighty God the Father, I petition You to release Angels of forefront warfare, wielding the most sophisticated divine weapons, and let them declare war, revolt, and destroy all satanic powers of the five Esoteric Seals of darkness that are fighting against my life and are subjecting me to their evil influences through Psychic manipulations.

I pull down every imagination and every high thing of the demon guardians of the four cardinal points seeking to destroy my ministry in Christ and by manipulation, reducing me to a doormat, victim, prisoner, lab rat, playground, test subject, candidate, and secret initiate of dark powers.

Let the light of Your word shine brightly in my steps and consume every planted and set destruction that is strategically placed on the ground before me.

It is written in Psalms 27:2, **"When the wicked, my enemies and my foes, came upon me to eat up my flesh, they stumbled and fell."** Lord Jesus, destroy the powers of the occult that are surrounding me, seeking to devour and eat me up.
By Your judgement oh Lord, give all these categories of demons and agents of Hell the portion of their cup, for it is written in Psalms 11:6, **"Upon the wicked he shall rain snares, fire and brimstone, and a horrible tempest: this shall be the portion of their cup."**

Thank you, O Lord, for listening to my prayer and breaking the backbone of the enemies and removing their teeth. I am grateful and therefore give you all the glory and honour, in Jesus Name.

75. Prayer Against The Octopus Demons

Lord God of the Heavens and the Earth, I come before Your throne of grace through the Holy Spirit and the judicial and redeeming blood of Jesus. It seems that my life is under the hold of an octopus demon, and by occurrences, my life is surrounded by continual calamities and continual disastrous manifestations by this water spirit, which have greatly caused sorrow, pain, misfortune, and mishaps in my life, and have compromised my destiny and the purposes of God in my life. Your word said in 1 Corinthians 6:20 that we are bought with a price; therefore, we must glorify God in our body and in our spirit, which are God's.

On this wise, I bring my body and soul to you, Lord Jesus, which is Your Temple. The Octopus demon is destroying my body, which is Your temple, but remember Your word said, if any man destroys Your temple, he shall be destroyed by God.
The Octopus spirit is destroying my body and soul, which are Your temples. Now, O Lord, destroy this demon.

Also, this octopus demon is stubborn and tough, and I am requesting Angelic reinforcement against this demon. Jesus, Son of Almighty God the Father, I petition you to release Angels of forefront warfare, wielding the most sophisticated divine weapons, and let them declare war, revolt, and destroy all satanic powers of the Cosmic Ocean of darkness that are fighting against my life and subjecting me to their evil influences by the psychic manipulations of the Octopus demon.
Every demonic water-based witchcraft through the Octopus demons projected to my home and life for vicious psychic attacks and manipulations, swift and progressive destructions, mind control, mind binding, mental torment, migraine, persistent predicaments, recurring calamities, repetitive failures, blockages, hindrances,

disappointments, marriage dismantlement, disgraces, and mutation of afflictions, shame, disgrace, and backwardness, and a mandate for my death, annihilation, madness, and destruction of my joy, peace, finances, health, and success, I call upon the Voice of the Lord in Psalms 29:3 to neutralize these water occult powers and destroy these psychic manipulations.

I separate the waters from the waters, and I neutralize all demonically charged turbulent waters, and destroy every and any occult water system or demonic substance that is covering my eyes, face, and body.

It is written in Mark 3:27, **"No man can enter into a strong man's house and spoil his goods, except he will first bind the strong man; and then he will spoil his house."**

Therefore, upon this authority, by the power of the Spirit of Jesus and the name of El-Shaddai, according to Mat 12:29 and Mark 3:27, I now bind with fiery barbed wire, with fiery iron hooks, and with an electric iron net any octopus spirit operating in my life or lurking in secret places seeking to strike me. I pierce its flesh with barbed hooks and neutralize it.

It is also written in Luke 11:22, **"But when a stronger than he shall come upon him, and overcome him, he taketh from him all his armour wherein he trusted and divides his spoils."**

It is written in 1 John 4:4, greater is he who is in me than he who is in the world. It is written in 1 John 5:4-5, **"For whatsoever is born of God overcometh the world: and this is the victory that overcometh the world, *even* our faith. Who is he that overcometh the world, but he that believeth that Jesus is the Son of God?"**

Therefore, by the power of Jesus and the charge of the Holy Angels of God, I overcome you, Octopus strong man, and I strip you of your defenses, artillery, and weapons of combat and manipulations, and I strip you of your armour wherein you trusted, and I divide your spoils.

I sever, block, and stop all your reception, communication channels, signals, frequencies transmitting beneath your waters and altars of the seas against my life.
I pray by fire against any Octopus demon that is allocated, assigned, and programmed to destroy my life via the enigma of water and various aquatic channels of witchcraft manipulations.

Wherever and by whatever aquatic power my life is submerged underwater spiritually, or brought to a place of deep-water trench, or placed in a crevice within the ocean bed, or trapped within bedrock prisons of the sea or ocean, or trapped among coral reefs, caught in the tides of spiritual rip currents, or covered with enchanted seaweeds, demonic sargassum, or any other form of sea algae by the octopus demons of water through witchcraft, and wherever my life is subjected to water demonic manipulations or is ambushed by any octopus spirit from any of the five occult zones of the marine kingdom: the zone Lumani, Banni, Lemuria, Gamma, or the occult realm of Atlantis, let my life be delivered from every watery environment surrounding me, in the name and power of Jesus Christ I pray.

Any altar that has formed a mutual relationship between the Octopus entities of the waters and my life, and every power of the octopus demons that have ambushed and claimed my body and soul as a property of the kingdom of darkness, because of an evil embargo, link, covenant, tie, contract, relationship, alliance, agreement by words, blood, handwriting, signature, ancestral truce, let all these astral and legal rights be nullified and condemned by the Blood of Jesus, and let my life, mind, emotions, etc., be set free from the power of every dark covenant of the octopus and waters, in the exalted name of Jesus of Nazareth.

I revolt with the lightning and thunder of the amber fire of Jesus Christ, and I pray against and banish every combined element of psychic and esoteric powers, astral poisons, and demons of the Octopus, propelling calamity, disaster, and chaos into my life.

Any octopus demon feeding on my brain and mind, retrieving my brain signals, and feeding on the energy of my thoughts, inducing confusion and other mental disorientations and thought disorders, I seared and burned you quickly with an intensely heated iron [1 Timothy 4:2].

You foul octopus demon, master of disguise and camouflage, I destroy your stealth ability and power of disguise and camouflage, and blend in with my surroundings, friends, enemies, etc., and your power to control multiple psychic elements simultaneously in my life.

I neutralize your ability to manipulate me by inflicting various categories of harm simultaneously.

I call forth fiery destruction and deconstruct, revoke, destroy, and banish from my life any octopus spirit creature, and nullify all psychic manipulations of the octopus demons and the powers of the Queen of Beta, the Queen of Shylon, the Queen of Yemunah, the Queen of Delta, the Queen of the Coast, the gods of the Tritons, the supreme elemental spirits, supreme Mermaids, the Sirens, and the Nymphs, or other evil powers that have subjected me to become a victim of continual calamities and frequent recurring disasters.

By the judicial verdict of the power of the Blood of the Lamb of God Almighty, these astral poisons, psychic spirits, and astral commands within the psychic layers of the Banwa kingdom are now disqualified and rendered useless, powerless, and ineffective against my life, and all demonic jurisdiction to my home; I hereby command you to be broken now with immediate effect, in the name of Jesus of Nazareth.

Let heavens and the Earth proclaim Your majesty, O Lord, and be magnified in all the Universe. Thank you for delivering me from the Octopus Demon and all its strongholds and influence. Your name be praised forever and ever. Amen and Amen.

76. Prayers Against Dreams Of Dead People

Abba Father, who is in Heaven, hallowed be Your name; let Your kingdom come and let Your will be done on Earth as it is in Heaven.

I praise Your great name today, for you are worthy to be praised in all kingdoms and realms. Thank you for the blood of the Lamb of God, through which I can stand in Your presence to declare my victory, blessings, and deliverance in Christ.
Father, I come before you today, seeking Your divine protection against disturbing dreams involving the dead. I petition by the blood of the Lamb for Your peace and comfort to fill my mind and heart as I sleep.

According to the Word of the Messiah Jesus in Mark 16:17, **"And these signs shall follow them that believe; in my name shall they cast out devils."**
Upon this authority, as commanded in Your word, I take up the whole armour of God to fight against the wiles of the enemies in the underworld, and every spirit of the dead that is attached to my life or this house, or any item in my possession.

In the Name of Jesus of Nazareth, by flames of lightning and thunder, I bind with chains of fire and fetters of hot iron, heated by the presence of the Holy Spirit of Jesus, every elemental spirit of masquerade from the underworld, every familiar spirit that is assuming the image of the dead in my dreams, and every high demon ruler from the kingdom of the dead and decay.

Let all these evil spirits fall to the ground. Banish them in heavy chains. Let them be tormented by the unbearable terror of God Almighty.

In the name of the Lamb who was slain, I also stand in the jurisdiction of the Blood that is sprinkled upon the Mercy Seat, and I summon the authority of the Blood, fire, and Spirit of the Living God, and I break and sever every seal, mark, covenant, alliance, relationship, link, tie, contract, agreement by words, blood, handwriting, signature, ancestral truce, and legal right that exists between me and the world of the dead, and any necro entity.

Through Jesus Christ, I invoke a Divine Judicial Order from the Courts of the Almighty God, who is the Grand Judge of the Heavens and the Earth, and I command by this Divine Judicial Order that all demons with the power of death, such as Hades, Hecate, Persephone, Erinyes, Anubis, Demeter, Pluto, Thanatos, Yama, Arae, Charon, Cronos, Erebus, Hel, Hypnos, Osiris, Shinigami, and any other prince, god, goddess, and queen of the realm of the dead and death, and the underworld be destroyed from my life, and every ethereal bridge, portal, doorway, or gateway be destroyed beyond repair, and all you gods be banished from my life and my children, effective immediately.

In the name of the Father, and of the Son, and of the Holy Spirit, I uproot every spirit, dream seed, deposit, and remnant of the dead, dead things, seed of the dead from my life, and every item of the dead that was given to me in a dream; I burn it to ash and send it back to the pit of Hell, in Jesus Name.

Any oil of a dead corpse that was placed upon me, I call upon the Altar of the Mercy Seat containing the Blood of Jesus, and I say, let the seraphic fire of God Most High burn out this oil and break the covenant and power of this oil from my life, that I may be set free from the realm of the dead, both in dreams and in reality.

Blood of Jesus, I ask that you purge my body and soul from any water or fluid from dead corpses that was given to me to drink in a dream, through earthly foods or drinks, by means of witchcraft and other esoteric operations and metaphysical homogeneity.

Any item in my home that is attached to a spirit of the dead and attracts dead people, known and unknown, let these items be revealed or destroyed by Your holy fire, in Jesus' name.
Heavenly Father, I pray, if there be any relic, buried corpse on the premises where I dwell, reveal or nullify the jurisdiction of the realm of death, rendering it incapable of using this buried corpse as a doorway to the earth's surface.

I nullify and cancel every marital certificate that may have been created through an ungodly union between me and the spirit of the dead in a dream, and I sever and nullify any soul tie that was forged between me and the dead in a dream.
Every eye contact, physical contact, sexual or sensual contact, exchange of passion in a dream with someone who is dead, and every communication with dead folks, let the soul tie, connection, link, and alliance that was created be destroyed from my life, effective immediately, in Jesus' mighty name.

All realms of the underworld—Hell, Death, and Hades—hear the word of the Lord in Luke 16:26: "**And beside all this, between us and you there is a great gulf fixed: so that they which would pass from hence to you cannot; neither can they pass to us, that** *would come* **from thence.**"
Therefore, you evil things and foul spirits from the realm of the dead, be gone from my life, dreams, visions, and trances in Jesus' name.

Every emotion that has me attached to a dead relative that I am still grieving over, which the demons are using as an open door, I separate my emotions from the influence of demons.

I renounce every cure, advice, direction, wisdom, information, etc., that was given to me by the dead in a dream, and I break that necro-friendship and spiritual bond with the spirit of the dead. I banish from my life all necro friends, dead friends, cemetery friends, etc., in Jesus' name.

I break the power of the Gnomes, the Necro demons, the spectral demons, demons of the undead, spirits of reanimated corpses, every ghost of the dead, poltergeists, and all other menacing and malevolent spirits, and all other evil spirits from the Cro-Magnon world and the underworld of Hades.

Today, by fire and light, lightnings, thunders, and the voice of the Almighty God in Psalms 29, I pull my soul, my mind, my body, my home, my assets, my belongings, my destiny, my star, my masterplan, my dreams, my visions, my future, my projects, my job, my business, and my household out from the land of the dead, from the Cemetery, from the Shades, from the gates of death, and from the kingdoms of every god and goddess, prince and princess, custodian and spirit of death, hell, and the grave, and I destroy the hold and folds of these demons, effective immediately, in Jesus' mighty name.

Every human agent of darkness: voodoo priest, grandmaster, demigod, or witch, who is working against me with cemetery magic, seeking to summon my spirit upon a witchcraft altar of the dead, or a magic mirror of the realm of the dead, I call down holy Fire from the fiery Coals that are at the feet of the Holy Altar in Heaven, to release a detonation and shatter to powder and cremate every altar, structure, entity, platform, shrine, monument, etc., that is working against my life from the realm of the dead and death.

I now decree by the divine law that governs the kingdom that any demon who seeks to take the image of a dead person in my dream will be roasted to ashes on-site by the thunderous voice of Jesus Christ, whose voice is like many waters (Revelation 1:15).

All realms of the dead, all astral and psychic vibrations, elemental spirits, and gods of the departed, hear my voice this day, as I speak under the jurisdiction of the fiery coals of God's holy altar; I am made free from Your presence because the Son of God has made me free. Henceforth, you will no longer afflict me, for the Lord God of hosts rebuke you.

I restrict you, spirits of masquerade and the dead, by a divine restraining order, and I command by fire that henceforth you shall not come near my dwelling.
You will not come after any of the people in my household. You will not invade my dream, nor seek to manipulate my dreams.

You will not cross over into the land of the living, for you are a foul spirit, rebuked by the blood of Jesus.
You will remove yourself from my bloodline and remove your contaminations with you, effective immediately.

From henceforth, every assignment given to you against my life, you will discard it and subject yourself to suffer the consequences at the hands of your superior demons.

Every torment, affliction, evil, calamity, and terror that you have placed upon my life, receive back unto yourself sevenfold, now, in Jesus' name.

Holy Father, now that I have rebuked the powers of darkness in Your name, Lord, I pray, shield me from any negative or harmful spiritual influences and atmospheres. Fill my dreams with Your light, love, and peace, so that I may rest securely in Your secret place and presence.

Also, fill me with strength and courage to overcome and disarm any fear factors or stimuli of anxiety that may seek to subject me to dream manipulations.

This I pray in the name of the Father, the Son, and the Holy Spirit. Amen and Amen.

77. Prayer Against The Demon Of Sleep Disorder

Heavenly Father, I come before you in the powerful name of Jesus Christ, my Savior and Deliverer. I acknowledge Your sovereignty over all spiritual forces, including every demon and evil spirit that interferes with the sleep of Your people. You have given me authority over all the powers of the enemy, and I claim that authority now, Psalms 127:2, **"for so he giveth his beloved sleep"**.
Blood of Jesus, arise against the highest council of darkness and condemn the demonic verdicts of the night that keep me awake and keep me restless.

I take up the authority of Jesus of Nazareth and by the lightnings of God's terror and the holy fire from Jesus Christ, I now banish every evil spirit of parasomnia, somni-phobia, [fear of sleep], confusional arousals, sleep nightmare disorder, isolated sleep paralysis, sleep apnea, excessive sleep inertia, and rhythmic movement disorder.

I also banish from my sleep and dream life every evil spirit of Somnam-bulism [sleepwalking], Sexsomnia, sleep-related eating disorder, post-traumatic stress disorder (PTSD), nightmares, heart arrhythmia, sleep behavior disorder, rapid eye movement, sleep bruxism (teeth grinding), sleep deprivation, obstructive sleep apnea, urinary incontinence (enuresis or bedwetting), nocturnal paroxysmal dystonia, sleep terrors, and terrifying cries and screams.

I also banish by the blood and name of Jesus of Nazareth all demons that are causing me to make nonsensical sounds, groans, and mumbles in my sleep, or are afflicting me with narcolepsy, restless legs syndrome, circadian rhythm sleep disorder, hypersomnia, snoring, excessive daytime sleepiness, shift work sleep disorder, movement disorders, nocturnal arousal, autonomic activation,

nocturnal penile tumescence, nocturnal emission, dream vaginal lubrication, and dream orgasm.
I activate my faith in Jesus' name (Acts 3:16) against the demon of insomnia and restlessness.

The word of the Lord came to us saying in Proverbs 3:24, **"When you lie down, you shall not be afraid; yea, you shall lie down, and your sleep shall be sweet."**
Proverbs 3:25 **"Have no fear of sudden disaster, nor of the desolation of the wicked when it comes."**
Proverbs 3:26 **"For the LORD shall be your confidence and shall keep your foot from being taken."**

By the power of the Lord God of hosts whose name is holy, I bind, frustrate, disarm, and banish from my life all the forces of darkness operating under the occult art of homogeneity, and all other occult esoteric crafts that are destroying my sleep through psychic manipulations, astral poisons, and sleep waves etc.

By the name of the Lord Jesus of Nazareth, I call you elemental forces out by your influence of manipulation, and banish from my life all you elemental demons of mood swings, irritability, anxiety, stress, depression, chronic pain, gluttony, pharmaceutical substances, spirits of environmental and atmospheric disturbances, and all you demons who are manipulating dopamine, serotonin, and melatonin in my body in order to cause troubled sleep.

I pray against the plan of the kingdom of darkness to keep me from having sleep difficulties, which contribute to daytime sleepiness, lack of concentration, slowness in activity, drowsiness, feeling tired upon waking from sleep, difficulty focusing on or remembering tasks, and increased errors or accidents.

By Fire, I call my sleep life into divine order, and I say to you demons of the night with faith, and all you psychic elements of the land, sea, and air to stand down, be disassembled, be scattered, and be banished in chains of powerlessness, defeat, uselessness, and ineffectiveness.

Fire of El-Eliyahu, descend for my sake, and let every psychic command launched into the invisible layers of the astral system with 'sleep-waves,' specifically designed and commanded to fight against me in the night be neutralized, vaporized, and destroyed.
I say into the atmosphere that when I lie down, my sleep will be sweet (Prov. 3:24). I cast all my cares upon Christ because He cares for me (1 Peter 5:7).

Sleep Apnea

Today, I pray against the demon behind the condition of sleep apnea that would prevent me from sleeping peacefully.
I command by the authority of the seven flames of the seven golden lamps of God that my tongue, throat, nasal passages, airways, and trachea cooperate in one accord to accommodate my peaceful, uninterrupted, and unobstructive sleep.
I stand in faith believing that when I lie down to sleep, my sleep will be sweet (Prov. 3:24). My sleep will be uninterrupted as I can breathe with ease, for the Holy Spirit is the breath that I breathe through Christ (Job 33:4). Let every factor of sleep apnea leave me now, as there will be no more collapsing of my windpipe; in the name of Jesus, I pray.
No weapon formed against me shall prosper (Isa. 54:17), including sleep apnea and any other obstructive sleep disorder. I call things that are not as though they already were (Rom. 4:17), and on the foundation of faith in the power of His name (Acts 3:16), my breathing is now regulated, with no more lingual obstruction to my throat passage and no more obstruction in my respiratory system.

Against Narcolepsy

Father, I pray against Narcolepsy.
By the Blood of Y'ahushua that speaks better things than that of Abel, I petition You, O Lord, for deliverance and healing from this chronic neurological disorder, narcolepsy. I pray that I will both lie down in peace and sleep, for the Lord only makes me dwell in safety (Ps. 4:8).

Yahuah Rapha, I pray for a healing of my brain's ability to regulate sleep-wake cycles normally, and get a good night's rest, and wake up refreshed, giving glory unto You for Your goodness, for Your mercy endures forever.
I say let my circadian rhythm be regulated in Jesus' name. All powers of the air and water that are interfering with my dream life, my sleep, circadian rhythm, my subconsciousness, my pituitary gland, my pineal gland. My hormones and dream state, subjecting my dreams to psychic manipulations, distortion, and confusions, I banish these demons in Jesus' name, and declare by fire my redemption from this curse, narcolepsy, according to Gal. 3:13).

Restless Leg Syndrome.

In the name of Jesus my Healer, the Lord God has sent His word to heal my diseases and sickness, and therefore I pray for deliverance and healing from this sleep movement disorder, restless leg syndrome. I pray that this evil will cease immediately, and the uncomfortable sensation and uncontrollable urge to move my legs as I try to fall asleep will stop.

I call fire from the altar of God to burn out every foreign demonic attachment to my neurological system, neurons, and to neutralize every demonic interference in the name of Jesus.
By the judicial verdict of the power of the Blood of the Lamb of God Almighty, these astral poisons, psychic spirits, and astral commands

within the psychic layers of the astral kingdom, etc., are now disqualified and rendered useless, powerless, and ineffective against my life.

Lord God, by the blood of Jesus Christ shed for me, I give You praise because You have delivered me from this curse of insomnia by becoming the curse for me (Gal. 3:13), and I rejoice for my freedom from every form of oppression, including nightmares caused by demonic entities. I will both lie down in peace and sleep, for You, Lord, only make me dwell in safety (Ps. 4:8).

Thank you, Lord, for giving me the victory in Christ. Surround me with Your angels, standing watch over me throughout the night.

Holy Spirit, fill me with Your peace that surpasses all understanding. Guard my mind and heart with Your truth and righteousness. All these I ask in the name of the Father, the Son, and the Holy Spirit of Yah, Amen.

78. Prayer Against Demons Of Dream Invasion

Lord Jesus, You are the Great High Priest. I come through Your grace to stand against the works of the Devil operating in my life.
I say by faith and the authority of Jesus Christ of Nazareth and the power of the Holy Spirit that I have the authority in Christ to disarm and destroy all powers of darkness, and nothing shall by any means hurt me according to Luke 10:19.

I pray against all evil forces working as dream catchers, dream eaters, dream invaders, dream manipulators, and all demons of forgetfulness who travel in the night to lay hands on me so that I will forget my dreams.

Every demon of the rank of elementals, aquatic vibrations, salamanders, sylphs, gnomes, undines, and familiar spirits who are receiving psychic commands through the vibrations of witchcraft, incantations, sins, and family iniquities in order to sustain various cycles of invasion and manipulation of my dreams, be subjected to and bound with chains of holy fire. I break your cycles and episodes of astral manipulation upon my dreams.

Therefore, by the power of the Holy Spirit, in the name of Jesus, let thunderclaps rain terrors of lightning storms, electric fire, hail, and brimstone from Heaven upon every evil spirit that has ambushed and captured my dream life, my sleep, circadian rhythm, my subconsciousness, my pituitary gland, my pineal gland, and dream state, subjecting my dreams to psychic manipulations, distortion, and confusion, and to the 52-day cycle of attack by the combined elemental forces of the five esoteric seals of darkness, which are responsible for **terrifying me with** episodes of nightmares and daymares, and are causing **me to get up in the middle of a good dream.**

I cancel every evil power, curse, and manipulation that was sent into my life through a dream in order to terminate my mission in life and sabotage the potential opportunities and blessings that are at my disposal throughout my life.

Evil seeds and serpents, eggs and larvae planted into me through dreams, let them dry up and die by the fervent heat of the Spirit of the Son of God, which is sent into my heart, crying, "Abba, Father." [Gal 4:6].

Any agent of darkness coming to me through dreams to terminate my glory and light, I destroy you, agent of darkness, by the Fire of the Spirit in the name of Jesus.

Every spirit seeking to spill my blood in a dream, I secure my life force, soul, virtue, and power with the fire of the Holy Spirit, and I claim the verdict of the blood of the Lamb to secure my blood.

Every evil in my dream is programmed to compromise my marital identity, spiritual identity, financial identity, marital identity, and social identity; be deprogrammed now, and go into torment by the fire of Jesus of Nazareth.

I take up the authority of Jesus of Nazareth and by the lightnings of God's terror and the holy fire from Jesus Christ, I now banish every evil spirit of parasomnia, somni-phobia, (fear of sleep), confusional arousals, sleep nightmare disorder, isolated sleep paralysis, sleep apnea, excessive sleep inertia, and rhythmic movement disorder.

I also banish from my sleep and dream life every evil spirit of Somnam-bulism [sleepwalking], sexsomnia, sleep-related eating disorder, post-traumatic stress disorder (PTSD), nightmares, heart arrhythmia, sleep behavior disorder, rapid eye movement, sleep bruxism (teeth grinding), sleep deprivation, obstructive sleep apnea, urinary incontinence (enuresis or bedwetting), nocturnal paroxysmal dystonia, sleep terrors, and terrifying cries and screams.

I also banish by the blood and name of Jesus of Nazareth all demons that are causing me to make nonsensical sounds, groans, and mumbles in my sleep, or are afflicting me with narcolepsy, restless legs syndrome, circadian rhythm sleep disorder, hypersomnia, snoring, excessive daytime sleepiness, shift work sleep disorder, movement disorders, nocturnal arousal, autonomic activation, nocturnal penile tumescence, nocturnal emission, dream vaginal lubrication, and dream orgasm.

King of kings Y'ahushua of Nazareth, I call upon Your power to destroy by Your holy fire of amber, voices, lightnings, and thunders, all these demonic entities who are interfering with my sleep and dreams, and all demonic strongholds and evil fortresses built and established in, over, and around my brain, mind, and dreams.

All demonic weapons formed against me in my dream, and every psychic program constructed for my destruction through dreams, I rise in authority and pull down every imagination and high thing that exalts itself against the knowledge of God, and I bring into captivity every evil thought to the obedience of Christ, and I destroy the powers of the Devil in this wise, in Jesus name.

Wherever I was killed, raped, wounded, beaten, fed, rejected, humiliated, sexually active, or restricted in a dream, I submit my vulnerability to the Lordship of Jesus the Christ, and I renounce, revoke, and declare all covenants, soul ties, curses, and manipulations that were set in my life to devalue and rob me of my dominion.

Let the rebuke of the Lord God be against all sirens who are blocking my mind so that I cannot remember my dreams, or who are distorting and mixing different scenes in my dreams in order to make it a confusion.

Let these demons of the elementals, aquatic vibration, salamander, sylph, gnome, undine, and familiar spirits be petrified of me and tremble at the name of Jesus in my mouth.

All demons who are creating dream scenes from my subconsciousness, and manipulations that are programmed by elemental spirits to cause dismantlement of the infrastructure of my finances, my marital life, my educational success, ministerial authority, social and economic status of influence, or to sabotage my destiny or to inflict upon me demonic wounds, may these demons be placed in hot chains of holy fire and be banished from my life now into the hands of their vile demon tormentors and oppressors.

And any agent of darkness who is taking the face of a family member or friend to attack me in sleep or dreams, and every familiar demonic spirit who would use the face of the dead in order to hide their evil identity, to attack me in dreams, I tear off their masquerade now and expose them by fire and subject them to destruction and torment.

By the amber fire of Yah, I also cancel and destroy any death curse, death incantation, bounty, death plot, death plan, death warrant, and death sentence that is placed upon my life through dreams, effective immediately.

O Lord God of hosts, hallowed be Your Name. Let the heavens and the Earth now proclaim Your majesty, O Lord, and be magnified in all the Universe. Thank you for delivering me from the powers of the elemental demons and all strongholds and influences. Your name be praised forever and ever. Amen and Amen.

79. Prayers Against Sexual Molestation

Heavenly Father, I come boldly before Your Throne of Grace, seeking Your divine intervention against the pains, hurts, and heaviness of heart and broken emotions because of sexual abuse from (__Name the sex offender/offenders__).

Father, I have been a victim, subjected to the manipulations of the forces of elemental spirits of sexual wickedness. Hence, I come before you with a heavy heart, for I have endured the unspeakable pain of sexual abuse.

My soul cries out for healing, and therefore I ask that you mend my brokenness and restore my sense of security and self-worth. Pour out Your divine love upon me, Father, and guide me on the path towards therapy that would aid my mental, emotional, and psychological healing and wholeness. Give me the strength to forgive and the courage to reclaim my life. Bring inner peace to me and let Your peace keep my heart and mind, according to your word in Philippians 4:7 that says, **"And the peace of God, which passes all understanding, shall keep your hearts and minds through Christ Jesus."** It is written in Colossians 3:15, **"And let the peace of God rule in your hearts."**
Heal and deliver me by Your Judicial Council and the intervention of Your Eternal Flame, and pour upon me songs of deliverance.

I forgive (_____ Speak the names of those who have molested you), so that you can forgive me.
I am requesting that Your fire would melt every chain, shackle, fetter, lock, knot, and bolt of evil and calamity and spiritual imprisonment that have come upon me as a result of sexual molestation and sexual abused.

Abba Father, I confess and ask for pardon for my sins, that which were done with and without my consent, and those that I have participated in - willingly or unwillingly.

I confess and ask for pardon for the sins of my ancestors in every area where there have been physical or spiritual, conscious or unconscious, direct or indirect participation in any unlawful sexual perversion, rape in the family bloodline, incest, sexual assault, sexual molestation, lesbianism, homosexuality, paraphernalia, sinful thoughts, sensual fantasies, sensual desires, or participation in sensual music, films, or songs that may have subjected me to become a victim and object of sexual abuse and sexual molestations.

Renounce Ties

Lord Jesus, Your word says to us in Luke 10:19, **"Behold, I give unto you power to tread on serpents and scorpions, and over all the power of the enemy; and nothing shall by any means hurt you."**
Therefore, upon the authority of Your word in Luke 10:19, Psalms 11:6, and Exodus 9:24, I stand in the Name of Y'ahushua HaMashiach of Nazareth, by the power of the judgement and the authority, and I renounce, denounce, and revoke all demonic acquaintanceship, contract, alliance, affiliation, connection, link, communication, covenant, and sexual partnership that was forcefully created in my life through sexual molestation and sexual abuse.

By the fire of the Holy Spirit of Yah, I renounce and reject all sexual spirit friends, sexual partners, sexual gamers, sexual playmates, sexual rapists, sexual offenders, and spirit spouses that have been given access to my body, soul, and mind through the contamination of sexual molestation.

Rebuke Directly

You foul, abominable, and detestable spirit of masturbation, you are an abomination unto the temple of God, which is my body, but the Word of God commands me in Proverbs 6:5 where it says, **"Deliver thyself as a roe from the hand of the hunter, and as a bird from the hand of the fowler."**

All demon spirits that have entered my life through sexual molestation and sexual abuse, I break your oath and demonic seal from my life, and renounce, reject, revoke, and banish you by the fiery terror of God's divine judgement.
I renounce you, spirit of sexual molestation and sexual abuse that was passed unto me through my family bloodline, that which I received in the womb.
Every evil seed implanted within me, I command it to shrivel and die immediately in the name and authority of Jesus Christ.
I renounce my spiritual heritage, marriage, and soul tie with the spirits of sexual molestation and sexual abuse that reigned in my ancestors, and I claim freedom from all bondage of the sexual molestation and sexual abuse demons that have captured my mind, thoughts, and emotions.

By the judicial verdict of the power of the Blood of the Lamb of God Almighty, these astral poisons, psychic spirits, and astral commands within the psychic layers of the seven kingdoms of darkness are now disqualified and rendered useless, powerless, and ineffective against my life, effective immediately.

Banishment

According to the words of the Messiah Jesus in Mark 16:17, **"And these signs shall follow them that believe; in my name shall they cast out devils."**

On this authority, by fire, thunderclaps, and lightning, I shatter, scatter, and banish from my life and into oblivion you unclean demonic spirits of perversity in my life, including you foul spirit of Baphomet, Pan, Satyr, Nymphomania spirits, Asmodeus, Mare, Hippocentaur, succubus spirits, and all you spirit of incubus.

I command you demons to get out of my life. Go, effective immediately.
I destroy your holds, your stronghold, your unclean settlement, your hooks, claws, nets, traps, shackles, and chains of sexual molestation, sexual abuse, and sexual cruelty from my life, mind, body, and soul, with immediate Effect.
I shatter, scatter, and banish from my life and into oblivion all demons of anger, rage, hatred, trauma, phobia, bitterness, unforgiveness, dishonour, hurt, embarrassment, scandal, condemnation, shyness, resentment, insecurity, and feelings of inferiority, reproach, fear, guilt, rejection, self-consciousness, timidity, hesitation, fear of rejection, withdrawal, apprehension, nervousness, bashfulness, low self-esteem, spirit of shame, and disgrace, by the name of Jesus the Messiah of Nazareth.

I command you demons to get out of my life, Go!
I destroy your holds, your stronghold, your unclean settlement, your hooks, claws, nets, traps, shackles, chains of sexual molestation and sexual abuse, from my life, mind, body, and soul. Effective immediately.

In the Name of Y'ahushua HaMashiach of Nazareth, by the power of fire, thunderclaps, and lightning from Jesus, I also shatter, scatter, and banish from my life every demon of lust, idolatry, lack of trust, hardheartedness, victimization, accusation, pornography, paedophilia, voyeurism, domination, homosexuality, confusions, pride, rebellion, every cord of sin, rape, sodomy, incest, brutality, and all demons responsible for soul ties, all demons behind generational spirits of molestation and abuse in my life, and all subjective spirits that have entered my life through sexual molestation and sexual abuse.

I command you demons to get out of my life, Go!
I destroy your holds, your stronghold, your unclean settlement, your hooks, claws, nets, traps, shackles, chains of sexual molestation and sexual abuse, from my life, mind, body, and soul. Effective immediately.
I humbly submit myself to the Lord Jesus Christ and the authority of His Holy Spirit. Let all principalities, powers, rulers, legislators, gods, and demons of Hell know that I am not the property of evil spirits and Hell, because I was purchased with a price, the precious Blood of Jesus of Nazareth, for it is written in 1Co 6:20, **"For ye are bought with a price: therefore, glorify God in your body, and in your spirit, which are God's."**

On the basis of 1 Corinthians 6:20 and Colossians 2:13-15, your sexual molestation and sexual abuse demons have no jurisdiction to live and be attached to my soul and body, because I am the temple of the Holy Spirit according to 1Co 6:19, where it is written, **"What? know ye not that your body is the temple of the Holy Spirit, *which is* in you, which ye have of God"**
The Word of God commands me in Proverbs 6:5, where it says, **"Deliver thyself as a roe from the hand of the hunter, and as a bird from the hand of the fowler."**

By the authority of the Word of God, and in the name of the King of kings and Lord of Lords, by the lightning, thunder, and fire of Jesus Christ of Nazareth, I loose myself from all demonic prisons of sexual victimization, resentment, reproach, shame, fear, insecurity, and feelings of inferiority that have come upon me as a result of sexual molestation.

I violently pray that wherever I am bound with iron chains and with the spirit of affliction because of sexual molestation and sexual abuse, wherever my life and soul are held behind astral iron bars and bronze gates because of sexual molestation and abuse, and wherever I am spiritually trapped and imprisoned in the astral realm in the land of the shadow of death [Isaiah 9:2], in the land of darkness [Job 10:21], in the shadow of death [Job 10:22], in the terrors of the shadow of death [Job 24:17], in the doors of the shadow of death [Job 38:17], in the valley of the shadow of death [Psalms 23:4], in the place of dragons and the shadow of death [Psalms 44:19], in perpetual desolation [Psalms 74:3], in the valley of dry bones, in the valley of desolation, within a spiritual cave, within an astral labyrinth, within a spiritual maze, a catacomb, a pit, grave, or any spiritual incarceration chamber within the forest, desert, water, and air because of sexual violation, that I be loosed, set free, and delivered, effective immediately.

Lord God, I petition by the blood of the Lamb that Your Angels bind, chain, and drag all demons of sexual molestation and sexual abuse out of my life, as it is done in Revelation 20:1-2 that says, **"And I saw an angel come down from heaven, having the key of the bottomless pit and a great chain in his hand. And he laid hold on the dragon, that old serpent, which is the Devil, and Satan, and bound him."**

I also call for the charge of God upon His Angels to rescue me from the spiritual prison where trauma has trapped my soul. In the name of Jesus of Nazareth.
Let any fragments of their souls return to them and let any scattered and fragmented parts of my soul return to me, in Jesus' name.

I receive by faith the healing for my mind, my emotions, my body, and spirit. I receive by faith the mind of Christ, and I choose this day to pull up the root of bitterness and replace it with the love of God. I ask You, Lord, to plant forgiveness, purity, obedience, peace, joy, and love in place of bitterness. Fill me with Your Holy Spirit and let the spirit of adoption be poured out into my heart in Jesus' name.

Let Your love and acceptance captivate my heart, O God. I thank You, Lord Jesus, for being my healer, restorer, redeemer, and protector. I thank You for replacing every lie in my belief system with the truth that will set me free. Thank You, Holy Spirit, for releasing revelation as to my true identity in Christ. . Father God, I thank You for overcoming victory. Please fill me with Your Holy Spirit and empower me to live for You. Help me to live a life that honours You and brings You glory. In Jesus' name, Amen and Amen.

80. Prayers Against The Spirit Of Paralysis

Heavenly Father, through the Blood of the New Covenant by Your Holy Spirit, I come to You, seeking Your grace and divine intervention. Behold, the forces of sirens and elemental psychic entities of darkness have been oppressing me with sleep paralysis, where I find myself immobilized, overcome by fear and uncertainty, unable to speak or move, and terrified with terror.

Proverbs 3:25-26, **"Be not afraid of sudden fear, neither of the desolation of the wicked, when it cometh. For the LORD shall be thy confidence, and shall keep thy foot from being taken."**

I petition by the blood of the Lamb for Your fiery presence to cover me as a blanket of light and neutralize all powers of darkness, bringing me comfort and peace.

Banish any darkness or oppressive presence that may seek to overshadow me in the night, and let terror fall upon the demon that causes sleep paralysis, causing this demon of terror to become terrified itself, seven times, for it is written in Pro 10:24, **"The fear of the wicked, it shall come upon himself: but the desire of the righteous shall be granted."**

By the power of Jesus of Nazareth, I stand in revolt against all demons of paralysis, and all other spirits that affect the nervous system, neurological system, and spinal region, who also manifest as demons of disability, stroke, palsy, atrophy, depression, hopelessness, despair, crippling, paraplegia, lameness, dumbness.

Every demon sitting on my chest, or manipulating my state of mind and consciousness, and perception, through Jesus of Nazareth, let every astral poison and the venom of tranquilization and neutralization be neutralized and lose all power and effectiveness against me.

In the Name of Jesus of Nazareth, by flames of lightning and thunder, with chains of fire and fetters of hot iron heated by the fire of the Holy Spirit of Jesus, I bind and disarm every one of you evil spirits of REM and sleep paralysis and demons under the Queen of the South, the spirits of the waters, or creatures of the forest and cemeteries that are haunting me. Whatever is giving you foul demon access to me to afflict me, I place it under the Blood of Jesus, and nullify this astral right, and bring to naught the law of homogeneity working against me in my sleep/wake moments.

Therefore, according to Job 29:17, **"And I brake the jaws of the wicked," I now break your jaws, you demons,** and I banish and render you demons and paranormal activities powerless, defenceless, ineffective, and useless to afflict me any longer. I command you foul spirit to get out and never return. It is written in Job 31:3, **"Is not destruction to the wicked, and a strange punishment to the workers of iniquity?"**

Every witchcraft placed upon my life, working through psychic vibrations of the spirit of night terror and troubled sleep, by lightning, thunder, and the fire of Jesus Christ of Nazareth, I renounce, revoke, shatter, and destroy these witchcraft curses in the name of Jesus the Christ.

81. Prayers Against The Spirit Of Alcoholism

Heavenly Father, I seek the intervention of Your eternal council, requesting that you set me free from the addiction and bad habit of alcoholism, which has been a stronghold in my life and has robbed, confiscated, and destroyed my life, and has tampered with my spiritual growth in Christ.

Oh Lord God of Israel, by psychic manipulations, I have become a victim of this habit and addiction to alcohol. I have been a victim of addiction, compulsive behaviors, obsession, and bad habits that have greatly injured my life, destiny, and inflicted damage on the purposes of God in my life.
But at this moment, Abba Father, I revolt against this stronghold.

I repent for my sin, transgressions, and the iniquities of my bloodline that may have opened a door for the spirit of alcoholic obsessive-compulsive behaviors in my life. Every sin of my forefathers that the enemy would be using as a legal right to build legal cases against me and to sabotage and ruin my destiny, I ask that the justifying blood of Jesus would wash them away and remove from my life the stigma of alcohol and the demon of mockery and shame. Break all curses of alcohol and addiction from my life and deliver me for Your glory.
I ask that every legal right the spirit of abuse is holding over me be hereby revoked, in Jesus' glorious name.
Heavenly Father, for my shame give me double; and for confusion let me rejoice in my portion: therefore, in my land I shall possess the double: everlasting joy shall be unto me according to Isaiah 61:7.

Restore to me the years that the locust hath eaten, the cankerworm, and the caterpillar, and the palmerworm, according to Your word in Joel 2:25.

By the power of the Holy Spirit, through Jesus of Nazareth, I pray against, renounce, and break the pattern and cycle of social drinking, binge drinking, functioning alcoholism, chronic-severe alcoholism, binge-eating alcoholism, high-functioning alcoholism, the demon of strong drink, the demon of mingled wines and drinks, the demons of wines, and every elemental spirit and demon of addiction and craving for alcohol; delirium tremens, intemperance, intoxication, and every spirit behind the bad habit and addictions of alcoholism, specifically against the demon Bacchus, that is embedded in the cornerstones and layers of my family foundation.

Every demon of intoxication and alcohol that is using and manipulating my past and current hurts and pain for the evil plan to destroy my life by alcohol, I bind them right now with the chains of the Holy Spirit in Jesus the Messiah's name.
Right now, I pray against every stronghold that has been built around my life, and in every place where my soul is held in astral prisons of this bad habit, may I be delivered. It is written in Genesis 29:32, **"Surely the LORD hath looked upon my affliction."**

Every demon that has robbed me of my happiness, emotional bliss, and stability, the Lord God of hosts rebukes you foul spirits, and I command the release of my stolen emotional benefits.
Abba Father, I pray, wherever I am bound with iron chains and with the spirit of affliction according to Psalm 107:10, wherever my life is held trapped within any land of darkness, within any hole, culvert, cave, gutter, drainage pipe, waste channel, roadside, under a bridge, railroad, inside a sewer or sewage pipe, or within the valley of the shadows of death, within an underground cave, within an astral labyrinth, within a spiritual maze, a catacomb, a pit, within a spiritual jail cell, or any spiritual incarceration chamber within the forest, desert, water, air, or within an underground astral chamber of the shadows of death and in every place where I am held by darkness as

a prisoner of alcohol, look upon my affliction and send Your Angel to rescue me.

Pull me out from any demonic pit that I am in, for it is written in Psalms 40:2, **"He brought me up also out of an horrible pit, out of the miry clay, and set my feet upon a rock, and established my goings."**
Every addiction of compulsive alcohol consumption and repetitive sins that have become weapons and devices of combat in the hands of the demons, to torment and destroy my life on earth, I pray against these and subject them to the blood of Jesus for destruction.

Demon of calamities, disaster, and chaos that follows oppression in my life, I deconstruct you foul spirits by fire now, and every satanic ambushment, psychic manipulation, and stronghold of the spirit of carnal addiction, I revoke, destroy, and banish from my life, by the power of Jesus.
Every habit, alcoholic obsession, which has attracted various demons to my home and surroundings and has created a lodging and nesting place in my life to brood, and has created a fort for combat, to inflict and afflict me and combat my angels. Let fire from Heaven descend and destroy the evil foundation, judicial grounds, legal rights, and powers of all demonic entities involved in this evil construction of addiction.
Chains of alcohol binding me and wrapping me, break into pieces now, in Jesus' name.

82. Prayers Against The Spirit Of Anorexia Nervosa

Heavenly Father, I seek the intervention of Your eternal council, requesting that you set me free from the fetish behaviour and addiction to food abstinence of which I am a victim of.
The spirit of Anorexia has been a stronghold in my life and has robbed, confiscated, and destroyed my life, and has tampered with my spiritual growth in Christ and physical well-being and health.

Oh Lord God of Israel, by psychic manipulations, I have become a victim of the demon of self-infliction, self-suffering, and self-sacrifice for addictive and compulsive behaviour and obsession with leanness. But at this moment, Abba Father, I revolt against this stronghold which has greatly injured my life, destiny, and inflicted damage on the purposes of God in my life. This altar of death that is attached to my body, let it be demolished by Jesus Name.

I repent for my sins, transgressions, and the iniquities of allowing this wrong mentality and influence to dominate my life.
Every personal sin or sins of my forefathers that have given the enemy legal right to build legal cases against me, to sabotage and ruin my destiny and physical life, I ask that the justifying blood of Jesus would wash my sins away and remove from my life the effects of Anorexia.
I petition by the blood of the Lamb that every legal right the spirit of abuse is holding on me to is hereby revoked, in Jesus' glorious name.

By the power of the Holy Spirit, through Jesus of Nazareth, I pray against, renounce, and break the pattern and cycle of eating disorders.
Demon of Anorexia characterized by the abnormal pursuit of gaining very low body weight, demon of intense fear of gaining weight, fat

phobia, eating disorder, starvation, death, fear of becoming fat, compulsive dieting, depression, self-rejection, and all other demons associated with Anorexia, I divorce you now. I disown you, reject you, renounce you, and banish you from my life by the power of Jesus, my Saviour.

It is written in Genesis 29:32, **"Surely the LORD hath looked upon my affliction."**

Every demon that has robbed me of my health and mental stability, the Lord God of hosts rebukes you foul spirits, and I command the release of my life now, in Jesus' name.

Chains of anorexia binding me and wrapping me, break into pieces now, in Jesus' name.

Every addiction of compulsive abstinence from foods that have become weapons and devices of death in the hands of demons, to torment and destroy my life on the earth, I pray against these and subject them to the blood of Jesus for destruction.

Demon of calamities, disaster, and chaos that is following and oppressing my life, I renounce all psychic manipulations and strongholds of the spirit of anorexia by the power of Jesus.

Father, thank you for delivering me from the demons of eating disorders and anorexia, in the name of Your holy Son, Jesus of Nazareth. Amen and Amen.

83. Prayers Against Spirit Of Backlash

In the name of Jesus of Nazareth, I pray against every demon of back-to-sender, who replicates the strategies of my prayers and sends them back to me. Every demon who launches countermeasure water strikes, air strikes, etc., against me, I neutralize every demonic strategy of backfiring my prayer procedures and tactics by the "god of thunder Thor" or any other demon.

Whatever I prayed seems to fall back on me, and this is not your will. I say, every open door, root cause, and legal right or covenant that has subjected me to become a victim of demonic forces of back-to-sender procedure, I decree against these demons that their expectation would fall back on them. None of my prayer weapons against the enemies will turn around and return to me.

O God who is clothed with fire and light, fight my battle against the seven princes of darkness and their kingdoms. Let the warfront battle wage hotter than blazing and raging fire and release angelic artillery and resistances against the sophisticated weapons of the Mephistophelian seals of the Occult. Arise to my help, Psalms 121:2, **"My help cometh from the LORD, which made heaven and earth."**

Let the three that bear witness in earth, the Spirit, the water, and the blood [1 John 5:8], arise against the highest council of darkness and condemn their verdict to destroy me in sleep, on the street, at home, by sudden sickness, or by any other way.
Fire of El-Eliyahu, descend for my sake, and consume every psychic command given to the evil higher powers of the Air who are representatives of the upper and lower darkness, in Jesus Name.

It is written in Psalms 71:13, **"Let them be confounded** *and* **consumed that are adversaries to my soul; let them be covered** *with* **reproach and dishonour that seek my hurt."**
Every high satanic weapon and strategy that is being used to backfire on my prayers or would try to make me a victim of my own destructive prayers against demons; let these strategies fail against my prayers. No weapon formed against me shall prosper, for greater is he who is in me than he who is in the world.

Let my prayers hit their demonic target with full impact and destroy them.

I decree and declare; my expectations shall not fail, for it is written in Isaiah 44:26, **"That confirms the word of His servant and performs the counsel of His messengers."**
Psalms 18:37, **"I have pursued my enemies and overtaken them; nor did I turn back until they were destroyed."**
Psalms 18:38, **"I have shattered them, and they cannot rise again; they have fallen under my feet."**
Psalms 18:39, **"For You have girded me with strength for the battle; You have subdued under me those who rose up against me."**
Psalms 18:40, **"Thou hast also given me the necks of my enemies; that I might destroy them that hate me."**

84. Prayers Against The Spirit Of Spiritual Blindness

Heavenly Father, I come to you for deliverance from the demon of spiritual blindness. You desire me to see spiritually, according to Your word in Revelation 3:18, **"and anoint thine eyes with eye salve, that thou mayest see."**

It is also written in Ephesians 1:18, **"The eyes of your understanding being enlightened; that ye may know what is the hope of his calling, and what are the riches of the glory of his inheritance in the saints."**
Ephesians 1:19, **"And what *is* the exceeding greatness of his power to us-ward who believe, according to the working of his mighty power,"**
I therefore submit my eyes to you, and I pray that the eyes of my understanding would be enlightened; and my eyes would be anointed with eye salve, that I may see.

I renounce every evil veil that is placed over my eyes; I pray against every scale that is placed over my eyes; I pray against every spiritual demonic membrane that is placed over my eyes; I pray against every pair of eyeglasses that is dimming and distorting my spiritual sight; I pray against every demonic eye shadow that is casting a shadow over my eyes that I cannot see, and I pray against every darkness that has been placed over my face.

May the light that was shown on Jesus' face on the Mount of Transfiguration, when his face shone like the sun, shine upon my face and melt, shatter, and destroy completely all astral material that is placed over my eyes to make me spiritually blind.

I call upon the fire that is in the Eyes of Jesus in Rev 19:12 to burn away every witchcraft, strange thing, evil eye, spell, demonic substance, demonic catarrh, and everything that keeps me from seeing spiritually.

It is written in Matthew 6:22, **"The light of the body is the eye: if therefore thine eye be single, thy whole body shall be full of light."**

Let my body be filled with light and let me be stripped of every religious spirit from the demonic realm of holy magic, the pandemonium kingdom, or any other realm that is operating to keep me in the dark concerning the truth and spiritual things; let these demons be roasted in Jesus name.

Every spirit of darkness, groping, veiled, lacking vision, hidden, covered, cataracts (natural and spiritual), hardness of heart, spiritual ignorance, dullness, deception, undiscerning, Pharisee, be gone from me now, and be chased by fire, in Jesus name.

Every foul bird assigned to pluck out my eyes, let fire consume them to ashes now.

Wherever my spiritual vision is, and whatever spirit that has my spiritual eyeballs in their necklaces, on a platter, within a box, or anywhere else, my eyes be restored to my head now, in Jesus' name, for it is written in Ecclesiastes 2:14, **"The wise man's eyes *are* in his head."**

I decree by fire of the Lord; I will see the dreams and visions from the Lord.

I will see the secrets of the enemies in dark places.

Psalms 119:18, **"Open thou mine eyes, that I may behold wondrous things out of thy law."** Let mine eyes behold wondrous things in the law of God.

I will see the darkness at noonday.

I will see the slickness and slyness of the Devil even in his camouflaged state. I will behold and see spiritual well in deserted places (Gen 21:19, and God opened her eyes, and she saw a well of water; and she went and filled the bottle with water and gave the lad a drink.)

I will see all upcoming attacks by darkness before they are launched into psychic motion.

Let my eyes be open to see the armies of Heaven round about, for there are more for us than those for them.

Let my eyes burn like a lamp, and my face like the sun in its strength.

My eyes are as the eyes of doves by the rivers of waters, washed with milk, and fitly set. [Song 5:12].

85. Prayers Against The Spirit Of Spiritual Deafness

Heavenly Father, I come to you for deliverance from the demon of spiritual deafness. You desire me to hear spiritually, according to Your word in Revelation 2:7, **"The one who has an ear, let him hear what the Spirit says to the churches. To the one who overcomes I will give** *the right* **to eat of the tree of life that is in** *the* **midst of the paradise of God."**
It is also written in Isaiah 30:21, **"And thine ears shall hear a word behind thee, saying, This is the way, walk ye in it, when ye turn to the right hand, and when ye turn to the left."**

Psalms 17:6, **"I have called upon thee, for thou wilt hear me, O God: incline thine ear unto me, and hear my speech."**
I therefore submit my ears to you, and I pray that the ears of my spirit would be open; and my ears would be anointed with oil, that I may hear. Proverbs 2:2, **"So that thou incline thine ear unto wisdom, and apply thine heart to understanding;"**
I renounce every evil stopper that is placed over my ears; I pray against every twister or demonic cork that is placed in my ears; I pray against every spiritual demonic snake placed in my ears so that I cannot hear.
May Your thunderous voice thunder over my ears so I can be spiritually inclined.

I call upon the sparks that are in the mouth of Jesus in Psalms to burn away every witchcraft, strange thing, spell, demonic substance, and everything that keeps me from hearing spiritually. It is written in Proverbs 8:6, **"Hear; for I will speak of excellent things; and the opening of my lips shall be right things."**

Every sword assigned to cut off my ears, let fire consume them to ashes now.

Wherever my spiritual hearing has been displaced, and whatever spirit has confiscated my spiritual ears, let my ears be restored to my head by fire now, in Jesus' name, for it is written in Ecclesiastes 2:14, **"The wise man's ears *are* in his head."**
I will hear the voice of the Lord in dreams and visions.
I will hear the secrets of the enemies in dark places.
Psalms 119:18, **"Open thou mine ears, that I may behold wondrous things out of thy law."** Let my ears behold wondrous things in the law of God.
I will hear of every secret plot being designed against me and my family. I will behold and hear clear directions of spiritual wells in deserted places (Gen 21:17-18). I will hear all upcoming attacks of darkness before they are launched into psychic motion.

Let my ears be open to hear the armies of Heaven roundabout, for there are more for us than those for them.
Therefore, all demons of spiritual deafness, I banish you from my life! Get out of my body and leave me now! Effective immediately! In the name of the LORD God of hosts, creator of the heavens and the earth.

86. Prayers Against The Spirit Of Regression And Backwardness

Through Jesus of Nazareth, let every astral poison and the venom of regression and backwardness be neutralized and lose all power and effectiveness against me.

Every witchcraft placed upon my life for reversion and regression, working through psychic vibrations against me to alter and demote my destiny of success, wealth, happiness, and completeness, to become a life of shame, poverty, failure, incompetence, and incompleteness and disgrace, by lightning, thunder, and the fire of Jesus Christ of Nazareth, I renounce, revoke, shatter, and destroy these witchcraft curses of regression and backwardness in the name of Jesus the Christ.

Every demon, every law, and every altar of regression & backwardness connecting me to any occult region, zone, realm, occult center, or sphere, within the Mephistophelian world through familiar spirits, elemental demons, terrestrial demons, demonic watchers, psychic naval forces, astral televisions, eaters of glory, psychic cameras, spirits of the dead and graveyards, let these demons be banished, and the witchcraft curse set upon my life to destroy my life, my reputation, my dignity, my mind, my purpose, future, and destiny, and to suck the potency, exuberance, and resplendence of my star; be destroyed and be banished now, In Jesus Name.

Spirit of backwardness from my father's house and mother's house affecting my destiny, I break your backbone by fire, in the name of Jesus.

All powers that hinder and destroy my blessings, conjure regression, and invoke backwardness in my life through dreams of being in my former school, my village, my hometown, my former apartment, former house, former class, former neighbourhood, or being with someone from the past who is already dead, I call upon the lightning of Jesus to destroy your demons by fire, in the name of Jesus.

All evil powers connecting my spirit, soul, and body to a village, a home, a family, a person, a school, a place, or an item, which are not known in reality but are only seen in my dreams, I break and banish these mysterious worlds and astral ties by the blood of Jesus, in Jesus' name.

Anything that was placed in my body by ingestion or incision, or entered my soul and body during any trauma or any demonic open door, or an evil dream that has subjected me to become the victim, a prisoner, an object and subject of the demon of regression, relapse, awkwardness, backwardness, reverse, failure, I call upon the God of the Heavens and Earth whose name is Holy, to destroy by fire, lightning, brimstone and hail of fire and a horrible tempest, all these evil powers, and I banish all foul spirits and curses of regression, relapse, backwardness, reverse, failure and all allegations, accusations and condemnations fighting against me. This I command in Jesus Name.

Curses of regression, relapse, backwardness, reverse, and failure in my life that are tied to a specific village, former hometown, former church, former friendship, city, neighbourhood, former apartment, and former school, or a friend's house, and any witchcraft charm that was buried in my village, hometown, former apartment, former house, former school, in a cemetery, or thrown in the sea, or a river, or a lake, or even a pond, or buried under the soil, which is working and speaking against me, waging war against me and blocking me from moving to the next level, progressing, advancing, going forward; may these evil charms be uprooted, self-destruct, and die now, in Jesus' name.

In Jesus' name, I banish from me every demon of the lobster, relapse, backsliding, setback, reversion, reversal, the skids, return, falling back, and all subjective spirits attached to the house of reversion and regression.

I destroy by fire all curses planted in my past, which are waging war against me and preventing me from moving to the next level, progressing, advancing, and going forward, right now by the blood of the Lamb. In the name of Jesus, I tread upon you serpents and scorpions and over all the powers of the enemy, and in Jesus' name, I destroy by lightning and fire the power of these strongholds, ties, leashes, and all curses working against me.

I call upon the God of the Heavens and Earth whose name is Holy, to destroy by fire, lightning, brimstone, and hail of fire and a horrible tempest, all these evil powers, demonic attachments attaching me to the past worlds.
I banish all foul spirits and curses of regression, relapse, backwardness, reverse, failure, and all allegations, accusations, and condemnations fighting against me, in Jesus' name.

Thank You Father for delivering me from these evil elemental spirits. May I represent who you are on the earth, and for this I ascribe greatness unto you, Deuteronomy 32:3, **"I will publish the name of the LORD: ascribe ye greatness unto our God."**

87. Prayers Against The Spirit Of Hard-Heartedness & Mercilessness

Lord our God, King of the ages, All-powerful and All-mighty who sits between the Cherubim of burning coals, you who made everything and transform everything by Your will, have mercy on me, and change my heart. I confess my heart of stone and express my need and desire for a new heart, fashioned after Yours. You have spoken in Ezekiel 36:26 and said, **"And I will give you a new heart, and a new spirit I will put within you. And I will remove the heart of stone from your flesh and give you a heart of flesh."**

Now, let Your gracious Holy Spirit breathe upon the chambers of my heart and let the heat of Your eternal flame of love melt away the wax, dross, and stoniness of my heart.

By the faith of the Son of God, by which I live [Gal 2:20], I address all psychic elements, entities, and mysterious powers of darkness manipulating my heart and soul, and I renounce the configurator demons, specifically the black heart, cold heart, and stony heart demons. It is written in Luke 6:35, **"But** love your enemies, and do good, and lend, hoping for **nothing again; and your reward shall be great, and you shall be the children of the Highest; for He is good to the unthankful and the wicked."**

Through Jesus of Nazareth, let all astral poisons and the venom of serpents and scorpions that have darkened, hardened, and neutralized my heart by instilling within me mercilessness, heartlessness, hardness of heart, cruelty, cold-bloodedness, and uncompassionate be neutralized and uprooted from my heart and lose all power and effectiveness against me.

Colossians 3:12, "**Put on therefore, as the elect of God, holy and beloved, bowels of mercies, kindness, humbleness of mind, meekness, longsuffering;**"

Colossians 3:13, "**Forbearing one another, and forgiving one another, if any man have a quarrel against any: even as Christ forgave you, so also *do* ye.**"

I banish from my heart every demon of mercilessness, heartlessness, hardness of heart, unforgiveness, cruelty, cold-bloodedness, cutthroat, sternness, pitilessness, harshness, and all subjective spirits attached to the stony heart demons. It is written in Ephesians 4:32, "**And be ye kind one to another, tenderhearted, forgiving one another, even as God for Christ's sake hath forgiven you.**"

Every witchcraft placed upon my life, working through the psychic vibrations of the black heart demons, the cold heart demons, the stony heart demons, the icy heart demons, the hard heart demons, and other heart configurator demons, who are working to transmute, change, alter, and downgrade my character, attitude, mannerism, personality, destiny of success, wealth, happiness, and completeness, now by lightning, thunder, and the fire of Jesus Christ of Nazareth, I renounce, revoke, shatter, and destroy these witchcraft curses from the 333 Mephistophelian seal, for it is written in Romans 12:10, "**Be kindly affectioned one to another with brotherly love; in honour preferring one another**".

Let every witchcraft curse set upon me to destroy my life, my reputation, my dignity, my mind, my purpose, future, and destiny be destroyed and be banished from all occult regions, zones, realms, occult centers, or spheres now, in the Name of Jesus the Christ. Ephesians 4:31, "**Let all bitterness, and wrath, and anger, and clamour, and evil speaking, be put away from you, with all malice:**"

Ephesians 4:32, "**And be ye kind one to another, tenderhearted, forgiving one another, even as God for Christ's sake hath forgiven you.**"
Galatians 2:20 says, "**I am crucified with Christ: nevertheless, I live; yet not I, but Christ liveth in me: and the life which I now live in the flesh I live by the faith of the Son of God, who loved me, and gave himself for me.**" Thank You Father for a heart change or a spiritual heart transplant. May my heart represent who you are on the earth, and for this I ascribe greatness unto you, Deuteronomy 32:3, "**I will publish the name of the LORD: ascribe ye greatness unto our God.**" Father, give me an excellent spirit. I make claim to the anointing to walk in divine distinction in every area of my life.
Psalms 96:7, "**Give unto the LORD, O ye kindreds of the people, give unto the LORD glory and strength**".

88. Prayers Against The Spirit Of Sabotage

Lord our God, King of the ages, All-powerful and All-mighty who sits between the Cherubim of burning coals, you who made everything and transform everything by Your will, have mercy on me, and change my heart's testimonies, and the outcome of my labour, sowings, plantings, and expectations and desires through Your name.
Where I have sabotaged, and now I am being sabotaged, and where my ancestors have sabotaged others, and now I am being sabotaged through the doorways of their sins, Father, I repent of my sins and the sins of my ancestors.

I petition by the blood of the Lamb that you remove the allegations, accusations, and condemnations against me and sever, overrule, and nullify every astral right, legislation, verdict, legally binding document, handwriting, and ordinance of the enemy through which my life and destinies are being sabotaged by the elemental spirits, day after day, week after week, month after month, and year after year.

from the judicial platform of Your divine council, grant unto me a full pardon from the penalty, reproach, and consequences of the sins of my mother's house and my father's house, and my own sins, based upon Yeshua's sacrifice on Calvary.
Father, I stand in the authority You have given me over the power of the elemental forces and the 52-day cycle of astral attacks which are programmed to bring sabotage, hindrances, obstacles, barriers, blockages, and resistance in my life that keep me from fulfilling Your prophetic destiny for my life.

According to (Hebrews 1:14), I petition by the blood of the Lamb the Lord to commission the angels that are assigned to me to go before me and destroy every negative projection of the enemy, conspiracy, obstacle, barrier, blockage, resistance, and sabotage against my life and bring me into the fullness of Your plans for me.

Every work of sabotage fashioned against me to derail my purpose, and my destiny is met with utter destruction. I decree that God shall frustrate evil workers and their weapons of sabotage. I sabotage the powers, schemes, and subtle manipulation within all seven kingdoms of the Mephistophelian world of darkness.

Every demon of sabotage attached to my life, specifically assigned to sabotage my destinies in my marriage, finances, career, ministry, and in my mission and commission, I render you demons inadequate, incapable, and ineffective in channeling any incantation and psychic commands into the psychic layers and astral planes against me.

By the power of the judicial blood of Jesus of Nazareth, these incantations and psychic spirits are now disqualified and rendered useless against my life. I release the fire of God against every attempt to sabotage and destroy my family, marriage, relationships, finances, career, health, ministry, and spiritual destiny.
I boldly declare that, like Haman's counsel against Mordecai, every evil counsel against me will turn around for my promotion; therefore, I cancel the assignment of the spirit of sabotage fashioned against my destiny. Every evil planting and secret plot of the spirit of Cain, the spirit of Potiphar's Wife, the spirit of Korah the son of Izhar, the spirit of Haman, the spirit of Ahitophel, the spirit of Absalom, the spirit of Jezebel, the spirit of Delilah, and the spirit of Judas programmed against me with evil be scattered by fire and be banished to ashes of shame and disgrace.

It is written, Psalm 21:11, **"For they intended evil against thee: they imagined a mischievous device, which they are not able to** perform." By fire, lightning and thunder, let every evil counsel against me turn to foolishness like how you turned the counsel of Ahithophel into foolishness, In Jesus Name.

O God of the eternal flame, fight my battle against the seven princes of darkness and their kingdoms. Let the warfront battle wage hotter than blazing and raging fire and release angelic artillery and resistances against the sophisticated weapons of the Mephistophelian seals of the Occult.

Arise to my help, Psalms 121:2, **"My help cometh from the LORD, which made heaven and earth."**
It is written in Daniel 6:23, **"Then was the king exceeding glad for him, and commanded that they should take Daniel up out of the den. So Daniel was taken up out of the den, and no manner of hurt was found upon him, because he believed in his God".**
Daniel 6:24, **"And the king commanded, and they brought those men which had accused Daniel, and they cast *them* into the den of lions, them, their children, and their wives; and the lions had the mastery of them, and brake all their bones in pieces or ever they came at the bottom of the den."**

All those who devised my hurt shall replace me in the Lion's Den and be devoured.
I send the fire of God against every spirit that would relegate me to a place of being forgotten, irrelevant, misunderstood, misrepresented, terminated, demoted, suspended, marginalized, criticized, and ostracized. I cancel the assignment of the enemy that is sent to sift me from my place of blessing, purpose, and destiny in the name of Jesus. Every witchcraft placed upon my life by day and by night, working through psychic vibrations of the demons of sabotage and ruin, seeking to transmute, change, alter, and demote my destiny of success, wealth, happiness, and completeness to become a life of shame, poverty, failure, incompetence, incompleteness, and disgrace.

By lightning, thunder, and the fire of Jesus Christ of Nazareth, I renounce, revoke, shatter, and destroy these witchcraft curses in the name of Jesus the Christ.

Thank you, Father, for delivering me from the powers of darkness, through Jesus and by Your Spirit. For thine is the kingdom, the power, and the glory now and forever, for it is written, **"Worthy is the Lamb that was slain to receive power, and riches, and wisdom, and strength, and honour, and glory, and blessing"**. [Rev 5:12].

89. Prayers Against Curses Of Cancer

Lord my God, King of the ages, All-powerful and All-mighty who sits between the Cherubim of burning coals, You are the Lord of all flesh; You know my frame and remember that we are mortal.

We come boldly unto the throne of grace, that we may obtain mercy, and find grace to help in time of need [Heb 4:16].
We seek help from the golden altar of Heaven through the sacrificial death of the Lamb of God and implore the judicial authority of the wounds of the Lamb who was slain against the cancer afflicting me. Have mercy upon me according to the multitude of Your lovingkindness and Your tender mercies. It is written in Isaiah 53:4-5 **"Surely he has borne my infirmities and carried my diseases..."**

Let my cry for help trigger an emergency alert to accelerate the velocity of mercy for intervention on my behalf. Psalms 70:1 says, **"Make haste, O God, to deliver me; make haste to help me, O LORD."**
Therefore, I summon a "Holy Rebuke" from the Courtroom and Divine Council in Heaven against all spirits of Cancer that have imprisoned me and have set themselves upon me to afflict me through ancient astral rights, legal grounds, and ethereal bridges coming from my ancestral genealogy.

O God, judge and vindicator, who is clothed with fire and light, arise and fight my battles with cancer and the spirit of premature death attached to it. By Your pillar of fire by night and cloud by day, let the warfront battle wage hotter than blazing and raging fire and release angelic artillery and resistances against the sophisticated weapons of the sting of death, the emperor of death, the agents of death, the bounty hunters, death hunters, and death reapers who seek to take my life by cancer.

My God and Father, I place my life upon the platform of Your judicial council. Behold, the tribunal of the night has ruled against me and has used legalities to strike me with cancer.
My God and Father, by the blood of Jesus of Nazareth, I invoke the judicial intervention of Heaven to rule against any and every processing, proceeding, and lawsuit in the tribunal of the night that has set itself against my life.
"And now, Lord, behold their threatenings: and grant unto thy servants that with all boldness they may speak thy word," as it is written in Acts 4:29.

By the authority of Jesus Christ and the power of the Holy Spirit of Jesus, we condemn every condemnation laid over my life by the grand juror of the judicial court of the kingdom of darkness, by the attorney general of Hell, by the magistrate of esoteric forces, and by the high judge of the Devil's kingdom.
Your word says, O Lord, in Psalms 94:21, **"They gather themselves together against the soul of the righteous and condemn the innocent blood"**. But it is written in Psalms 109:31, **"For he shall stand at the right hand of the poor, to save *him* from those that condemn his soul"**.
All decisions taken in the courts of darkness against my life to destroy my body by cancer, let Heaven overrule these evil decisions now.

By the name of Jesus Christ, with hot chains of fire and by force, I bring into subjection to the power of Jesus Christ of Nazareth, every imagination and high thing, every judicial platform, demonic judge, satanic juror, evil bailiff, occult attorney, demonic false witnesses, every evil perpetrator, instigator of evil, and every satanic law and order.

Arise to my help, Psalms 121:2, **"My help cometh from the LORD, which made heaven and earth."**

Let the three that bear witness on earth, the Spirit, the water, and the blood [1 John 5:8], arise against the highest council of darkness and condemn their verdict to destroy us by cancer.
Your word says you sent forth Your word and healed my diseases; therefore, I stand erect in the authoritative capacity of the blood, water, and Spirit of Jesus of Nazareth, and by the authority of Your word and name, O Yah, I address Cancer by inheritance, paternal, genealogical, traits, ethnic, racial, family line, bloodline, roots, family tree, ancestral, and hereditary curses that are the result of the sins of the fathers (Jeremiah 32:18), especially witchcraft, occultism, perversion, and idolatry. I call upon the judicial blood of Jesus to acquit me from these evil allegations, accusations, condemnations, and strongholds by which the spirit of Cancer has set itself in my body.

By the Throne of El-Shaddai, and by the authority of the Word of the Almighty, I bind with hot chains of holy fire the spirit of death, the curse of cancer, and cancer caused by abnormalities in the body.
Psalms 41:2, **"The LORD will preserve him and keep him alive; and he shall be blessed upon the earth: and thou wilt not deliver him unto the will of his enemies"**.
Anything that was placed in my body by ingestion or incision, or entered my soul and body during any trauma or any demonic open door, or an evil dream that has subjected me to become the victim, a prisoner, an object and subject of the demon of Cancer, and every psychic entity or agent of darkness that has placed a sigil or mark of cancer upon my forehead, or in the palm of my hand in order to strike me with:
Breast cancer
Leukemia
Bowel cancer

Lung cancer
Lym-phoma
Brain tumour
Bladder cancer
Mela-noma
Prostate cancer
Cervical cancer
Colon cancer
rectal cancer
Kidney cancer
Head and neck cancer
Liver cancer
Sarcoma
Bile duct cancer
Bone tumour
Skin cancer
Endometrial cancer
Pancreatic cancer
Myeloma
Esophageal cancer
Appendix cancer
Cancer of unknown primary origin
Bone cancer, cancer of the cardiovascular system.

1 Peter 2:24: **"He Himself bore my sins' in His body on the cross, so that we might die to sins and live for righteousness; 'by His wounds you have been healed."**
Let Respiratory, Digestive, Psychological, Circulatory, Lymphatic, Skeletal, Nervous, Integumentary, Endocrine, Urinary, Mental, Dermatological, and Neurological failures be cancelled and condemned in Jesus' name.

I call for the holy fire of Yah, and the blood of the Lamb of God that was sprinkled upon the mercy seat to intervene and erase every mark, trace, and presence of cancer that was placed in any part of my body by demonic spirits and genetic inheritance.

Psalms 103:2 **Bless the LORD, O my soul, and forget not all his benefits:**
Psalms 103:3 **Who forgiveth all thine iniquities, who healeth all thy diseases;**
Psalms 103:4 **Who redeemeth thy life from destruction;**

Send Your angels, O Lord, to recover the health and organs of these my people from darkness. Psalms 103:20, "Bless the LORD, ye his angels, that excel in strength".
By the power of the Holy Spirit of Jesus, I revoke all witchcraft incantations done over my body, and I destroy any witchcraft hex and cage that are over my health, and I retrieve by fire my health and organs from the Gates of Hell; I smash to pieces every pendant, cauldron, black box, vase, bottle, or any other vessel in which my health is trapped.

Your word says in Exodus 23:25, **"You shall serve the Lord your God, and He will bless your bread and your water, and I will take sickness away from among you."**

Jeremiah 17:14, says, **"Heal me, O LORD, and I shall be healed; save me, and I shall be saved: for thou art my praise."**

Jeremiah 30:17, says, **"For I will restore health unto thee, and I will heal thee of thy wounds, saith the LORD".**

Isaiah 53:5 says, "But he was wounded for my transgressions, he was bruised for my iniquities; the chastisement of my peace was laid upon him, and by his wounds we are healed."

Matthew 10:1 says, "Jesus called his twelve disciples to him and gave them authority to drive out impure spirits and to heal every disease and sickness."

Mark 5:34 says, "He said to her, 'Daughter, your faith has healed you. Go in peace and be freed from your suffering."

3 John 1:2 says, "I pray that you may be in good health and prosper,"

90. Prayers Against The Spirit Of Monsters

Heavenly Father, I come before You, seeking Your protection and peace from the monstrous world of evil creatures who are hunters of the night and terrors of sleep. Many monsters have crossed over the barrier of the spirit world into the natural world and are programmed with the mandate to terrorize and destroy me.

O God of the eternal flame, release Your forefront angels to fight against them and fight my battle against the seven princes of darkness and their kingdoms. Let the warfront battle wage hotter than blazing and raging fire and release angelic artillery and resistances against the sophisticated weapons of the Mephistophelian seals of the Occult. Arise to my help; Psalms 121:2 says, **"My help *cometh* from the LORD, which made heaven and earth."**

I pray against the spirit of monsters, and by electric fire from Heaven, in the name of the Lord God of hosts, I banish from my life with immediate effect the spirit of the Dragon, the gargoyle, griffin, sea monster, ghoul, phantom, behemoth (Job 40:15-24), Gog and Magog, banshee, Beast, behemoth, bogeyman, centaur, Cerberus, Cyclops, demon, devil, djinn, dragon, elf, fairy, fire-breathing dragon, Frankenstein's monster, genie, ghost, giant, gnome, Godzilla, Golem, gorgon, leprechaun, leviathan, mermaid, merman, mummy, ogre, orc, Pegasus, sprite, troll, reanimated dead corpse, vampire, werewolf, yeti, zombie, brute, incubus, succubus, horror, terror, and even the spirit of panic that is haunting, taunting, or afflicting me in dreams, nightmares, trances, by flashes, sensory perceptions, by phobias, horrors, or in any other way.

By my authority through Jesus of Nazareth, I now take authoritative commands over all monster demons of the four kingdoms of the Air, the kingdom of the waters, the kingdom of the Land, and the kingdom of the subterranean region, and over the four elements of the four cardinal dimensions, and I call upon the glorious light of Jesus Christ to destroy and banish all monster spirits stalking and haunting me with severe nightmares, physical assault, sudden wakes from sleep, unexplainable prints, auditory hallucinations, visual hallucinations, olfactory hallucinations, gustatory hallucinations, tactile hallucinations, algesic hallucinations, general somatic hallucinations, and strange ambiances of monstrous voices, hideous laughter, or whispers.

Right now, by the power of El-Shaddai, I bind and disarm every combined element of psychic and esoteric operation, and I banish all these evil monsters and occult activities taking place with me. I declare war and revolt against, neutralize, destroy, and banish these creatures of hell from every area of my life.

Whatever link exists between me and any demon monster, let it be broken now, effective immediately.

Father in heaven, guard my mind and heart from all fears, nightmares, territorial evil, and residential evil.

Surround me with Your loving presence and dispel any darkness that tries to invade my thoughts with fear and terror. Hence, I say, I will not be bullied, not be scared, or paralyzed by fear and terror in Jesus' mighty name, Amen and Amen.

91. Prayers Against The Spirit Of Anxiety

Heavenly Father, I come before You in the powerful name of Jesus Christ, my Saviour, Redeemer, and Deliverer. I acknowledge Your sovereignty, that You are the God of peace and the giver of peace, and have power over all spiritual forces in every realm, sphere, dimension, etc. You said in Your word in Isaiah 26:3, **"You will keep him in perfect peace, whose mind is stayed on You; because he trusts in You."**

Anointed One Y'ahushua, I come now to Your throne of Glory to obtain deliverance from the spirit of anxiety and all connected and subordinate demons that have been disturbing, afflicting, and incarcerating me and my peace of mind. Deliver me, for it is written, Psalms 50:15, **"call on Me in the day of trouble; and I will deliver you, and you shall glorify Me"**.

In thee, O LORD, do I put my trust; let me never be ashamed: deliver me in thy righteousness [Psalms 31:1].
"Bow down your ear to me; deliver me speedily: be my strong Rock, for a house of defence to save me", according to Psalms 31:2.

By my authority through Jesus of Nazareth, by the Throne of El-Shaddai, and by the authority of the Word of the Almighty, I now take authoritative commands in the name of Jesus over the Mephistophelian occult seal 333, and all spirits and demons of anxiety afflicting my life, and I bind with hot chains of holy fire the spirit of mental and emotional abnormalities in my body. By thunders of fire and lightnings, I address, banish, and terminate the existence of every demon behind generalized anxiety disorder, agoraphobia, panic disorder, specific phobias, social anxiety disorder, separation anxiety disorder, selective mutism, and all other mental disturbances and spirits of traumatic stress disorder (PTSD), acute stress disorder, and obsessive-compulsive disorder (OCD post-) that have entered and are sitting, dwelling, and dominating my life.

Arise, my God, and set me free, for it is written in Psalms 68:1-2, **"God arise, let his enemies be scattered: let them also that hate him flee before him"**.
"As smoke is driven away, so drive them away: as wax melteth before the fire, so let the wicked perish at the presence of God".

As you deliver me from fear and anxiety, send the calming presence of the Holy Spirit to overtake my heart and mind and let the heat of Your eternal flames of love burn out from my heart and surround any unclean thing that contaminates my heart and serves as an ethereal bridge or open door. Psalm 42:11, **"Why art thou cast down, O my soul? and why art thou disquieted within me? hope thou in God: for I shall yet praise him, who is the health of my countenance and my God."**

Father in Heaven, let my demonic enemies melt like wax, and let the wax of their defeat drip down to the lowest hell in shame.
Disturb the spirit of anxiety and everything that disturbs my glory, honour, ministry, and destiny.
Arise, O Lord, let me now be released from captivity, and from the sin and curses from paternal and maternal sides, up to ten generations of both my mother's house and my father's house, and open the prison of my bondage to liberate me, spiritually, emotionally, socially, psychologically, and mentally, in the Almighty Name of Jesus.

It is written in Isaiah 61:1, **"The Spirit of the Lord GOD is upon Me because the LORD has anointed Me to preach the Gospel to the poor; He has sent Me to bind up the broken hearted, to proclaim** liberty to the captives, and the opening of the prison to those who are bound."

You have given me authority over all the powers of the enemy, and I claim that authority now over the demon of anxiety.
It is written in Philippians 4:6, "**Do not be anxious about anything; but by prayer and supplication with thanksgiving, let your requests be made known to God in everything;**"
Philippians 4:7, "**And the peace of God, which surpasses all understanding, shall guard your hearts and your thoughts in Christ Jesus.**"

Holy Father, in the name of the Lord Jesus Christ, cut off all spiritual umbilical cords through which the spirit of anxiety has flowed into my life from my ancestral bloodline.
Deliver me, I pray, from the insurrection of the kingdom of darkness that is fighting against me, and Lord Jesus, as I banish from my life every elemental spirit programmed to destroy me through anxiety, using various techniques and psychic manipulations, let Your fire and terrifying lightnings descend from heaven upon all demonic spirits and sirens.

It is written in Psalms 12:5, "**For the oppression of the poor, for the sighing of the needy, now will I arise, saith the LORD; I will set him in safety from him that puffeth at him.**"
I banish by the name of Jesus all constructed demonic ties, knots, and bolts in my mind. I also banish every spirit of fear of death, phobia, dread, worry, defeat, depression, stagnation, affliction, delay, panic, social anxiety, nervousness, suicidal thoughts, unhappiness, tension, restlessness, confusion, frustration, rejection, doubt, and all other demons of anxiety.

I banish by the name of Jesus all constructed demonic ties, knots, and bolts placed in my mind.

I also banish every spirit of fear of death, phobia, spirit of dread, worry, defeat, depression, stagnation, affliction, death, delay, panic, apprehension, social anxiety, fear, nervousness, uneasiness, suicidal thoughts, unhappiness, tension, fretfulness, restlessness, confusion, frustration, rejection, doubt, and all other demons attached to anxiety, which make me feel continually irritable, tense or restless, nauseated or give me abdominal distress, having heart palpitations, uncommon sweating, bodily tremors or shaking, trouble sleeping, having a sense of impending danger, feeling of panic, doom and trouble concentrating or making decisions; and every astral attack that comes against me through esoteric occult sciences, orders, formulas, codes, channels, vibrations and frequencies, for it is written in Psalms 34:19, **"Many are the afflictions of the righteous: but the LORD delivereth him out of them all"**.

It is also written in Psalms 31:15, **"My times are in thy hand: deliver me from the hand of mine enemies, and from them that persecute me."**

Father, this I pray in the name of the Father, the Son, and the Holy Spirit. Thank you for healing me from anxiety, and for giving me Your light and mercy and Your word, which delivers me. In Jesus' name, Amen and Amen.

92. Prayers Against The Spirit Of Shame And Disgrace

Heavenly Father, I give You thanks and praise as I come into prayer against shame and disgrace. It is not Your will that I walk in shame and disgrace; therefore, I revolt against this evil that besets me on every side.

Therefore, in the name of Jesus, and through Jesus of Nazareth, I say let every astral poison and the venom of shame and disgrace be neutralized and lose all power and effectiveness against me.

In the name of Y'ahushua, Son of the Living God, I banish from my life every demon of dishonour, hurt, embarrassment, scandal, condemnation, shyness, reproach, fear, guilt, ejection, self-consciousness, timidity, fear, hesitation, fear of rejection, withdrawal, apprehension, nervousness, bashfulness, low self-esteem, and all subjective spirits attached to the house of shame and disgrace.

Every witchcraft placed upon my life by day and by night, working through psychic vibrations of the spirit of shame and disgrace, seeking to transmute, change, alter, and demote my destiny of success, wealth, happiness, and completeness to become a life of shame, poverty, incompetence, incompleteness, failure, and disgrace,
By lightning, thunder, and the fire of Jesus Christ of Nazareth, I renounce, revoke, shatter, and destroy these witchcraft curses from my life, effective immediately, in the name of Jesus the Christ.

By the Fire of the Holy Spirit, I pray against every demon, law, and altar of shame and disgrace that is connecting me to any occult region, zone, realm, occult Centre, or sphere within the Mephistophelian world through familiar spirits, elemental demons, terrestrial demons, demonic watchers, psychic naval forces, astral televisions, psychic cameras, succubus demons, incubus demons, spirits of the dead, and graveyards. Let every demon, law, and altar of shame and disgrace, witchcraft curse, and connection set upon me to destroy my life, my reputation, my dignity, my mind, my purpose, future, and destiny, and to suck the potency, exuberance, and resplendency of my star; be destroyed and banished into realms of no return, now, in Jesus' Name.

I send the fire of God against every dragon spirit ready to devour my God-given vision.
Let every evil entity setting a trap of failure for me fall into its own pit of destruction.
Lion of Judah, roar over me and silence all my accusers. Let every assignment of slander be silenced that is meant to destroy my character. Father, please cause me to flourish in Your hands.
Let any covetous person trying to malign my name with the intention of assuming my position fail in his or her crafty and devious ways.
I declare that those who have gone too far in their attack on my commitment to fulfil God's purpose for my life shall be embarrassed and put to shame.
I receive God's immunity from every attack of the enemy. I shall fulfil God's purpose for my life unhindered. I shall not be put to shame.
Father, thank You for the wisdom to bridle my tongue and not expose the secrets You have spoken concerning my life.
I boldly declare that those who have made themselves agents of hindrance, frustration, sabotage, resistance, and barriers shall be put to shame.
Father, thank You for hearing me and delivering me from the astral poisons of shame and disgrace, and setting me free so that I can glorify You in all the earth. I pray these prayers in no other name but the name of Y'ahushua HaMashiach, for Yours is the kingdom, the power, and the glory forever. Amen and Amen.

93. Prayers Against Curses Of Spiritual Partitions

Heavenly Father, I come to You in desperation to be set free from the hold of evil.
You have surrounded us with walls of salvation, but I identify foreign walls and partitions in my life.
Father, I refuse to live any longer under affliction and failure and hereby revolt against all demonic spiritual partitions that are separating me from my destiny.
It is written in Ephesians 2:14, **"For he is our peace, who hath made both one, and hath broken down the middle wall of partition *between us;"***

By the jurisdiction of the finished work of Christ, I subject all partitions in my life to be judged and broken down after the like manner of the walls of partition broken down by Christ in Ephesians 2:14, and I say, all partitions in my life, be broken down in like manner, effective immediately, in Jesus' name.
Today I pray against every evil partition that is separating me from my career, health, finances, academics, business, ministry, family, and destiny helpers, supporters, and my God-approved spouse (if you are Single].

I condemn, renounce, revoke, overturn, and overthrow all evil invisible barriers and partitions, and shatter beyond repair every power within the invisible realm that has me under the force of detention and retention.

Let hot chains of holy fire fall upon all demons who are part of the construction of the partition in my life, or who are responsible for the partition and walls.

By force, I neutralize every venom, and I arrest, bind, and bring into captivity under subjection all demons of spiritual partition and walls of separation in my life.

I call to judgement and destruction, eradication, annihilation all demons in my life responsible for division, separation, isolation, partition, unhealthy self-protection, unhealthy self-preservation, fear of rejection, fear of hurt, introversion, withdrawal, pride, demonic walls of rejection, hurt, fear etc.

Wherever I am under affliction between realms, being trapped within darkness by demonic partitions and walls of separation, O God my Saviour, I petition by the blood of the Lamb that You destroy the powers of the Occult that are continually surrounding me. I pray for the disintegration of every evil wall and partition and evil agenda in my life, that they be demolished by the thunderbolts of God's thunderous voice.

May the schemes of the rulers of darkness of this world operating in my life collapse, and their intents be turned to foolishness, in Jesus' precious name.

For it is written in Psalms 21:11, **"For they intended evil against thee: they imagined a mischievous device, which they are not able to perform."**

In the powerful name of Jesus of Nazareth, I destroy and banish by fire, lightning, and thunder all you demons of:

Partitions for limitations.
Partitions for reduction.
Partitions for loss.
Partitions for wastage.
Partitions for failure.
Partitions for disappointment.
Partitions for depression.
Partitions for sighing.

Partitions for crying and weeping.
Partitions for confusion of face.
Partitions for sorrow.
Partitions for frustration.
Partitions for disdain.
Partitions that create the feeling of being overwhelmed and lost.
All you demons of evil partitions mentioned here by name, and every power and influence from the four corners of the heavens, working contrary to me and fighting the will of God for my life, receive severe and critical destruction: crumble and be vaporized from my life now, in Jesus' name, effective immediately.
Therefore, through travailing prayer, in the battles of confrontations and resistance, I build barricades and barriers of incomprehensible force, and permanent walls and defences of Light and Fire, around my life against the kingdom of darkness.
In the mighty name of Jesus.
Father, thank You for hearing me and delivering me from evil partitions and setting me free, so that I can glorify You in all wisdom. I pray these prayers in no other name but the name of Y'ahushua HaMashiach, for Yours is the kingdom, the power, and the glory forever. Amen and Amen.

94. Prayers Against The Spirit Of Slothfulness

Father, I come before You in acknowledgment of Your word and power, which says you have given us the power to gain wealth.

But I also acknowledge that I am slothful in many things, and I repent and ask for Your forgiveness.
I come seeking Your intervention for my total deliverance from slothfulness and laziness, and I thank You that I can overcome it, for it is written, **"I can do all things through Christ which strengtheneth me."** (Philippians 4:13).

I have allowed that spirit to stop me from accomplishing what is written in the master plan of my destiny, but Father, this ends here.
I want to achieve what Heaven wants me to accomplish in my life, and therefore I pray for courage to address my encounter with the spirit of sluggardness, slothfulness, and laziness. For it is written in 1 John 4:4, **"Ye are of God, little children, and have overcome them: because greater is he that is in you than he that is in the world."**
Therefore, Father, I rebuke laziness right now and I pray that You will give me the power to destroy the forces of the occult regime of darkness and their psychic manipulations, and the strength and courage to overcome it, to gain victory over it".
Give me wisdom and ways to overcome laziness, as I ask for guidance on priorities, and give me the wisdom to establish accountability among my circle of friends and family, give me the grace to start with small steps and the intelligence for setting manageable goals, creating a detailed plan, channeling positive energy, and striving for progress and perfection, and the discipline to take short breaks.

In Jesus Almighty Name, I command the thunder and lightning of God to break into pieces any statue in any occult zone, occult sphere,

occult realm, occult dimension, occult center, occult region, and occult kingdom representing my slothfulness and the obstruction of my destiny, productivity, and materialization of my wealth and prosperity.
Through Jesus of Nazareth, let every astral poison and the venom of slothfulness be neutralized and lose all power and effectiveness over me.

I banish from me every demon of slothfulness, laziness, slumber, idleness, lethargy, passivity, heaviness, sluggard, shame, and disgrace, for it is written in Romans 12:11, **"not slothful in business; fervent in spirit; serving the Lord."**
Every witchcraft placed upon my life by day and by night, working through secret psychic vibrations of the spirit of slothfulness, laziness, heaviness, sluggard, and all shadows that are seeking to keep my destiny of success, wealth, happiness, and completeness from coming forth.
Every power of darkness seeking to subject me to become a vessel of shame, poverty, failure, incompetence, incompleteness, and disgrace, by lightning, thunder, and the fire of Jesus Christ of Nazareth, I renounce, revoke, shatter, and destroy these witchcraft curses that restrain me in the prison of slothfulness.
Proverbs 10:5 says, "**He who gathers crops in summer is a prudent son, but he who sleeps during harvest is a disgraceful son."**
I am not a disgraceful son/daughter; therefore, I keep my body under and bring it into subjection, lest by any means, when I have preached to others, I myself should be a castaway. [1Co 9:27].

Father, grant me the spirit of success and competence, for it is written in 1 Corinthians 9:24-27, **"Don't you know that those who run a race all run, but only one receives the prize? That is the way you are to run in order that you may obtain the prize."**

1Corinthians 9:26, "I therefore so run, not as one who is uncertain; so also I fight, not as beating the air."

I declare by the authority of my position sitting in heavenly places in Christ Jesus, according to Ephesians 2:6, Poverty eating my destiny through slothfulness, laziness, and unproductivity, die now and release my wealth and finances.
I declare by the authority of my position sitting in heavenly places in Christ Jesus, according to Ephesians 2:6, that I will walk in my prosperity and blessings and eat from the bounty and fruitfulness of my efforts, labour and sacrifices.
By the authority of my position sitting in heavenly places in Christ Jesus, according to Ephesians 2:6, I call fire of the Lord Jesus to burn upon my head and melt every crown of poverty and lack by which I was made a dignitary in poverty because of my slothfulness, laziness, and procrastination, in Jesus' name.
It is written in Colossians 3:23-24,
"And whatever you do, do it heartily, as to the Lord and not to men, knowing that from the Lord you will receive the reward of the inheritance; for you serve the Lord Christ."

Luke 16:10
"He who is faithful in what is least is faithful also in much; and he who is unjust in what is least is unjust also in much."

Hebrews 6:11-12
"And we desire that each one of you show the same diligence to the full assurance of hope until the end, that you do not become sluggish, but imitate those who through faith and patience inherit the promises."

Proverbs 10:4 says, "Lazy hands make for poverty, but diligent hands bring wealth."

It is also written in Proverbs 20:4, **"The sluggard will not plow by reason of the cold; therefore, shall he beg in harvest, and have nothing."**

Therefore, I come against the Sloth demon, the slug demon, the snail demon, the demon of procrastination, sleepiness, the demon of drowsiness, daydreaming, fantasy, mental drifting and wandering, and all other demons, laws and altars connected to slothfulness, laziness, heaviness, and sluggardliness, which have reduced me to become a victim and vessel of the spirits of failure and unaccomplishment. in the name of Jesus, the Christ.

In the Name of Jesus the Christ, I remove my feet from the ground and pedestal of laziness, slothfulness, and sluggardness, for it is written in Ecclesiastes 9:10, **"Whatsoever thy hand findeth to do, do it with thy might."**

Holy Spirit, fill me with Your peace that surpasses all understanding. Guard my mind and heart with Your truth and righteousness. Surround me with Your angels, standing watch over me throughout the day and night.

Thank You, Lord, for Your protection and for the victory I have in Christ. I trust in Your unfailing love and care. In Jesus' name, I pray. Amen.

95. Prayer Against The Spirit Of Guilt & Self-Condenmation

My Father and Most High God, I come to You, seeking the presence and sweet wisdom of Your precious Holy Spirit, and a judicial intervention by the precious Blood of the Lamb of God [which was shed for me], and was sprinkled upon Your holy altar.

Lord Jesus, by Your mercy, Your Blood pleads for my deliverance and salvation; hence, I am imploring the ruling and verdict of the council of Your divine eternal Blood, wisdom, and light so that I may be delivered from the spirit, stronghold, and curse of perpetual guilt.
I have been carrying the weight of my past mistakes, and it burdens my soul with guilt. I petition by the blood of the Lamb for Your divine guidance and strength to release these heavy emotions that are holding me back and weighing me down. Help me find and accept forgiveness within myself and from others, and grant me the clarity to learn from my past while embracing the present and future with an open heart. For it is written in Proverbs 4:18, **"But the path of the just *is* as the shining light, that shineth more and more unto the perfect day."**

It is written in Isaiah 53:5, **"But he was wounded for our transgressions, he was bruised for our iniquities: the chastisement of our peace was upon him; and with his stripes we are healed."**
Father, I have erred, but have since asked for forgiveness, and by faith believed that You have forgiven me; yet the guilt of my actions is eating me up, and I am consumed by this heaviness of guilt.
My heart and soul are clouded with guilt, no matter how much I try to focus on Your word and forgiveness. But You said in Exodus 31:13, **"…I am the LORD that doth sanctify you."**

Therefore, I seek help from Your holy council to overrule and overthrow the verdict of my conviction, and the condemnation that is documented in Hell because of my sins, and acquit me from all allegations, accusations, and condemnations that are brought against me in the tribunal of the night, and in the courts of accusations by the Devil.

In Your word, in 1 John 1:9 it says, **"If we confess our sins, he is faithful and just to forgive us our sins, and to cleanse us from all unrighteousness".**
I have confessed my sins and renounced all open doors in the name of Jesus Christ.

Now Lord Jesus, I am asking You to rebuke the demon of guilt and condemnation that has infiltrated my mind and heart, making me feel guilty and unforgiven. I am requesting that Your fire would melt every chain, shackle, and fetter, lock, knot, and bolt of the spirit of guilt and self-condemnation that has been placed upon me, for You said in Romans 5:1, **"Therefore being justified by faith, we have peace with God through our Lord Jesus Christ." It is also written in Romans 5:9, "Much more then, being now justified by his blood, we shall be saved from wrath through him."**
By the authority of the Blood, fire, and Spirit of the Living God, I highlight by fire every spirit of guilt, condemnation, every crossbreed, hybrid, and siren operating in my life, which has constricted, imprisoned, and neutralized me within the prison cells of guilt, through psychic manipulations, through the Aramau astral poisons, the elemental psychic forces of the four elements of darkness, water, earth, fire, and wind, and through any other astral poison.
In the name of Jesus of Nazareth, by the dynamic and terrifying coals of the altar and fires of amber, which have a most vehement flame [Son 8:6].

I bind you with hot chains of holy fire and neutralize you, venom of guilt, condemnation, and unforgiveness of self, and I arrest, bind, and bring you into captivity under subjection, you, demon of guilt, condemnation, and unforgiveness of self, which are destroying my life.
I burn to ash all your roots of guilt, your regiment, your barracks, your fortress, your infrastructure, any barricade of guilt, every fortress of my imprisonment, and any monument of condemnation built around my life.

I also call upon the eternal light and the dynamic and terrifying fire coals of God's altar to descend from Heaven now and shatter, deconstruct, and vaporize any megalith, structure, tower, or any black stone of guilt that has been placed upon my shoulders, any demon of guilt sitting upon my life, and to vaporize all prison walls of the valley, the land, and the gates of the shadows of death, of darkness and desolation, that have been built in and around my life.
Hence, according to Psalms 11:6 and Exodus 9:24, I call rain of snares and terrors, rain of fires, brimstone, horrible tempests, destruction, desolation, degradation, annihilation, liquidation, and eradication upon all elemental psychic entities and evil powers from darkness holding me captive under the weight of grievous guilt, shame, unforgiveness, and self-condemnation.
Therefore, all plots, plans, snares, lairs, and evil expectations have already failed in my life, In Jesus name.
I claim full functionality of my strength, my will, and my power to walk in justification by the blood and not in self-condemnation and perpetual guilt.

Psalms 18:2, **"The LORD is my Rock, and my fortress, and my deliverer; my God, my Rock in Whom I take refuge; He is my shield, and the horn of my salvation, my high tower."**

You demon of guilt and self-condemnation, you have no jurisdiction to rule and reign in my life any longer, for I am bought with a price according to 1 Corinthians 6:20, and redeemed with the precious blood of Christ according to 1 Peter 1:19. Now be banished and release my destiny, soul, and prosperity, now! Effective immediately!
I rebuke and resist the devil in Jesus' name.

You demon of guilt and self-condemnation, I reclaim my joy, my peace, and my freedom in Christ from your kingdom of despair, sadness, and gloom. I now command the immediate release of my destiny, soul, and prosperity, for it is written in 1 Samuel 30:8, "**...And the Lord answered him, Pursue: for thou shalt surely overtake them, and without fail recover all.**" Hence, I recover all and rebuke and resist the devil, in Jesus' name.
Therefore, by the dynamic power of the Name of Y'ahushua HaMashiach, I declare that I am no more a victim, subject, candidate, or captive of the demons of grievous guilt and self-condemnation, but I am a rod of power, a bundle of joy, rejoicing with joy unspeakable and full of glory, with my peace restored, my freedom made permanent through Christ, and all despair, sadness, gloominess, guilt, and self-condemnation are dispelled and vanquished into oblivion, now effective immediately.

For I can do all things through Christ who strengthens me, as it is written in Philippians 4:13.
Father, I thank You for delivering me from the power and spirits of guilt and condemnation.
I will praise thee with my whole heart: before the gods will I sing praise unto thee (Psalms 138:1).
I will declare thy name unto my brethren; in the midst of the church will I sing praise unto thee (Hebrews 2:12).

96. Prayers Against Hermaphrodite Demon (Bisexual Spirit)

Heavenly Father, I come boldly before Your Throne of Grace, seeking Your divine intervention against the hermaphrodite spirit and every serpentine spirit of sexual twistedness and corruption that is in me.
Father, I have been a victim and vessel of the hermaphrodite spirit, and other serpentine spirits of sexual wickedness. The influence of this demon possessing both male and female genitalia has been dominating my life, and I have been subjected to the stimulation for sensual satisfaction by both genders.

I seek the intervention of Your Eternal Flame and songs of deliverance that are projected from Your judicial council.
I am requesting that Your fire would melt every chain, shackle, fetter, lock, knot, and bolt that the hermaphrodite and spirit of Bisexuality have placed upon me all these years, for You said in Exodus 31:13, "...I *am* the LORD that doth sanctify you."
In the name of Jesus Christ, I confessed my sins of participation in bisexual actions, thoughts, fantasies, and desires that have subjected me to the manipulations of the demon of sexual wickedness.

Abba Father, I repent for any sinful door that I or my ancestors have opened unto this hermaphrodite spirit, whether in the dream world, the natural world, through the possession of an item, by sexual intercourse or contact, through an invitation by witchcraft, or through inheritance from the ancestral bloodline.
I confessed and asked for pardon for my sins and the sins of my ancestors in every area where there has been physical or spiritual, conscious or unconscious, direct or indirect participation in any occult alphabet, symbol, sigil, seal, marking, or secret ceremony, divination, initiation, or ritual, or participation in any sexual paraphernalia, occult

sexual arrangement, conjuring of sexually oriented spirits, or participation in sensual music, films, or songs that may have channelled the hermaphrodite demon into me.

In the Name of Y'ahushua HaMashiach of Nazareth, I renounce, denounce, and revoke all acquaintanceship, embargo, contract, alliance, affiliation, connection, link, communication, covenant, and sexual partnership that I have with the hermaphrodite spirit, and with the kingdom of darkness through personal or ancestral open sinful doors and gates of iniquities.

I renounce and reject all sexual spirit friends, sexual partners, sexual gamers, sexual playmates, sexual rapists, sexual offenders, and spirit spouses that have been given access to my body, soul, and mind through my contamination by the hermaphrodite spirit, and all allegiance that I have pledged to the bisexual spirit.

It is written in Matthew 6:24, **"No man can serve two masters: for either he will hate the one and love the other; or else he will hold to the one and despise the other."**
It is also written in James 1:8, **"A double-minded man is unstable in all his ways."** Also, it is written in James 4:8, **"Draw nigh to God, and He will draw nigh to you. Cleanse your hands, ye sinners; and purify your hearts, ye double-minded."**

In the Name of Y'ahushua HaMashiach of Nazareth, I also renounce any witchcraft substance that was given to me in a dream, or any sexual contact or intimacy that I had in a dream that may have subjected me to become a prisoner of the hermaphrodite demon.

I renounce the inherited hermaphrodite spirit that was passed unto me through my family bloodline, that which I received in the womb or as a neonate.

I renounce my spiritual heritage, marriage, and soul tie with the hermaphrodite spirits of my ancestors, and I claim freedom from all dark powers of Hermaphroditus covering my mind, thoughts, and emotions.

I call upon the Name of Yahushua HaMashiach of Nazareth, and the fire of the Holy Spirit of Christ and the holy Blood of the Lamb of God according to Revelation 12:11, to banish every hermaphrodite demon occupying, controlling my life, and possessing my sensual preferences and desires. By whatever way I have inherited this hermaphrodite demon, I petition by the blood of the Lamb that Your Angels bind, chain, and drag this demon out of my life, as it is done in Revelation 20:1-2 that says, **"And I saw an angel come down from heaven, having the key of the bottomless pit and a great chain in his hand. And he laid hold on the dragon, that old serpent, which is the Devil, and Satan, and bound him."**

You hermaphrodite spirit and bisexual demon, by the power of the judgement and the authority of the Word of God in Luke 10:19, Psalms 11:6, and Exodus 9:24, I call down a rain of fire mingled with grievous hail; I call down rains of snares and terrors, rain of fires, brimstone, horrible tempests, upon you.
You foul spirit of androgyny and effeminate men, and you intersex deity, bisexual spirit, hermaphrodite spirit, and sexual pervert demon under the order of Hermaphroditus, etc., you are detestable and an abomination unto the temple of God, which is my body.

You demons have been poisoning my life with dual sexual characteristics, but the Lord of hosts rebuke and disarm you foul spirit and your army, and render you shield-less, defenceless, weaponless, useless, impotent, clueless, ineffective, and powerless against me, in the Name of Y'ahushua the Messiah, for I am the Temple of God sanctified, according to Exodus 29:43, Hebrews 13:12, Ephesians 2:21, and is therefore written in 1Corinthians 3:17, **"for the temple of God is holy, which temple ye are."**

I notify you that I am a heterosexual being and will walk according to the law of God, the order of nature in creation, and by sanctification, for Hebrews 10:10 says, **"And by that will, we have been sanctified through the sacrifice of the body of Jesus Christ once for all."**

Evil spirit of the Hermaphrodite species, I break your oath and demonic seal, and renounce, reject, revoke, and banish you by the fiery terror of God's divine judgement, according to the Words of the Messiah Jesus in Mark 16:17, **"And these signs shall follow them that believe; in my name shall they cast out devils."**

Let all principalities, powers, rulers, legislators, gods, and demons of Hell know that I am not the property of evil spirits and Hell, because I was purchased with a price, the precious Blood of Jesus of Nazareth, for it is written in 1 Corinthians 6:20, **"For ye are bought with a price: therefore, glorify God in your body, and in your spirit, which are God's."**

On the basis of 1 Corinthians 6:20 and Colossians 2:13-15, you hermaphrodite demon have no jurisdiction to live and be attached to my soul and body, because I am the temple of the Holy Spirit according to 1 Corinthians 6:19, where it is written, **"What? know ye not that your body is the temple of the Holy Spirit, *which is* in you, which ye have of God, and ye are not your own?"**

It is written in John 17:19, **"And for their sakes I sanctify myself, that they also might be sanctified through the truth."**

On this authority, I drive you out by force and banish you, hermaphrodite demon, by fire, thunderclaps and thunder breaks, lightning and terror, and I command you to get out of my life, Now!

I destroy your hold, your stronghold, your unclean settlement, your hooks, claws, nets, traps, shackles, chains, astral poison of Effeminacy [if you are a man], astral poison of Masculinity [if you are a woman], and by lightnings storms, tempests, by coals of fire, which hath a most vehement flame, and a vehement east wind; [Jonah 4:8], and I burn your roots to ashes, and I burn to the ground your regiment, your fortress, your kingdom and barrack that you have built in my life.

Through Jesus of Nazareth, let every astral poison and the venom of this shameful and disgraceful two-sexed demon be neutralized and lose all power and effectiveness in my life, for I release upon you, hermaphrodite demon, destruction, desolation, degradation, annihilation, liquidation, and eradication, for I will not have unnatural sexual preferences, for it is written in Romans 1:26, "**...for even their women did change the natural use into that which is against nature.**"

Rom 1:27, "**And likewise also the men, leaving the natural use of the woman, burned in their lust one toward another; men with men working that which is unseemly, and receiving in themselves that recompense of their error which was meet.**"

I accept the salvation of Yahushua the Messiah of Nazareth into my spirit, soul, and body.

Lord, let my eyes be clear to see in the spirit realm as well as the natural realm. Matthew 6:22, "**The light of the body is the eye: if therefore thine eye be single, thy whole body shall be full of light.**"

Mat 6:23, "**But if thine eye be evil, thy whole body shall be full of darkness.**"

Open my eyes to see, and I thank You for receiving my prayers.

97. Spirits Of Gaslighting

Heavenly Father, in the name of Jesus, I come to You through the blood of the Lamb which gives me access to Your throne of grace by the Holy Spirit, to petition You against the gaslighting spirit. It is important that You fill my heart with Your love and grace, so that I may reflect Your goodness in all my actions and interactions according to Deuteronomy Chp. 10 and 11. It is written in Deuteronomy 10:16, **"Circumcise therefore the foreskin of your heart, and be no more stiff-necked."**
Heavenly Father, I acknowledge that I often use this designed technique to manipulate other people's emotions to achieve my selfish desires by preying on their emotions and feelings of guilt or responsibility. My inconsideration and lack of empathy is at the expense of their wellbeing; therefore.

I repent and ask for Your forgiveness and royal pardon, and royal prerogative of mercy for being a gaslighter in trying to manipulate or confuse others into doubting themselves in order to gain power and control over them, seeking to make them question their own judgement and reality.
For trying to downplay the significance of the feelings or experiences of others, and trying to make them deny events, experiences, and realities that they know to be true, and instead embrace a lie, delusion, or illusion.

For trying to make them question their judgement and perceptions, which usually reduces them to a fear of speaking up or expressing their emotions and instead makes them stay silent.
For trying to make them feel vulnerable and insecure about themselves and around others and to have a lack of self-esteem.

For the attitude of making others feel alone, powerless, and convinced that everyone around them thinks they are strange, crazy, or unstable.
For trying to make them feel like they are always wrong, unintelligent, inadequate, or insane and are the perpetrator, and also for trying to make them feel that they need to apologize all the time for everything they do or for expressing themselves.

Your word commands in Malachi 2:16, **"...therefore take heed to your spirit, that ye deal not treacherously."**
Thus says the Lord Jesus to us in Luke 10:19, **"Behold, I give unto you power to tread on serpents and scorpions, and over all the power of the enemy; and nothing shall by any means hurt you."**
Therefore, through Jesus of Nazareth, let every astral poison and venom of beguiling serpents that are poisoning my soul with the manipulative character of gaslighting others be neutralized and lose all power and effectiveness within my heart and mind, and be gone from me now, In Jesus name.
Your word says, Matthew 10:16, **"Behold, I am sending you forth as sheep in *the* midst of wolves. Therefore, be wise as serpents and harmless as doves"**.

In the Name of Y'ahushua HaMashiach of Nazareth, by the power of the judgement and the authority of the Word of God in Luke 10:19, I banish from me every demon of gaslighting, and all subjective spirits of manipulation, demon of beguile, condemnation, pride, arrogance, self-righteousness, and demon of oppression, bullying, and victimization attached to the spirit of gaslighting.

I quench every fiery serpent sent into my life, and cast out every viper of gaslighting, beguile, and emotional manipulation that is operating in my soul.

I break all power and cut all cords of the spirit of Nehushtan, blind occultism, astral poisons, and combined forces of psychic elements that are sent out to demonize me.
Let the stronghold and pattern of this wickedness in my life be broken, and the manipulations of demonic spirits of gaslighting that are seeking to transmute, change, alter, and demote my character, personality, behaviors, thinking systems, and practical methods be banished.

Let all spirits of trickery, manipulation, subtle witchcraft propensities, the demon of control, hypnotic poisons, and crafty manipulation in my life, programmed to destroy my reputation, my dignity, my mind, my purpose, and my future, be destroyed and banished now, in Jesus' name.

Now, Lord Jesus, I petition by the blood of the Lamb for You to cultivate a heart that is pure, kind, and full of compassion in me. Remove any negativity, anger, or selfishness that resides within me.
I petition by the blood of the Lamb for a humble heart, seeking Your guidance and wisdom in the expression of the character of Your love.

Teach me to love others as You love me, to forgive as You forgive, and to extend kindness and understanding to everyone I meet. May my heart be a vessel of Your peace and joy, shining Your light in the world around me.
Teach me how to align my heart with Yours, because I choose to seek Your face (Psalms 27:8). Open my heart to receive Your revelation and understand Your divine principles. Hide me in the shelter of Your tabernacle (Psalms 27:5).
It is written in Psalms 18:19, **"He brought me forth also into a large place; He delivered me because He delighted in me"**.
In Jesus' name, I pray, Amen and Amen.

98. Protection From People Trying To Gaslight You

Father, I come to Your throne of power and might to seek Your hand of strength in my life.
I identify the strategy of the demonic realm to degrade the human race and prey on our ignorance of Your holy Word.
By faith, I call forth the light of Your Holy Son Jesus the Christ into all aspects of my life, and I call into the light of our presence of judgement the spirit of Gaslighting, a psychological abusive demon, which seeks to terrorize me.
Lord God, I pray for divine strength because it is written in Galatians 5:1, **"Stand fast therefore in the liberty wherewith Christ hath made us free and be not entangled again with the yoke of bondage."**

Therefore, I am standing in the liberty wherewith Christ hath made me free and revolt against the demon of gaslighting, that I would not be entangled in its web, snare, and lair.
Hence, I stand my ground in the authority of Jesus the Christ, and I declare the war of offensive warfare against all manipulative techniques programmed to gaslight me. Every power of manipulation that would reconfigure my emotions through cunning, crafty people, let it be disarmed.

I pull these venoms of manipulation down to naught before they rise; I abort them before they are conceived, I banish them before they are formed against me, and I claim full functionality of my strength, my will, and the power to walk in justification by the blood and not in guilt and perpetual self-condemnation. I am not condemned by Jesus, for I am already redeemed from the powers of guilt, shame, and condemnation. Hence, I rebuke and resist the devil, In Jesus Name.

Psalms 18:2, **"The LORD is my Rock, and my fortress, and my deliverer; my God, my Rock in Whom I take refuge; He is my shield, and the horn of my salvation, my high tower."**

I declare war, and revolt, and the neutralization of every snare and plot that would be laid to ensnare me through other humans, and that any attempt to gaslight and manipulate me would be met with resistance and defences of lightning.

Every astral poison and all venom of tranquilization and neutralization that demons would try to vaccinate me with, though manipulative people, let them be neutralized now, in the powerful name of Jesus.

All gaslighters who would attempt to manipulate or confuse me into doubting myself in order to gain power and control over me, seeking to make me question my own judgement and reality, I barricade my mind and emotions with barriers of fire, permanent walls of reinforced protection and emotional, psychological, mental, and spiritual fortification against all potential gaslighters.

All gaslighters who would try to downplay the significance of my feelings or experiences and try to make me deny events, experiences, and realities that I know to be true, and instead embrace a lie, delusion, or illusion, I barricade my mind and emotions with barriers of fire, permanent walls of reinforced protection, and emotional, psychological, mental, and spiritual fortifications against all potential gaslighters.

All gaslighters who would try to make me question my judgement and perceptions, which usually reduce me to fear of speaking up or expressing my emotions or staying silent instead, I barricade my mind and emotions with barriers of fire, permanent walls of reinforced protection, and emotional, psychological, mental, and spiritual fortification against all potential gaslighters.

All gaslighters who would try to make me feel vulnerable and insecure around my partner, friend, or family member, having a lack of self-esteem, I barricade my mind and emotions with barriers of fire, permanent walls of reinforced protection, and emotional, psychological, mental, and spiritual fortifications against all potential gaslighters.

All gaslighters who would try to make me feel alone and powerless and convinced that everyone around me thinks I am "strange," "crazy," or "unstable," I barricade my mind and emotions with barriers of fire, permanent walls of reinforced protection, and emotional, psychological, mental, and spiritual fortifications against all potential gaslighters.

All gaslighters who would try to make me feel like I am always wrong, unintelligent, inadequate, or insane, or that I am always the perpetrator, I barricade my mind and emotions with barriers of fire, permanent walls of reinforced protection, and emotional, psychological, mental, and spiritual fortifications against all potential gaslighters.

All gaslighters who would try to make me feel that I need to apologize all the time for everything I do, or for expressing who I am, I barricade my mind and emotions with barriers of fire, permanent walls of reinforced protection, and emotional, psychological, mental, and spiritual fortifications against all potential gaslighters.

All gaslighters who would try to make me feel like everyone is disappointed in me or would try to make me wonder if there's something fundamentally wrong with me, or if I am the one who is always making the mistake, I barricade my mind and emotions with barriers of fire, permanent walls of reinforced protection, and emotional, psychological, mental, and spiritual fortifications against all potential gaslighters.

All gaslighters who would try to make me feel distrust in myself and that I am inadequate and incapable of decision-making, I barricade my mind and emotions with barriers of fire, permanent walls of reinforced protection, and emotional, psychological, mental, and spiritual fortifications against all potential gaslighters.

I speak to that land, the sea, and the air that all efforts to gaslight me shall fail miserably, by the power of the Holy Spirit, in Jesus' name.

99. Spirits Of Guilt-Tripping

Heavenly Father, in the name of Jesus, I come to You through the blood of the Lamb which gives me access to Your Throne of Grace by the Holy Spirit, to petition You against the demon of guilt-tripping and subtle emotional blackmail. It is important that You fill my heart with Your love and grace, so that I may reflect Your goodness in all my actions and interactions according to Deut. 10 and 11. It is written in Deuteronomy 10:16, **"Circumcise therefore the foreskin of Your heart, and be no more stiff-necked."**

Heavenly Father, I acknowledge that I often use this designed technique to manipulate other people's emotions to achieve my selfish desires by preying on their emotions and feelings of guilt or responsibility. My selfishness is at the expense of their well-being; therefore, I call this forth as a toxic behaviour that can have detrimental effects on a person's well-being as well as our relationship.

Thus says the Lord Jesus to us in Luke 10:19, **"Behold, I give unto you power to tread on serpents and scorpions, and over all the power of the enemy: and nothing shall by any means hurt you."**
Therefore, through Jesus of Nazareth, let every astral poison and the venom of the beguiling serpent that is poisoning my soul with the manipulative character of guilt-tripping be neutralized and lose all power and effectiveness against me, and be gone from me.

In the Name of Y'ahushua HaMashiach of Nazareth, by the power of the judgement and the authority of the Word of God in Luke 10:19, I banish from me every demon of guilt tripping, and all subjective spirits of scrupulosity, demon of beguile, condemnation, pride, arrogance, and self-righteousness attached to the spirit of guilt tripping.

I quench every fiery serpent sent into my life and cast out every viper of guilt-tripping, beguilement, and emotional manipulation that is operating in my soul.

I break all power and cut all cords of the spirit of Nehushtan, blind occultism, witchcraft, and voodoo, all sorts of hexes, and spiritual locks, which are sent out to demonize me.

In Jesus' name, you demon of guilt-tripping, beguilement, and emotional manipulation, I am no longer your subject, candidate, or captive.

Let the stronghold and pattern of this wickedness in my life be broken, and the manipulations of demonic spirits of guilt-tripping that are seeking to transmute, change, alter, and demote my character, personality, behaviors, thinking systems, and practical methods be banished.

Let every witchcraft curse set upon my life to destroy my life, my reputation, my dignity, my mind, my purpose, my future, and my destiny be destroyed and banished now, in Jesus' name.

Every power that has made me a collaborator and subject of the evil rulers, legislators, governors, and dignitaries of land, sea, and air, through the spirits of trickery, manipulation, subtle witchcraft propensities, and the demon of control, hypnotic poisons, and crafty manipulation, I banish you, elemental and foul spirits, from my life; now get out, in Jesus' name.

Now, Lord Jesus, I petition by the blood of the Lamb for You to cultivate a heart that is pure, kind, and full of compassion in me. Remove any negativity, anger, or selfishness that resides within me.

I petition by the blood of the Lamb for a humble heart, seeking Your guidance and wisdom in the expression of the character of Your love. Teach me to love others as You love me, to forgive as You forgive, and to extend kindness and understanding to everyone I meet. May my heart be a vessel of Your peace and joy, shining Your light in the world around me.

Teach me how to align my heart with Yours, because I choose to seek Your face (Psalm 27:8). Open my heart to receive Your revelation and understand Your divine principles. Hide me in the shelter of Your tabernacle (Psalm 27:5). It is written in Psalms 18:19, **"He brought me forth also into a large place; He delivered me because He delighted in me"**.
In Jesus' name, I pray, Amen and Amen.

100. Protection From People Trying To Guilt-Trip You

I call forth the light of Jesus Christ in all aspects of my life and request that I be armed and shielded from the satanic assaults of the demons of guilt tripping.

Hence, I stand my ground in the authority of Jesus the Christ, and I declare the war of offensive warfare against all outside venomous stimuli programmed for the manipulation of my emotions by cunning, crafty people around me.

I pull these venoms of manipulation down to naught before they rise; I abort them before they are conceived; I banish them before they are formed against me, and I claim full functionality of my strength, will, and power to walk in justification by the blood and not in self-condemnation and perpetual guilt. I am not condemned by Jesus, for I am already redeemed from the powers of guilt, shame, and condemnation. Hence, I rebuke and resist the devil, In Jesus Name.

Psalms 18:2, **"The LORD is my Rock, and my fortress, and my deliverer; my God, my Rock in Whom I take refuge; He is my shield, and the horn of my salvation, my high tower."**

I declare war, and revolt, and neutralization of every snare and plot that would be laid to ensnare me through other humans, and that any guilt trip and manipulation would be met with resistance and defences.

Every astral poison and all venom of tranquilization and neutralization that demons would try to vaccinate me with, though manipulative people, let them be neutralized now, in the powerful name of Jesus.

Any strategy and spirit of guilt-tripping that would seek to lure me into its lair, I barricade my mind and emotions with barriers of fire.

In Jesus' name, I will not be the victim, subject, candidate, or captive of the demons of guilt-tripping, beguilement, and emotional manipulation.
I call for permanent walls of scriptural protection and emotional, psychological, mental, and spiritual fortification against all upcoming and forthcoming advances of the spirits of trickery, manipulation, subtle witchcraft propensities, demons of control, hypnotic poisons, guilt-tripping, beguilement, emotional manipulation, and crafty manipulation.

Plots, plans, snares, and lairs have already failed in the near and far future of my life, In Jesus name.
Father, I thank You for Your mercy and grace to sustain my protection in Christ my saviour, and Your will to protect me from the evil one.
I will praise thee with my whole heart: before the gods will I sing praise unto thee (Psalms 138:1).
I will declare thy name unto my brethren; in the midst of the church will I sing praise unto thee (Hebrews 2:12).

101. Spirits Of Blame Shifting

Heavenly Father, in the name of Jesus, I come to You through the blood of the Lamb which gives me access to Your Throne of Grace by the Holy Spirit, to petition You against the demon of blame shifting and subtle self-denial. It is important that You fill my heart with Your love and grace, so that I may reflect Your goodness and self-accountability in all my actions and interactions according to Deut. 10 and 11. It is written in Deuteronomy 10:16, **"Circumcise therefore the foreskin of your heart, and be no more stiff-necked."**
Heavenly Father, You have circumcised my heart through Christ, yet I acknowledge that I often use this designed technique to escape from the responsibilities of my own actions and seek to place another as the scapegoat. I have the habit of making others feel that they are the ones in error for something that I have done.

I am manipulating other people into adopting self-guilt and condemnation to escape my responsibilities. I have sinned by preying on them psychologically, and my selfishness has been at the expense of their well-being. Therefore, this toxic behaviour can have detrimental effects on a person's well-being as well as our relationship.

Thus says the Lord Jesus to us in Luke 10:19, **"Behold, I give unto you power to tread on serpents and scorpions, and over all the power of the enemy: and nothing shall by any means hurt you."**
Therefore, through Jesus of Nazareth, let every astral poison and the venom of the beguiling serpent that is poisoning my soul with the manipulative character of blame-shifting be neutralized and lose all power and effectiveness against me, and be gone from me.

In the Name of Y'ahushua HaMashiach of Nazareth, by the power of the judgement and the authority of the Word of God in Luke 10:19, I banish from me every demon of blame shifting and all subjective spirits of beguilement, condemnation, pride, arrogance, and self-righteousness attached to the spirit of blame shifting.

By the power of the Holy Spirit, through Jesus of Nazareth, I quench every fiery serpent sent into my life and cast out every viper of blame-shifting, beguilement, and emotional manipulation that is operating in my soul.

By the authority of God, I pray against and drive out every spirit that manipulates me to perform blame shifting by building a defence mechanism to shield myself from shame or guilt, to avoid responsibility, justify my bad behaviour, or to protect my ego, for social comparison, protection from my vulnerability.

Hence, I break all power and cut all cords of the Demon of Narcissism in my life, and all spirits of blind occultism, selfishness, pride, arrogance, pompousness, and rebuke any narcissistic personality disorder and inflated sense of self-importance that are controlling me.

Let the stronghold and pattern of this wickedness in my life and the manipulations of demonic spirits of blame shifting that are seeking to transmute, change, alter, and demote my character, personality, behaviors, thinking system, practical methods be broken by the thunder of the power of the Lord God of hosts, and every power that has made me become a collaborator and subordinate of the evil rulers, legislators, governors, and dignitaries of land, sea, and air through the spirits of blame shifting, trickery, manipulation, subtle witchcraft propensities, and the demon of control, hypnotic poisons, and crafty manipulation, let these be banished now from my life, effective immediately.

Let every witchcraft curse set upon my life to destroy my life, my reputation, my dignity, my mind, my purpose, my future, and my destiny be destroyed and banished now, in Jesus' name.

I declare that I am no more your subject, candidate, or captive of you, demon of blame-shifting, beguilement, and emotional manipulation, in Jesus' name.

Now, Lord Jesus, I petition by the blood of the Lamb that You cultivate a heart that is pure, kind, and full of compassion in me. Remove any negativity, anger, or selfishness that resides within me.

I petition by the blood of the Lamb for a humble heart, seeking Your guidance and wisdom in the expression of the character of Your love. Teach me to love others as You love me, to forgive as You forgive, and to extend kindness and understanding to everyone I meet. May my heart be a vessel of Your peace and joy, shining Your light in the world around me.

Teach me how to align my heart with Yours. I choose to seek Your face [Psalms 27:5]. Open my heart to receive Your revelation and understand Your divine principles. Hide me in the shelter of Your tabernacle [Psalms 27:5]. It is written in Psalms 18:19, **"He brought me forth also into a large place; He delivered me because He delighted in me"**.

In Jesus' name, I pray. Amen and Amen.

102. Prayers Against Curses Of Singleness

Father, I repent for my sins and iniquities, and those of my ancestors and parents from my mother's house and my father's house. I detest all personal and family transgressions and trespasses, and ask You to remove from me every sin, evil covenant, and iniquity that have given demons and astral right to keep me in singleness, and not being able to find a spouse in the will of God.

By the Judicial Council of Your mercy, judgement and compassion, O Lord, revive the verdict of the judicial Blood of the Lamb and the Mercy Seat, and acquit me of all allegations, accusations and condemnations, and of all sins, evil and wickedness blocking my marital destiny.
By the power of Jesus, the Christ of Nazareth, and through His holy blood, I break and banish from my life the curse of any Greek and Roman deity or deities from the eastern and western rivers, seas, or seven oceans.

By the power of Jesus, the Christ of Nazareth, I also destroy and banish from my life every power, stronghold, curse, and spirit of singleness and unmarriedness that has ambushed, shut up, and rendered me incapable of finding a God-given mate because of my use and possession of the products of Victoria's Secret, Hypnotic Poison, Versace, Chanel, Hugo Boss, Midnight Rose, Midnight Poison, Scandal, Dhoon Glen Perfume, Flower Bomb, Cabello, Giorgio Armani, Dolce & Gabbana, Sigma Products, and Hermès.

Uber Universal, Carol Beauty Products, Beauty Clear, Clear Hair Products, Louis Vuitton, etc., and I curse all curses from the demons and sirens of the waters and forests.

Every curse of singleness that was placed upon me by my parent or grandparent, aunty, uncle, or any family member, and any curse of singleness and unmarried that I have brought into my life, through ignorance or disobedience, I command by the power of Jesus Christ that this curse of singleness be broken off me, effective immediately, for it is written in Numbers 23:23, **"Surely there is no enchantment against Jacob, neither is there any divination against Israel."**

Wherever my spouse is held up by guardian demons, or placed inside a tree, watery facility chamber, locked within any cage, hex, spell, witchcraft box, bag, pot, desert incarceration, etc., I demand the release of my destined spouse, for I will not remain single and unmarried; this I declare in Jesus' mighty Name.

I call for the holy fire of Yah, and the blood of the Lamb of God that was sprinkled upon the mercy seat to intervene and erase every mark of singleness that was placed upon my forehead, hand, or any other part of my body by demonic spirits.

By the power of Jesus, Son of the Living God, I also break and banish from my life every curse and spirit of singleness and unmarried that came into my life through any love portion, love pendant, love charm, words or prayers of the law of attraction, goddess of false love, enchanted incenses, accessories, fragrances, make-up, witchcraft enchantments concocted with herbs, animal urine, dung, blood of animals or humans, or any paraphernalia.

Any human, nymph, or avatar occult agent of darkness responsible for the misfortunes and calamity of singleness surrounding my life, I call the judgement of Jesus Christ upon them, and I say to these occult agents be rendered mute, maimed, deaf, and blind effective immediately, in Jesus' name.

Wherever the kingdom of darkness has tied or is hiding my destined spouse, I loose my spouse from this place with the power in the verdict of the judicial blood of Jesus.

I pray, any evil power holding my destined spouse captive, in order for me to remain single, I invoke the fire, lightning, and thunder of the presence of Jesus upon this evil power, and I loose my spouse right now by the verdict of the Temple of the Most High, in Jesus' name.

My destined spouse, wherever you are now, come back to your senses and locate me for marriage in Jesus' name. I decree and declare that I will not be overlooked, I will not be desolate, I will not be rejected; I have been found, chosen, and accepted by my destined spouse.

In the name of Jesus, and with the fire of the blood of Jesus Christ, I wash away every evil mask placed on my face, which diverts people away from me.

Mighty God, I pray that every veil that is placed over my face, or any false image replacing my facial image, causing my destined spouse to not see or recognize me, let this veil and false image and mask be burned out and removed from me, effective immediately.

Every human agent of the occult who was hired to curse my potential and opportunity of finding a destined spouse and getting married, I strike this hired occultist with madness for a season, and I break the curse of singleness that is upon me now, in Jesus' name.

I decree by the verdict of the Council of El-Shaddai that all expectations, decrees, evil prayers, and bad wishes of men sent into the psychic layers against me, and all elemental spirits programmed to block my opportunity for betrothal to my destined soulmate are hereby rendered disappointed, nullified, barren, and infertile in the name of Jesus of Nazareth.

I banish from my life any strange lover that is keeping my true lover away from me, or from finding me. I speak by fire, and I say, any strategy the Devil is using to keep my spouse away from me, may the thunder of God scatter those strategies in Jesus' name.

- FOR A MAN - By the Divine Judicial Council of the Grand High Court of the God of the Heavens and Earth, O God, make me a help as promised, and let there be manifestations of her, in Jesus' name, for it is written in Genesis 2:18, **"And the LORD God said, It is not good that the man should be alone; I will make him an help meet for him."**
- FOR A WOMAN - By the Divine Judicial Council of the Grand High Court of the God of the Heavens and Earth, I command by the judicial fire of Christ that my God-given man be released from his mother and his father, and cleave unto me as his wife now, effective immediately, for it is written in Genesis 2:24, **"Therefore shall a man leave his father and his mother, and shall cleave unto his wife: and they shall be one flesh."**

By the light, the death, the burial, and the resurrection of Jesus Christ of Nazareth, I take authority over and banish from my life and destiny all the principalities, against every ruler, against all powers of darkness, and every spiritual wickedness in high places, against all psychic commands and psychic elemental and sound vibrations within the astral plane that are sustaining and maintaining singleness and being unmarried in my life.

I take authority over every shame and disgrace of singleness that I have inherited from my father's house and from my mother's house. I break this stronghold of shame, disgrace, and humiliation that came about because of my singleness.

Lord, I come to petition Your Judicial Council of Truth, and I request that you put a mark upon me, that no hygiene condition, hair condition, physical birth defect, characteristic, attitude, mannerism, accent, personality, behaviour, financial disposition, or outward appearance will keep me from finding my destined soulmate and lover; in Jesus' name, it is done.

Fire of the Holy Spirit, draw my destined spouse to me by the bond of Your love and kindness. Allow my life to be fulfilled by Your grace and will, and make me a devout spouse to my soulmate, that I may rejoice in your bounty, mercy, and blessings.

Thank You that singleness is broken from me, and I am set free, for it is written in John 8:36, **"If the Son therefore shall make you free, ye shall be free indeed."**

To You be all the glory for the great things You have done in my life in this way; Amen and Amen.

103. Prayer For Women Of God

In the mighty name of Y'ahushua Ha-Mashiach, by the power and authority of the lightnings and thunderings and voices: and the seven burning lamps of fire which are the seven Spirits of God, [Rev 4:5], I stand in the capacity of a woman of purpose and divine destiny, clothed with the power and authority of the name King of Kings and Lord of Lords, and I now declare my position in Christ as a woman of God and a mother in Zion.

Decrees

By the authority of the seven golden lamps, which are the seven Spirits of God, I decree by fire in all realms of the Heavens and the Earth, in the Terrestrial and the Astral planes, that as a woman, I am clear-sighted, I am perceptive, and I can see decisions clearly.

- I decree by fire that, as a woman, I am astute; I have clever solutions to problems based on my sharp perception.
- I decree by the glory that I am a woman of dignity, class, and intelligence, and I possess impeccable qualities beyond my years.
- I decree by fire that I am a woman and minister of the Altar of burning Coals, and Seraphim, Cherubim, and Archangels are my companions.
- I decree by fire that, as a woman, I am creative and have ideas that others have not considered before.
- I decree by fire that, as a woman, I am decisive and possess the principles to commit to a decision after properly weighing the outcomes.
- I decree by fire that, as a woman, I am discerning, and I have the capability to demonstrate good judgement and taste that can save lives.

- I decree by fire that, as a woman, I am innovative and have the capability to apply new ideas to old problems to find creative solutions in this time and season.
- I decree by fire that, as a woman, I am inquisitive about the mysteries of the knowledge of the Son of God. My thirst for the things of God is impeccable.
- I decree by fire that, as a woman, I am intuitive and observant and am able to notice small but important details that others may have overlooked.
- I decree by fire that I am sharp and skillful in utilizing spiritual materials of divine intelligence.
- I decree by fire that, as a woman, I am resourceful, and I am able to make use of what I have available to solve problems and situations. Like Moses, may my rod become a rod of power; like Samson, may my tool of warfare become dangerous to the enemies.

Declare your position among the coals of the altar.

Holy Father, I petition You by the jurisdiction of the altar and throne of God upon Mount Zion, and I request that You place me this day among the fiery coals of Your holy altar and let me become electrified by the flames of the wheels of Your Throne.
O Lord, cause my garment to become resplendent, radiating the light of Your greatness in me as a warrior in Zion.

Father, I declare that as a woman and mother in Zion, I am a carrier of greatness and power, and everything that I conceive and bring forth shall possess the image of magnificence in the spirit of excellence.
Therefore, I come before Your Throne of Grace, as a woman who is called by God, and I ask You to pour into my heart the coals of fire that are around Your holy feet, and fill my heart with Your divine wisdom,

so that I may make decisions that honours You and bring blessings to myself and others.

I declare my place in the kingdom as a woman of destiny, a woman of purpose, a woman of valour, and a woman of excellence, and I speak unto the heavens and the Earth, and say, O Heavens, O Earth, hear my voice, for I stand as a woman of power amongst the fiery coals in the presence of the Adonai, and I say unto you, be silent and give way to my coming forth in this season, for my manifestation cometh forth as the brightness of the sun [Dan 12:3].
Let the Gentiles come to my light, and kings to the brightness of my rising according to Isaiah 60:3.

By the verdict of the Council of ElShaddai, let the glory of the LORD go up from the cherub, and stand over the threshold of my heart; and let the chambers of my heart, mind, soul, spirit, body, and home be filled with the cloud of Your presence, and my courts be filled with the brightness of the LORD's glory. [Ezekiel 10:4], in Jesus' name.
As a woman, I take my divine and strategic position in the kingdom of Mount Zion, and I command the four corners of the heavens to release the wisdom of the ancient path of the men and women of God in the scriptures, and let my life become a rod of power, set on fire by the Holy Ghost, of which the heavens and the earth will bear witness and testify.

In the name of the Most High Yah, I command the heavens and earth to be reconditioned and reconfigured to accommodate the greatness of my glory as a woman, wife, and mother, for wisdom has become my sister (Proverbs 7:4).

I call for a judicial order from the Holy Council of Mount Zion, and I request and claim upon my head the crown of excellence, glory, and perfect wisdom.

In the name of Jesus, I take hold of the four horns of the altar of mercy and fragrance, and lay claim to my blessings, anointings, power, levels, dimensions, and spiritual assets, and I declare that I am a woman of excellence.

I say unto the gates of the Heavens, lift up your head O ye gates, and be lifted up you everlasting doors, in the North, South, East, and West, and let the Lord God of hosts impart unto me the mantles of the great women of Zion, and the mighty women of valour: Deborah, Esther, Mary, Ruth, Abigail, Sarah, Hannah, Elizabeth, Rebekah, Rachel, Lydia, Leah, and Anna, in the name of Y'ahushua of Nazareth.

Be polished after the similitude of a palace:
Heavenly Father, the enemy has set many snares and traps for me, and now, Lord, behold their threatenings; and grant unto thy servants that with all boldness they may speak thy word, as it is written in Acts 4:29.

I, as a woman, have suffered from great calamities that have challenged my walk with you. My father, they have tried to stop us as women, so that we cannot function with power. They said that we, as women, cannot teach Your word or preach the Gospel, but should remain silent in the Church. This, Lord Jesus, is contrary to Your will and Word; therefore, LORD God of Abraham, Isaac, and Israel, grant unto me power to manifest Your greatness in the earth, and let it be known this day that You alone *are* God in Israel, and that I am Your servant, and that I have done all these things at Your word (1 Kings 18:36).

Father, send now Your treasured Holy Spirit of comfort, for I have been a victim of criticism, shame, rejection, abuse, and violence in various ways, and have suffered from suppression, depression, oppression, humiliation, disgrace, victimization, mistreatment, and exploitation, but You have kept me. Psalms 124:2-3 says, **"If it had not been for the LORD Who was on our side when men rose up against us, then they would have swallowed us up alive."**

Father, turn this day my shame into glory, and erase from my heart all traces of hurt, pain, and emotional abuse that have negatively affected me and my walk with You.
Because of these pains, my actions have been negatively modified and mutated, but Father, You are the Most High God.
You said in Your word in Isaiah 40:2, **"Speak comfortably to Jerusalem, and cry unto her that her warfare is accomplished, that her iniquity is pardoned; for she has received of the LORD's hand double for all her sins."**
You also said in Your words in Isaiah 61:7, **"For your shame, you will receive double."**

Abba Yah, who is in Heaven, let all hurts and abuse that I have suffered from my co-workers, friends, family members, church members, strangers, acquaintances, neighbours, and past lovers serve to my advantage and become a weapon that will equip me to fight against the kingdom of darkness.
Turn my mourning into dancing, my darkness into light, my weaknesses into strength, my sadness into joy unspeakable and full of glory, and turn all my hurts and pain into vigorous boldness and forwardness, that I may stand and, having done all, to stand.

It is written in Psalms 144:12, **"that our daughters may be as corner stones, polished after the similitude of a palace:"**
Therefore, polish me, Father, as a cornerstone, after the similitude of a palace, that Your holy name may be glorified in me in all the Earth.

Abba Father Yah, it is written in Your word, Lord God, in Isaiah 54:11, **"O thou afflicted, tossed with tempest, and not comforted, behold, I will lay thy stones with fair colours, and lay thy foundations with sapphires."**
Vs.12, **"And I will make thy windows of agates, and thy gates of carbuncles, and all thy borders of pleasant stones."**

O God of Zion, arise by Your divine council; and restore unto me my stones that are of fair colours, and restore my foundations of sapphires, my windows of agates, my gates of carbuncles, and all my borders of pleasant stones.

Heavenly Father, according to Your word in Isaiah 61:3, I also request of Your Judicial Council that You repair and restore my wholeness and wellness and give unto me beauty for ashes, the oil of joy for mourning, the garment of praise for the spirit of heaviness; that I might be called trees of righteousness, the planting of the LORD, that You might be glorified.
For my shame, give me double; and for confusion, let me rejoice in my portion: therefore, in my I shall possess the double: everlasting joy shall be unto me, according to Isaiah 61:7.

Lord Y'ahushua, I petition You this day, that I will not only be of the Rib of man, but the Rib of Christ himself, and that You place upon me the flesh of his divine mission on Earth. Attire me with the garment of fire for the mission, as I articulate the burden of the Lord for divine service in the vineyard. I decree by fire that I have wisdom and instruction to perceive the words of understanding; Proverbs 1:2.

Warfare Against the Kingdom of Darkness

Abba Father, You have given me authority to fight against the powers of darkness and prevail, and have anointed me with the fire to disarm the powers of darkness.

Today in Your holy name, which upholds the 10 Heavens, I declare war against every diabolical weapon, astral poison, astral device, surveillance system and devices, weapons, arrows, and devices of destruction, the tridents, sickles, astral stones, magical powders, and witchcraft nets that are formed against me from beyond the 12 gates of Hell.
They shall not prevail, according to Your word in Matthew 16:18 that says, **"I will build my church, and the gates of hell shall not prevail against it."**

In the name of Y'ahushua, hear me, all you hosts of the kingdom of darkness, the land, the sea, and the air.
The Lord Y'ahushua of Nazareth has given me authority in Luke 10:19, where He says, "Behold, **I give unto you power to tread on serpents and scorpions, and over all the power of the enemy: and nothing shall by any means hurt you"**.

By the power of Y'ahushua Son of God, with chains of fire and fetters of hot iron, I bind, disarm, and banish from my life the powers and influence of the grand dukes of hell, the grand generals, the captain demons, principalities, powers, the attorney general, the head-hunters, destiny eaters, star eaters, flesh eaters, blood drinkers, spirit guides, occult naval forces, gods, princes, highlanders, demons of the Elements, and the high council of darkness etc.
I also declare by fire that all you Transporter demons, Genies, Serpents, Scorpions, Mammon, Abaddon, Elemental Spirits, Supreme Elementals, Divas, Gnomes, Sirens, and all other satanic holds that have placed my life under siege, that your power, influence, and

essence around, over, and in my life, space and atmosphere, finances, ministry, and destiny are hereby broken now, effective immediately, in Jesus' name.

By the rays of the light and fire of Adonai Tzeva'ot, the Lord God of hosts, I pray and overthrow the jurisdiction and operation of all Aquatic, Aerial, Subterranean, and Land occult forces of the Inner Esoteric framework and Hierarchy of the Astral and Terrestrial dimensions, who are programmed to attack and destroy my life through sound vibrations and other frequency channels.

I pray, let fire descend from the Throne of El-Shaddai and scatter these occult forces and their evil gatherings, meetings, and conferences, and telecommunication in the North, East, South, and West, and in the heights above, on the Earth beneath, in every realm, kingdom, zone, region, plane, and sphere.

In Jesus' name, I destroy and banish from my life, my home, and my surroundings every entity working with the enigma of the four elements—water, fire, earth, and air, or with the enigma of the forest, or with intergalactic, interstellar, planetary, and cosmic elements.

I clothe myself with Your power by faith, and in the name of Y'ahushua I destroy and banish from my life all evil agendas and subtle psychic manipulation, which are programmed in the psychic layers, and I destroy by fire, lightning, and thunder all psychic commands of incantations of witchcraft, voodoo, magic spells, necromancy, injuring, conjuring, projecting, herbal divination, ritual, and every plot, plan, weapon, curse, net, web, snare, and lair, and any other esoteric craft deployed to destroy me; let them be met with incomprehensible destruction by fire, in Jesus' name.

Let all satanic schemes intended to annihilate me collapse and turn into foolishness, in Jesus' precious name.

Psalms 21:11 says, **"For they intended evil against thee: they imagined a mischievous device, which they are not able to perform."**

Every midnight terror, or arrows of the midday gate of the sun, pestilence that walks in darkness and destruction at noon that is sent towards me for my destruction or death, shall be dead on arrival. I call them to destruction by fire, in Jesus' name.
Let the forces of the Twilight Zone and the Gates of the Dawn who are blocking and obstructing my blessings, successes, and increase be banished by the fire of God's holy altar, in Jesus name.

Claiming A Judicial Order from the Courts of GOD

In the power of the name of Jesus and the Kingdom of God, I plunder the treasures of the seven kingdoms of darkness in the land, sea, air, and subterranean world, and by the judicial court order from the Courts of the Throne Room of God, I demand compensation, restitution, and restoration of all spiritual and material things that the kingdom of darkness has taken from me.

I invoke a judicial intervention from the mercy seat that is covered with the Blood of the Lamb of God, and I unlock supernatural strengths, I unlock divine intelligence, I unlock angelic intervention, and I unlock the windows of heaven in my life, and I call forth, recover, and take back my joy, my peace, my happiness, my finances, my business, my mind, my health, my boldness, my anointing, my zeal, my passion for God, my praise, my success, my advancement, my promotion, my children, my marriage, and I lay hold of my influence to initiate changes, all in the name of Jesus of Nazareth.
Lord, by the Divine Judicial Council of the Grand High Court of the God of the Heavens and Earth, I speak into my past and I command by fire that my lost glories, which are buried under the rubble and debris of

hurts, pains, and shames, will in this season manifest with full resplendence, as I command restoration at my gates, effective immediately, in Jesus name.

O Lord God of Noah, Abraham, Moses, Daniel, and Elijah, come to my aid, as I request a Holy Restraining Order from the Judicial Courts of Heaven against every evil fighting against me under a satanic verdict because of a legal ground.

Render a holy verdict of the Blood of Christ in my favour and surround me with the Angels of Your divine presence, to set guard over, around, and under my home day and night.
Surround me with Your loving embrace, shielding me from all harm, snares, traps, and dangers lurking in secret places.
I request a divine injunction to neutralize and stop all satanic operations that have been fighting and destroying my life since my youth.

Guard me from the battles of contestation and confrontation that surround me on every side, which are set by the forces of the fresh and salty occult water kingdom.

I request from Heaven a divine injunction and divine restraining order against the four satanic kingdoms of the air, and also against the kingdom of the subterranean world, the land world, and the water occult kingdom: against the Queen of Beta and her husband, the Queen of the Coast and her husband, the Queen of Shylon and her husband, the Queen of Yemunah and her husband, or the Queen of Delta and her husband, and against all five occult zones of the marine kingdom: the zones Lumani, Banni, Lemuria, Gamma, and Atlantis.

I pray by the Holy Spirit that my steps be guided away from perilous paths, and that every web, net, and barbed wire (which are placed in my path) will be consumed to dry ashes, and every pit and trench covered.

Lord Jesus, I pray, let dynamic flames of fire, lightning, and thunder shatter and banish every astral prison facility and coven where evil weapons, devices, evil thoughts, and wicked imaginations are being formed and fashioned against my life.
Holy Father, in the name of Y'ahushua, give me protection and safety as I walk this path that You have set before me as a woman, a mother, and a wife.

I petition Your Divine Judicial Council and request that the chariots of Your Mounting Angels surround me with their chariots of fire; and cause Your Warring Angels to stand guard and defend me from the diabolical assaults of the five esoteric Occult Seals and Mephistophelian forces of the seven kingdoms of darkness, which are fighting against me.

Defend me, O God of hosts, from the 'Avatars' and demi-gods who are on the earth in human form, seeking ways to stop women from preaching, teaching, and walking in Your grace.
By the highest authority of the eternal Heaven, and by the power of His Name Yah, I build barricades and barriers of incomprehensible resistance against every evil spirit.
I barricade my life, home, and surroundings with reinforced barriers of divine power and permanent defences of electric fire, light, lightning, and incomprehensible resistance, effective immediately.

Father, I pray that You lead me on the path of righteousness and grant me the discernment to navigate life's complexities with grace and conviction. Give me divine intelligence and revelation to build my altar of good character.

My family altar, my financial altar, altar of fervent prayer, my altar of celestial worship, and my altar of strategic praise.
All these I pray in the name of Y'ahushua HaMashiach of Nazareth, Amen and Amen.

104. Destroying Curses

- By authority in Jesus Christ of Nazareth, by the jurisdiction of the Blood of the Holy Altar, and in the name of the Son of God, Y'ahushua, I destroy from my life every curse of Misfortune that is sitting upon me.
- I destroy from my life every curse of living from paycheck to paycheck.
- I destroy from my life every curse of sowing good things and not reaping 30, 60, and 100 fold.
- I destroy every curse of lack, want, and emptiness from my life.
- I destroy from my life the curse of scavenging coins to feed my family.
- I destroy from my life every curse of losing good jobs after a wonderful interview.
- I destroy from my life every curse of sudden termination in my jobs.
- I destroy from my life every curse of difficulty in finding a job suitable to my education, qualifications, and skills.
- I destroy every curse of Azazel from my life.
- I destroy every curse of Medusa from my life.
- I destroy every curse of the Queen of the Coast from my life.
- I destroy every curse of the Queen of Heaven from my life.
- I destroy from my life every curse of the supreme elementals and gnomes.
- I destroy from my life every curse of the elemental forces of air, water, and forest.
- I destroy from my life every curse placed by Asmodeus.
- I destroy from my life every curse of the gods of India (Ganesha, Kali, Krishna, Vishnu, Brahma, and Shiva).
- I destroy from my life every curse of all African gods, goddesses, and Orishas in Jesus' name.
- I destroy from my life every curse of disgrace that is sitting upon me.
- I destroy from my life every curse of poverty that is sitting upon me.

- I destroy from my life every curse of rejection that is sitting upon me.
- I destroy from my life every curse of insufficiency that is sitting upon me.
- I destroy from my life every curse of calamity that is sitting upon me.
- I destroy from my life every curse of terror, dread, and torment that is sitting upon me.
- I destroy from my life every curse of fear and fright that is sitting upon me.
- I destroy from my life every curse of sickness that is sitting upon me.
- I destroy from my life every curse of sexual immorality that is sitting upon me.
- I destroy from my life every curse of sin and iniquity that is sitting upon me.
- I destroy from my life every curse of bitterness, unforgiveness, or hatred that is sitting upon me.
- I destroy from my life every curse of premature and sudden death that is sitting upon my life.
- I destroy from my life every curse of shadow and darkness that is sitting upon my life.
- I destroy every curse of singleness, divorce, or childlessness that has been my life.
- I destroy every curse of nightmares and sleep paralysis that others have placed upon me from my life.
- I destroy from my life every curse of educational failure that was placed upon me.
- I destroy every curse of forgetfulness, madness, and mental displacement that others have placed upon my life.
- I destroy from my life every curse of miscarriage or stillbirth that is placed upon me.
- I destroy from my life every curse of marital abuse, rejection, and frustration that is placed upon me.

- I destroy from my life every curse of singleness that is placed upon me.
- I destroy from my life every curse of a beggar and pauper that is upon my life, in Jesus' name, Amen and Amen.

105. Transformer Of Minds

My God and my Lord, I praise You today and say worthy is the Lamb that was slain to receive power, and riches, and wisdom, and strength, and honour, and glory, and blessing. You are exalted on high, blessed be Your name forever.

Jesus, I come to You, seeking deliverance from the stronghold of the demons, imploring the ruling of the council of Your divine eternal flame of wisdom and light, seeking the intervention of Your seven golden altars against the Transformer of Minds, the mind-bending demon, mind-blinding spirits, the hypnotic poison, the demon of illusion, delusion, deception, and all associated demons who have ambushed my mind, and all other psychic entities working through metaphysical homogeneity against my mind.

Your word says to us in Ephesians 4:23, **"And be renewed in the spirit of your mind;"** hence I approach Your Throne of Grace to obtain mercy and find grace to help in this time of need, so that my mind can be renewed.
You promised in Your word according to Hebrews 8:10 where you say, **"For this *is* the covenant that I will make with the house of Israel after those days, saith the Lord; I will put my laws into their minds,"**

However, the kingdom of darkness, through the transformer of minds, has placed a dark law in my mind and has perverted my knowledge and understanding.
Your word says in the book of Proverbs 4:7, **"Wisdom *is* the principal thing; *therefore,* get wisdom: and with all thy getting, get understanding."**

In the Name of Y'ahushua HaMashiach of Nazareth, I renounce, denounce, and revoke all power of acquaintanceship, link, and communication between me and the transformers of mind from the gates of Hell, for it is written in 1 Corinthians 2:16, "**...But we have the mind of Christ."**
I desire wisdom and understanding by Your Holy Spirit, but my mind has been ambushed by the demonic world, where confusions in understanding, mental blocks, disorientations, drowsiness, etc., have taken over my mind.

Lord Jesus, Your word says to us in Luke 10:19, **"Behold, I give unto you power to tread on serpents and scorpions, and over all the power of the enemy; and nothing shall by any means hurt you."**

Therefore, in the Name of Y'ahushua HaMashiach of Nazareth, by the dynamic power of the Lord Jesus of Nazareth, by the dynamic and terrifying fires of Amber, thunderclaps, lightnings, and the fear of the Lord, by the power of the judgement and the authority of the Word of God in Luke 10:19, Psalms 11:6 and Exodus 9:24, I call down a rain of fire mingled with grievous hail; I call down the fiery terror of God's divine judgement, rains of snares and terrors, rain of fires, brimstone, horrible tempests, destruction, desolation, degradation, annihilation, liquidation, and eradication, upon all elemental psychic entities, upon you demon of transformer of minds, you mind-bending demon, mind-manipulating demon, mind-blocker demon, and you demons who are brain eaters and mind consumers, and all psychic forces of darkness working in my mental life.

With hot chains of holy fire and by force, I neutralize every venom, and I arrest, bind, bring into captivity under subjection, and in the powerful name of Jesus of Nazareth, I banish and destroy by fire, lightning, and thunder all you demons of transformer of minds, astral poisons, elemental demons, you mind-bending demon, mind-blinding spirits, mind-manipulating demon, mind-blocker demon, mind readers, and you demon of mind puzzle, mental perplexity, demon of illusion, delusion, deception, misunderstanding, mental confusion, mind control, hypnotic poison, and you demons who are brain eaters and mind consumers, and all connected psychic forces of darkness of the same category working in my mental life.

Alongside the angelic forces of the hosts of the Lord, I charge against the transformer of mind, and by the name of the King of kings and Lord of lords and by the dynamic power of the Lord Jesus of Nazareth, by dynamic and terrifying fires of Amber, thunderclaps, lightnings and terror, I drive you out by force and I destroy and banish from my life the law of metaphysical homogeneity, and all astral forces of mental and psychological destruction, every portal of hell created in my brain to steal, upload and download my brain signals, frequencies and information, and any astral chip, strap, and evil seed placed in my brain, every evil helmet, demonic channel for mental manipulation, every limitation and resistance placed in my mind towards the truth of God, everything that is tampering and compromising my mind, and all forces of darkness working, conspiring and devising evil and destruction against my life and destiny in the occultic world.

Let each of these evil powers be met with holy fire, judged by fire and be destroyed by fire, and every stronghold be broken down to ash and useless powders, now! in Jesus name.
By coals of fire, which hath a most vehement flame, and a vehement east wind; [Jonah 4:8], I burn your roots to ashes, and I burn to the ground your regiment, your fortress, your kingdom, and barrack that you have built in my mind, through Books of Evolution, Books of false philosophy, Book of Mormon, Watch Tower, Wake, You Magazine, People Magazine, Jerusalem Bible, Gideon Bible, New World Translation, and the Censorship Commission.

It is written in 1 Peter 1:13, **"Wherefore gird up the loins of your mind, be sober."** It is also written in Philippians 2:5, **"Let this mind be in you, which was also in Christ Jesus."**
On this basis, I reclaim my mind from the hands of the demons.

I break down every psychological wall and stronghold of demons built in my mind and infiltrate the work of the transformer of the mind.
Through Jesus of Nazareth, I pray against and destroy all dark energy that is set upon my mind to retard the development of my logic, comprehensive skills, mental organization skills, fluent memory, and other vital mental capacities to achieve a good mental ability to reason and understand, and any astral acid destroying my brain and mind, that it be neutralized and lose all power and effectiveness now.

Father, I call upon Your anointing to destroy the yoke from over my mind and give me a clear mind, alert, bright, intelligent, stable, peaceful, and uncluttered, where there is no confusion, no dullness, and no absentmindedness.
It is written in Luke 10:17, **"And the seventy returned again with joy, saying, Lord, even the devils are subject unto us through thy name"**.

Lord, I thank You that the demons are subjected to me through Your name, and by faith I have a sound mind. I am NOT a victim and candidate for the demons of mind-bending and transformers of mind anymore.

Father, thank You for deliverance from these evil entities of mind destruction, which have tormented me these many years. I ascribe greatness unto You, and I say blessing, and honour, and glory, and power *be* unto You that sit upon the throne, and unto the Lamb for ever and ever. Amen and Amen.

106. Prayers Against Aquatic (Marine) Friends

Heavenly Father, I come boldly before Your Throne of Grace, seeking Your divine intervention against psychic aquatic friends who have befriended me in the astral realm and always show up in my dreams as humans.

I seek intervention and deliverance at the hand of Your divine judicial council. I am requesting that Your fire would melt every chain, shackle, fetter, lock, knot, and bolt that these aquatic friends have placed upon me. Sanctify me according to Exo 31:13, "...I *am* **the LORD that doth sanctify you."**

Abba Father and Lord Jesus the Christ, I repent for any sinful door that I have opened unto these aquatic friends, and I confess and ask for pardon for my personal sins and iniquities, and the sins and wickedness of my ancestors in every area where there have been physical or spiritual, conscious or unconscious, direct or indirect participation in anything that has opened a door to relationships with aquatic friends over time.
In the Name of Y'ahushua HaMashiach of Nazareth, I renounce, denounce, revoke, and sever all soul ties, yokes, acquaintanceships, contracts, alliances, affiliations, connections, links, communications, covenants, and sexual partnerships that I have with the aquatic friends.
I renounce, reject, and destroy the power and influence of all my aquatic friends, aquatic partners, and aquatic playmates who have been given access to befriend my body, soul, and mind through psychic manipulation, homogeneity, and metaphysical intercourse.

It is written in 1 Thessalonians 4:7, **"For God hath not called us unto uncleanness, but unto holiness."**

By the Fire and Blood of Jesus of Nazareth, I bring into subjection and destruction all marine powers from the five zones of the water kingdom of darkness affiliated with me through dreams, creating dream scenes, various manipulations in my dreams, and initiating and instigating influences in my dreams.

I pray against all aquatic friends who are infiltrating, invading, intruding, lodging, and violating my home and dreams, using subtle psychic manipulations to harass, torment, and destroy me.

According to the words of the Messiah Jesus in Mark 16:17, **"And these signs shall follow them that believe; in my name shall they cast out devils,"** and according to the Word of God where the Lord Jesus said to us in Luke 10:19, **"Behold, I give unto you power to tread on serpents and scorpions, and over all the power of the enemy: and nothing shall by any means hurt you."**

Through the Lord of hosts, I rebuke and disarm you foul marine friends, and render you all shieldless, defenseless, weaponless, useless, impotent, clueless, ineffective, and powerless against me, in the Name of Y'ahushua the Messiah.

The Word of God commands me in Proverbs 6:5, where it says, **"Deliver thyself as a roe from the hand of the hunter, and as a bird from the hand of the fowler."**

It is also written in Proverbs 12:6, **"but the mouth of the upright shall deliver them."**

Therefore, according to Proverbs 6:5 and Proverbs 12:6, I speak with my mouth by faith, and I deliver myself from all your aquatic friends, as a roe from the hand of the hunter, and as a bird from the hand of the fowler. It is also written in Luke 10:17, **"And the seventy returned again with joy, saying, Lord, even the devils are subject unto us through thy name"**.

By the power and jurisdiction of the Word of Christ of Nazareth, I cast you marine demons out of my life and command you all to Get Out! Now! In Jesus' name.

According to the words of the Messiah Jesus concerning us Christians in Mark 16:17, it is written, **"And these signs shall follow them that believe; in my name shall they cast out devils."**

- All astral poison of the waters set to fight me for a 1,095-day cycle, or The Seven Cycles of Attack fighting against me through marine demons posing as good friends in my dreams, by the laws of the Divine Council of Heaven, I roast you marine demons by lightnings of fire and banish you into the realm of oblivion, in Jesus' name.
- Marine friends, feeding on my flesh, blood, and emotions, I dislodge you foul spirits of the waters, I roast you by lightnings of fire and banish you into the realm of oblivion and consume you all to nothingness, In Jesus Name.
- All marine elemental demons masquerading as human friends in my dreams, I unmask you demons by fire and melt your human image to reveal your true identity, and command that you be consumed to nothingness. I roast you by lightning of fire and banish you into the realm of oblivion.
- Every brooding and nesting serpent, and other demonic creatures, lodging and resting in my body and soul, catch fire and are consumed to nothingness, and all demonic eggs, larvae, and hatchlings are roasted to powder by the heat of the fire of Jesus Christ.
- Marine friend feeding me and influencing me with bad habits and evil compulsions, and carnality, I roast you by lightnings of fire and banish you into the realm of oblivion. Let your weapons, tactics, schemes, and manipulations be vaporized into uselessness in the wind of God, in Jesus Name.

- Marine friends secretly sniffing, snitching, and plotting my destruction, I roast you by lightning of fire and banish you to the realm of oblivion.
- I command all evil materials and friendship pendants, friendship rings, friendship necklaces, friendship marks, etc., given to me by marine friends to catch fire and vaporize from me now, in Jesus' name.
- Aquatic friends and all spirits that have entered a union with me through items in the spirit, in the name of Jesus, I return to you every property of yours that is in my possession.

107. Prayers Against Pestiferous Friends (Forest Demons)

Heavenly Father, I come boldly before Your Throne of Grace, seeking Your divine intervention against psychic forest friends who have befriended me in the astral realm and always show up in my dreams as humans.
I seek intervention and deliverance at the hand of Your divine judicial council. I am requesting that Your fire melt every chain, shackle, fetter, lock, knot, and bolt that the psychic forest friends have placed upon me. Sanctify me according to Exodus 31:13, "...I *am* **the LORD that doth sanctify you."**

Abba Father and Lord Jesus the Christ, I repent for any sinful door that I have opened unto these psychic forest friends, and I confess and ask for pardon for my personal sins and iniquities, and the sins and wickedness of my ancestors in every area where there have been physical or spiritual, conscious or unconscious, direct or indirect participation in anything that has opened a door to relationships with psychic forest demons over time.

In the Name of Y'ahushua HaMashiach of Nazareth, I renounce, denounce, revoke, and sever all soul ties, yokes, acquaintanceships, contracts, alliances, affiliations, connections, links, communications, covenants, and sexual partnerships that I have with psychic forest friends.
I renounce and reject all my psychic forest friends, who have been given access to my dreams to befriend my body, soul, and mind through psychic manipulation, homogeneity, and metaphysical intercourse.

By the Fire and Blood of Jesus of Nazareth, I bring into subjection and destruction all forest powers affiliated with me through dreams, creating dream scenes, various manipulations in my dreams, and initiating and instigating influences in my dreams.

I pray against all psychic forest friends who are infiltrating, invading, intruding, violating, and lodging in my home and dreams, using subtle psychic manipulations to harass, torment, and destroy me.

According to the Words of the Messiah Jesus in Mark 16:17, **"And these signs shall follow them that believe; in my name shall they cast out devils,"** and according to the Word of God where the Lord Jesus said to us in Luke 10:19, **"Behold, I give unto you power to tread on serpents and scorpions, and over all the power of the enemy: and nothing shall by any means hurt you."**

By the power of the judgement and the authority of the Word of God in Luke 10:19, Psalms 11:6, and Exodus 9:24, I call down a rain of fire mingled with grievous hail; I call down rains of snares and terrors, lightnings of fires, brimstone, thunder, and horrible tempests upon all you Monera demons, Protista demons, Fungi demons, the Plantae demons, the Animalia demons, upon the Moss Folks, Wood Wives, nymphs, familiar animals, animal spirit guides, dwarves, elves, fae, fairies, tree giants, Dryads, gnomes, satyrs, goblins, orcs, trolls, totems, leprechauns, halflings, centaurs, and upon the meta-physical projecting spirits, miniature demons, elemental spirits, and all forest demons within the Delvic and occult forest world who have befriended me, masquerading as humans in my dreams, for it is written in Psalms 11:6, **"Upon the wicked he shall rain snares, fire and brimstone, and a horrible tempest: this shall be the portion of their cup."**

Through the Lord of hosts, I rebuke and disarm you foul psychic forest friends, and render you all shieldless, defenseless, weaponless, useless, impotent, clueless, ineffective, and powerless against me, in the Name of Y'ahushua the Messiah.

You forest friends in my dreams, be scattered by arrows of fire and be electrocuted by lightning of flames that proceed from the garment of Jesus Christ and his holy angels.
According to the Words of the Messiah Jesus in Mark 16:17 that say, **"And these signs shall follow them that believe; in my name shall they cast out devils,"** by the dynamic power of the Lord Jesus of Nazareth, by dynamic and terrifying fires of Amber, thunderclaps, lightnings, and fear of the Lord, I drive you out by force and I banish you forest demon friends out of my life. I command you all to get out! Now Go! in Jesus' name.

It is written in 2 Samuel 22:15, **"And he sent out arrows, and scattered them; lightning, and discomfited them."** Get out and leave me and my dreams; never return! In Jesus' name.
- Psychic forest spirits who have forged a friendship with me or who are trying to forge a friendship with me in my dreams self-destruct and die now, in Jesus Name.
- Psychic forest friends, feeding on my flesh, blood, and emotions, I dislodge you foul spirits of the forest, I roast you by lightnings of fire and banish you into the realm of oblivion and consume you all to nothingness, In Jesus Name.
- Every psychic forest elemental demon masquerading as a human friend in my dreams, I unmask you demons by fire and melt your human image to reveal your true identity, and command that you be consumed to nothingness. I now roast you by the lightning of fire and banish you into the realm of oblivion.
- Psychic forest friend feeding me and influencing me with bad habits and evil compulsions and carnality, I roast you by lightnings of fire and banish you into the realm of oblivion. Let

your weapons, tactics, schemes, and manipulations be vaporized into uselessness in the wind of God, in Jesus Name.
- Psychic forest friends secretly sniffing, snitching, and plotting my destruction, I roast you by the lightning of fire and banish you to the realm of oblivion.
- I command all evil materials and friendship pendants, friendship rings, friendship necklaces, friendship marks, etc., given to me by psychic forest friends to catch fire and be vaporized from me now, in Jesus' name.
- Psychic forest friends and all spirits that have entered a union with me through items in the spirit, in the name of Jesus, I return to you every property of yours that is in my possession.

108. Prayers Against The Spirit Of The Masturbation Demon

Heavenly Father, I come boldly before Your Throne of Grace, seeking Your divine intervention against the spirit of masturbation and every serpentine spirit of sexual lewdness and corruption that is controlling my life.
Father, I have been a prisoner of the spirit of masturbation and other serpentine spirits of sexual wickedness that have been dominating my life through psychic manipulations and spiritual remote stimulation. Your word says in 2 Timothy 2:22, **"Flee also youthful lusts; but follow righteousness."**

I seek intervention and deliverance at the hand of Your divine judicial council. I am requesting that Your fire would melt every chain, shackle, fetter, lock, knot, and bolt that the masturbation spirit has placed upon me. Sanctify me according to Exodus 31:13, **"...I *am* the LORD that doth sanctify you."**
Lord Jesus the Christ, I confess my sins of participation in masturbation, where I have willingly subjected myself to sexual fantasies, sexual imagery, lust, mental corruption, and visualization, which have greatly corrupted my relationship with Your Holy Spirit over time.

Abba Father, I repent for any sinful door that I have opened unto this masturbation spirit, and I confess and ask for pardon for my personal sins and iniquities, and the sins and wickedness of my ancestors in every area where there have been physical or spiritual, conscious or unconscious, direct or indirect participation in erotica, hardcore, X-rated books, movies, videos, sensual music, peep shows, obscenity, HBO TV station, soap opera, incest, rape, fornication, pornography, lust of the flesh, sex in dreams, eating in dreams, laying on of hands, rejection, unforgiveness, loneliness, bitterness, rebellion, fear, anger, wrath, rage, contact and association, or through inheritance from the ancestral bloodline, or by participation in any enchanted material, symbol, sigil, divination, blind initiation, or participation in any sex paraphernalia, philia, sexual arrangements, belly dancing, conjuring of sexual spirits, which may have opened my body to the demon of masturbation.

In the Name of Y'ahushua HaMashiach of Nazareth, I renounce, denounce, and revoke all soul ties, acquaintanceships, contracts, alliances, affiliations, connections, links, communications, covenants, and sexual partnerships that I have with the demon of masturbation and its subordinates.

I renounce and reject all my sexual spirit friends, sexual partners, sexual gamers, sexual playmates, sexual rapists, sexual offenders, and spirit spouses that have been given access to my body, soul, and mind through my contamination by the masturbation spirit, and all allegiance that I have pleaded to the masturbation spirit. It is written in 1 Thessalonians 4:7, **"For God hath not called us unto uncleanness, but unto holiness."**
It is written in Matthew 6:24, **"No man can serve two masters: for either he will hate the one and love the other; or else he will hold to the one and despise the other."**
It has also commanded me in Proverbs 4:23, **"Keep thy heart with all diligence; for out of it *are* the issues of life."**

By Y'ahushua HaMashiach of Nazareth, I henceforth renounce any witchcraft substance that was given to me in a dream, or any sexual contact or intimacy that I had in a dream that may have subjected me to become a prisoner of the masturbation demon.
I renounce the demon of masturbation that may have been passed on to me in the womb or as a neonate.

I renounce my spiritual heritage, marriage, and soul tie with the masturbation spirits of my ancestors, or those I have invited to myself.

Right now, I now take charge of the powers of the seven kingdoms of darkness and the five Mephistophelian occult seals, and stand upon the authority of the Word of God where the Lord Jesus said to us in Luke 10:19, **"Behold, I give unto you power to tread on serpents and scorpions, and over all the power of the enemy: and nothing shall by any means hurt you."**
It is also written in Luke 10:17, **"And the seventy returned again with joy, saying, Lord, even the devils are subject unto us through thy name"**.

Therefore, upon this divine jurisdiction, in the mighty name of Y'ahushua Ha-Mashiach, by the judicial verdict of the Blood of Jesus that is sprinkled once and for all, I declare war and combat of the highest order against you, demon of masturbation.

I call down a rain of fire mingled with grievous hail; rain of snares and terrors, rain of fires, brimstone, and a horrible tempest upon you, Elemental spirit of Masturbation and your subordinates, and with hot chains of electric fire and force, I bind, disarm, bring into captivity and under subjection, and banish you, demon of masturbation, out of my body, my soul, and my life.

I banish from my life your presence, your stronghold, your unclean settlement, your hooks, claws, nets, traps, shackles, chains, your tentacles, astral poison, your oath and demonic seal, and all your subordinate forces: the demon of fantasy, lust, perversion, oral sex, anal sex, homosexuality, lesbianism, orgies, mind control, lewdness, lasciviousness, uncleanness, sensuality, carnality, whoredom, prostitution, voyeurism, fetishism, lust of the eyes, nudity, sexual curiosity, shame, guilt, condemnation, sexual impurity, and defilement.

I bind the evil altar of Masturbation, its custodian, sacrifices, rituals, and incantations that are working in and against my life, within the forest, streams, rivers, lakes, pools, ponds, and the ocean in the occult world.

In Jesus' name, I withdraw my blood, my sperm [if you are a man], my vaginal fluids [if you are a woman], and my genitalia or any other part of my body from the altar of the spirit husband/wife.

You masturbation spirit and your subordinates that have been poisoning my life with masturbation, controlling my life, and possessing my sensual preferences and desires, by the power of the judgement and the authority of the Word of God in Luke 10:19, Psalms 11:6 and Exodus 9:24, I renounce, reject, revoke and nullify your power and jurisdiction that's in my life.
According to the Words of the Messiah Jesus in Mark 16:17, "And these signs shall follow them that believe; in my name shall they cast out devils,"

I therefore cast you, demon of masturbation, out of my life and command you to Get Out! Now! In Jesus' name, for it is therefore written in 1 Corinthians 3:17, **"for the temple of God is holy, which temple ye are."**
You foul, abominable, and detestable spirit of masturbation, you are an abomination unto the temple of God, which is my body, but the Word of God commands me in Proverbs 6:5 where it says, **"Deliver thyself as a roe from the hand of the hunter, and as a bird from the hand of the fowler."**
It is also written in Proverbs 12:6, **"but the mouth of the upright shall deliver them."**

Therefore, according to Proverbs 6:5 and Proverbs 12:6, I speak with my mouth by faith, and I deliver myself from you, demon of masturbation, sexual lust, and lewdness, as a roe from the hand of the hunter, and as a bird from the hand of the fowler.

I claim freedom from all dark powers of the Queen of Masturbation and any other masturbatory influences.
and hereby destroy by fire the psychic manipulation of the law of metaphysical homogeneity, vaccine of the law of repetition and resistance, and all astral poisons that manipulate my behaviour, character, desire, and cravings in order to plunge me deeper into the obsession with masturbation, for it is written, 1 Corinthians 6:18 says, **"Flee fornication. Every sin that a man doeth is without the body; but he that committeth fornication sinneth against his own body."**

I purge myself of all evil desire and demonic practice and addiction, for it has been commanded to me in Colossians 3:5, **"Mortify therefore your members which are upon the earth: fornication, uncleanness, inordinate affection, evil concupiscence, and covetousness, which is idolatry."**
Kingdom of demons, hear the word of the Lord God Almighty; I was purchased with a price, the precious Blood of Jesus of Nazareth, for it is written in 1 Corinthians 6:20, **"For ye are bought with a price: therefore, glorify God in your body, and in your spirit, which are God's."**

On the basis of 1Corinthians 6:20 and Colossians 2:13-15, you masturbation demon have no jurisdiction to live and be attached to my soul and body any longer, because I am the temple of the Holy Spirit according to 1Corinthians 6:19, where it is written, **"What? know ye not that your body is the temple of the Holy Spirit, *which is* in you, which ye have of God, and ye are not your own?"**

It is written in John 17:19, **"And for their sakes I sanctify myself, that they also might be sanctified through the truth."**

Therefore, by the name King of kings and Lord of Lords, and by the lightning, thunder, and the fire of Jesus Christ of Nazareth, I pray wherever I am bound with iron chains and with the spirit of affliction according to Psalm 107:10, wherever my life and soul are held behind astral iron bars and bronze gates, because of the bad habit of masturbation, and wherever I am spiritually trapped and imprisoned in the astral realm in the land of the shadow of death [Isaiah 9:2], in the land of darkness [Job 10:21], in the shadow of death [Job 10:22], in the terrors of the shadow of death [Job 24:17], in the doors of the shadow of death [Job 38:17], in the valley of the shadow of death [Psalms 23:4], in the place of dragons and the shadow of death [Psalms 44:19], in perpetual desolation [Psalms 74:3], in the valley of dry bones, in the valley of desolation, within a spiritual cave, within an astral labyrinth, within a spiritual maze, a catacomb, a pit, or any spiritual incarceration chamber within the forest, desert, water, and air, because of the addiction to masturbation, I call for the charged angel of God to rescue me now.

Let me be pulled out from the projection, wall, and hellish cell of the queen of masturbation, and from any demonic pit, trench, slum, and prison that I am in because of masturbation, for it is written in Psalms 107:14, **"He brought them out of darkness and the shadow of death and brake their bands asunder."**
And also in Psalms 40:2, it is written, **"He brought me up also out of an horrible pit, out of the miry clay, and set my feet upon a rock, and established my goings."**

- All astral poison set to fight me for a 1,095-day cycle, or The Seven Cycles of Attack fighting against me through masturbation, seeking to subject me to zero point, you have

failed terribly by the laws of the Divine Council of Heaven, in Jesus' name.
- Every lodging and nesting place created in my life to brood serpents and other demonic creatures catches fire and be consumed to nothingness, now. All demonic eggs, larvae, and hatchlings, I command that you be roasted to powder by the heat of the fire of Jesus Christ.
- In every way, the habit and repetitive sin of masturbation (or participating in masturbation) are used as weapons against me in combat; let these weapons vaporize in the wind of God.
- You spirit husband/wife of masturbation and other sensual acts consuming my life, I bind you with hot chains and fetters of God and cast you out of my life, and I command you to never come into my life again, in the name of Jesus.
- I command all evil materials deposited in my body because of masturbation to be flushed out of my body and soul by the fire and water of the Word of God, in Jesus' name.
- Demon of masturbation, and all spirits that I have entered a marital union with through masturbation, in the name of Jesus, I return to you every property of yours in my possession in the spirit world, including the dowry and whatsoever was used for the marriage and covenants between us.
- By whatever way I have inherited this masturbation demon, I petition by the blood of the Lamb that your Angels bind, chain, and drag this demon out of my life, as it is done in Revelation 20:1-2 that says, **"And I saw an angel come down from heaven, having the key of the bottomless pit and a great chain in his hand. And he laid hold on the dragon, that old serpent, which is the Devil and Satan, and bound him."**

Angels who are given charge over me according to Psalms 91:11 excel in strength and fight for me according to Psalm 34:7. Psalms 35:5 says,

"Let them be as chaff before the wind; and let the angel of the LORD chase them."

Lord, let my hands be cleansed [James 4:8], so I can work the work of the Lord [Acts 19:11], for it is written in Job 17:9, **"The righteous also shall hold on to his way, and he that hath clean hands shall be stronger and stronger."**

Psalms 24:4-5, **"He that hath clean hands and a pure heart; He shall receive the blessing from the LORD, and righteousness from the God of his salvation."**

109. Prayers Against The Pornography Demon [Pornography Spirit]

Heavenly Father, I come boldly before Your Throne of Grace, seeking Your divine intervention against the pornography spirit and every serpentine spirit of sexual lewdness and corruption that is in me.

Father, I have been a prisoner of the pornography spirit and other serpentine spirits of sexual wickedness that have been dominating my life through psychic manipulations and spiritual remote stimulation. Your word says in 2 Timothy 2:22, **"Flee also youthful lusts; but follow righteousness, faith, charity, peace, with them that call on the Lord out of a pure heart."**
I seek the intervention of Your Judicial Council for the songs of deliverance.

I am requesting that Your fire would melt every chain, shackle, fetter, lock, knot, and bolt that the pornography spirit has placed in me, sanctify me according to Exodus 31:13, **"...I *am* the LORD that doth sanctify you."**

In the name of Jesus Christ, I confessed my sins of participation in pornography, where I have willingly subjected myself to sexual materials that, in times past, influenced my actions, thoughts, fantasies, and desires.

Abba Father, I repent for any sinful door that I have opened unto this pornography spirit, and I confess and ask for pardon for my personal sins and iniquities, and the sins and wickedness of my ancestors in every area where there have been physical or spiritual, conscious or unconscious, direct or indirect participation in erotica, hard-core, X-rated books, movies, videos, sensual music, peep shows, obscenity,

HBO TV station, soap operas, drugs, drunkenness, incest, rape, fornication, lust of the flesh, sex in dreams, eating in dreams, laying on of hands, rejection, unforgiveness, loneliness, bitterness, rebellion, fear, anger, wrath, rage, contact and association or through inheritance from the ancestral bloodline, or by participation in any occultic alphabet, symbol, sigil, seal, marking, divination, blind initiation, or participation in any sexual paraphernalia, occult sexual arrangement, belly dancing, conjuring of sexually oriented spirits, which may have channelled the pornography demon into me, and serves as the legal ground and open door. It is written in James 4:8, **"Draw nigh to God, and he will draw nigh to you. Cleanse your hands, ye sinners; and purify your hearts, ye double-minded."**

In the Name of Y'ahushua HaMashiach of Nazareth, I renounce, denounce, and revoke all soul ties, acquaintanceships, contracts, alliances, affiliations, connections, links, communications, covenants, and sexual partnerships that I have with the pornography spirit and with the kingdom of darkness.

I renounce and reject all my sexual spirit friends, sexual partners, sexual gamers, sexual playmates, sexual rapists, sexual offenders, and spirit spouses that have been given access to my body, soul, and mind through my contamination by the pornography spirit, and all allegiance that I have pledged to the pornography spirit.

It is written in Matthew 6:24, **"No man can serve two masters: for either he will hate the one and love the other; or else he will hold to the one and despise the other."**
It is also written in Proverbs 4:23, **"Keep thy heart with all diligence; for out of it *are* the issues of life."**
By Y'ahushua HaMashiach of Nazareth, I also renounce any witchcraft substance that was given to me in a dream, or any sexual contact or

intimacy that I had in a dream that may have subjected me to become a prisoner of the pornography demon.

I renounce the inherited pornography spirit that was passed unto me through my family bloodline, that which I received in the womb or as a neonate.
I renounce my spiritual heritage, marriage, and soul tie with the pornography spirits of my ancestors, and I claim freedom from all dark powers of the Queen of Masturbation in the Kingdom of Hell.

You foul spirit of pornography, you are detestable and an abomination unto the temple of God, which is my body, for it is written in Proverbs 6:25, **"Lust not after her beauty in thine heart; neither let her take thee with her eyelids."**
You demons have been poisoning my life with pornography, controlling my life, and possessing my sensual preferences and desires, but the Lord of hosts rebuke and disarm you foul spirit and your army, and render you shieldless, defenceless, weaponless, useless, impotent, clueless, ineffective, and powerless against me, in the Name of Y'ahushua the Messiah, for I am the Temple of God sanctified, according to Exodus 29:43, Hebrews 13:12, Ephesians 2:21, and is therefore written in 1Co 3:17, **"for the temple of God is holy, which *temple* ye are."**
The Word of God commands me in Proverbs 6:5, where it says, **"Deliver thyself as a roe from the hand of the hunter, and as a bird from the hand of the fowler."**
It is also written in Proverbs 12:6, **"but the mouth of the upright shall deliver them."**

Therefore, according to Proverbs 6:5 and Proverbs 12:6, I speak with my mouth by faith, and I deliver myself from you demon of pornography, sexual lust, and lewdness, as a roe from the hand of the hunter, and as a bird from the hand of the fowler."

I stand upon the authority of the Word of God where the Lord Jesus said to us in Luke 10:19, **"Behold, I give unto you power to tread on serpents and scorpions, and over all the power of the enemy; and nothing shall by any means hurt you."**
It is also written in Luke 10:17, **"And the seventy returned again with joy, saying, Lord, even the devils are subject unto us through thy name"**.

On this authority, with hot chains of electric fire and by force, I bind, disarm, and bring into captivity and under subjection you, Pornography demon that is in my life, and all your subordinate forces. By the dynamic power of the Lord Jesus of Nazareth, by dynamic and terrifying fires of Amber, thunderclaps, lightnings, and terror, I drive you out by force and I banish you, demon of fantasy, lust, perversion, oral sex, anal sex, homosexuality, lesbianism, orgies, mind control, lewdness, lasciviousness (1 Peter 4:3), uncleanness (Ephesians 5:3), sensuality, carnality, whoredom, prostitution, voyeurism, lust of the eyes, masturbation, nudity, a marriage-breaking spirit, sexual curiosity, shame, guilt, condemnation, sexual impurity, and defilement, out of my life, which are connected to the streams, rivers, lakes, pools, ponds, and ocean occult world or forest occult world.

I bind the evil altar of pornography, its priest, sacrifices, rituals, and incantations that are working in and against my life.
In the mighty name of Y'ahushua Ha-Mashiach, by the judicial verdict of the Blood of Jesus that is sprinkled once and for all, you pornography spirit and your subordinates, by the power of the judgement and the authority of the Word of God in Luke 10:19, Psalms 11:6, and Exodus 9:24, I renounce, reject, revoke, and nullify your power and jurisdiction that is in my life, and I declare war and combat of deliverance against you.

Hear the words of the Messiah Jesus in Mark 16:17, **"And these signs shall follow them that believe; in my name shall they cast out devils."**

By this authority, I call down a rain of fire mingled with grievous hail; rain of snares and terrors, rain of fires, brimstone, and a horrible tempest upon you, Elemental spirit of the Pornography species, and I destroy your works and banish out of my body, my soul, and my life, your essence, ethereal substance, your stronghold, your unclean settlement, your hooks, claws, nets, traps, shackles, chains, your tentacles, astral poison, your oath, and demonic seal.

Demon of Pornography, I call you out into the light of Christ, and I cast you out of my life and command you to GO! Now, for it is written [Psalms 101:3], **"I will set no wicked thing before mine eyes: I hate the work of them that turn aside;** *it* **shall not cleave to me."**
Kingdom of demons, hear the word of the Lord God Almighty; I was purchased with a price, the precious Blood of Jesus of Nazareth, for it is written in 1 Corinthians 6:20, **"For ye are bought with a price: therefore, glorify God in your body, and in your spirit, which are God's."**

On the basis of 1Corinthians 6:20 and Colossians 2:13-15, you pornography demon have no jurisdiction to live and be attached to my soul and body any longer, because I am the temple of the Holy Spirit according to 1Corinthians 6:19, where it is written, **"What? know ye not that your body is the temple of the Holy Spirit,** *which is* **in you, which ye have of God, and ye are not your own?"**
It is written in John 17:19, **"And for their sakes I sanctify myself, that they also might be sanctified through the truth."**

Therefore, wherever I am bound with iron chains and with the spirit of affliction according to Psalm 107:10, wherever my life is held behind astral iron bars and bronze gates because of the addiction, compulsive behaviors, obsession, and bad habit of pornography, and wherever I am trapped within any land of darkness, within the valley of the shadows of death, within an underground cave, within an astral labyrinth, within a spiritual maze, a catacomb, a pit, within a spiritual jail cell, or any spiritual incarceration chamber within the forest, desert, water, air, or within an underground astral chamber of the shadows of death or in any place where I am held by darkness, incarcerated and afflicted because of the addiction of pornography, I call for the charged Angel of God to rescue me now.

Let me be pulled out of any demonic pit, trench, slum, and prison that I am in because of pornography, for it is written in Psalms 40:2, **"He brought me up also out of an horrible pit, out of the miry clay, and set my feet upon a rock, and established my goings."**

- All astral poison set to fight me for a 1,095-day cycle, or The Seven Cycles of Attack fighting against me through pornography, seeking to subject me to zero point, you have failed terribly by the laws of the Divine Council of Heaven, in Jesus' name.
- Every lodging and nesting place created in my life to brood serpents and other demonic creatures, catch fire and be consumed to nothingness, and all demonic eggs, larvae, and hatchlings be roasted to powder by the heat of the fire of Jesus Christ.
- In every way, the habit and repetitive sin of watching pornography or participating in pornography are being used as weapons against me in combat; let these weapons be vaporized in the wind of God.
- You spirit husband/wife of pornography and other sensual acts consuming my life, I bind you with hot chains and fetters of God

and cast you out of my life, and I command you to never come into my life again, in the name of Jesus.
- I command all evil materials deposited in my body because of pornography to be flushed out of my body and soul by the fire and water of the Word of God, in Jesus' name.

Demon of pornography, and all spirits that I have entered a marital union with through pornography, in the name of Jesus, I return to you every property of yours in my possession in the spirit world, including the dowry and whatsoever was used for the marriage and covenants between us.

I break every evil power of seduction, lust, veil, scale, or evil eye that was placed in my eyes through watching pornography; I call upon the fire that is burning in the eyes of Jesus, the King of kings and Lord of lords (Rev 19:12), to burn out from my eyes all evil covenants, sin, iniquity.

By whatever way I have inherited this pornography demon, I petition by the blood of the Lamb that your Angels bind, chain, and drag this demon out of my life, as it is done in Revelations 20:1-2 that says, **"And I saw an angel come down from heaven, having the key of the bottomless pit and a great chain in his hand. And he laid hold on the dragon, that old serpent, which is the Devil, and Satan, and bound him"**
Angels who are given charge over me according to Psalms 91:11 excel in strength and fight for me according to Psalm 34:7. Psalms 35:5 says, **"Let them be as chaff before the wind: and let the angel of the LORD chase them"**.
Matthew 6:22 says, **"The light of the body is the eye: if therefore thine eye be single, thy whole body shall be full of light."**
Matthew 6:23, **"But if thine eye be evil, thy whole body shall be full of darkness."**

Lord, let my eyes be clear to see in the spirit realm as well as the natural realm, and to see your glory and behold wondrous things in your law (Psalms 119:18).

Open my eyes to see, and I thank You for receiving my prayers, in Jesus' name, Amen.

110. Prayer Against The Demon Of Bully

Oh Lord God of Israel, I have been a victim of bullying and have been subjected to bullying and abuse emotionally, mentally, physically, and psychologically by the words and brutal actions that have greatly injured my life, attitude, character, self-esteem, and destiny, and have inflicted damage to the purpose of my walk with God, but it is written in Genesis 29:32, **"Surely the LORD hath looked upon my affliction."**

I pray against the spirit of Tobiah and the spirit of Sanballat, and any hidden agenda of Moloch to destroy me.
I stand upon the authority of the word of God where the Lord Jesus said to us in Luke 10:19, **"Behold, I give unto you power to tread on serpents and scorpions, and over all the power of the enemy: and nothing shall by any means hurt you."**

By this authority in the name of the King of Kings and Lord of Lords, I banish the demon of bullying that has made me a laughingstock, an object of scorn and ridicule, and by the power of the 7 eyes of the Lamb of God that was slain [Rev 5:6], I unleash terror and banish and shatter by lightning and the power of Jesus Christ all demons by name that have entered my body and life through being bullied: demons of criticism, shame, rejection, abusive and violent suppression, depression, oppression, guilt, humiliation, disgrace, withdrawal, hurt, wounds, victimization, offense, curses, mistreatment, torment, exploitation, perversion, mind control, domination, cruelty, and every demon of unforgiveness, bitterness, rage, murder, violence, hatred, anger, resentment, and fear, in Jesus' name.

All you demons mentioned that have subjected my life to become an arena for various afflictions by bullying spirits, be banished from my

life! Get out of my body and leave me now! Effective immediately! In the name of the LORD God of hosts, Creator of the heavens and the earth.
It is also written in Luke 10:17, **"And the seventy returned again with joy, saying, Lord, even the devils are subject unto us through thy name"**.

Therefore, by the dynamic power of the Name of Y'ahushua HaMashiach, I declare that I am no more a victim, subject, candidate, or captive of the demons of bullying, but I am a rod of power, a bundle of joy, rejoicing with joy unspeakable and full of glory, with my peace restored, my freedom made permanent through Christ, and all despair, sadness, gloominess, guilt, and self-condemnation are dispelled and vanquished into oblivion, now, in Jesus name.

Abba Yah, who is in Heaven, let all hurt and abuse that they have done to me serve to my advantage and become a stepping stone to my advancement in life.

Equip me to fight against the kingdom of darkness and turn all hurts and pain into vigorous boldness and forwardness, where I will stand and love my enemies with a perfect love. Your word says all things work together for good to those who love Christ.
It is written in Psalms 6:9, **"The LORD hath heard my supplication; the LORD will receive my prayer."**
Psalms 6:10, **"Let all mine enemies be ashamed and sore vexed: let them return *and* be ashamed suddenly."**

111. Prayer Against Demons Of Stealing

Dear Heavenly Father, I petition by the blood of the Lamb for forgiveness for stealing from my neighbours, and I repent for any manipulative and evil desire to become rich on behalf of others and for covetousness.

I have been stealing things from my workplace, neighbours, family, etc., and have therefore violated your law that says in Exodus 20:15, **"Thou shalt not steal."**
Abba Father, I acknowledge that I have been a prisoner of the Kleptomania demon, of which I am ashamed. Every curse of stealing that is passed unto me from my mother's house or my father's house, I renounce, reject, and curse it at the root.
I charge against the satanic kingdom of the Occult Seal 333 and release the judgement of the word of God against the kleptomania demon that is controlling my life.

You demon of stealing in my life, it is written in Eph 4:28, **"Let him that stole steal no more: but rather let him labour, working with *his* hands the thing which is good, that he may have to give to him that needeth"**.
It is written in Matthew 19:18, **"He saith unto him, Which? Jesus said, Thou shalt do no murder, Thou shalt not commit adultery, Thou shalt not steal, Thou shalt not bear false witness."**
It is also written in Romans 13:9, **"For this, Thou shalt not commit adultery, Thou shalt not kill, Thou shalt not steal,"**
Let chains of stealing that are binding me melt like wax, and by the word of God I command you, evil spirit of stealing, to go away from me and get out of my blood.

Through Jesus of Nazareth, let every astral poison and the venom of stealing be neutralized and lose all power and effectiveness against me, and let these poisons of stealing be filtered from my soul through the blood of Jesus.
Let every evil power and curse that drives me to steal be broken with immediate effect.

I therefore resist you, foul demon of stealing, for it is written in James 4:7, **"Submit yourselves therefore to God. Resist the devil, and he will flee from you."** Now flee away, you unclean spirit. I break your seal, and I destroy your mark, sigil, and jurisdiction by the fire of the Holy Spirit.

O Lord, I destroy every connection, relationship, embargo, truce, and alliance that I have made with the evil spirit of stealing and with the kingdom of darkness through stealing.
I pray against every evil altar that was built in the astral planes through my habit of stealing. I demolish the altar that was built in my life and the altar of theft that is standing in my family bloodline, which is speaking against my life and controlling my life.

I destroy every covenant that was made against my material and spiritual wealth, and every law of conversion and exchange that is implemented upon my life to ruin my finances, destroy my finances, steal my finances, and exchange my finances for poverty and lack.

I will no longer be a victim and prisoner of stealing, for it is written in Proverbs 13:11, **"Wealth gotten by vanity shall be diminished; but he that gathereth by labour shall increase."**
1 Timothy 6:9, **"But they that will be rich fall into temptation and a snare, and into many foolish and hurtful lusts, which drown men in destruction and perdition."**

Ecclesiastes 5:10, "**He that loveth silver shall not be satisfied with silver; nor he that loveth abundance with increase: this is also vanity."**
Luke 12:15, **"And he said unto them, Take heed, and beware of covetousness: for a man's life consisteth not in the abundance of the things which he possesseth."**

Every witchcraft placed upon my life seeking to transmute, change, alter, and demote my destiny of success, wealth, happiness, and completeness to become a life of shame, poverty, failure, incompetence, incompleteness, and disgrace be destroyed by lightning, thunder, and the fire of Jesus Christ of Nazareth.

Let every demon, law, and altar of shame and disgrace connecting me to any occult region, zone, realm, occult center, or sphere, within the Mephistophelian world through familiar spirits, elemental demons, terrestrial demons, demonic watchers, psychic naval forces, astral televisions, psychic cameras, spirits of the dead, and graveyards, be destroyed and be banished now, In Jesus Name.

By the word of God, I sever myself from the demon Mammon, for it is written in 1 Timothy 6:10, **"For the love of money is the root of all evil; which while some coveted after, they have erred from the faith and pierced themselves through with many sorrows."**

I bind the arrows of many sorrows in midair, and I banish from me every demon of dishonour, embarrassment, shame, and disgrace that comes with stealing.

I say through Christ that I am content and fulfilled, for it is written in Hebrews 13:5, **"Let your conversation be without covetousness; and be content with such things as ye have: for he hath said, I will never leave thee, nor forsake thee."**

Also, it is written in Philippians 4:11, **"Not that I speak according to need, for I have learned to be content in whatever state I am."**
Philippians 4:12, "**I know both how to be abased, and I know how to abound. In everything and in all things, I am instructed both to be full and to be hungry, both to abound and to suffer need".**
Philippians 4:13, "**I can do all things through Christ who strengthens me".**

112. Praying Against Estranged Marine Babies

Psalms 58:3 **The wicked are estranged from the womb; they go astray as soon as they are born, speaking lies.**
Psalms 58:4 **Their poison is like the poison of a serpent; they are like the deaf adder that stoppeth her ear.**
Psalms 58:5 **Which will not hearken to the voice of charmers, charming ever so wisely.**
Psalms 58:6 **Break their teeth, O God, in their mouths: break out the great teeth of the young lions, O LORD.**
Psalms 58:7 **Let them melt away as waters which run continually: when he bendeth his bow to shoot his arrows, let them be cut in pieces.**
Psalms 58:8 **As a snail which melteth, let every one of them pass away: like the untimely birth of a woman, that they may not see the sun.**
Psalms 58:9 **Before your pots can feel the thorns, he shall take them away as with a whirlwind, both living and in his wrath.**

Through Jesus of Nazareth, let every estranged baby and agent of the venom of serpents and asps be neutralized and lose their power and effectiveness against me.

O Lord God, deliver me from the holds of evil, and let not the wicked come nigh me. Destroy their tridents, darts, and arrows of destruction that are fashioned against me, and let me not be led into the secret snares of the ambush of the esoteric crafts of darkness.

I banish from me every demon and wicked estranged from the womb, every straying spirit, all voices of charmers, and I break your teeth, you young lions, and destroy your bow and arrows, and I cut in pieces all flying, fiery serpents, venomous snakes from hell and death adders.

I will not be pulled into your nets; neither will I be a punching bag for your diabolical assaults and mischievous games.

Every witch baby attacking from the mother's womb is attacking as a neonate; I block their channel of attack and sabotage their astral right, jurisdiction, and stealth operation.

I charge their path with destruction and destroy their ability to astral project into my arena.

By lightning, thunder, and the fire of Jesus Christ of Nazareth, I renounce, revoke, shatter, and destroy these witchcraft curses, and let every witchcraft curse set upon my life to destroy my life and my reputation, my dignity, my mind, my purpose, future, and destiny, by the hands of these estranged babies of the Mephistophelian world, be destroyed and be banished now, in Jesus' name.

Father, thank you for Your protection and assurance that I am safe in Your holy hands. To You be all the glory, honour and praise, forever Amen and Amen.

113. Prayer To Deflect Evil Arrows

In the name of the Lord God Almighty, I approach the realm of warfare in the name of the Lord my God with the authority of my position in Christ above principalities and powers.

I say by fire, arrows sent by the second heaven and the air; I address you by authority in Christ Jesus my Lord. In the name of Jesus of Nazareth, every arrow that was sent towards me by you evil entities of the Air: you demi-gods, you metallic council, planetary spirits, watchers, guardians of the flame, solar lords, inter-planetary lords, inter-galactic lords, guardians of fate and the cycles of life, powers, principalities, legions of the air or the sylphs, using intergalactic gates, lunar gates or solar gates, I block, stop, neutralize by an invisible shield all your arrows, and I say, let all your arrows be deflected and redirected with seven times more destructive force to the regions of the habitation of demons in the second heaven.

Let all your kingdoms and regions of demons experience severe destruction by fire and lightning now, in the name of Jesus, the Son of the Living God, creator of the heavens and the Earth.

Every evil arrow of death, [sudden or progressive], infirmity, madness, or arrows that carry the formula for emotional destruction, mental destruction, physical destruction, spiritual destruction, psychological destruction, hormonal wreckage, bad habits, etc., which were sent against me from the cosmic ocean and astral sea, from the Delvic world of the Land, from the Marine kingdom and the Bermuda Triangle, from the fiery region of the elemental demons, the Salamanders; from the underground psychic elementals, the Gomes and Gnomes, or from the Pestifer world.

I say to you evil spirits, let all your arrows be deflected and redirected with seven times more destructive force to the regions, herds, and den of demons, in the land, deserts, seas, oceans, and underground, and to Lilith and her children in the desert, to the Satyr in the rocky wilderness, to Azazel in the desert in Dudael, to the four psychic kingdoms of the firmament, to the hold of every foul spirit and to the cage of every unclean and hateful bird, [Rev 18:2].

Let all your kingdoms and regions of demons experience severe destruction by fire and lightning, now, effective immediately, in Jesus name.

Arrows sent by forest demons; I address you by authority in Christ Jesus, my Lord. You demon archers of the forest, you left-handed demon archers, you spirit of Pan, spirit of the Satyrs, spirit of the Centaur demons, you 12-fingered archer demon, Sagittarius, and all other demons who possess archery skills, I bind you with chains of vehement fire, and I neutralize your base camp, confuse your archery, and destroy your bows, and by Jesus of Nazareth, I deflect and redirect your arrows seven times more destructive to the regions of the habitation of demons in the land, deserts, seas, oceans, and underground, and to Lilith and her children in the desert, to the Satyr in the rocky wilderness, to Azazel in the desert in Dudael, to the four psychic kingdoms of the firmament, to the hold of every foul spirit and to the cage of every unclean and hateful bird, [Rev 18:2].

Arrows sent by witches; I address you by authority in Christ Jesus, my Lord. By lightning, thunder, and the fire of Jesus Christ of Nazareth, I also block, stop, neutralize, and render powerless and ineffective all arrows that are sent towards me from within any gate of witchery, and I renounce, revoke, shatter, and destroy in midair all arrows of witches and sorcerers, in the name of Jesus the Christ.

Let all arrows sent towards me by witches, or other occult agents of darkness collide with immense heat from the garment of the Lord and

melt, for it is written in Psalms 68:2, **"as wax melts before the fire, let the wicked perish in the presence of God."**
I call upon the fiery breath of the Holy Spirit and say, "Breathe fire, Lord Jesus, upon these arrows, in Jesus' name."
It is written in Psalms 18:3, **"I will call upon the LORD, who is worthy to be praised: so, shall I be saved from mine enemies."**

Also, in the name of Y'ahushua I pray that every deflective strategy, device, and mechanism that is used and established by demons and witches to deflect my arrows sent against them, I now destroy and shatter these deflective strategies, devices, and mechanisms by fire and lightning, in the name of Jesus of Nazareth.

By the name and power of Jesus of Nazareth, I invoke a holy divine jurisdiction and judicial order against the kingdom of darkness, and I say to the hordes of the 12 gates of Hell, my arrows sent against demons and human occult agents will not be deflected to any of my blood relatives, neighbours, friends, or anybody with whom I have a natural relationship.

It is written, No weapon formed against me shall prosper [Isaiah 54:17]; also, it is written for greater is he who is in me than he who is in the world [1 John 4:4]; and it is also written Fear not: for they that are with us *are* more than they that are with them - the enemies, [2Kings 6:16].
I pray this in the name of Jesus, Amen and Amen.

114. Prayers Against Curses Of Poverty And Lack

Heavenly Father, I come boldly before Your Throne of Grace, seeking Your divine intervention against the curse of poverty embedded in my foundation and family foundation. I acknowledge that You are El-Shaddai, the many-breasted One, who nurtures and gives power to gain wealth and success on the earth, and there is nothing too difficult for You.

I come through the Blood of Your Son Y'ahushua to petition You today against the curse and spirit of poverty and lack, that I would be set free from all inbuilt poverty, built poverty, borrowed poverty, or inherited poverty that is destroying my life.

I repent for my sins and iniquities, and those of my ancestors and parents from my mother's house and my father's house. I detest all personal and family transgressions and trespasses, and ask You to remove from me every sin, evil covenant, and iniquity that have brought poverty upon my life and subjected me to be a victim of chronic poverty. By the Judicial Council of Your mercy, judgement and compassion, revive the verdict of the judicial Blood of the Lamb and the Mercy Seat, and acquit me of all allegations, accusations, and condemnations, and of all sins, evil, and wickedness embedded in me from my youth till now.

Please appease Your anger, O Ancient of Days and God of Eternity, and turn Your anger away from me, and turn Your face of loving-kindness towards me right now, in Jesus name.
It is written in Psalms 35:27, **"Let them shout for joy, and be glad, that favour my righteous cause: yea, let them say continually, Let the LORD be magnified, which hath pleasure in the prosperity of his servant."**

You cannot take pleasure in my prosperity as Your servant if I do not have prosperity.

Therefore, I say in the name of the God of the heavens and the Earth, wherever my prosperity destiny and financial destiny were exchanged and replaced with poverty, with a demon of poverty, with a demon of shame and disgrace, a demon of failure, a demon of incompetence, a spirit of incompleteness, a demon of mental and psychological shutdown, lack, scarcity, insufficiency, neediness, and always wanting and never getting, by the authority of my position sitting in heavenly places in Christ Jesus according to Ephesians 2:6, by lightning, thunder, and the brazen fire of the feet of Jesus Christ of Nazareth [Rev 1:15, Rev 2:18], I break the power of poverty and renounce and revoke this evil transaction.

Wherever my prosperity destiny and financial destiny were taken captive by the Genies, by Mammon, by the spirit of Judas Iscariot, or by any other psychic transporter spirit, demon of poverty, or by the treasurer of Hell, I now take authority by the power of the throne of the Lamb of God, by the sceptre of his right hand, by his name King of kings and Lord of Lords, and by the lightning, thunder, and the fire of Jesus Christ of Nazareth, and I now renounce and revoke the law of the incarceration of my prosperity destiny and financial destiny, and I now demand and command by fire that Hell retrieve its spirit of poverty from my life and restore my destiny of prosperity and financial wealth back to my life, effective immediately.

In the mighty name of Y'ahushua Ha-Mashiach, today I declare war and combat of reclamation and retrieval, and by the power of God's word in 1 Samuel 30:8, by fire and by force I call forth, **pursue, overtake, and without fail recover** *all, retrieve all* and reclaim all my prosperity and financial wealth, and all other components of my financial life, wealth, and prosperity from any cemetery, from the wastelands, from the barren lands, from the desolate places, from the woodlands, the wetlands, from any catacomb or grave, from any enchanted forest, the monsoon forest, the tropical forest, from the Swamp, from the sacred grove, from the mangroves, from the everglades, from the crossroad, the fork road, or the roundabout, or from any metropolitan, megapolitan, jurisdiction, principality, municipality, neighbourhood, township, borough, city, town, urban, exurb, suburb, county, district, state, nation, archive, and from any of the seven kingdoms of darkness according to 1Samuel 30:8.

It is written in 1 Samuel 30:8, **"And David enquired at the LORD, saying, Shall I pursue after this troop? shall I overtake them? And he answered him, Pursue: for thou shalt surely overtake *them*, and without fail recover *all*."**

Also, in the mighty name of Y'ahushua Ha-Mashiach, I call forth, retrieve, reclaim, and recover by fire and by force my prosperity and financial wealth, and all other components of my financial life, wealth, and prosperity from all terrestrial realms, sub-aquatic regions, astral layers, occult plains, zones, regions, and kingdoms, or from any glass jar, iron or bronze vessel, black box, wooden box, iron box, or from any tree root, calabash, vase, altar, shrine, river, sea, pond, pool, or lake, and from any of the five occult zones of the marine kingdom: the zone Lumani, Banni, Lemuria, Gamma, and the occult zone of Atlantis. I pray and command my destiny of prosperity and financial wealth to surface and be restored into my life sevenfold, and let every watery environment and chaos surrounding my prosperity and financial wealth dry up now, by the power of Jesus Christ.

Whoever is holding my wealth and finances in their hand, let my success become like a burning fire coal, too hot to hold any longer, and wherever my finances are being held, let them become like a burning fire coal, too hot for the kingdom of darkness to hold any longer.

Right now, by the dynamic power of the Lord Jesus of Nazareth, in the mighty name of Y'ahushua Ha-Mashiach of Nazareth, and by my position sitting in heavenly places in Christ Jesus, according to Ephesians 2:6, I declare war and combat of reclamation and retrieval.

I rain terror of fire, brimstone, tempest, terrible windstorm, a terrible earthquake, a horrible destruction mixed with fiery hails upon all demi-gods, astral forces, planetary spirits, avatars, grand masters, witches, warlocks, satanists, wiccans, sorcerers, watchers, guardians of the flame, ascended masters, solar lords, inter-planetary lords, inter-galactic lords, guardians of fate and the cycles of life, and upon dark principalities, powers, rulers of darkness, legions of the air, aquatic forces, subterranean forces, earth masters, highlanders, mermaids, sirens, the elemental spirits, and every other category of demons who are holding me in poverty, trapping me in poverty, and feeding me with poverty, who have clothed me with poverty, confiscated my prosperity, my success, and my financial wealth.

Every dangerous power of diverse esoteric crafts, manipulations, weapons, systems, and techniques that any human occult agent, demon, or spirit is using to destroy my life, through acute and chronic poverty, I call for the power of the fire of the Holy Spirit to descend into the space between spaces, within every crevice in the cosmic cracks, portals, elevated realms, upper dimensions of the cosmic layers, and lower regions of darkness, to dismantle and destroy these evil armed forces that are governing poverty in my life.

For it is written in Psalms 11:6, **"Upon the wicked he shall rain snares, fire and brimstone, and a horrible tempest: this shall be the portion of their cup."**

Blood of Jesus, arise against the highest council of darkness and condemn their verdict to destroy me through poverty, lack, and insufficiency.

Blood of Jesus and fire of the judicial altar of God Almighty, remove any generational curse of poverty and lack that has hindered my progress all these years.

I revolt by my liberty in the covenant of the Blood of Jesus and by the power of his salvation against every degree of stronghold, operating under the velocity of the five Mephistophelian occult seals, which are mandated to fight against my destiny. By the power of the Holy Spirit, in the name of Jesus of Nazareth, and by the three witnesses on earth: the water, the blood, and the Spirit, I banish by fire all these evil entities and doorways of poverty established in my home and life.

I detach every enforced link that is built to hold me bound under the curse of poverty and lack, and by the power of the Messiah Jesus of Nazareth, I break that pattern and cycle of poverty from my life, effective immediately.

I condemn and revoke all prayers that were made against my life for advanced poverty, for a broken and sad life, for sorrowful discoveries in life, for advanced distress syndromes, for failure in everything that I do, for bankruptcy in my business, loss of my job, and evil prayers that were made for me to become a victim of advanced poverty.

In the Name of Jesus the Christ, by lightning, thunder, and the fire of Jesus Christ of Nazareth, I render powerless, ineffective, useless, and barren every demon of poverty and witchcraft curses of lack, operating in my life. I renounce, revoke, shatter, and destroy every power within the invisible world that has spiritually plunged me into a detention camp of witches and wizards so that I would continually live in poverty, despite my efforts to work hard, bring in much, and work multiple jobs.

By the Blood of Jesus and by the power of His victorious resurrection from the dead, I call for a judicial verdict from Heaven to overthrow

any judicial law that was set over my life by darkness to destroy me by poverty, lack, and failure.
Let God arise and let His angels from Heaven intervene.
It is written that if the thief is caught, he shall restore sevenfold.

Let the God of abundance now break this spiritual enslavement that is keeping me in poverty, and I call forth my sevenfold restoration from the North, the South, the East, and the West.
Therefore, every power that has stolen this shout of joy and gladness from my mouth because of continual poverty in my life, I revolt against these demons right now by the power of the Holy Spirit in the name of Jesus of Nazareth.

I charge, revolt, and pray against every mark of poverty placed upon my forehead or in the palm of my hand, and against every curse, hex, or cage placed upon my life from my mother's house, my father's house, or my spousal house.

Wherever my life was placed in a knot by witchcraft, or a knot was placed in a witchcraft ceremonial rope to represent my life as a knotted life and stricken with poverty, by the power of the redemptive blood of Jesus of Nazareth, let my life be unknotted now, and every knotted witchcraft rope that represents poverty in my life and my generation's bloodline, let these knotted ropes catch fire and be burned to ash in Jesus Name.

I renounce, revoke, overturn, and overthrow every law that was placed on my life for the shutting down and lockdown of my prosperity destiny, and the destiny of my financial wealth, and I renounce, revoke, overturn, and overthrow the eternal curfew and constitution that Hell has placed upon my life to keep me in constant poverty because of the poverty spirit that was passed unto me through the womb of my mother and the seed of my earthly father.

I destroy every lock, law, chain, and shackle of poverty that is placed upon my life, and I renounce, revoke, overturn, and overthrow, annihilate, liquidate, dissolve, and eradicate all evil astral forces of combined elements, sustaining daily psychic attacks and poverty, lack, and insufficiency in my life up to this day.

I revoke and overturn the verdict of any and every tribunal of darkness within any of the occult zones, occult regions, or occult centers, or within the cosmic planes and psychic layers that have ruled against my destiny in order to build strongholds of poverty around my life.
Wherever my finances are submerged in blood, or in enchanted water or witchcraft solution, let my finances be released from the clutches of darkness now, by the holy fire and lightning of the eternal flames that surround the throne of Almighty God.

Any blood money or ritual money that has passed through my hands and has caused a mark to be placed on my hands for degradation, consumption, and eradication of my wealth and finances may the blood of Jesus of Nazareth, the Lamb of God, condemn the condemnation placed over my finances and wealth because of these cursed and blood monies.

Wherever my wealth is buried under soil, in the cemetery, or given as an offering to demons, or sacrificed upon an altar, I boldly invoke the electrical voltage of the blood of Jesus to intervene and vindicate my wealth and finances. In Jesus name.
Any hole placed in my bag or hand by psychic entities, robbers, thieves, financial manipulators because of open doors, ethereal bridges, astral rights, coming from my family heritage or personal errors, I place myself now under the mercy of the Blood of Jesus, and I demand that all powers of darkness release my money and wealth now, in Jesus' name.
Poverty that is eating my destiny, die now and release my wealth and finances.

Poverty from my mother's house and father's house releases my family wealth, and I command a family wealth transfer into my life, in Jesus Name.

In Jesus' Name, I call fire of the Lord Jesus to burn upon my head and melt every crown of poverty and lack by which I was made a dignitary in poverty.

Wherever my wealth is held, or being sold in the Den of Thieves, or is locked up in a treasury of darkness by the evil spirit Mammon, the grand treasurer of Hell, I call on the fires of Heaven to fight my battles against Mammon and release my wealth and money from the darkness.

I will no longer drink from the cup of poverty, and poverty is not my portion and inheritance; neither am I any longer a beneficiary of poverty. The womb of my destiny will conceive productivity and success financially. I declare I am a conceiver of success, of great and mighty things, and my paths are successful paths.

Let money become my hired servant and work for me and answer all things that pertain to my needs and wants.
Let wealth run after me and find me, even if I am hiding from success.

Let wealth surround me like a wealthy garment, and let my days, weeks, months, and years be filled with unexpected accumulation and amounts of wealth, to the glory of God the Father.
Let financial prosperity and the prosperity of favour rain upon me like the dew of Mount Zion and the dew of Mount Hermon, where the Lord has commanded his blessings.

Psalms 23:5, **"You prepare a table for me in the presence of my enemies. You anoint my head with oil; my cup runs over."**

Psalms 2:8 says, **"Ask of me, and I shall give thee the heathen for thine inheritance, and the uttermost parts of the earth for thy possession."**

I say, the season of poverty in my life is hereby permanently terminated, effective immediately, in the name of Jesus of Nazareth, Amen and Amen.

115. Pulling Your Life From The Rivers

Wherever River my life, my future, my destiny, my children, my success, my soul, my mind, health and spirit, my wealth was thrown in, I call upon the Lord God, and I say let the Angels of God Almighty locate all the rivers I call by name today and bind their dragon, goddess, god, ruling entity with chains of fire, and let whatever item of mine be released from this river with immediate effect.

By the Authority of the Golden Altar of Heaven, the Throne of God and of the Lamb, and the verdict of the Blood and the Divine Council in Heaven, in the name of Y'ahushua, I bind and release my life, future, destiny, belongings, children, and blessings from the:
Nile River
Amazon River
Yangtze River- China
Mississippi River United States
Yenisey River
Yellow River
Ob–Irtysh River
Paraná River
Congo River - Congo
Amur–Argun River
Lena River
Mekong River
Mackenzie River - Canada
Niger River
Volga River
Ganges River – India
The Niagara River
Missouri River – United States
Volga River
Danube River
Zambezi River
Rio Grande

Indus River
Yenisei River
Orinoco
Irrawaddy River
Ural River
Dnipro River
Salween River
Tigris River
Murray River
São Francisco River
Japurá River
Purus River
Yukon River
Tocantins River
Paraguay River
Rhine River
Songhua River
Ohio River
Sepik River
Colorado River
Paraná River
Lena River
Orange River
Brahmaputra
Elbe
Irtysh River
Limpopo River
Don River
Pilcomayo River
Vilyuy River
Ishim River
Kolyma River
Juruá River

Every evil river in my place of birth, swallowing my prosperity, my life, and destiny, and great opportunities in life, dry up now, in the name of Jesus.

Rivers of the Sirens, Mermaids, Dragons, and Nymphs, where the jewels of my destiny and life are held, dry up now and release my destiny, effective immediately, in Jesus' name.

116. Rounding Up Demons In Your Life For Perpetual Destruction

In the name of Jesus of Nazareth, I establish and build up myself upon my most holy faith, praying in the Holy Ghost, Jude 1:20; therefore, I take hold of the grace of God to bind and loose, to pull down strongholds and evil imaginations, to cast out demons and tread upon serpents and scorpions through Christ Jesus.

Father, You have called me to walk before You in perfection [Deuteronomy 18:13], in perfect love [1Jn 4:17] and faith [Jas 2:22], and desire that Christ be formed in me [Galatians 4:19]. Hence, I desire that I be made perfect by Your Spirit in every good work to do Your will, working in me that which is well-pleasing in Your sight, through Jesus Christ; to whom be glory for ever and ever. Amen. [Heb 13:21]

I also desire that patience would have her perfect work, that I may be perfect and entire, wanting nothing. [James 1:4]
But Father, behold the kingdom of darkness is surrounding me like packs of wolves and dogs, like hungry lions, and serpents and scorpions. But Your word says to us in Psalms 91:13, **"You shall tread upon the lion and adder: the young lion and the dragon shall you trample under feet."**
Psalms 101:3, **"I will set no wicked thing before mine eyes: I hate the work of them that turn aside; it shall not cleave to me."**
Therefore, by the power of the Holy Spirit, in the name of Jesus of Nazareth, and by the three witnesses on earth—the water, the blood, and the Spirit—stand against and revolt against the daily demons, the besetting demons, and the wandering spirits, and all elemental spirits seeking to place my life in a realm of gloom, doom, darkness, and despair.

You said in Deuteronomy 30:19, **"I have set before you life and death, blessing and cursing. Therefore, choose life, so that both you and your seed may live,"**
Lord Jesus, I choose life so that I and my generation may live.
But Your word also says in Joshua 24:15, **"And if it seems evil to you to serve the LORD, choose this day whom you will serve."**

On this wise, I declare my allegiance to you, to serve you for all of my days.
Therefore, I stand in your authority of the Lamb of God, and I call into judgement, destruction, and banishment all spirits that I call forth this day.
Powers of darkness, hear my voice for I stand in the presence of the holy angels, and in the presence of the Lamb [Rev 14:10], and I say to you, demons, be gone from my life as I nullify, renounce, break, and rebuke all links that I have with the kingdom of darkness.
By the power of the Most high God, by the blood and the fire, I banish from my life:

117. Prayer Arrows Of Declarations

- I decree that at the end of my battles, I will be anointed with fresh oil, in the name of Jesus.
- Doors of divine opportunities open unto me in the North, South, East, and West in the name of Jesus.
- From henceforth, I will not miss my divinely appointed time with the Lord, neither in Dream, Vision, Trance, or Visitation, in the name of Jesus.
- I curse the lean calf trying to enter my life, and I curse the lean ears of corn trying to grow in my life, in Jesus name.
- [Lay your right hand on your head and say] Power of inherited poverty in my life, die, in the name of Jesus.
- Power of borrowed poverty resting on my head, and in my life, I cast you out from me, now, in the name of Jesus.
- Power of built-in poverty resting on my head, and in my life, I cast you out from me, now, in the name of Jesus.
- Power of inherited poverty resting on my head, and in my life, I cast you out from me, now, in the name of Jesus.
- Power to gain poverty in my life, that is resting upon my head, and in my life, I cast you out from me now, in the name of Jesus.
- Trademark of poverty, I am not your candidate; die and be banished in the name of Jesus.
- Every foundational witchcraft sitting on my prosperity, I overthrow you. Self-destruct now, effective immediately, in the name of Jesus.
- Power to gain wealth, come upon me like streams of living water, and flourish me now, in Jesus name.
- Cobwebs of darkness in my family line, in my blood, in my children, in my home, around my destiny and blessings, be consumed and be vaporized now, in the name of Jesus.
- I shall continue in the truth of God's word, clothed with the light of life, and shall never depart from it in the name of Jesus.
- I decree and declare, the Word of Yah is a lamp unto my feet and a light unto my path, in Jesus' name.

- Uncommon divine wisdom, knowledge, and understanding from Yah, that the spirit of error and folly cannot comprehend, possess, and fill me now, in the name of Jesus.
- I dissociate and withdraw myself from the company of fools in the name of Jesus.
- Power to make the right decisions at all times, enter into my life by the Holy Spirit in the name of Jesus.
- I shall not despise wisdom and divine instruction in the name of Jesus.
- My soul shall not be lost in hellfire as a result of foolishness, in the name of Jesus.
- Spirit of foolishness, I am not your candidate; be banished from my life now, effective immediately, in the name of Jesus.
- Garment of fools, be torn from me now, and turn to powder, in Jesus' name.
- I declare according to Ecclesiastes that I shall sow good seeds and reap my harvest in the name of Jesus.
- The power of God that turned Jabez's life around for good and enlarged his borders, locate my life today in the name of Jesus.
- Anointing that breaks the yokes, descend upon me now, and break every yoke of bondage. Loose me and set me free from all strongholds of the occult kingdoms of the land, sea, underground, and air, in the name of Jesus.
- Every witchcraft power using my placenta to summon me in their magic mirror, or to some places in the dream, or is being used to entrap my life by witchcraft, let fire descend from Jesus and destroy this operation, and banish the witches, in Jesus' name.
- I call lightning to destroy every tree in which my soul, life, and destiny are held imprisoned, and to destroy every soul-tie covenant between me and any evil enchanted tree in my village or community, in the name of Jesus.
- Any kind of curse that is making me dream about my former places I have lived long ago, my former places of education,

and past lovers, etc., I neutralize and destroy this astral poison today, in Jesus' name.
- Any curse in my father's house or my mother's house that is making me dream about in the dream, be revoked by fire and die now, in Jesus' name.
- All terrain of desolation mimicking the appearance of greener pastures, so that I can leave my current position in vain, be unveiled and rebuked now, in Jesus' name.
- Enemies of my progress and prosperity, let my name and address be lost from your memory now. Be gone from my life, and know my path no more, in Jesus' name.
- Expectations of the enemies for me and my household this week scatter unto desolation, in the name of Jesus.
- Powers, personalities waiting to hear evil news concerning me, I cancel every situation for bad news and disappoint the expectations of the enemy in the name of Jesus.
- This week, my enemies will hear my testimonies and be converted to Jesus Christ in the name of Jesus.
- Good opportunities that will move me to my next level, locate me now in the name of Jesus.

118. 58 Scripture Prayers - God's Judgement Upon Your Enemies

- Psalms 11:6 Upon the wicked he shall rain snares, fire and brimstone, and a horrible tempest: this shall be the portion of their cup.
- 1Samuel 2:9 He will keep the feet of his saints, and the wicked shall be silent in darkness; for by strength shall no man prevail.
- Job 8:22 They that hate thee shall be clothed with shame; and the dwelling place of the wicked shall come to nought.
- Job 11:20 But the eyes of the wicked shall fail, and they shall not escape, and their hope shall be as the giving up of the ghost.
- Job 18:5 Yea, the light of the wicked shall be put out, and the spark of his fire shall not shine.
- Job 20:5 That the triumphing of the wicked is short, and the joy of the hypocrite but for a moment?
- Job 21:17 How oft is the candle of the wicked put out! and how oft cometh their destruction upon them! God distributeth sorrows in his anger.
- Job 29:17 And I brake the jaws of the wicked and plucked the spoil out of his teeth.
- Job 31:3 Is not destruction to the wicked? and a strange punishment to the workers of iniquity?
- Psalms 7:9 Oh let the wickedness of the wicked come to an end; but establish the just: for the righteous God trieth the hearts and reins.
- Psalms 10:15 Break you the arm of the wicked and the evil man: seek out his wickedness till you find none.
- Psalms 17:13 Arise, O LORD, disappoint him, cast him down: deliver my soul from the wicked, which is thy sword.
- Psalms 27:2 When the wicked, even mine enemies and my foes, came upon me to eat up my flesh, they stumbled and fell.
- Psalms 32:10 Many sorrows shall be to the wicked: but he that trusteth in the LORD, mercy shall compass him about.

- Psalms 34:21 Evil shall slay the wicked: and they that hate the righteous shall be desolate.
- Psalms 37:17 For the arms of the wicked shall be broken but the LORD upholdeth the righteous.
- Psalms 37:20 But the wicked shall perish, and the enemies of the LORD shall be as the fat of lambs: they shall consume; into smoke shall they consume away.
- Psalms 64:2 Hide me from the secret counsel of the wicked; from the insurrection of the workers of iniquity:
- Psalms 68:2 As smoke is driven away, so drive them away: as wax melteth before the fire, so let the wicked perish at the presence of God.
- Psalms 75:10 All the horns of the wicked also will I cut off; but the horns of the righteous shall be exalted.
- Psalms_91:8 Only with thine eyes shalt you behold and see the reward of the wicked.
- Psalms 92:11 Mine eye also shall see my desire on my enemies, and mine ears shall hear my desire of the wicked that rise up against me.
- Psalms 106:18 And a fire was kindled in their company; the flame burned up the wicked.
- Psalms 112:10 The wicked shall see it and be grieved; he shall gnash with his teeth, and melt away: the desire of the wicked shall perish.
- Psalms 125:3 For the rod of the wicked shall not rest upon the lot of the righteous; lest the righteous put forth their hands unto iniquity.
- Psalms_129:4 The LORD is righteous: he hath cut asunder the cords of the wicked.
- Psalms_141:10 Let the wicked fall into their own nets, whilst that I withal escape.
- Psalms_145:20 The LORD preserveth all them that love him: but all the wicked will he destroy.
- Proverbs 2:22 But the wicked shall be cut off from the earth, and the transgressors shall be rooted out of it.

- Proverbs 3:25 Be not afraid of sudden fear, neither of the desolation of the wicked, when it cometh.
- Proverbs 3:33 The curse of the LORD is in the house of the wicked: but he blesseth the habitation of the just.
- Proverbs 10:3 The LORD will not suffer the soul of the righteous to famish: but he casteth away the substance of the wicked.
- Proverbs 0:24 The fear of the wicked, it shall come upon himself: but the desire of the righteous shall be granted.
- Proverbs 10:25 As the whirlwind passeth, so is the wicked no more: but the righteous is an everlasting foundation.
- Proverbs 10:27 The fear of the LORD prolongeth days: but the years of the wicked shall be shortened.
- Proverbs 10:28 The hope of the righteous shall be gladness: but the expectation of the wicked shall perish.
- Proverbs 10:30 The righteous shall never be removed: but the wicked shall not inhabit the earth.
- Proverbs 11:5 The righteousness of the perfect shall direct his way: but the wicked shall fall by his own wickedness.
- Proverbs 11:8 The righteous is delivered out of the tribulation, and the wicked takes his place.
- Proverbs 2:2 A good man obtaineth favour of the LORD: but a man of wicked devices will he condemn.
- Proverbs 12:21 There shall no evil happen to the just: but the wicked shall be filled with mischief.
- Proverbs 13:9 The light of the righteous rejoiceth: but the lamp of the wicked shall be put out.
- Proverbs 14:11 The house of the wicked shall be overthrown but the tabernacle of the upright shall flourish.
- Isaiah 14:5 The LORD hath broken the staff of the wicked.
- Jeremiah 15:21 And I will deliver thee out of the hand of the wicked, and I will redeem thee out of the hand of the terrible.
- Psalms 6:10 Let all mine enemies be ashamed and sore vexed: let them return and be ashamed suddenly.
- Psalms 9:3 When mine enemies are turned back, they shall fall and perish at thy presence.

- Psalms 18:37 I have pursued mine enemies, and overtaken them:
- Psalms 18:40 You hast also given me the necks of mine enemies; that I might destroy them that hate me.
- Psalms 27:2 When the wicked, even mine enemies and my foes, came upon me to eat up my flesh, they stumbled and fell.
- Psalms 27:6 And now shall mine head be lifted up above mine enemies round about me.
- Psalms 54:5 He shall reward evil unto mine enemies.
- Psalms 54:7 For he hath delivered me out of all troubles.
- Psalms 143:12 And of thy mercy cut off mine enemies, and destroy all them that afflict my soul: for I am thy servant.
- Proverbs 16:7 When a man's ways please the LORD, he maketh even his enemies to be at peace with him.
- Miciah 5:9 Thine hand shall be lifted up upon thine adversaries, and all thine enemies shall be cut off.
- Deuteronomy 23:9 When the host goeth forth against thine enemies, then keep thee from every wicked thing.
- Proverbs 14:32 The wicked is driven away in his wickedness: but the righteous hath hope in his death.

119. Prayer Against The List Of Evil Spirits

In the name of the Lord God of hosts, Father, I make petitions today, and I request by the verdict of your Judicial Council that the Angelic host of the Commander of the Armies of the host of the Lord be given to my assistance in banishing from my life every demon that I call out during this prayer.

By the authority and jurisdiction of the death, burial, and resurrection of Christ, by the authority of the Throne of the Almighty God whose name is holy, I cast out and banish from my life, my home, and my children, with immediate effect, all Spirits of error.
Spirit of insatiability in the belly
Spirits of fighting in the liver and the gall.
Spirits of fawning and trickery
Spirits of lying
Baphomet Spirits
Spirits of manipulation
Spirit of mischief
Spirits of Lust of the Eyes
Spirits of Lust of the Flesh
Spirit of Pride of Life
Spirit of Azazel
Spirit of Baal
Spirit of Jezebel
Spirit of Asmodeus
Spirit of the Triton
Spirit of the Titans
Spirit of the Reptilians
Spirit of the Pleiadians
Spirit of the Sirian
Spirit of the Arcturians
Spirit of the Andromedans
Spirit of the Lemurians

Spirit of the Atlanteans
Harassing Spirits
Spirits of Unrighteousness Judgement
Spirits of Self-Righteousness
Spirit of Distraction
Spirit of Error
Vagabond Spirits
Spirits of slumber
Spirits of the wisdom of this world
Spirits of Carnal Mind
Spirits of Carnal Reasoning
Spirits of Demonic Recorders
Spirits of financial exchange and devourers.
Spirits of destiny exchange.
Spirits of destiny devourers
Ancestral spirit worship
Ahab Spirits (spirit of people-pleasing)
Spirits of delusion
Delilah Spirits
Absalom Spirits
Spirit of Lilith
Spirit of alienation
Spirits of parental favouritism
Enabling Spirits
Parental Abuse Spirits
Spirits of Masturbation
Spirits of Trauma Bonding
Spirits of Divination
Spirits of anger
Spirit of the Gorgons,
Spirit of Gargoyle
Spirit of Stheno,
Spirit of Euryale
Spirit of Medusa
Spirits of vengeance

119. Prayer Against The List Of Evil Spirits

In the name of the Lord God of hosts, Father, I make petitions today, and I request by the verdict of your Judicial Council that the Angelic host of the Commander of the Armies of the host of the Lord be given to my assistance in banishing from my life every demon that I call out during this prayer.

By the authority and jurisdiction of the death, burial, and resurrection of Christ, by the authority of the Throne of the Almighty God whose name is holy, I cast out and banish from my life, my home, and my children, with immediate effect, all Spirits of error.
Spirit of insatiability in the belly
Spirits of fighting in the liver and the gall.
Spirits of fawning and trickery
Spirits of lying
Baphomet Spirits
Spirits of manipulation
Spirit of mischief
Spirits of Lust of the Eyes
Spirits of Lust of the Flesh
Spirit of Pride of Life
Spirit of Azazel
Spirit of Baal
Spirit of Jezebel
Spirit of Asmodeus
Spirit of the Triton
Spirit of the Titans
Spirit of the Reptilians
Spirit of the Pleiadians
Spirit of the Sirian
Spirit of the Arcturians
Spirit of the Andromedans
Spirit of the Lemurians

Spirit of the Atlanteans
Harassing Spirits
Spirits of Unrighteousness Judgement
Spirits of Self-Righteousness
Spirit of Distraction
Spirit of Error
Vagabond Spirits
Spirits of slumber
Spirits of the wisdom of this world
Spirits of Carnal Mind
Spirits of Carnal Reasoning
Spirits of Demonic Recorders
Spirits of financial exchange and devourers.
Spirits of destiny exchange.
Spirits of destiny devourers
Ancestral spirit worship
Ahab Spirits (spirit of people-pleasing)
Spirits of delusion
Delilah Spirits
Absalom Spirits
Spirit of Lilith
Spirit of alienation
Spirits of parental favouritism
Enabling Spirits
Parental Abuse Spirits
Spirits of Masturbation
Spirits of Trauma Bonding
Spirits of Divination
Spirits of anger
Spirit of the Gorgons,
Spirit of Gargoyle
Spirit of Stheno,
Spirit of Euryale
Spirit of Medusa
Spirits of vengeance

Spirits of Necromancy
Spirits of the demon Legion
Spirits of hatred for the opposite sex.
Spirits of hatred for your own people
Willie Lynch Spirits
Spirits of Whoredom
Spirits of Molestation
Spirits of Incest
Spirits of Premarital Sexual Activity
Spirits of tattoos
Spirits of alternative sexual lifestyle
Spirits of Idolatry
Spirits of Baphomet
Spirits of the Queen of the Heavens
Spirits of the Queen of the Coasts
Spirits of the Queen of the South
Spirits of the Pride of Life
Spirits of lover of pleasure more than lover of God
Spirits of ignorance,
Spirit of the foolishness,
Spirit of the Swine [2 Pet 2:22, Mat 7:6]
Spirit of the Dog [Pro 26:11, 2 Pe 2:22]
Spirit of the Fox
Spirit of the Wolf.
Air Bender,
Water Bender,
Fire Bender
The Mare,
Mermaids
Sirens,
Peeping Demons
Whistling Demons
Monitoring Demons
Familiar Spirits
Marine Friends

Marine Children,
Environmental Demons
Tracing Demons.
Kleptomania Demon
Demon of Bed Wetting
Sex Mania Demons
Nymphomania Demon
Satyr-Mania Demon,
Dual Demons,
Daily Demons,
Predatory Demons,
Destructive Demons,
Slimy Demons,
Secretive Demons,
Sticky Demons,
Armored Demons,
Hidden Sins Demons
Black Heart Demons
Icy Demons,
Phantom,
Zombie Demons,
Cro-Magnon,
Serpents,
Scorpion,
Nymphs

I banish by fire all you evil entities and doorways that are opened in my life, and I shut all doors, block all holes, and repair all cracks through which you would seek to come into my life. All you demons and foul spirits mentioned here by name, title, and characteristic, be famished and vanish from my life and surroundings, now, for I destroy all your holds, jurisdiction, and operations in my home, life, and family, effective immediately. All these I do by faith through the Son of God, for it is written, **"And having spoiled principalities and**

powers, he made a shew of them openly, triumphing over them in it,." [Col 2:15].
I command by the jurisdiction of the fire of the highest Altar, and the Altar of Altars in Heaven, that you evil powers of Hell holding my life under lockdown, oppression, and spiritual chains, be condemned by the Blood of the Lamb of God and the Holy Altar, and that you receive from the hand of the Lord double defeat and destruction of the highest proportion, each one of you beings, until you release everything that the Occult has holding of mine, now in Jesus' name.

Kingdom of darkness, I disarm and rebuke you and destroy your powers and forces. By the lightnings and arrows of 2 Samuel 22:15, I scatter you by arrows and discomfit you by lightning and render you speechless and motionless in shame and disgrace and defeat in Jesus' name, for it is written in Psalms 18:38, "**I have wounded them that they were not able to rise: they are fallen under my feet.**"
It is also written, "**For this purpose the Son of God was manifested, that he might destroy the works of the devil.**" [1Jn 3:8].

Cause me to walk worthily of the LORD, pleasing in all, being fruitful in every good work, and increasing in the knowledge of God, [Col 1:10].
I pray this, in the name of the Father, the Son, and the Holy Spirit, Amen and Amen.

120. Prayer Against Dying In Your Sleep

Heavenly Father, Lord, and God of the Universe, I come to you recognizing your will to give me sweet sleep and to wake up in the morning to see your sunshine. Your word says weeping endures for a night, but joy comes in the morning (Psalms 30:5).

Heavenly Father, I know that the enemy is seeking to kill me in my sleep, through astral arrows, tridents, spears, javelins, and darts, so that I will not fulfill Your purpose on Earth.
Destroy their jurisdiction, formula, codes, and the powers and laws of homogeneity, the force of the Astro Omni-dictator, and the powers of the guardians of fate and cycles of life that are set to destroy me while I am asleep.

Lord Y'ahushua, I cancel every death threat and death sentence that is hanging over my head and over the head of any one of my family members. Any one of us who is scheduled to die in sleep, I cancel this sentence, overthrow the verdict of death, cancel the funeral, destroy the burial clothes, shatter the evil coffin, destroy the tombstone, cover the graves, shut the gates of the cemetery opened to me and my children, and erase the date of death from our foreheads, effective immediately, in Jesus' name.

I pull my name from the register of the butchery, and the death register of the gates of Hell, and also the names of my children from the register of sudden death, in the name of Jesus Christ.
I invoke the glorious fire that is burning within the eyes of Y'ahushua the Son of God, and I call for the intervention of the bronze fire of his feet in Revelation 1:14-15, to fall upon the demoness Lilith, and upon the demon Mare, upon the Demon reaper, the Death hunter, the Demon hunter, the demon annihilator, the demon of high destruction,

the destroyer demons, the highlanders, and all demons who kill on demand, who kill for sport and show, or who kill with or without a purpose. Let these demons be roasted by the judgement of the soles of the feet of Christ Jesus.

I invoke perpetual coals of fire from around the feet of Jesus to fall upon these demons mentioned. Let them be banished from my life, and from time, space, matter, and all layers of the psychic and terrestrial realms, as I now implement upon these evil spirits of "death in sleep" and "sudden destruction," the judgement written: for I have this honour according to Psalms 149:9. Praise ye the LORD.

Father, I pray against all evil of the night and call forth the judgement of the 7 lamps of fire and the 7 horns of the Lamb of God upon every evil power that creeps in the night unaware to strike me with sudden death in my sleep, the various astral poisons and the forces of combined elements.

I call for the intervention of the hierarchy of the Mounting Angels and Chariots of flames, to fight on my behalf and destroy forever the powers of the Stampa or Voltra Bolt astral poison, that is set and programmed to operate against my life through the air between 1:00 a.m. and 2:30 a.m., in order to kill me suddenly in my sleep. I also pray that the person who is operating this astral poison, who must sit naked in an open place without being seen by another human, that he or she be seen by human eyes and suffer the repercussions of sudden death.

I stand against the Dark Overlords of the night, and the Emperor of Death, and I also destroy the Nkpitime astral poison, and every diabolic esoteric process within the psychic layers of the Mephistophelian world.

Lord, your promise to be an enemy to my enemies and an adversary to my adversaries is clear. Now, Lord, be my advocate and banish every terror of the night that would seek to enter my subconsciousness, and sleep with weapons for mysterious annihilation.

By the authority of the sapphire Throne of God, and the amber of His flames, I pray against and destroy with severe destruction all Incubus demons who would seek to sit upon my chest and reduce me to the state of sleep paralysis, and who would seek to drink my blood in order to kill me, or who would seek to suffocate me to death.

Lord Jesus, God of hosts, by my heavenly rights through the Blood of Jesus, I invoke the verdict of your divine council, and hereby call for the intervention of the hierarchy of the Mounting Angels and Chariots of flames, to fight on my behalf, and destroy by wars of lightning, thunder, and fire, every situation, secret technique, and strategy these evil spirits would use to kill me in my sleep.

Release Angels attired with the most sophisticated weapons, and armed with heavy divine artillery, and let them destroy the powers of highly strategized troops of the pandemonium, namely: the demon god Hypnos (the demon god of sleep), Pasithea (goddess of sleep resting), the demon Morpheus, and the demon Incubus, who would seek to interfere with my sleep to suffocate me, and kill me through obstructive sleep apnea, block airways, demon of cardiac arrhythmia, cardiac arrest, sudden cardiac death, diaphragm paralysis, hypoxemia, sudden unexpected nocturnal death syndrome (SUNDS), long QT syndrome, Brugada syndrome, and hypertrophic cardiomyopathy, congenital heart defects, sudden cardiac arrest, congestive heart failure, lung failure, end-stage or terminal disease, sudden unexpected death in epilepsy, familial dysautonomia, sudden adult death syndrome (SADS), and sudden arrhythmia death syndrome (SADS), inherited heart conditions, structural heart abnormalities, arrhythmias, underlying health conditions, previous heart attack, congestive heart failure, stroke or previous stroke, and other demons who are called into order to kill or allow me to die during my sleep.

I call forth holy lightnings from the amber of the divine fire of God to wrap around the necks of these evil demons. Let these demons of death who strike in sleep now be hanged by holy lightning and be suspended by their necks between the heavens and the Earth, and let every molecule of their essence be vaporized into oblivion, in Jesus' name.

Father in Heaven, I also pray against all evil and request protection by fire against all demons who would be sent or programmed to kill me in my sleep.

By the verdict of your Throne of Sapphire, and the authority of the 7 Horns of the Lamb of God, I request and petition that you release the fiery troops of Archangels and surround my home with barriers of fire. Let the amber of the fire of the holy Altar burn around me while I sleep. Cover every window and door with a curtain of fire and cover my bed with a blanket of light.

Set walls of light and fire that release lightning around my sleep and protect me from demons who would seek to enter and destroy me through my Beta state of sleep, through my Alpha state of sleep, through my Theta or through my Delta state of sleep, when deep sleep falls upon men.

Let all manipulative techniques of these evil spirits to kill me in my sleep fail, for it is written no weapon that is formed against me shall prosper.

I clothe myself with light and fire by faith, and I release a detonation immediately, by God's judgement, upon all evil around me within a 2-mile radius.

I destroy by light and fire every sickle, trident, or arrow of death that is formed against me in my sleep.

I decree by the verdict of the word of God that I will not be afraid of sudden fear, nor for the desolation of the wicked when it comes, for the Lord shall be my confidence and shall keep my soul from being taken [Proverbs 3:26-28].

By the fire of the Holy Spirit, let me be protected from every deflected arrow, misguided arrow, stray arrow, and all arrows of death that would be shot in my way.

The snares of the fouler will not take me in my sleep, nor will the shadow of death overshadow me while I sleep, for the Lord is my light and my salvation.

Father, I also pray that no arrow sent to kill me in my sleep would be deflected to any one in my household, nor neighbour, but would return to the head demons who rule over lesser demons.

Lord Jesus, King of kings and Lord of lords, give me prayer techniques for disarming the powers of witchcraft and other satanic operations working against me and others, and allow me to grow in stature, grace, and power, in Jesus' name.

I thank you for saving me and delivering me from death in my sleep, in the name of Jesus, Amen and Amen.

Isaiah 60:1

Arise, shine; for thy light is come, and the glory of the LORD is risen upon thee.
Vs.2 For, behold, the darkness shall cover the earth, and gross darkness the people: but the LORD shall arise upon thee, and his glory shall be seen upon thee.
Vs.3 And the Gentiles shall come to thy light, and kings to the brightness of thy rising.